✤ THE BURDENS OF INTIMACY ✤

THE BURDENS OF INTIMACY

Psychoanalysis
&
Victorian Masculinity

Christopher Lane

THE UNIVERSITY OF CHICAGO PRESS
Chicago & London

CHRISTOPHER LANE is associate professor of English at Emory University. He is the author of *The Ruling Passion: British Colonial Allegory and the Paradox of Homosexual Desire* and editor of *The Psychoanalysis of Race*.

The University of Chicago Press, Chicago 60637
The University of Chicago Press, Ltd., London
© 1999 by The University of Chicago
All rights reserved. Published 1999
09 08 07 06 05 04 03 02 01 00 1 2 3 4 5

ISBN: 0-226-46859-3 (cloth)
ISBN: 0-226-46860-7 (paper)

Library of Congress Cataloging-in-Publication Data

Lane, Christopher, 1966–
    The burdens of intimacy : psychoanalysis and Victorian masculinity
/ Christopher Lane.
        p. cm.
    Includes bibliographical references (p.   ) and index.
    ISBN 0-226-46859-3 (hardcover : alk. paper). — ISBN 0-226-46860-7
(pbk. : alk. paper)
    1. English literature—19th century—History and criticism. 2. Masculinity in
literature. 3. Psychoanalysis and literature—Great Britain—History—19th century.
4. Homosexuality and literature—Great Britain—History—19th century. 5. English
literature—Men authors—History and criticism. 6. Schreiner, Olive, 1855–1920—
Knowledge—Psychology. 7. Intimacy (Psychology) in literature. 8. Friendship in
literature. 9. Desire in literature. 10. Men in literature. I. Title.
PR468.M38L36 1999
820.9'353—dc21   98-17100
                                                                                CIP

If human nature is the highest nature to man, then practically also the highest and first law must be the love of man to man. . . . This is the great practical principle:—this is the axis on which revolves the history of the world.

—Ludwig Feuerbach, *The Essence of Christianity* (1841) 271

Oh! the difference of man and man.
To thee a woman's services are due:
A fool usurps my bed.

—William Shakespeare, *King Lear* (1605) IV.ii, 26–28

[W]e are never so defenceless against suffering as when we love . . .

—Sigmund Freud, *Civilization and Its Discontents* (1929; 1930) 82

CONTENTS

ACKNOWLEDGMENTS

I began writing this book as a Mellon Fellow at the University of Pennsylvania, during the 1995–96 academic year, and I owe a debt of sincere thanks to the Mellon Foundation and the English Department at Penn for supporting me financially and in countless other ways. Nina Auerbach, Stuart Curran, Jim English, Jean-Michel Rabaté, and especially David De-Laura were true interlocutors, shaping this book in ways they probably couldn't foresee. Wendy Steiner and Alan Filreis helped in other ways too numerous to mention. I also thank James Sappenfield, former Chair of English at the University of Wisconsin, Milwaukee, as well as Patrice Petro and Barbara Kuster, for their assistance during my year's leave.

Several other people supported me while I wrote this book, offering invaluable counterpoints and ways to improve the manuscript, and it's a pleasure to thank them here: Robert Caserio, Richard Dellamora, Kevin Kopelson, and Joe Valente. I am especially grateful to Jason Friedman, who copyedited the manuscript with remarkable care and insight, and Tim Dean, who pushed me to explain my argument with Foucault's *History of Sexuality;* the book would have suffered immeasurably without their input. Two anonymous readers gave excellent advice on revising the manuscript, for which I thank them, and Doug Mitchell, at the University of Chicago Press, offered encouragement, wonderful support, and timely advice when all were needed. Jason Jones was a tireless assistant during the final stages of research, and Donald Whitfield assisted generously with references and translations from the Greek; I thank Jerry Beaty, Joe Bristow, Michael Koplow, Matthew Howard, and Panivong Norindr, too, for related help. Jacqueline Rose and Leo Bersani each contributed numerous insights that shaped my overall claims; the influence of their work on mine should be apparent throughout this book.

I am grateful to Cathy Davidson, Michael Moon, and Carol Rigsby at *American Literature,* as well as Robert Martin, George Piggford, and Judith Scherer Herz, for their assistance with the chapters on James and Forster, respectively. Andy Medhurst and Sally Munt refined several arguments in the first section of my introduction, which appears in their collec-

tion, *Lesbian and Gay Studies: A Critical Introduction;* and William Holzberger and William Halloran raised important points about Santayana's
poetry and prose fiction that improved chapter 6. Lauren Berlant, Carolyn
Dinshaw, David Halperin, Carlos Alberto Pereira, and Elizabeth Weed all
contributed ideas and useful responses to my afterword, helping me refine
its primary thesis; I appreciate their assistance. And the College of Arts and
Sciences at Emory University provided a generous subvention to finance
the cover of this book.

I owe a special debt of thanks to my parents and brother in England,
who provided fine support while I finished writing this book among them,
and to John David Smith, whose calls from the U.S. were a delightful distraction, and whose thoughtful perspective on intimacy continues daily to
influence mine.

Slightly different versions of chapters 5 and 7 appeared, respectively,
in *American Literature* 68.4 (Winter 1996) © Duke University Press, and
Queer Forster, ed. Robert K. Martin and George Piggford © The University of Chicago Press, 1997. Material from the first section of my introduction appears in *Lesbian and Gay Studies: A Critical Introduction,* ed. Andy
Medhurst and Sally R. Munt © Cassell Press, London. I am grateful to
these presses for permission to reprint. I also acknowledge Bucknell University Press for allowing me to reproduce material from *The Complete
Poems of George Santayana: A Critical Edition* (1979).

PREFACE

This is a book about the elements drawing men together and pushing them apart in Victorian literature. It is a book, fundamentally, about the desires and conflicts tormenting male protagonists in Victorian novels, culminating in violence and even death. In attempting to explain why these conflicts recur with such intensity, I argue that our perception of Victorian repression and sexuality may be faulty. My basic claim is simple in scope, but extensive in its effects: By displaying a prescient understanding of the unconscious, nineteenth-century literature repeatedly challenges a strictly materialist understanding of identity. In this respect, the very tools we commonly use to interpret Victorian literature hinder our grasp of its meaning.

When considering why male characters in Victorian fiction are often erotically drawn together and phobically flung apart, we might be tempted to claim that their passions are marred only by the violent intrusions of culture and society. This book explicitly challenges that view. Every chapter revokes the assumption that culture alone is responsible for spoiling love and desire between men. I argue that culture sometimes is a factor enabling—even eliciting—same-sex desire, and, more important, that internal difficulties emerge in individuals and literary characters that don't fall easily under the rubric of "cultural homophobia." I refine this distinction between culture and subjects, but argue throughout that desire conveys and masks *internal difficulties*—a thesis that defined this project from the outset, but that now seems to me, at the book's completion, something of an understatement.

The Burdens of Intimacy engages an expectation of intimacy on the part of authors and readers alike, and an almost perverse fascination with intimacy's failures and disappointments—with affective conflicts that belie comfort, ease, and satisfaction. My book is as much about love, including love's sometimes nonidentical relation to desire, as it is about friendship. In *From Man to Man; or Perhaps Only . . .* (begun in 1873 but published posthumously in 1926), Olive Schreiner's narrator asks whether "a man [can] ever fully realise his ideal, or even attempt to realise it, without acute suffering and many-sided failure" (194); the writing I examine highlights very similar concerns. And though my understanding of "the agony of life" and its "absolutely conflicting ideals" differs from Schreiner's (479), my study nonetheless examines why, in Victorian literature, men's intentions often spectacularly diverge from their desires.[1] I focus on actions that back-fire with appalling consequence, and desires so extreme and antisocial they seem almost to unravel a number of troubled protagonists. Representing these psychic extremes as a woman perplexed by their manifestation in men, one of Schreiner's heroines asks whether "truth, the thing to be loved and sought after more than life, can be only a knowledge of *the will of the arbitrary ruling individual,* and [whether] the only thing of real importance in life [is] . . . the relation between that one indestructible element in man and the ruling individuality" (179; my emphasis). My book asks too what "ruling individuality" means in novels grappling with similar enigmas.

Why does passion bewilder and torment so many Victorian protagonists? The question is farther-reaching than it may at first appear, asking us to reflect carefully on factors that bedevil Victorian expressions of desire. "There is something in the heart of everything, if we can reach it, that we shall not be inclined to laugh at," remarks John Ruskin in *Modern Painters* (1843, 1846; 166), before elaborating on "the peculiar power of the imagi-nation over the feelings of the spectator" (176)—in this case, of Tintor-etto's study of the Crucifixion. According to Ruskin, Tintoretto's work "an-nihilates locality," documenting forms of "fear, rage, and agony [that], at their utmost pitch, sweep away all character" (180, 176). "Those who have so pierced and seen the melancholy deeps of things, are filled with the most intense passion and gentleness of sympathy" (166), he claims, noting that "all egotism, and selfish care, or regard, are in proportion to their con-stancy, destructive of imagination" (187), an argument that in modified form recurs throughout this book.

Ruskin vacillates between Romantic (that is, Coleridgean) and mid-Victorian conceptions of the psyche, arguing first that "there is in every word set down by the imaginative mind an awful under-current of mean-ing," before suggesting that if we "dwell upon it and trace it" with sufficient care and patience, "it will lead us always securely back to that metropolis of the soul's dominion" (162). Juxtaposing doubt and inspiration, antago-nism and creativity, Ruskin's claim is instructive, informing the first two chapters of this book. I argue that Edward George Bulwer-Lytton's *Pelham; or, The Adventures of a Gentleman* (1828; reprinted 1835 and 1840) and Algernon Charles Swinburne's poetry and prose fiction are also haunted by Romantic conceptions of spirit and passion.

Ruskin's argument in *Modern Painters* anticipates what Swinburne called "the weariness of pain and the bitterness of pleasure—the perverse happiness and wayward sorrows of exceptional people" (*Complete* XIII: 419). Swinburne here describes Charles Baudelaire's *Les Fleurs du mal* (1857), praising the collection because "it seems as if all failure and sorrow on earth, and all the cast-out things of the world—ruined bodies and souls diseased—made their appeal" (426). While for Swinburne Baudelaire captured "the sharp and cruel enjoyments of pain, the acrid relish of suffering felt or inflicted, the sides on which nature looks unnatural" (421), his observations summarize related forms of unrest and turbulence besetting male protagonists in his own novels, as well as in widely different works by Bulwer-Lytton, George Meredith, Olive Schreiner, Thomas Hardy, Henry James, Oscar Wilde, George Santayana, and E. M. Forster.[2]

My emphasis on internal unrest and turbulence—what I'm calling "the burdens of intimacy"—points up the limitations of materialist, historicist, and Foucauldian approaches to Victorian culture. My book engages psychoanalytic theory because it offers a subtle account of the fantasies and often troubled identifications that drive a wedge between couples, friends, groups, and even communities. Underpinning all of these conflicts, according to psychoanalysis, is an additional factor—the insurmountable division between consciousness and the unconscious that belies all hope of unifying personal objectives, and (for authors) of representing love and desire without crises of doubt and uncertainty. Beginning from the assumption that sexual desire is not *constructed* as such, but is instead the point of identificatory *failure,* psychoanalysis alone grasps the "internal difficulties"—the lapses, fault lines, and blind spots—that desire inevitably fosters.

Questions may arise at this point: Why engage a theoretical model that emerged only at the end of the Victorian era? And is it not counterintuitive and historically misleading to run together these "discourses," particularly when psychoanalysis seems better aligned with modernism? The answers to these questions appear in the introduction on "Victorian asymmetry," where I elaborate on the conceptual inadequacy of materialist approaches to desire and identification, and on the reasons Victorian culture and society endlessly manifest related concerns about individuals' turbulent inner lives—a turbulence, I argue, to which psychoanalysis partly emerged as one interpretive response. The cultural repercussions of Freud's investigations into hypnosis and hysteria became clear only in the mid-1890s, it is true, but Victorian literature was, I argue, prescient in its understanding of psychic conflicts, anticipating theoretical investigation into the psychic complexities on which it elaborated with such urgency.[3] Thus Schreiner observes in *The Story of an African Farm* (1883): "This thing we call existence; is it not a something which has its roots far down below in the dark, and its branches stretching out into the immensity above, which we among the branches cannot see?" (118). When reproducing Maggie Tulliver's internal strife, the narrator of George Eliot's *The Mill on the Floss* (1860) asks a similar question: "When was that first hateful moment in which she had been conscious of a feeling that clashed with her truth, affection, and gratitude, and had not shaken it from her with horror, as if it had been a loathsome thing?" (583). Below Maggie's "quiescence and even torpor of manner," the narrator observes, was a "new passionate tumult . . . It seemed to her as if all the worst evil in her had lain in ambush till now and had suddenly started up full-armed with hideous, overpowering strength" (582). And in Arnold Bennett's *The Old Wives' Tale* (1908), a novel written when many psychoanalytic insights already had been popularized, this "passionate tumult" surfaces occasionally as "a malignant and exhaustless pleasure" in others' suffering (124). When the invalid John Baines dies suddenly during a moment's neglect, after fourteen years of constant nursing, Maggie, the Baines's domestic servant, "perceiving darkly that disaster was in the air," is "instantly filled with . . . a sort of black joy" (110).

The Burdens of Intimacy considers the impact and significance of this "black joy" on friendships in Victorian literature. Several chapters also endorse my argument about history and prescience, confirming the interpretive accuracy of Randolph Hughes, the infamous critic who once remarked that "Swinburne, writing some half-century before Freud, gives the impression of having read the latter and other writers of the same school" (Swinburne, *Lesbia* 373).[4] Instead of taking Hughes's statement as a bio-

graphical claim—and thus as an opportunity to "psychoanalyze" Swinburne, as many have tried, generally with poor results—I reflect on its
conceptual repercussions, taking seriously the suggestion that someone of
Swinburne's intelligence alighted in the mid-1860s on a set of concerns
that Freud began to theorize thirty years later.[5] The introduction highlights
similar "prepsychoanalytic" moments in fiction by Meredith, Hardy,
Schreiner, and Elizabeth Gaskell.

"Who shall determine the limits of pleasure?" asks Lady Wariston in
Swinburne's unfinished novel, *Lesbia Brandon* (1864, published posthumously in 1952), a book that often tries to answer this radical question
(148). When the eponymous heroine lies dying from illness and heartache,
the narrator of this extraordinary novel remarks, "Far out of sight, deep
down in her sense of things, *intangible to reason and invisible to thought*,
there lived a cruel fear of every instant, lest this perhaps were the instant
. . . of agony and death" (134; my emphasis). *Lesbia Brandon* is replete
with such observations. We read that after Lesbia realizes the futility of
loving Herbert Seyton, "her sides heaved and shook as if with violent
laughter" (132). And when Herbert has a strange, almost surreal dream in
which "the star of Venus" appears to him as "a white rose . . . with a redden-
ing centre that grew as it descended liker and liker a living mouth . . . [and]
that only laughed, and came closer," the narrator notes that "instead of
desire [Herbert] felt horror and sickness at the sight of it, and averted his
lips with an effort to utter some prayer or exorcism" (97). Waking after "a
violent revulsion of spirit," he spends "an hour's beating of the brain
against and about such fancies and the fears engendered from them" (97).

Toward the end of Swinburne's novel, we read that Herbert is "oppressed . . . [by] a profitless repugnance against things that were." "He did
not seem effeminate or dejected," the narrator adds, "and hoisted no signs
of inward defeat; but at heart he was conscious of weakness and waste"
(157). Lesbia concludes on her deathbed, "I was haunted with the fear that
there might be nothing new behind death after all. . . . Even by dying I
suppose sometimes one can hardly escape what torments us, it would be
too easy" (162, 161). These and other passages make it difficult to ignore
Hughes's observation about Swinburne and Freud. More important, Swinburne in these passages illustrates his distance from Romantic, Gothic, and
other transcendentalist and broadly supernatural conceptions of fantasy

and the unconscious: he suggests that "lust[ing] after death" is *neither exceptional nor pathological,* and that "inward defeat" is often endemic among his characters.

We might consider another example more relevant for a study of male homoeroticism, a passage from Benjamin Disraeli's 1844 novel, *Coningsby; or, The New Generation.* "At school," Disraeli's narrator writes,

> friendship is a passion. It entrances the being; it tears the soul. All loves of after-life can never bring its rapture, or its wretchedness; no bliss so absorbing, no pangs of jealousy or despair so crushing and so keen! What tenderness and what devotion; what illimitable confidence; infinite revelations of inmost thoughts; what ecstatic present and romantic future; what bitter estrangements and what melting reconciliations; what scenes of wild recrimination, agitating explanations, passionate correspondence; what insane insensitiveness, and what frantic sensibility; what earthquakes of the heart and whirlwinds of the soul are confined in that simple phrase, a schoolboy's friendship! (72)

"All loves of after-life can never bring its rapture": This is quite an admission! But the passage interests me most for its interest in passionate joy's *excessive* dimension. When Disraeli writes of this homoerotic desire's "tear[ing] the soul" and "melting reconciliations" with "scenes of wild recrimination" and "agitating explanations," he is close to calling these attachments, at their most extreme, almost joyless. At such points Disraeli's and others' observations on passion complicate and depart from Phaedrus's account of Dionysian, manic love in Plato's *Phaedrus,* instead anticipating psychoanalytic arguments about the structurally *indissoluble,* unconscious relation between Eros and Thanatos.[6]

"We must observe," notes Phaedrus, "that in each one of us there are two ruling and leading principles, which we follow whithersoever they lead; one is the innate desire for pleasures, the other an acquired opinion which strives for the best. Now . . . when desire irrationally drags us toward pleasures and rules within us, its rule is called excess" (*Phaedrus* 237E–38A).[7] Advancing a philosophy of restraint and self-knowledge that greatly informed Victorian culture, Plato and other Greek philosophers also heavily influenced Freud, as he acknowledges in *Three Essays on the Theory of*

Sexuality (1905) and *Beyond the Pleasure Principle* (1920).⁸ However, these philosophers' conceptions of excess differ from Freud's, which detailed a form of joy and pleasure over which the individual often has no conscious control, and toward which he or she may yearn in a perverse—and counterintuitive—hunger for death. As Swinburne's narrator observes of Lesbia Brandon, "She lusted after death with the violent desire underlying violent fear" (132). Freud was willing to call this type of desire perverse, but—like Swinburne and others before him—by the middle of his career he differed from Plato in no longer deeming exceptional Plato's suggestion that desire can "irrationally drag . . . us toward pleasures and rules within us"; by 1915—if not earlier—such claims represented Freud's primary thesis about the complex vicissitudes of all sexual drives (see "Instincts" 124–26; *Beyond* 50–53).

Summarizing these claims here, I wish to identify a powerful shift in cultural and philosophical accounts of passion. This shift differs radically from the elements of fear and sexual aversion that Michel Foucault identifies in ancient Greek and Roman thought. In *The Use of Pleasure* (1984) Foucault shows how these cultures represented passion as a potential threat—even "danger"—to an individual's "self-rule [*pouvoir sur lui-même*]" (79, 81; *L'Usage* 94). However, he resists the suggestion, voiced differently by the cultures of antiquity and the nineteenth century, that sexuality's complex relationship to ontology is not always *reducible* to history and cultural concerns. The result in Foucault's work—a consistent refusal to engage sexuality's immanence and internal force—is oddly limiting, allowing him to represent desire only in its relationship to "models," "ideals," "rules," and "images" (*Use* 17–20). Such emphasis certainly tells us how passion became tied to "(1) the expression of a fear, (2) a model of conduct, (3) the image of a stigmatized attitude, and (4) an example of abstinence" (15). In eclipsing all suggestion of interiority, however, it can understand passion's ontological *difficulty* and relationship to failure only as antiquity represented these phenomena—that is, as "the effects of errors of regimen [*les erreurs de régime*]" (16; *L'Usage* 23).⁹

Since for historical reasons Foucault is obliged to engage both the cultural *and* psychic mechanisms of nineteenth-century repression in volume one of *The History of Sexuality*, his methodology is more vulnerable there and his argument about repression correspondingly less assured. I revisit these methodological problems in the introduction, arguing that psychoanalytic theory falls *between* constructivist and essentialist theories of sexuality because, despite its historical emphasis, psychoanalysis is a theory and practice that alters our relationship to history. In recognizing the disbelief, ridicule, and even contempt with which various intellectuals respond to these and other psychoanalytic arguments, I'll provide in the introduction and subsequent chapters many more examples of the perverse joy eliciting profound degrees of psychic unpleasure.

Victorian culture's "grasp" of psychic issues has not always struck contemporary critics as benign. In Victorian scholarship, we read over and again that such investigations into characters' psyches are disciplinary procedures, designed coercively to mold characters into "better" citizens; Victorian literature apparently does this by sloughing off their idiosyncrasies and "wayward" desires. In one sense, these claims are correct: Victorian novels often do seem to depict behaviors and propensities in order to curtail them, thus establishing a paradox about silence and repression that many critics—following Foucault—cast as reprehensible hypocrisy. Yet I contend that Victorian literature, sometimes oblivious of the wider culture's various (and rarely coherent) designs, aimed to voice internal difficulties without always trying to divine their political meaning. We have, I think, lost an ability to read (and perhaps even to tolerate) the psychic repercussions of these conflicts, maintaining with sometimes tedious rigidity that these conflicts—regardless of their content—are *always already* moments of political crisis or significance, as if psychic life were merely an effect of cultural pressure or historical events.

In representing the rigidity and occasional banality of these approaches to Victorian literature and culture, I offer a type of reading that is, I believe, more faithful to the grain of this material's diverse impulses— and, ironically, more faithful to Foucault's remarks about Victorian repression. I don't claim that this style of reading is new—indeed, I acknowledge my debt to such brilliant readers and theorists as Leo Bersani, Joan Copjec, Tim Dean, John Kucich, Jacqueline Rose, and Kaja Silverman. But despite the number of studies now grappling with Victorian literature's diverse fantasies and anxieties, particularly about gender and sexuality, this emphasis on the "grain" of literature's conflicting impulses is curiously undeveloped.

Revisiting key psychoanalytic arguments about repression and "deferred action," the introduction shows that psychoanalytic theory is not—as many critics still think—a crude, universalizing, and historically insensitive approach to literature, but just the reverse: When exploring inter- and intrapersonal conflicts in Victorian writing, psychoanalytic theory is *more* historically and interpretively subtle than is historicism (see Copjec, *Read* 6, 14; Dean, "Eve" 121, 133). This claim may seem grandiose—even preposterous—to some critics, but I believe the introduction and subsequent chapters show otherwise.

"Victorian Asymmetry" opens rather than completes this theoretical dialogue; critical debates arise in almost every chapter, especially in my afterword, where I engage several interpretive dilemmas in recent gay literary criticism and queer theory. My afterword outlines a set of critical assumptions and precepts I wanted to avoid in this book and my last, *The Ruling Passion: British Colonial Allegory and the Paradox of Homosexual Desire* (1995). Indeed, this afterword sounds a caution against various forms of critical and historical idealism in gay, lesbian, and gender studies. Here—as in *The Ruling Passion*—I try to show why the *burdens* of intimacy revoke ideas about the simple destiny of desire, pointing instead to its psychic resonance and sometimes traumatic effects in Victorian fiction.

The working title for this book was "Between Desire and Virility," a phrase the Lacanian analyst Joël Dor adopts in his fine study *The Clinical Lacan* (1997; 103). Dor underscores that while virility tries to efface desire, desire in turn represents the "symptom" of this effacement, proving the means by which virility is shattered and undermined. For various reasons, "the burdens of intimacy" better illustrates men's often agonistic relations, but Dor's phrase still captures a perception that recurs frequently and sometimes violently in Victorian literature: that effeminacy is the sign of a man's *ruin*, a phenomenon—even propensity—that "unravels" identity by turning virility into its haunting and frightening underside. Invoking Dor's phrase alongside my present title establishes my book's fundamental interest: the reason a perceptual gap between virility and effeminacy emerged with renewed intensity in Victorian literature.

When regarding the effects of this perceptual gap in the twentieth century, the psychoanalyst Jacques Lacan remarked that "virile display in the human being itself seem[s] feminine" ("Signification" 291). Refuting conventional wisdom and a plethora of studies examining contemporary forms of machismo, Lacan claimed that "virile display" *exaggerates* (rather than conceals) the gap separating men from the phallus—the signifier that represents men and women's castration, *not* their power; this gap gives these men a "feminine" aspect. The obvious irony here is that when men try to display machismo, they instead reveal the inherent vulnerability of "lack-in-being." Lacan also indicates why, "in the case of men, . . . the dialectic of demand and desire engenders the effects . . . of a specific depreciation (*Erniedrigung*) of love" (290); indeed, chapter 4 of this study, on *The Mayor of Casterbridge* (1886), endeavors to explain why this scenario besets Hardy's protagonist, Michael Henchard.

Although this perceived split between virility and effeminacy is centuries old—in many respects, it could be called a defining principle of ancient Greek culture—I discuss in chapter 6 why the *erastēs* (ἐραστής) and *erōmenos* (ἐρωμένος) (that is, the "lover" and "beloved") of ancient Greece held pivotal meanings in Victorian Hellenism.[10] As many recent studies have shown, effeminacy and virility shifted dramatically in Victorian culture, in part the result of definitional changes in the late 1860s that gathered increasing momentum toward the end of the century. As Foucault argues famously in his *History of Sexuality, Volume One* (1976), "The nineteenth-century homosexual became a personage, a past, a case history, and a childhood, in addition to being a type of life . . . The sodomite had been a temporary aberration; the homosexual was now a species" (43). *The Burdens of Intimacy* doesn't contest this claim so much as flesh out its literary and identificatory repercussions. What matters here is how this shift was received, modified, and perceptually recast.

Despite helping us understand this shift, psychoanalysis neither resolves it nor reduces it to historical causes. Indeed, psychoanalysis indicates that castration and sexual difference are not phenomena we simply *resolve*. Our diverse psychic reactions to anatomy generally don't correspond neatly to biological explanations of sex differences and political arguments that we promote androgyny to downplay or subvert these differences. By focusing carefully on the manifestations of our desire—which can differ widely from cultural expectations of what is considered acceptable and appropriate—psychoanalysis helps us realize our unconscious perspective on sexual difference.

This is just one way that psychoanalytic approaches to sexuality and sexual difference differ conceptually from queer theory and cultural studies' approaches to homosexuality and effeminacy. Indeed, we can build on Lacan's point about the phallus's revealing our deficiency to reframe slightly the dialectical relationship between individuals and culture. Although the introduction elaborates on this point at greater length, I should state here that *The Burdens of Intimacy* resists the still-widespread assumption that individuals ultimately are imprints of culture and society—an assumption that Judith Butler, for one, repeats as a premise of her recent book, *The Psychic Life of Power: Theories in Subjection* (1997).[11] My book examines an aspect of this dialectic that materialism tends to eclipse—a perspective on fantasy and psychic dilemmas that gets effaced when critics argue that our culture determines everything "in advance." As the above literary examples demonstrate, this book amplifies a less defined and infinitely messier sense of process, of ideas being worked out in texts trying to make clear their own understanding of desire, intimacy, and gender. This clarification is rarely successful—one reason texts by Bulwer-Lytton, Swinburne, Schreiner, James, Hardy, Santayana, Forster, and of course Freud are so varied and fascinating.[12] But if we see literature in this way, and psychoanalysis in some sense as its "respondent"—an implicit commentator on issues begging an infinite number of questions—we can't view Victorian literature as fully complicit in its culture's quest for interpretive and epistemological control. We might instead see this literature as a conduit for the expression of a remarkable set of doubts—a type of uncertainty or "negative capability" I point up repeatedly in the following readings. The wager of this book is simply this: If we represent literature in this way, we better understand the diverse influences affecting sexuality—and thus friendship and intimacy—in the Victorian age.

INTRODUCTION

Victorian Asymmetry: The Study of Repression and Desire

Writing novels is . . . thinking about one's self.
—William Makepeace Thackeray, *Letters* 3: 645

The chief thing is the subject, the divine *Ego*.
—Ludwig Feuerbach, *The Essence of Christianity* 260

"A man who doubts his own love," wrote Freud in 1909, "may or rather *must* doubt every lesser thing" ("Notes" 241). Although published when the Victorian era had ended, Freud's claim gives us insights into why many male Victorian protagonists are beset by doubt about the meaning and value of their love and affection. If we reflect seriously on these last two factors, Freud suggests, we engender a host of questions about our lives, cultures, communities, even religions. And though these questions spiral beyond our understanding, stemming partly from unknown causes, they nonetheless derive, Freud insists, from our basic expectations about intimacy.

To explain more fully why Freud's claim points up enigmas in Victorian literature, I'll begin with my first thesis: Psychoanalysis and Victorian culture share a profound interest in asymmetry, a term I'll adopt throughout this study when referring to Victorian culture's large epistemological gaps in the realms of sexuality, fantasy, and identification. These gaps surface when characters and narrators reflect seriously on the literal and conceptual distance separating one individual from another. The term *asymmetry* helps us gauge this distance by bringing to our attention a "lack of proportion"; indeed, the fictional relationships I discuss in this book are often "ill-proportioned" and "incommensurable" (*Webster's*).

Because Victorian literature reveals that characters' desires can differ widely from their identifications, it also illustrates the second thesis of this book: Homosexuality has a complicated relationship to this asymmetry,

1

for it represents an intermediary point between the individual—frequently defined as a solitary, even "narcissistic" unit—and the group, which Victorian culture often represents as an entity built on, and out of, sublimated homosexual desire. Since my claims about asymmetry and homosexuality will reveal in Victorian literature much more than "cultural homophobia," I suggest that we revisit contemporary theories of individual and group identity before addressing Victorian accounts of repression and desire. Many critics use the term "cultural homophobia" too freely, in the process overlooking the *relational* failures that prevail in nineteenth-century accounts of male friendships.

"Some [men] have the language on their tongues," announces Sir Willoughby Patterne, George Meredith's "egoist," "and some have not. Some are very dry sticks; manly men, honest fellows, but so cut away, so polished away from the sex, that they are in absolute want of outsiders to supply the silken filaments to attach them" (*Egoist* 77). That Sir Willoughby describes "manly men" as "cut away" and "polished away from the sex" indicates what is for him an interesting gap between men's surfaces and depths—their appearance and ontology. That such men also "are in absolute want of outsiders to supply the silken filaments to attach them" underscores their *internal* inability to cohere, which ensures that Sir Willoughby, the foppish protagonist of *The Egoist: A Comedy in Narrative* (1879; 1897), displays a desperate self-ignorance when attempting to marry.

I use this example of internal tension partly to explain why *The Burdens of Intimacy* differs from related studies of Victorian manhood. For me, engaging masculine desire in Victorian literature meant rethinking key assumptions and expectations we have inherited—often from modernists concerned to shake off the legacy of Victoria's reign. In focusing carefully on the stark differences between materialist and psychoanalytic conceptions of desire, I also began to grasp the profound limitations of the former.[1]

Many literary and cultural critics interpret power, desire, and even fantasy in Victorian culture without considering the psychic relevance of these elements; they try to explain this period solely through its social policies and legal mandates. Accompanying these moves, one characterization of psychoanalysis after another has dismissed this field and its body of writing as irrelevant or politically coercive.[2] While attempting to account for this attitude, let us consider what we would gain by resisting the tendency to read nineteenth-century manhood as a coherent construction, following Meredith instead in emphasizing that this factor—like all elements of sexuality—is prone to failure.

In adopting this latter emphasis on internal and relational failures, this book revises some of Foucault's arguments about Victorian sexuality and this period's apparent "incitement to discourse" (*History* 17), showing that none of these discourses held a lasting or unequivocal sway in Victorian culture. *The Burdens of Intimacy* undertakes this task by asking us, among other things, carefully to review what Foucault dismissed as the "repressive hypothesis" (10–12). I argue that Foucault advanced his thesis about Victorian society's "incitement to discourse"—an incitement chiefly concerning homosexuality, incest, masturbation, and feminine hysteria— by downplaying the extent to which psychoanalysis pursued a related set of questions about the meaning of repression, fantasy, desire, and identification. Additionally, Foucault's definition of *repression* is strangely unclear. In *The History of Sexuality, Volume One* (1976), Foucault states that his "main concern will be to locate the forms of power, the channels it takes, and the discourses it permeates in order to reach the most tenuous and individual modes of behavior" (11). One wonders whether Foucault can achieve this aim, though, for he immediately concedes, rather vaguely, "all this entail[s] effects that *may be* those of refusal, blockage, and invalidation, *but also* incitement and intensification: in short, the 'polymorphous techniques of power' [tout ceci avec des effets qui *peuvent être* de refus, de barrage, de disqualification, *mais aussi* d'incitation, d'intensification, bref les 'techniques polymorphes du pouvoir']" (11; *Histoire 1* 20; my emphases).[3] Such equivocation doesn't exactly promise a clear argument about "the most tenuous and *individual* modes of behavior." Most important, Foucault's remarks about the "repressive hypothesis" concern the work of Wilhelm Reich and Herbert Marcuse, theorists who revised—and perhaps entirely disbanded—Freud's account of repression.[4]

Reopening this debate about "repression" is vital in determining *how* we approach and interpret Victorian sexuality, masculinity, and literature. Indeed, rethinking the intricacies of masculine desire and identification helps us grasp Victorian masculinity's turbulent relation to beauty and passion, femininity and culture, individualism and self-control. By quoting crucial passages from *The History of Sexuality, Volume One,* and noting discrepancies between this text's French and English editions, I'll show that Foucault's thoughts about the "repressive hypothesis" bring him closer to Freudian psychoanalysis than many of his Anglo-American followers have realized or cared to admit.[5] For complex reasons, some concerning the vexed relationship between homosexuality and psychiatry that properly emerged after Freud's death in 1939, many Foucauldians underestimate this proximity between Foucault and Freud and consequently misrepresent some of Foucault's claims in *The History of Sexuality, Volume One.*[6]

Foucault argued that psychoanalysis changed radically in the 1940s. He also dramatized a split between Freud's work and that of many of his followers, confirming that Reich's and Marcuse's claims often eclipsed careful examination of Freud's most important arguments about repression, desire, and identification.[7] However, in his attempt to refute the "repressive hypothesis," Foucault downplayed that ideological manipulation and psychic repression are *not the same thing:* though policies and legislative measures aimed at controlling sexuality may intensify a society's interest in this phenomenon, one cannot thereby deduce causal relationships between those measures and their psychic repercussions. One must either infer the effect of these measures on individuals or generalize from historical documents and cultural texts, which tends to reinforce the study of ideology at the expense of psychic understanding.

Let us put this another way to illustrate Foucault's conceptual dilemma: If political manipulation and oppression lead *causally* to psychic repression (the hydraulic model), favorable political conditions should liberate people sexually (the fantasy underpinning much of Reich's work). As we'll see, Foucault wisely rejected both the hydraulic model and the notion that sexuality is a prelude to our political and even personal emancipation. However, he failed properly to interpret the *ontological* effects of an "incitement to discourse," and so ignored what happens to the subject when the "repressive hypothesis" is abandoned (Stoler 166). A vacuum arises here, which Foucault's later essays and interviews don't address, and which arguably derives from his lack of interest in immanence and overreliance on ideological forces: Foucault considers desire largely an effect of cultural production, which partly defines our problem. This dilemma besets the work of such historians of sexuality as Françoise Barret-Ducrocq, Michael Mason, and F. Barry Smith: Like Foucault, all three write compellingly about the discursive explosion of sexuality in Victorian culture; and all are somewhat at a loss in theorizing the effects of this expansion on the subject, in part because they periodically reintroduce hydraulic assumptions that Foucault was careful to disband, in particular that repressive aspects of culture produce corresponding repressions within individuals.[8]

By asserting only that "repression" *tended* to lead to an explosion of interest in "deviance" and "pathology," Foucault has allowed scholars of this period to sidestep the pressing, contemporaneous questions that psychoanalysis struggled to raise about sexual difference and identification.[9] John Kucich is a notable exception to this scholarly trend and I discuss his study of repression and Victorian literature in section 3 of this introduction. Kucich's argument is important for this study because it comes closest—although not close enough—to recognizing Foucault's *ambivalence* about the concept of repression and the implications of that ambivalence for studies of Victorian literature. However, Kucich retains some reservations about psychoanalysis and he repeats some of Foucault's ambivalence in his own work. In the last two sections of this introduction, I assess the implications of this conceptual uncertainty for studies of Victorian culture and masculinity.

Partly recognizing that psychoanalysis in fact has a great deal to teach us about this period, recent critics have tried to incorporate elements of psychoanalytic vocabulary into their work, while simultaneously upholding Foucault's rejection of the "repressive hypothesis."[10] The result is a good deal of substantive and conceptual confusion, in which psychoanalysis seems to be both the perpetrator of a monstrous crime—heightened sexual scrutiny, increased social surveillance—and an interrogative force challenging society's insistence on sexual conformity. Several questions arise at this point: What does it mean to adopt a discourse suffused with such terms as "fetishism," "disavowal," "projection," and "displacement," only to contend that one hundred years ago these terms signified only egregious sexual oppression? Can we also maintain Foucault's important point about incitement alongside indisputable evidence that Victorian culture was grossly repressive? And what happens to Foucault's argument about incitement when *literature's* tensions between "repression" and "incitement" foster profound insights into the very bases of ontology and desire?

Let us consider two examples, offered here because they touch on Victorian masculinity as well as complicating the idea that incitement and repression are mutually exclusive. In his preface to *The History of Pendennis: His Fortunes and Misfortunes, His Friends and His Greatest Enemy* (1848–50), William Makepeace Thackeray laments:

> Even the gentlemen of our age . . . , even these we cannot show as they are, with the notorious foibles and selfishness of their lives and their education. Since the author of Tom Jones was buried, no writer of fiction among us has been permitted to depict to his utmost power a MAN. We must drape him, and give him a certain conventional simper. Society will not tolerate the Natural in our Art. Many ladies have remonstrated and subscribers left me, because, in the course of the story, I described a young man resisting and affected by temptation. My object was to say, that he had the passions to feel, and the manliness and generosity to overcome them. (xv–xvii)

Foucauldians might consider Thackeray's attempt to describe "a young man resisting and affected by temptation" as an example of the "incitement and intensification" of desire (*History* 11), but in doing so they would downplay both Thackeray's lament about social repression and the *internal narrative means* by which he highlights the ontological price of this desire. In *Pendennis,* Thackeray engages what he famously calls "the lassitude of the sick appetite palled with pleasure" (2: 210). The result is a palpable struggle among "resign[ation]," "disappoint[ment]," "defeat," and the "manly and humble heart" that must tolerate these failures with a "submissive repose" (2: 210–11). Applying Foucault's argument about "incitement" would tell us little about Thackeray's preoccupation with the psychic ramifications of fantasy and temptation. Implicitly, too, it would end up substituting "incitement" for "repression," suggesting that this literature can serve only conservative ends. Such claims ultimately would miss the radical effects of Thackeray's work, particularly in such remarkable texts as *Lovel the Widower* (1861).

Illustrating these psychological complexities with even more nuance than Thackeray, Thomas Hardy argued in "Candour in English Fiction" (1890): "Life being a physiological fact, its honest portrayal must be largely concerned with, for one thing, the relations of the sexes, and the substitution for such catastrophes as favour the false colouring best expressed by the regulation finish that 'they married and were happy ever after,' of catastrophes based upon sexual relations as it is [*sic*]. To this expansion English society opposes a well-nigh insuperable bar" (127–28).[11] Like Thackeray's statement, Hardy's illustrates concerns about "refusal, blockage, and invalidation" (Foucault, *History* 11)—concerns that Foucault must limit effectively to dismiss the "repressive hypothesis." Foucauldians—ignoring Foucault's primary objective of refuting Marcuse's and Reich's "hydraulic" conception of desire—push these claims even further, tending to dismiss Freud's work as crudely oppressive, and thus rejecting the very interpretive tools that would help us unpack the *political* ramifications of Victorian repression.[12] Still, in order to finesse their accounts of sexuality's "queer" properties, Foucauldians are obliged, as Tim Dean observes, "to *reinvent* fundamental psychoanalytic concepts, such as the unconscious and sexuality—that is, to eschew Freud while nonetheless insisting on all the ways in which sexuality is unnatural, difficult, perverse" ("Eve" 122).

The Burdens of Intimacy steers a path between Foucault and sexual conservatism. My study doesn't deny that the Victorian age fostered an intense and often oppressive interest in sexuality; however, it also doesn't dismiss psychoanalytic interest in this subject because conservatives in the 1940s and 1950s reoriented psychoanalytic arguments toward sexual and social adaptation, as Russell Jacoby has shown in *The Repression of Psychoanalysis: Otto Fenichel and the Political Freudians* (see esp. 5–8, 12–15, 77, 112–13, 115). Corroborating only some of Foucault's claims, *The Burdens of Intimacy* argues that we have too quickly dismissed the conceptual work informing the "repressive hypothesis." As a result, we unthinkingly repeat quite impoverished notions of sexual desire and identification.

Many scholars in critical theory and gender studies have brought these psychoanalytic arguments to our attention. Among others, Leo Bersani, Arnold I. Davidson, Tim Dean, Teresa de Lauretis, John Fletcher, Judith Roof, and Kaja Silverman have repeatedly stressed the astonishing implications of Freud's undertaking and the immense benefits of noting the mutability of psychic fantasy, not least for the history of homosexuality.

Additionally, Henry Abelove has carefully outlined the political repercussions of Freud's death and ego-psychology's consequent emergence in North America, arguing that such psychology and related forms of psychiatry completely revised Freud's arguments about male and female homosexuality (67). And Ann Laura Stoler has underscored why "saying 'yes' to Foucault has not always meant saying 'no' to Freud, not even for Foucault himself" (168). "Despite Foucault's rejection of the repressive hypothesis," she adds, "there are surprising ways in which their projects can and do converge" (168–69). Rather than simply revisiting all this important work in critical theory and gender studies, *The Burdens of Intimacy* inflects it through specific attention to Freud's account of masculine identification and his accompanying interest in sublimation, homosexuality, groups, and death.[13]

Freud's claims about masculine identification, discussed at length in chapter 3, lead us back to my earlier point about asymmetry, for Freud argues that there is a specific and ineradicable *default* within human relations. By preventing individuals from sustaining perfect reciprocity, the unconscious defeats the idea that we'll find lasting unity in social groups and across such wider networks as nations and empires.[14] But while Freud clearly influenced a whole generation of modernist writers, many mid-Victorian novelists and thinkers grappled with related arguments about the problems besetting individual and group unity (see Polhemus 37). Indeed, John Kucich points up the *social* repercussions of these literary investigations when arguing, "Victorian novelists clearly manifest a growing nineteenth-century distrust of collective life not only in their occasional images of mobs and their political conservatism but, more important, . . . in their conceptualization of *an impassable gulf between individual libidinal dynamics and group life* through the association of self-negating libido with repression" (29; my emphasis; see also Showalter, *Sexual* 8–11). Psychoanalysis is crucial for this study (and for Victorian thought), however, because it takes us beyond the suggestion that individual and group disunity obtain only from such identifiable causes as political and class alienation. My use of psychoanalysis—specifically its focus on internal psychic conflicts and constraints—will show that I am not referring simply to alienation when discussing Victorian asymmetry; rather, I interpret how Victorian novels and novelists convey the representational difficulties that arise from their preoccupation with sexuality and identification.

As I argued at the start of this introduction, asymmetry emerges in Victorian literature whenever characters and narrators reflect seriously on the literal and conceptual distance separating one individual from another. Here is Meredith's pompous fool Sir Willoughby announcing his thoughts to his fiancée, Lætitia Dale: "[A] breath of difference between us is intolerable. Do you not feel how it breaks our magic ring? One small fissure, and we have the world with its muddy deluge!" (*Egoist* 76). The narrator of Hardy's *The Mayor of Casterbridge* (1886) comments similarly on protagonists Michael Henchard and Lucetta Templeman, "The gulf between them was growing wider every day" (310), emphasizing too the price of repression. Henchard strives to maintain a secret that "would leave [his] shady, headstrong, disgraceful life as a young man absolutely unopened" (144), though his adopted daughter, Elizabeth-Jane, is said to "keep . . . in all signs of emotion till she was ready to burst" (271) and to "cork . . . up the turmoil of her feeling with grand control" (290).

In Hardy's later novel *Tess of the d'Urbervilles: A Pure Woman* (1891), the narrator highlights even more keenly the violent effects of asymmetry. Reframing Aristophanes' theory of desire and division in Plato's *Symposium,* he avows: "completeness is not to be prophesied, or even conceived as possible. Enough that in the present case, as in millions, it was not the two halves of a perfect whole that confronted each other at the perfect moment; a missing counterpart wandered independently about the earth waiting in cross obtuseness till the late time came. Out of which maladroit delay sprang anxieties, disappointments, shocks, catastrophes, and passing-strange destinies" (83).[15] Because of this "maladroit delay" and the selfish desire it elicits from Alec d'Urberville, "an immeasurable social chasm . . . divide[s] our heroine's personality thereafter from that previous self of hers" (119).

Before explaining why this "missing counterpart" engenders so many "anxieties, disappointments, shocks, [and] catastrophes," let me offer more examples. Pushing back Hardy's interest in asymmetry and repression three decades, Algernon Charles Swinburne's eponymous heroine announces to Herbert Seyton in *Lesbia Brandon* (1864), "I don't know if you would like it or not, but I should like to feel thoroughly that we were not less than brother and sister. It would not make the gulf between us wider than it is" (100). In Samuel Butler's *The Way of All Flesh* (begun in 1873 but published posthumously in 1903), the narrator declares that Theobald Pontifex "was by nature secretive, and had been repressed too much and too early to be capable of railing or blowing off steam where his father was concerned" (80). Failed and misdirected repressions lead Theobald to vent this anger on his wife and children, and so become a cornerstone of Butler's scathing account of Victorian hypocrisy and cruelty. And in Olive Schreiner's novel *From Man to Man; or Perhaps Only . . .* (1873; 1926), the protagonist Rebekah, reflecting on what "makes us feel so infinitely more removed from the worthy Christian fathers and the sometimes gifted writers and thinkers of the Middle Ages," asks whether "the absence of this passionate desire to penetrate into the nature of all things and know them exactly as they are" isn't responsible for the sense that "we, who to-day share the new spirit [and] strive to come near them . . . seem to be looking at them across an impassable mental chasm and through the haze of an almost infinite moral distance" (178).[16]

Mary Poovey has usefully addressed related concerns in Elizabeth Gaskell's *Mary Barton: A Tale of Manchester Life* (1848). "Gaskell," she writes,

> begins to delineate a domain that does not precisely coincide with the social domain her domestic narrative supposedly illuminates. Many of the characteristics of this emergent psychological domain bear distinct affinities to features of the narrative plots that compete so ostentatiously in *Mary Barton*. As Freud was to describe the psychological domain, its dynamics are characterized by a sublimity that simultaneously baffles representation and insists on being known. . . . *Mary Barton* helped delineate the psychological in a way that facilitated its disaggregation as an autonomous domain, whose operations are governed by a rationality specific to it, not to social relations more generally understood. (*Making* 147; see also Anderson 108–11)

As Poovey usefully explains, psychoanalysis adds to Victorian culture's already intense focus on alienation a further account of asymmetry: Psychoanalysis argues that the gap separating consciousness from unconsciousness, and thus distinguishing agency from psychic drives, throws awry the very idea of coherent individualism; Gaskell calls the result a "dark lurid gulf" representing "the heart['s] . . . capacity for evil" (*Ruth* 245; see also *Mary Barton* 45). The repercussions of this dark gulf are devastating for many forms of Victorian epistemology, and we must assess these repercussions alongside such related phenomena as social Darwinism.[17]

These examples bring us back to my second thesis, about homosexuality's complex relation to this asymmetry. *The Burdens of Intimacy* interprets a crucial distinction in Victorian culture between same-sex identification, which was actively promoted, and same-sex desire, which generally was prohibited: Henry Labouchère's amendment to the 1885 Criminal Law Amendment Act made all male homosexual acts, whether public or private, an "act of gross indecency." The law stated that the culprit "shall be guilty of a misdemeanour, and being convicted thereof shall be liable at the discretion of the court to be imprisoned for any term not exceeding two years, with or without hard labour" (Criminal Law Amendment Act, 1885, 48 and 49 Vict., c. 69, sec. 11; see also Smith, "Labouchère's"). This distinction between same-sex acts and masculine identification greatly informs most Western cultures, though strangely it is a subject on which little ink has been shed.[18] Throughout this book I suggest the repercussions of this distinction for Victorian culture and interpret the many different forms it took.

Thus far I have provided only an overview of this book's central claims and interests. Before elaborating on these claims, I must retrace my steps and offer a more detailed account of the "repressive hypothesis" and the reason Foucault wanted to reject it. Having done so, I'll elaborate on Freud's account of "repression" and its interpretation by the French psychoanalysts Jacques Lacan and Jean Laplanche, aiming to show what psychoanalytic theories add to our understanding of subjectivity. I'll also substantiate my related claims about "Victorian asymmetry" by engaging John Kucich's intricate account of repression in Victorian literature. In general, this dialectic between psychoanalysis and literature is central to my book, for the two mediums raise mutually involved questions about subjectivity and its vicissitudes that greatly affect our understanding of Victorian masculinity. As the passages above from Meredith, Thackeray, Hardy, Swinburne, Schreiner, and Gaskell illustrate, nineteenth-century novels were grappling with psychological questions before they were theorized by Freud.[19] And though chapter 7, on Forster's short stories and *Maurice,* is an obvious historical exception to this claim, I argue that Forster's writing repeatedly invokes late Victorian (Carpenterian) models of friendship and homosexual desire while struggling with early twentieth-century psycho-analytic accounts of sexuality.

1. FOUCAULT AND PSYCHOANALYSIS

Foucault has much to say about repression in his first volume of *The History of Sexuality,* though his argument is hard to summarize, as the book's first two sections—"We 'Other Victorians'" and "The Repressive Hypothesis"—cite few sources, resort frequently to paraphrase, and often are uncertain about the exact meaning of "repression." The volume begins ringingly, "For a long time, the story goes, we supported a Victorian regime, and we continue to be dominated by it even today. Thus the image of the imperial prude is emblazoned on our restrained, mute, and hypocritical sexuality" (3). Yet Foucault's shift in argument from the first sentence to the second is subtle: While implicitly rejecting the suggestion that we "continue to be dominated" by this "Victorian regime," Foucault suggests that the "regime" did not foster a "restrained, mute, and hypocritical sexuality" but instead created "a veritable discursive explosion . . . that gathered momentum from the eighteenth century onward" (17–18). What haunts us of this "discursive ferment," he claims, is an idea that Victorian culture was sexually repressive and that sexuality in the future will connect with the free and joyous sexual times that apparently preceded Queen Victoria's reign: "[W]e ardently conjure away the present and appeal to the future, whose day will be hastened by the contribution we believe we are making. Something that smacks of revolt, of promised freedom, of the coming age of a different law, slips easily into this discourse on sexual oppression" (6–7).

This "something" slips into Foucault's studies of sexuality. In one sense, it would be strange if it did not, for Foucault must balance an argument against the "repressive hypothesis" with some attention to changes in the structure of law, policing, and social codes. He does this by representing the law and social codes as instruments "inciting" more discourse than they do—or can—control. In Foucault's model, the law rapidly becomes an agent soliciting—rather than merely punishing or criminalizing—sexual "deviance."[20] We might accept that the law never simply prohibits or impedes, but Foucault's emphasis on "regulation" also begins to appear productive, even benign, as if in promoting sexuality's "veritable discursive explosion" (17), "the bourgeois order" is something we might almost thank for promoting today's sexual visibility (5).

Foucauldians are more conflicted than Foucault was in their response to this sexual visibility,[21] for Foucault preferred to represent sexuality as a set of acts rather than a form of speech. Indeed, Foucauldians generally ignore this interesting dimension of *The History of Sexuality* and Foucault's related essays, which actually is the logical outcome of his contention in the first volume of *History:* "Not only did ['the society that emerged in the nineteenth century'] speak of sex and compel everyone to do so; it also set out to formulate the uniform truth of sex. As if it suspected sex of harboring a fundamental secret" (69).

Contemporary queer theory is ambivalent about this point. It accepts, for instance, that sexuality marshaled in the name of identity is bound to reproduce a "discursive regime" remarkably similar to the one Foucault critiqued when he remarked, "The sodomite had been a temporary aberration; the homosexual was now a species" (43). In response to these constraints, queer theory aims toward a fluid politics that tries to displace binary logic (heterosexuality vs. homosexuality)—and especially "heteronormativity"—by promoting polymorphous perversity.[22] Yet many proponents of queer theory forget that radical psychoanalysis has advanced comparable anti-identitarian arguments since Freud's *Three Essays on the Theory of Sexuality* (1905). These psychoanalytic arguments derive from Freud's claim that the ego is hostile to difference and desire.[23] In *The Freudian Body,* Leo Bersani substantiates Freud's claim by arguing that the ego fails to produce a lasting rapport with external forces: "far from having any original aptitude for dealing with reality, [the ego] is in a state of radical hostility to the external world" (87). In formulating this intrapsychic antagonism, Freud did not excuse psychoanalysis from cultural prejudice, intolerance, and homophobia, as many Foucauldians claim.[24] On the contrary, to invoke only three examples, in "'Civilized' Sexual Morality and Modern Nervous Illness" (1908), "Thoughts for the Times on War and

Death" (1915), and in *Civilization and Its Discontents* (1929, revised 1930), Freud consistently criticized modern Western societies for compelling their subjects to live "beyond [their psychic] means" ("Thoughts" 284). In such circumstances, Freud argued, neurosis is the subject's only reprieve from society's relentless and intolerable demands. "Experience teaches us," he wrote in 1908, correcting Christian von Ehrenfels, W. Erb, Ludwig Binswanger, and Richard von Krafft-Ebing "that for most people there is a limit beyond which their constitution cannot comply with the demands of civilization. All who wish to be more noble-minded than their constitution allows fall victims to neurosis; they would have been more healthy if it could have been possible for them to be less good" ("Civilized" 191).

As we'll see, Foucault willingly concedes this point. Indeed, in *The History of Sexuality, Volume One,* he states unequivocally that it is *incorrect* to equate early psychoanalysis with sexual normativity. Here we must slightly revise Robert Hurley's translation, which gives us: "And the strange position of *psychiatry* at the end of the nineteenth century would be hard to comprehend if one did not see the rupture it brought about in the great system of degenerescence" (119; my emphasis). Foucault actually wrote: "Et la position singulière de la *psychanalyse* se comprendrait mal, à la fin du XIXe siècle, si on ne voyait la rupture qu'elle a opéré par rapport au grand système de la dégénérescence" (*Histoire 1,* 157; my emphasis). The meaning of this sentence is critical because while *singulière* refers to psychoanalysis, and not psychiatry, it also means "remarkable," "odd," "unusual," "special," and "queer." In the following passage, too, we see why this "situation . . . would be thoroughly misunderstood," as Foucault anticipated:

> It is very well to look back from our vantage point and remark upon the normalizing impulse in Freud; one can go on to denounce the role played for many years by the psychoanalytic institution; but the fact remains that in the great family of technologies of sex, which goes so far back into the history of the Christian West, of all those institutions that set out in the nineteenth century to medicalize sex, [psychoanalysis] was the one that, up to the decade of the forties, *rigorously opposed* the political and institutional effects of the perversion-heredity-degenerescence system [*la psychanalyse . . . fut, jusqu'aux années*

1940, celle qui s'est opposée, rigoureusement, *aux effets poli-tiques et institutionnels du système perversion-hérédité-dégénéres-cence].* (119; *Histoire 1* 157–58; my emphases)

Those who insist to the contrary, Foucault implies, have simply not read Freud.[25] When characterizing the arguments of Reich's and Marcuse's read-ers, however, Foucault asks archly,

> But have we not liberated ourselves from those two long centu-ries in which the history of sexuality must be seen first of all as the chronicle of an increasing repression? Only to a slight ex-tent, *we are told*. Perhaps some progress was made by Freud; but with such circumspection, such medical prudence, a scientific guarantee of innocuousness, and so many precautions in order to contain everything, with no fear of "overflow," in that safest and most discreet of places, between the couch and discourse: yet another round of whispering on a bed. . . . *We are informed that* . . . the least glimmer of truth is conditioned by poli-tics. . . . Thus, one denounces Freud's conformism, the nor-malizing functions of psychoanalysis, the obvious timidity of Reich's vehemence, and all the effects of integration ensured by the "science" of sex and the barely equivocal practices of sexol-ogy. (5; my emphases)

These remarks are obvious caricatures of others' perspectives on Freud. And since Reich and Marcuse substantially revised Freud's work on civilization and repression to produce what Foucault calls—quite accu-rately in this context—a "repressive hypothesis" (10–12), his objections to their work are justified. Reich's account of the allegedly functional relations among society, libido, and sexual response misconstrues Freud's stress on the precise *asymmetry* of these elements, given their disturbance by the un-conscious.[26] In similar ways Marcuse tended to represent social oppression (and less commonly the superego) as responsible for the subject's "repres-sive de-sublimation," a concept Freud never advanced.[27] Foucault can therefore legitimately claim, "This discourse on modern sexual repression holds up well, owing no doubt to how easy it is to uphold . . . [but] a suspicious mind might wonder if taking so many precautions in order to give the history of sex such an impressive filiation does not bear traces of the same old prudishness" (5–6). This point—even tautology—seems rather to beg the question, since it hinges on the accuracy of Foucault's own reading of Victorian sexuality. I repeat it here merely to illustrate Foucault's distance from the politics and arguments of his followers.

Unlike Foucault, whose allegiance to anti-identitarian politics recurs emphatically throughout his work, queer theory, despite its professed concerns, is consistently torn between identitarian and anti-identitarian conceptions of desire. In her introduction to *Epistemology of the Closet* (1990), for instance, Eve Kosofsky Sedgwick writes: "[O]ne main strand of argument in this book is deconstructive, in a fairly specific sense. The analytic move it makes is to demonstrate that categories presented in a culture as symmetrical binary oppositions—heterosexual/homosexual, in this case—actually subsist in a more unsettled and dynamic tacit relation" (9–10). Yet although Sedgwick is keenly aware that the distinction between homosexuality and heterosexuality stems primarily from nineteenth-century sexological arguments about sexuality and ontology, she is not prepared to revoke these categories and so tries casting them in an altered form: "Ultimately, I do feel, a great deal depends—for all women, for lesbians, for gay men, and possibly for all men—on the fostering of our ability to arrive at understandings of sexuality that will *respect a certain irreducibility in it* to the terms and relations of gender" (16; my emphasis). In this respect, Sedgwick ends up reinforcing suggestions that these categories are in fact adequate keys to our identity: "To alienate conclusively, *definitionally,* from anyone on any theoretical ground the authority to describe and name their own sexuality is a terribly consequential seizure. In this century, in which sexuality has been made expressive of the essence of both identity and knowledge, it may represent the most intimate violence possible" (26). Here Sedgwick differs radically from Foucault, whose concern *not* to advance a "reverse discourse" was such that he supported only "movements of affirmation" rescinding ontological arguments about sexuality (*History* 101; "Power" 155).

My reference to "anti-identitarian" conceptions of desire binds Foucault's arguments about sexuality to his antihumanist perspective in *The Order of Things* (1966) and *The Archaeology of Knowledge* (1969), which strive to decenter man from history, time, and consciousness. As Foucault explained in this now famous claim, "man would be erased, like a face drawn in sand at the edge of the sea" (*Order* 387). By insisting that "man" is subject to the unconscious, psychoanalysis, as we'll see, is also "anti-identitarian." Indeed, that psychoanalysis comes closest to offering the type of sexual fluidity queer theory wants to promote bears intimately on the way the latter has promulgated rather confused and contradictory notions of the unconscious, fantasy, and identification.[28]

On all these points, we must reread Foucault more carefully. Foucault rejected the "repressive hypothesis" because such claims imply a misleading *rapport* between sexuality and political emancipation. Recall: "Something that smacks of revolt, of promised freedom, of the coming age of a different law, slips easily into this discourse on sexual oppression" (7). Accordingly, *The History of Sexuality, Volume One,* tries to reconceive sexuality's relation to power so that power needn't imply repression and sexuality doesn't anticipate emancipation:

> To say that sex is not repressed, or rather that the relationship between sex and power is not characterized by repression, is to risk falling into a sterile paradox. . . . The question I would like to pose is not, Why are we repressed? but rather, Why do we say, with so much passion and so much resentment against our most recent past, against our present, and against ourselves, that we are repressed? By what spiral did we come to affirm that sex is negated? What led us to show, ostentatiously, that sex is something we hide, to say it is something we silence? (8–9)

The "sterile paradox" that bores Foucault is the suggestion that if sexuality is repressed, favorable political conditions will sexually liberate people. We can accept Foucault's frustration with Reich's and Marcuse's arguments about sexual emancipation, but the problem about repression isn't solved by invoking this "sterile paradox"—Foucault simply renders it enigmatic. Those accepting Foucault's premise forget that sexuality for him *no longer can function as the subject's truth.* This is where essentialists and constructionists part company, the former adamant that the history of homosexuality is not reducible to discourse (see Boswell), the latter certain that Foucault's emphasis on discourse helps them interpret diverse constructions of homosexuality (see Weeks, "Discourse" 86–103; Halperin, *One* 15–40, 41–53). This is also the point at which psychoanalysis contends that Foucault has thrown out the baby with the bathwater: So concerned is he to disband an insistence that sexuality is the subject's truth that he ignores *psychical* history and resistance, arguing instead that different formations of discourse can radically transform a subject's desire. These arguments ultimately produce a theoretical voluntarism about gender and sexuality, particularly the fantasy that we can reinvent at will our gender and sexuality.[29]

Thus far we have established only that Foucault wants to disband the "repressive hypothesis" and to refute the claims of Neo-Freudians, though it's still unclear what he means throughout *The History of Sexuality, Volume One,* by *repression.* In the opening pages of this volume, Foucault again characterizes other people's understanding of repression as silence and prohibition, a definition he clearly doesn't share:

> These are the characteristic features attributed to repression, which serve to distinguish it from the prohibitions maintained by penal law: repression operated as a sentence to disappear, but also as an injunction to silence, an affirmation of nonexistence, and, by implication, an admission that there was nothing to say about such things, nothing to see, and nothing to know. Such was the hypocrisy of our bourgeois societies with its halting logic. (4)

The logic is "halting [*boiteuse*]" because certain concessions were imperative: "If it was truly necessary to make room for illegitimate sexualities, it was reasoned, let them take their infernal mischief elsewhere: to a place where they could be reintegrated, if not in the circuits of production, at least in those of profit" (4).

Since Foucault "defines" repression in this way—as a hypothesis formulated by unnamed sources (implicitly Reich and Marcuse) whom Foucault represents in turn by *self*-characterizations—one sees why his "adversaries" are easy to defeat (82). One can't even hold Foucault responsible for these characterizations, for the agency they describe apparently has vanished, absorbed by a vast system of "power/knowledge." Indeed, Foucault implies conveniently, even bizarrely, that the very *act* of probing these characterizations "bear[s] traces of the same old prudishness" and thus compels us to reproduce bourgeois discourse (6). The point is that Foucault—in a veiled, almost authoritarian way—compels his readers to choose between two false alternatives.

It is quite feasible to claim that Victorian culture was simultaneously "expansive" *and* "repressive" in its elaboration of sexuality. And Foucault eventually has to make this point to show why legislative measures accompanying the "discursive explosion . . . tended to function as a norm [that] was stricter, perhaps, but quieter" (38). This admission immediately muddies the waters, however, for it concedes much ground to those advocating the "repressive hypothesis." Hence, one might speculate, Foucault repeatedly substitutes caricature for historical agency and dates, relies increasingly on passive voice, and softens his opening rhetoric about power and hypocrisy when describing legal situations that illustrate precisely the most repressive aspects of Victorian society:

> What does the appearance of all these peripheral sexualities signify? Is the fact that they could appear in broad daylight a sign that the code had become more lax? Or does the fact that they were given so much attention testify to a stricter regime and to its concern to bring them under close supervision? *In terms of repression, things are unclear* [*En termes de répression, les choses sont ambiguës*]. There was permissiveness if one bears in mind that the severity of the codes relating to sexual offenses diminished considerably in the nineteenth century and that law itself often deferred to medicine. But an additional ruse of severity, if one thinks of all the agencies of control and all the mechanisms of surveillance that were put into operation by pedagogy or therapeutics. (40–41; my emphasis; *Histoire 1* 56)

The net effect is that Foucault has it both ways. In the interest of saying everything about medicine, psychiatry, sexology, and the law, Foucault says nothing precise about their immediate repercussions. Why? Specific details surely would push Foucault too close to his "adversaries" (82), forcing closer scrutiny of claims that sound magnificent when charting the sociosexual terrain of four or more centuries, but less convincing when applied to such crucial decades as the 1880s and 1890s.

Let's reflect on the "example" Foucault postulates: "the codes relating to sexual offenses," which "diminished considerably in the nineteenth century." Considering his emphasis on late Victorian society and related discussion of emergent sexual categories in Western Europe, Foucault partly refers to the fact that in 1861 English and Welsh law revoked Henry VIII's statute of 1533 that criminalized buggery as a "crime against nature" punishable by hanging (Scotland revoked this law in 1889; Weeks, *Coming Out* 12; "Sins"). One could say immediately that one of the last enactments of this law was in February 1816, when four crew members of H.M.S. *Africaine* were hanged for buggery after a major naval scandal (Weeks, *Sex* 100) and that Henry VIII's statute became ineffective, even before being revoked, because its punitive terms were too harsh to enforce in late-nineteenth-century England.[30] For this and other reasons, the 1861 Offences Against the Person Act removed the death penalty for buggery, "replacing it by sentences of between ten years and life" (Weeks, "Discourse" 85). However, in 1885, largely in response to greater demands for social and sexual control,[31] section 11 of England and Wales's Criminal Law Amendment Act—the Labouchère amendment—designated *all* male homosexual acts, whether public or private, illegal and punishable for a term "not exceeding two years, with or without hard labour" (qtd. in Weeks, *Coming Out* 14; Smith, "Sexuality"). Since buggery alone was previously illegal, Labouchère's amendment actually signified a *marked increase* in the law's purview and repressive power;[32] it is more difficult to invoke this amendment as a factor *soliciting* the acts it criminalized, as even the staunchest Foucauldians concede.[33] We could add that William Coote, secretary of Britain's National Vigilance Association, wrote in 1902: "There is a very popular cant phrase that you cannot make men good by [an] Act of Parliament. It is false to say so. . . . You can, and do, keep men sober simply by an Act of Parliament; you can, and do, chain the devil of impurity in a large number of men and women by the fear of the law" (qtd. in Mort, *Dangerous* 105).

    Where does this leave the status of "repression" in Foucault's text? Foucault himself seems unable to decide. "All this garrulous attention which has us in a stew over sexuality, is it not motivated by one basic concern: . . . to constitute a sexuality that is economically useful and politically conservative? I still do not know whether this is the ultimate objective. But this much is certain: reduction has not been the means employed for achieving it" (36–37). Here and elsewhere, Foucault wants to refute narratives characterizing Western society since the seventeenth century as simply "repressive." Yet he also wants to produce a discourse about "resistance" that responds to generic forms of "power": "Where there is power, there is resistance, and yet, or rather consequently, this resistance is never in a position of exteriority in relation to power" (95). Foucault's solution to this conceptual impasse (one can't have resistance without at least *implying* that it responds to repressive measures) is to make "power" *nonspecific,* detached from identifiable causes. In this way, he advances the paradoxical claim that one can have resistance responsive to power, *but not power with strictly repressive means or ends.*

We can give Foucault credit for rescinding many stale and implausible conceptions of subjectivity (a project he inherited from Freud, Nietzsche, and Marx), but the net effect of his project is to render subjectivity either a model of replete consciousness that displaces the unconscious or a nomadic principle devoid of all coherence *except* "desire," since power and desire conflict and meld in Foucault's account without identifiable forms of repression. The paradox is that in dismissing the principle of repression, Foucault provides a startling account of fantasy and desire that consistently returns us to an unanswered question: Did psychoanalysis prescribe or demythologize gender and sexuality? Given Freud's concern to highlight the "violent opposition" between identity and sexuality ("Resistance" 294), he points up both the psychic constituents of these phenomena and the reason neither can lead to perfect fulfillment and lasting happiness. It is nonetheless remarkable that Foucault ultimately *reproduces* this binary between sexuality and identity in his later work. Aiming to include all forms of psychoanalysis in the "repressive hypothesis," Foucault's Anglo-American readers downplay or simply ignore these conceptual links between Foucault and Freud.

Am I therefore arguing that Foucault was a closet Freudian? Not quite. Foucault's disparaging remarks about psychoanalysis at the end of *Madness and Civilization* (1961) are well known, not least his claim that psychoanalysis "has not been able, will not be able, to hear the voices of unreason" (278). Less well known(and certainly less quoted) is the fact that Foucault concluded his later study *The Order of Things* (1966) by saying *the exact opposite,* valuing psychoanalysis far above ethnology because it reveals "the outer confines of representation" (378). The following passage is sufficiently important to quote at length:

Psychoanalysis stands as close as possible, in fact, to that critical function which, as we have seen, exists within all the human sciences. In setting itself the task of making the discourse of the unconscious speak through consciousness, psychoanalysis is advancing in the direction of that fundamental region in which the relations of representation and finitude come into play. Whereas all the human sciences advance towards the unconscious only with their back to it, waiting for it to unveil itself as fast as consciousness is analysed, as it were backwards, psychoanalysis, on the other hand, points directly towards it, with a deliberate purpose—not towards that which must be rendered gradually more explicit by the progressive illumination of the implicit, but towards what is there and yet is hidden, towards what exists with the mute solidity of a thing, of a text closed in upon itself, or of a blank space in a visible text, and uses that quality to defend itself. *It must not be supposed that the Freudian approach is the combination of an interpretation of meaning and a dynamics of resistance or defence;* by following the same path as the human sciences, but with its gaze turned the other way, *psychoanalysis moves towards the moment—by definition inaccessible to any theoretical knowledge of man, to any continuous apprehension in terms of signification, conflict, or function—at which the contents of consciousness articulate themselves, or rather stand gaping, upon man's finitude.* (374; my emphases)

Considering the importance of this and other passages on psychoanalysis in *The Order of Things,* it is odd that many Anglo-American readers of Foucault have consistently ignored this dimension of his work. Here and elsewhere, Foucault did not argue that psychoanalysis is axiomatically repressive. In *The History of Sexuality, Volume One,* he acknowledged instead that Freudian psychoanalysis does *not* logically fall within the purview of Victorian repression. We should note that this argument differs radically from his claim that Reich and Marcuse interpreted the relation between subjects and societies by a "repressive *hypothesis.*" Put bluntly, Foucault realized that the proponents of a theory can be distinct from the actual phenomenon that theory aims to describe.

Without grasping this obvious point, Foucauldians must be surprised to see Foucault draw heavily on Freudian-Lacanian arguments to conceptualize his claims about power-without-repression. Unfortunately, Foucault makes the following admission only at the start of part four of *Volume One*. Had this passage appeared in the opening section, where it surely belongs, he would have averted much interpretive confusion:

> In point of fact, the assertion that sex is not "repressed" is not altogether new [!]. Psychoanalysts have been saying the same thing for some time [Que le sexe ne soit pas "réprimé," ce n'est pas en effet une assertion bien neuve. Il y a bon temps que des psychanalystes l'ont dit]. They have challenged the simple little machinery that comes to mind when one speaks of repression; the idea of a rebellious energy that must be throttled has appeared to them inadequate for deciphering the manner in which power and desire are joined to one another; they consider them to be linked in a more complex and primary way than through the interplay of a primitive, natural, and living energy welling up from below, and a higher order seeking to stand in its way; *thus one should not think that desire is repressed,* for the simple reason that the law is what constitutes both desire and the lack on which it is predicated [il n'y aurait pas à imaginer que le désir est réprimé, pour la bonne raison que c'est la loi qui est constitutive du désir et du manque qui l'instaure]. (81; my emphasis; *Histoire 1* 107, 108)

At this point it should be clear that Foucault's "thus," in the passage above ("thus one should not think that desire is repressed"), is doing quite a lot of work. Considering the deceptive ease with which Foucault here redefines the very *repression* that the "repressive hypothesis" tries to theorize, before paraphrasing one of Lacan's fundamental axioms ("la loi . . . est constitutive du désir et du manque qui l'instaure"),[34] we might wonder why the final sentence in this passage contains no quotation marks or even a footnote referencing Lacan's *Les quatre concepts fondamentaux de la psychanalyse*. Lacan published this seminar in 1973, three years before Foucault's *La Volonté de savoir* appeared, though he presented it in Paris throughout 1964 and copies of this and other seminars by Lacan were disseminated widely among Parisian intellectuals; Lacan's *écrits* were published much earlier, however, in 1966. According to his most recent biographer, David Macey, Foucault attended Lacan's seminars in the 1950s and followed his work with keen interest (245, 513 n. 26; see also James Miller 62, 135–36, 150). Macey notes also that Foucault wrote a brief tribute to Lacan, after his death in 1981, calling him "the liberator of psychoanalysis" (qtd. 422).

In his 1964 seminar, Lacan advanced Freud's perspective on the significance of psychic drives. In "Instincts and Their Vicissitudes" (1915), Freud had argued that the drive is neither organic nor socially constructed, but an *involuntary* sign of the subject's alienation, a phenomenon Lacan would later call "lack-in-being" (122–23; Lacan, *Four* 29):

> What is the relation of 'instinct' to 'stimulus'? There is nothing to prevent our subsuming the concept of 'instinct' under that of 'stimulus' and saying that an instinct is a stimulus applied to the mind. But we are immediately set on our guard against *equating* instinct and mental stimulus. . . . [A]n 'instinct' appears to us as a concept on the frontier between the mental and the somatic, as the psychical representative of the stimuli originating from within the organism and reaching the mind, as a measure of the demand made upon the mind for work in consequence of its connection with the body. ("Instincts" 118, 121–22; original emphasis)

In light of Freud's and Lacan's arguments, Foucault surely is right to suggest that the law "constitutes both desire and the lack on which it is predicated," yet he also confuses Lacan's distinction between symbolic Law and political laws. The former *causes* desire by intervening between the subject and "the Thing" it wants, an intervention responsible for ontological alienation because the subject's identity can begin only when this traumatic separation occurs (*Four* 218).

Since Foucault's argument appropriates elements of Lacanian psychoanalysis, we can see why he wanted immediately to distance himself from Lacan's conception of repression, to which I'll soon turn. The result, however, is simply confusing—unusually so in a philosopher of Foucault's stature:

> Where there is desire, the power relation is already present: an illusion, then, to denounce this relation for a repression exerted after the event [illusion donc, de le dénoncer dans une répres-

sion qui s'exercerait après coup]; but vanity as well, to go questing after a desire that is beyond the reach of power.

But, in an obstinately confused way, I sometimes spoke, as though I were dealing with equivalent notions, of *repression,* and sometimes of *law,* of prohibition or censorship [Or, d'une manière obstinément confuse, j'ai parlé, comme s'il s'agissait de notions équivalentes, tantôt de la *répression,* tantôt de la *loi,* de l'interdit ou de la censure]. Through stubbornness or neglect, I failed to consider everything that can distinguish their theoretical implications [J'ai méconnu—entêtement ou négligence—tout ce qui peut distinguer leurs implications théoriques ou pratiques]. And I grant that one might justifiably say to me: By constantly referring to positive technologies of power, you are playing a double game where you hope to win on all counts; you confuse your adversaries by appearing to take the weaker position, and, discussing repression alone, you would have us believe, wrongly, that you have rid yourself of the problem of law; and yet you keep the essential practical consequence of the principle of power-as-law, namely the fact that there is no escaping from power. (81–82; *Histoire 1* 108; original emphases)

In this passage Foucault ventriloquizes some of the arguments I'm making here, but his strategy doesn't answer the doubts he raises; instead, it allows him to sidestep the questions altogether: Foucault doesn't respond to the "charges" he lists above in the form in which he presents them. Instead, he introduces the term "juridico-discursive" (82), proposing that

[i]t is this conception that governs both the thematics of repression and the theory of the law as constitutive of desire. In other words, what distinguishes the analysis made in terms of the repression of instincts from that made in terms of the law of desire is clearly the way in which they each conceive of the nature and dynamics of the drives, not the way in which they conceive of power [c'est à coup sûr la manière de concevoir la nature et la dynamique des pulsions; ce n'est pas la manière de concevoir le pouvoir]. . . . Moreover, one must not imagine that this representation is peculiar to those who are concerned with the problem of the relations of power with sex. In fact it is much

more general; one frequently encounters it in political analyses of power, and it is deeply rooted in the history of the West. (82–83; *Histoire 1* 109)

The problem here is that, as Foucault acknowledges and then strangely forgets, "the analysis made in terms of the repression of instincts" is *not commensurate* with "that made in terms of the law of desire." Generalizing the "relations of power with sex" in a way that seems to engage both phenomena simply interprets the latter in terms of the former. Thus the "juridico-discursive" model won't do as a comprehensive explanation of repression. As Foucault seemed to accept when ventriloquizing his adversaries' arguments, his appeal to the broader regulation of "power" doesn't address "the analysis made in terms of the repression of instincts": "[I]n an obstinately confused way, I sometimes spoke as though I were dealing with equivalent notions, of *repression,* and sometimes of *law,* . . . [and] failed to consider everything that can distinguish their theoretical implications."

2. Lacan's Rereading of Freud

What Lacan says about repression challenges Foucault's account of sexuality and culture. Lacan argued that the subject's "integration into history evidently brings with it the forgetting of an entire world of shadows which are not transposed into symbolic existence" (*Seminar I* 192). He insisted that one cannot have identity without "forgetting," by which he means that identity is not possible until the subject encounters separation and alienation. And he characterized this alienation as a profound gap between "being" and "meaning," in which the subject gains the latter only by relinquishing and suspending elements of the former (in being able to speak, for instance, the subject gives up aspects of its jouissance): "The being of the subject . . . is there beneath the meaning. If we choose being, the subject disappears, it eludes us, it falls into non-meaning. If we choose meaning, the meaning survives only deprived of that part of non-meaning that is, strictly speaking, that which constitutes in the realization of the subject, the unconscious" (*Four* 211).

Foucauldians and cultural materialists may respond to these arguments by claiming that if repression proceeds according to the ego's supposedly "ethical" and cultural aspirations,[35] psychoanalysis merely illustrates the particular forms and effects of repression found in Victorian society. What this ignores is the psychoanalytic argument that repression does not exist *only* in response to social prohibitions; this gets us to the heart of the confusion. Psychoanalysis argues that repression exists *regardless of the historical and cultural conditions in which it occurs,* a claim that doesn't thereby ignore how certain elements of repression are contingent on social forces. The ego's identifications don't fall neatly within the purview of cultural imperatives, a point illustrating why Foucault's argument that repression is socially specific ignores the fraught, and sometimes impossible, relation between discourse and sexual desire. The psychic determinants of identification and desire are rarely self-evident, Freud and Lacan argue, because the relations between society and subject—and between being and nonbeing—are asymmetrical and not causal:

> [W]hat has to be recognised, Freud teaches us, is not expressed, but repressed. With a machine, whatever doesn't come on time simply falls by the wayside and makes no claims on anything. This is not true for man, the scansion is alive, and whatever doesn't come on time remains in suspense. That is what is involved in repression.
>
> No doubt something which isn't expressed doesn't exist. But the repressed is always there, insisting, and demanding to be. The fundamental relation of man to this symbolic order is very precisely what founds the symbolic order itself—the relation of non-being to being. (*Seminar II* 307–8)

Lacan argues that the subject is torn between several incommensurate demands: social law, psychic Law operating by injunctions and guilt, and an internal resistance to satisfaction, based on the psychoanalytic precept that the subject's ultimate pleasure orients it not toward its own good, but toward its extinction in death. Concerning the influence of resistance on psychic pleasure, for example, Freud argued as early as 1912: "[W]e must reckon with the possibility that something *in the nature of the sexual instinct itself* is unfavourable to the realization of complete satisfaction" ("On the Universal" 188–89; my emphasis). This tearing and the subject's related internal antagonism give us less and more than a political statement about Victorian, modern, or contemporary societies because the antagonism, although related to discourse, is not reducible to it. As I outlined above, Freud did complain about the impossible demands society places on its subjects, but he framed this complaint in an unconventional way. In *Civilization and Its Discontents* (1929, 1930), he argued that "it is impossible to overlook the extent to which civilization is built up upon a renunciation of instinct, how much *it presupposes precisely the non-satisfaction* . . . of powerful instincts" (97; my emphasis).

Many critics paraphrase Freud's claim to suggest that "civilization" merely deprives us of satisfaction. But Freud meant that "civilization," in trying to prevent us from realizing the "satisfaction . . . of powerful instincts," not only protects us from what we want, but compels us to forget the reasons for this central "non-satisfaction." Such a forgetting doesn't produce a benign education, in which the subject gladly accepts its constraints.[36] Since Freud argues that desire itself is not ontologically benign, given the subject's orientation toward a satisfaction "beyond pleasure,"[37] he doesn't claim that we can divert desire toward utilitarian ends—that is, by turning the sacrifice into productive labor—without paying an immense price. Nor does Freud add insult to injury by telling us all to "school" ourselves and thus enjoy our deprivation. He argues instead that *society* adds insult to injury by demanding that we repress the constitutive trauma of subjectivity (the distinction between "being" and "meaning" described above). This "insult" obviously varies from one culture to the next, but we should not forget that the resultant trauma *surpasses* politics and representation, due to the resistance of aspects of subjectivity to meaning. Following Freud and Lacan, *The Burdens of Intimacy* points up the repercussions of this self-surpassing—or "excess" of subjectivity—but it doesn't try to incorporate the excess into philosophical and literary texts in order to render it meaningful. Instead, by asking us to rethink conventional accounts of cultural and sexual meaning—accounts that can understand sexuality and identity only as self-evident and rational phenomena—this book tries to use the subject's partial resistance to meaning to highlight significant fault lines of Victorian society.

Why does psychoanalysis insist that repression is not in fact suppression? Because in rejecting the principle that subjects have either replete consciousness or entire mastery of language and themselves, Freud came to see that "[a] repression is something very different from a condemning judgement" (*From the History* 79–80). Repression proceeds largely from the preconscious, he claims, which acts in the interests of the ego but without the latter agent being aware of this action. In this respect, repression is involuntary and not a conscious activity (Freud, "Unconscious" 179–83; see also Lacan, *Seminar I* 43). If repression were a conscious affair (a psychic contradiction in terms), one could easily persuade others to disband their repressions and accept the things they find abhorrent, repulsive, and intolerable. Yet as psychoanalysis knows, people not only "irrationally" hate phenomena they could enjoy, but often find themselves drawn to objects or activities jeopardizing their entire well-being.

To all these claims about repression, psychoanalysis adds that sexuality impacts on the subject not as a "construction" or simple element of discourse, but as a *shock:* As Jean Laplanche remarks on a passage in Freud's letters and notes to Wilhelm Fliess, "the ego is 'attacked,' so to speak, on the side where it 'least expected it'" (*Life* 43), which means that sexuality arrives "too early" and "too late" for the ego to consider it tolerable (Freud, *Origins* 416). Laplanche usefully glosses Freud's claim:

> Fundamentally, what is at stake is the relation in the human being between his "acculturation" and his "biological" sexuality, on the condition that it be understood that the latter is already, for its part, partially "denatured." What exactly is too late? Biological sexuality with its maturational stages and above all the moment of puberty; such organic sexuality comes too late, failing to furnish the child (who constitutes the principal subject of the *Three Essays*) with "affective" and "ideational" counterparts sufficient to allow him to assimilate the sexual scene and to "understand" it. But at the same time sexuality comes too early as an interhuman relation; it comes from without, imported from the world of adults. (*Life* 43–44)

Despite drawing on biology ("maturational stages," "the moment of puberty," and "organic sexuality") and on materialism ("the world of adults"), psychoanalytic arguments about sexuality aren't reducible to either register. While as Laplanche shows, psychoanalysis discusses psychic *drives*—rather than biological *instincts*—"the world of adults" impacts the child "too early," influencing consciousness with stimulants and fantasies that far exceed its capacity to grasp their physical and sexual significance.

More important, Laplanche's argument takes us beyond biological and organicist notions that sexuality is wholesome, instinctual, and ontologically benign. According to psychoanalysis, sexuality *shatters* consciousness by breaking through the tenuous boundaries the ego erects to oppose psychic drives: Sexuality is thus *of* the subject, but *not within consciousness.* "Sexuality," notes Bersani, summarizing Laplanche's claims, "is a particularly human phenomenon in the sense that its very genesis may depend on the *décalage,* or gap, in human life between the quantities of stimuli to which we are exposed and the development of ego structures capable of resisting or, in Freudian terms, of binding those stimuli" (*Freudian* 38). That is why Freud emphasized the sexual constituency of the unconscious, and why Lacan in turn saw Freud's claim as an argument about representation and meaning: "The unconscious," he tells us, "is that chapter of [our] history that is marked by a blank or occupied by a falsehood: it is the censored chapter" ("Function" 50; see also Žižek 231).

In *Jude the Obscure* (1894; 1895), Hardy repeatedly illustrates this argument, even coining the term *erotolepsy*—or "love-seizure"—to emphasize the shock of desire (146). Similar crises of desire also recur in *Teleny; or, The Reverse of the Medal* (1893), a novel critics generally attribute to Oscar Wilde and his friends. Camille des Grieux, the narrator, wants Teleny so badly he tells his friends, "my inward self seemed to disintegrate itself from my body and to follow like his own shadow the man I loved. I unconsciously threw myself into a kind of trance and I had a most vivid hallucination, which, strange as it might appear, coincided with all that my friend did and felt" (73). Later, when des Grieux and Teleny have sex, Teleny is said to be "overpowered by enjoyment" (79)—"shattered by such an excess of wantonness" (119)—while des Grieux experiences "an unbearable voluptuousness of mingled pain and pleasure, [which] shattered my body and blasted my very soul; then everything waned in me. He clasped me in his arms, and I swooned away whilst he was kissing my cold and languid lips" (127).[38]

3. Repression in Victorian Literature

A fine example of literary criticism can illustrate these arguments about repression and sexuality. The body of critical work addressing these arguments in Victorian literature and repression is vast, and feminist accounts of the period's definitions of femininity, privacy, and domesticity have greatly enriched this field, seeing in Victorian repression what John Kucich has called "a certain efficacy as strategies for the exercise of social power" (9).[39] But Kucich's own astute study *Repression in Victorian Fiction: Charlotte Brontë, George Eliot, and Charles Dickens* (1987) is most relevant to our discussion because it comes closest to identifying Foucault's ambivalence about the concept of repression and the implications of that ambivalence for studies of Victorian literature. Kucich acknowledges that repression may have affected men and women quite differently, but he doesn't entirely accept a related feminist argument that women's strength and rebellion emerged by default as hysteria, covert rebellion, or mythic defiance:[40] Such claims reproduce the hydraulic model that Kucich, with Foucault's help, wants to dismantle. At the same time, Kucich pauses before accepting Foucault's cavalier dismissal of the "repressive hypothesis"; he wants to advance a thesis that is both supportive and critical of Freud, and certainly of much interest to psychoanalysis: "[N]ineteenth-century novels show us how, through the insular dynamics of repression, private and exclusive emotional experience can be rendered more intense, and more central to self-definition than any form of interpersonal experience" (2).

This thesis radically transforms the deadlock between materialism and psychoanalysis, for psychoanalysis cuts both ways in Kucich's book: If it partly endorses an understanding of secrecy that Kucich wants to disband, it is also not a simple perpetrator of coercive "power/knowledge": "My argument does not dispute the existence of a Freudian mechanism of repression, nor would I deny that many nineteenth-century individuals were victimized by paralyzing inhibitions. We must also not forget that repression is a contested practice in Victorian culture that could be shaped toward many different ends" (4). What is perhaps most interesting here is the relation between psychoanalysis and the intensification of libidinal pleasure, for according to Kucich psychoanalysis helps advance "unrecognized and pleasurable aspects of Victorian repression—its relationship to a libidinal model that develops and enriches desire" (30). And "[a]lthough the force of repression has always rightly been seen as anti-individualistic," he writes, "repression's attack on the self need not be understood only as a sterilizing one. Rather, repression can produce a *euphoric enlargement* precisely because it creates a destabilizing split within the self, and transforms assertive energy into self-negating energy" (22–23; my emphasis).

This argument highlights interesting tensions in Kucich's interpretive model. He claims that repression may occasionally puncture conventional forms of selfhood and that the subsequent "destabilizing split within the self" can intensify the subject's experience of desire. Yet these arguments partly imply a causal relation between social suppression and psychic repression, and it's difficult to see how *repression* itself produces a "euphoric enlargement": "splitting," "dissociation," and "condensation" are terms closer to Kucich's argument, but the psychic principles they describe differ radically from that of repression. Finally, although Kucich's reading of "euphoric enlargement" does accord with my previous discussion of the tension between sexuality and identity, Kucich seems uncertain how to read this "euphoric enlargement," arguing initially that it is "anti-individualistic" but not always "sterilizing"; that it can produce a "destabilizing split within the self" that is nonetheless "euphoric"; and, finally, that such "euphoric enlargement" ultimately "transforms assertive energy into self-negating energy."

Let me ask contentiously, Is "self-negation" necessarily problematic? Must we accept Kucich's claim that repression "smuggles an eroticized self-disruption out of the range of collective life" (27), as if "self-disruption" entirely derived from, or could be absorbed by, "collective life"? We are often told that self-negation jeopardizes group ties, community involvement, and even self-esteem, but if we pursue the arguments I raised above that sexual desire is largely inimical to selfhood, we might in fact represent this last factor as driving people apart—indeed, as the very reason Freud characterized the ego as "His Majesty" and a "constitutional monarch" ("On Narcissism" 91; *Ego* 55). We might also begin to see self-negation as an appropriate corrective to what Bersani has called "a hyperbolic sense of self" and a "phallicizing of the ego" ("Rectum" 218), a point to which I'll return.[41]

The French philosopher Georges Bataille allows Kucich to rethink suggestions that repression "causes" political and sexual paralysis, yet he also punctures conventional readings of Freud that can understand psychoanalysis only as the cause of our social and sexual misery. Bataille, that is, pushes whatever "Freudian" conceptions we have of "repression" toward an expansive—not entirely depletive—model, in which psychoanalysis *destroys* nineteenth-century models of self-aggrandizement by intensifying the conflict between sexuality and identity (the model is "expansive" in its attention to drives, but "depletive" in its conception of the ego). In this respect, Freud's insistent critique of "His Majesty the Ego" is not only profoundly anti-imperialistic, but of immense service to subjects finding the gap between "private" fantasy and "public" life increasingly intolerable.[42] Bataille also makes clear that the most radical dimensions of psychoanalysis have fallen by the wayside, despised by empiricists wanting "proof" of the unconscious (symptoms and phobias apparently aren't proof of the unconscious), materialists and many feminists misunderstanding Freud's relation to his sexual culture,[43] and philosophers appalled at Freud's insistence that self-negation wasn't something psychoanalysis invented (*Erotism* 200).[44]

If we debunk these egregious mischaracterizations of Freud—and Kucich partly encourages this—*we can't align Freudian psychoanalysis with cultural forms of repression,* as we discovered when reading Foucault's critique of Reich and Marcuse:

> Given the premium our culture has placed on knowledge and on desire, psychoanalysis has helped make it seem urgent to penetrate the inauthenticities of repression, if not actually to destroy them. Freud's notion of repression, and the wide theme of self-deception it has situated at the core of our ideas about psychic ill-health, is part of a universal modern stigmatization of forms of self-negation as enemies of truth. And it is precisely that stigmatization that I want to help dispel, for it blinds us (among other things) to the constitution of Victorian subjectivity. (Kucich, *Repression* 2)

In this passage, Kucich asks us to dispel the "universal modern *stigmatization* of forms of self-negation," which our culture considers "enemies of truth." This thesis has radical implications for our understanding of Victorian culture—even if, as I'm contending, it makes Freud partly responsible for the trauma and misery he tried to alleviate. Kucich doesn't fully claim that self-negation is an error or simple response to oppression; instead, he suggests that in stigmatizing self-negation, "our culture" gives us the impression that self-negation is *equivalent* to psychic ill-health. For Kuc-ich, the reverse may be true: Self-negation intensifies the libidinal intensity he finds attractive in such thinkers as Bataille (19–23). And when describ-ing the tendency to "slide away from symbolic connection to collective life" (31), Kucich reinvokes the problem of asymmetry as a critical gap between sexuality and identity, and between subjects and social groups. My book slightly revises this point, arguing that "collective life" is rarely a benign entity in which the subject best "realizes" itself, and that it's a mis-take to consider the subject's "slid[ing] away . . . toward the isolation of self-disruptive libido" as politically neutralizing or as producing only "the closed integrity of a repressed self" (31). *The Burdens of Intimacy* unpacks these assumptions about "isolation," "otherness," "symbolic connection," "self-disruptive libido," and "closed integrity" in order to view them afresh. Suffice that I raise only a set of competing questions here to anticipate my later readings: Why does the "collective" always recur in cultural and Marx-ian criticism as a benign entity promoting individual well-being, and yet an emphasis on the diverse violences that collectivity permits—and even encourages—falls out of discussion, only to emerge later as a concern about nationalism and imperialism? Why does society figure in this criti-cism as a redemptive counterforce to individual selfishness, while solitary and detached figures represent alienation rather than a strident individual-ism resisting the "tyranny" of social mandates? Why is an individual's satis-faction "potentially anti-individualistic," whereas at the level of groups it is empowering and politically efficacious? And why, finally, do we assume that "experience of the self" is a private affair and that our "experience of a group" is not?

These questions ask us to consider whether self-negation takes us toward others or pushes us away from them, a debate I restage at several points in this book. Let us pause here, however, and consider how these questions alter our perspective on Victorian sexuality.

4. Victorian Manhood

During the Victorian period the line between affectionate friendship and sexual intimacy seemed increasingly important to maintain. We can add, following Richard Dellamora, Linda Dowling, Jeffrey Richards, and Elaine Showalter, that the Victorians' attempt to distinguish friendship from sexual intimacy emerged partly in response to such cultural influences as Tractarian faith, Victorian Hellenism, and Paterian aestheticism, which strove to refine (and sometimes eclipse) this distinction altogether.[45] In "The New Chivalry" (1894), for example, Charles Kains-Jackson occasionally summarizes earlier endeavors in the nineteenth century: "Of companionship . . . there is much to be said. Here it is enough to ask how much do ordinary engaged couples, how much even do husband and wife, see of each other?" (qtd. in Reade 318). Arguing that overpopulation was a social and cultural burden (so endorsing the Rev. Thomas Malthus's concerns), and that male homosexual love represents "a more advanced type" than its heterosexual equivalent (qtd. 316), Kains-Jackson considered love between men a social and erotic imperative:

> Wherefore just as the flower of the early and imperfect civilization was in what we may call the Old Chivalry, or the exaltation of the youthful feminine ideal, so the flower of the adult and perfect civilization will be found in the New Chivalry or the exaltation of the youthful masculine ideal. The time has arrived when the eternal desire for Love which nature has implanted in the breast of man requires to be satisfied without such an increase in population as has characterized the past. (qtd. 315)

Kains-Jackson's argument illustrates that Victorian accounts of narcissism and same-sex friendship, such as Meredith's *Egoist,* cited earlier, had a profound effect on notions of decadence informing the 1880s and 1890s. This context underscores the ramifications of what Sedgwick and Showalter have called the "gender-transitive" and "gender-intransitive" theories that surfaced in Britain and Europe in these decades (Sedgwick, *Epistemology* 1–2, 88–89, 219–20; Showalter, *Sexual* 170–73). Such theories highlight instructive tensions in the definition of male and female homosexuality, especially homosexuality's relation to contemporaneous arguments about "appropriate" masculine and feminine behavior. Showalter therefore interprets the discussion of homosexuality after Oscar Wilde's 1895 trials, arguing that

> two conflicting models of homosexual identity began to emerge, opposing possibilities sometimes held simultaneously by the same individuals, which continue to coexist with power-

ful consequences today. The first was the paradigmatic fin-de-siècle model of sexual inversion, illustrated by the work of Karl Ulrichs and Magnus Hirschfeld in Germany and Edward Carpenter and John Addington Symonds in England. According to this model of border-crossing and liminality, gay people were an "intermediate sex," "exactly at the threshold between genders." . . . The second model, however, saw homosexuality as the "highest, most perfect evolutionary stage of gender identification." According to this model, the male-identified man and the woman-identified woman expressed heightened forms of masculinity and femininity and were the most purely "manly" or "womanly" representatives of their sex. Their sexual preference for their own sex was seen as determined by their shared disgust for the opposite sex rather than by their sharing of its desires. (*Sexual* 172–73)

In this passage, Showalter cites Edward Carpenter, followed by Sedgwick's article on Willa Cather and Benedict Friedländer's "Seven Theses on Homosexuality" (1908). The dualism she describes is instructive and informs the ensuing chapters in this book. In chapter 4, for instance, I consider Hardy's *The Mayor of Casterbridge* as a novel torn between these "conflicting models of homosexual identity" because Hardy represents his protagonist, Michael Henchard, as incapable of fulfilling the masculine ideal to which he and his closest friend, Donald Farfrae, aspire. After Henchard and Farfrae fight almost to the point of death, given their erotic rivalry for Lucetta Templeman, the narrator remarks: "Henchard took his full measure of shame and self-reproach. The scenes of his first acquaintance with Farfrae rushed back upon him—that time when the curious mixture of romance and thrift in the young man's composition so commanded his heart that Farfrae could play upon him as on an instrument. So thoroughly subdued was he that he remained on the sacks in a crouching attitude, unusual for a man, and for such a man. Its womanliness sat tragically on the figure of so stern a piece of virility" (348).

In Hardy's novel—and in related texts I interpret in this book—masculine identification emerges almost as a "vertical" idea, while effeminacy seems to be sandwiched *beneath* virility, betraying its presence only when protagonists such as Henchard fail to sustain their masculine ideals.

However, Showalter's and related arguments about masculine friendship usefully invert this "vertical" model of virility/effeminacy, presenting it as a "lateral" problematic in which cultural pressures beset a continuum of masculine identifications. These arguments help us interpret the pressure and violence compelling men to identify with such rigid sexual categories as "homosexuality" and "heterosexuality"—categories often inadequate to the diversity of thoughts, acts, and desires that Victorian fiction frequently represents.

Such arguments about virility and effeminacy remind us of Alfred C. Kinsey's suggestion that a continuum best represents sexual characteristics among men and women. As he argued in 1948 (against popular wisdom),

> Males do not represent two discrete populations, heterosexual and homosexual. The world is not to be divided into sheep and goats. Not all things are black nor all things white. It is a fundamental of taxonomy that nature rarely deals with discrete categories. Only the human mind invents categories and tries to force facts into separated pigeon-holes. The living world is a continuum in each and every one of its aspects. The sooner we learn this concerning human sexual behavior the sooner we shall reach a sound understanding of the realities of sex. (639)[46]

Sedgwick notes further that this continuum affects men and women quite differently, impeding "gender symmetry" (*Between Men* 21–27; *Epistemology* 27–35). We can hazard that the resistance still facing Kinsey's and Sedgwick's arguments stems from a pervasive cultural idea that virility is inherently superior to effeminacy, an idea we've inherited from ancient Greece without properly acknowledging its homoerotic foundations.

Despite these suggestions of a divide between gender-transitive and -intransitive theories, Showalter usefully shows that many advocates of each argument vacillated from one side to the other. While in principle supporting notions of an "intermediate sex," Edward Carpenter was fascinated by "manly" homosexual men (to speak of "gay people" in the 1890s is anachronistic). And though Karl Heinrich Ulrichs advocated the idea of a "third sex," believing that male homosexuals were congenitally disposed to femininity as "inverts," his work highlights dramatic conceptual tensions between masculine identification and what he called "man-manly" love. Ulrichs asked in 1868, "Are there particular physical characteristic differences between Urnings and Men?," his question presupposing that these types are mutually exclusive. Yet his discussion becomes equivocal when trying to account for "Mannlings" (manly Uranians, surely an oxymoron for Ulrichs):

> Everything feminine that is found in the Urning's physical sphere is only the effect of an overlapping of the feminine sexual power of the psyche into the sphere of the body, which is itself completely integrated as masculine (an overlapping that does not quite occur in the case of the Mannling). The masculine body shape is hardly ever transformed in any respect into an organically female one by that overlapping, never more than in the assumption of a feminine coloring or complexion. . . . The reverse phenomenon, the Mannling's psychical masculinity or manliness, I consider, on the other hand, to be the effect of that formative overlapping of the male physical power, that is, of an overlapping that automatically gives form to the female love drive, and not somehow as the effect of the residue of original psychical masculinity. That is because the psyche, differing from the body, in general exhibits no original masculine aspects, just as it exhibits no original feminine ones; on the contrary, in its original state the psyche is simply asexual. There is much more research to be done in this field. (2: 386–87)[47]

Why does "the Mannling's psychical masculinity or manliness . . . *automatically* give form to the female love drive"? This conclusion arises from Ulrichs's insistence on congenital inversion, for the "third sex" apparently lacks a "residue of original psychical masculinity." The argument becomes inconsistent here, for this "residue" necessarily distinguishes Mannlings from other Uranians. In later chapters in this book, the trace of this conceptual difficulty will recur in distinctions between "manly" homosexuality and heterosexuality. And we'll see psychoanalysis reject the congenital model of homosexuality, with Freud insisting that "Psycho-analytic research is most decidedly opposed to *any* attempt at separating off homosexuals from the rest of mankind as a group of a special character" (*Three* 145 n; my emphasis; see also chapter 3 below). Freud's insistence has extensive repercussions for theorizing the nebulous terrain between heterosexuality and "manly" homosexuality, for this dimension of Victorian asymmetry emerges overall as a concern about the social and cultural significance of masculinity. Let me therefore repeat this introduction's opening quotation, taken from Freud's "Notes upon a Case of Obsessional Neurosis" (1909): "A man who doubts his own love may or rather *must* doubt every lesser thing" (241; original emphasis).

Considering these arguments, that many critics downplay psychoanalysis's role in promoting gender-transitive discussion truly is remiss (see D. A. Miller, *Novel* 190; and Sedgwick, *Epistemology* 84, 90). Psychoanalysis does not draw on gender-transitive theories to endorse heterosexual complementarity; it argues instead that *fantasy* is the transitive element overriding men and women's sexual asymmetry.[48] More than any of the thinkers above, Freud consistently elaborated on the psychic and political repercussions of instances in which same-sex desire is congruent *and* incongruent with same-sex identification. And so while Showalter summarizes scientific arguments about "the male-identified man and the woman-identified woman," psychoanalysis adds that both phrases veil much psychic and conceptual turbulence. To offer only the most obvious possibilities, a "male-identified man" could refer to an effeminate heterosexual or a virile homosexual, as Ulrichs discovered; it would also include all conceivable shades of masculinity between. For psychoanalysis, the very phrase "the male-identified man and the woman-identified woman" begs a question to which we'll need an entire book to respond.

5. MODERN MASCULINITY

Later chapters will illustrate this point. I want to conclude this introduction by sketching how this context shifted at the turn of the century; the relevance of this identificatory question for Victorian culture can be grasped by noting briefly how later writers viewed it. That several male modernists recoiled from the "taint" of Romantic and Pre-Raphaelite sensibility, averse to its more extreme manifestation in fin-de-siècle decadence, tells us a great deal about effeminacy in the nineteenth century and perceptions of it in the first decades of the twentieth. Such comparisons don't give us legible history, it is true, but they allow us to consider why several modernists rejected the seemingly florid, ornate, and effete styles of Romantic and Pre-Raphaelite poetry. As several critics have noted, T. E.

Hulme advanced in "Romanticism and Classicism" (c. 1911–12) an early Imagist doctrine that tried to distance itself from the alleged effeminacy and emotionalism of "parts of Keats, Coleridge, Byron, Shelley and Swinburne" (119).[49]

Hulme claims strikingly that Romanticism has "debauched us" (127); he calls it "damp" and "leak[y]" (127, 135), a movement replete with "sloppiness" and "vagueness" (126, 114). And while the "perverted rhetoric" and "receptive attitude" of Romantic poetry apparently have "run dry" (118, 126), "the awful result of romanticism," he writes, "is that, accustomed to this strange light, you can never live without it. Its effect on you is that of a drug" (127). In "the classical attitude" Hulme admires, however, there is a "holding back, a reservation" (120), this perspective being "all dry and hard" (126, 133); "arid" (127); "accurate, precise" (132); "exact" (132); "sincer[e]" (133); "fresh" (134, 135); "physical" (135); "cheerful, dry and sophisticated" (137). Such claims are more pronounced in Hulme's "Lecture on Modern Poetry" (c. 1908), in which he reflects on "the decay of an art form . . . and . . . religion": "The carcass is dead, and all the flies are upon it. Imitative poetry springs up like weeds, and women whimper and whine of you and I alas, and roses, roses all the way. It [Romanticism] becomes the expression of sentimentality rather than of virile thought" (69).

T. S. Eliot, Ezra Pound, and W. B. Yeats all characterized nineteenth-century aestheticism and decadence in similar ways. "I took the usual adolescent course with Byron, Shelley, Keats, Rossetti, Swinburne," laments Eliot in *The Use of Poetry and the Use of Criticism* (1933; 33). "At this period, the poem, or the poetry of a single poet, invades the youthful consciousness and assumes complete possession for a time. We do not really see it as something with an existence outside ourselves. . . . It is not [the] deliberate choice of a poet to mimic, but writing under a kind of daemonic possession by one poet" (34). Upping the ante, Pound remarks: "I have different degrees of antipathy or even contempt . . . for the softness of the 'nineties'" (362); of Swinburne's poetry he notes, "[T]he unconscious collapse into this sort of writing has wrecked more poets in our time than perhaps all other faults put together" (294). Finally, rejecting the "womanish introspection" of his early poetry (its "exaggeration of sentiment and sentimental beauty . . . I have come to think unmanly"), Yeats calls aestheticism "a region of brooding emotions full of fleshly waters and vapours which kill[s] the spirit and the will, ecstasy and joy equally" (*Letters* 434). "As so happens with a thing one has been tempted by and is still a little tempted by," he adds, "I am roused by it to a kind of frenzied hatred which is quite out of my control. . . . I cannot probably be quite just to any poetry that speaks to me with the sweet insinuating feminine voice of the dwellers in that country of shadows and hollow images" (434).

These and other commentaries on the "softness" of aestheticism and on "womanish introspection" justify my book's interest in psychoanalysis and effeminacy.[50] Indeed, in his book-length essay, *Per amica silentia lunæ* (1918 [1917]), Yeats reflects extensively on ingenuousness and passivity:

> Some years ago I began to believe that our culture, with its doctrine of sincerity and self-realisation, made us gentle and passive, and that the Middle Ages and the Renaissance were right to found theirs upon the imitation of Christ or of some classic hero. . . . When I had this thought I could see nothing else in life. I could not write the play I had planned, for all became allegorical, and though I tore up hundreds of pages in my endeavour to escape from allegory, my imagination became sterile for nearly five years and I only escaped at last when I had mocked in a comedy my own thought. (34–35)[51]

In pushing for greater understanding of what aids and defeats ingenuousness and creativity, Yeats engages popular superstitions about temptation, suggesting that "the Daemon comes not as like to like but seeking its own opposite, for man and Daemon feed the hunger in one another's hearts. Because the ghost is simple, the man heterogeneous and confused, they are but knit together when the man has found a mask whose lineaments permit the expression of all the man most lacks, and it may be dreads, and of that only" (37–38).

"The expression of all the man most lacks": Yeats seems ardently to want this, but tolerating this type of speech entails a fascinating internal compromise. "Within ourselves Reason and Will, who are the man and woman, hold out towards a hidden altar, a laughing or crying child" (90), he claims, suggesting that if a writer is to aid creativity, he (the masculine personal pronoun is apposite; Yeats's essay is largely autobiographical) must tolerate a type of "passiv[ity]" where the vehicle [of the Will] is coarse, we become mediumistic, and the spirits who mould themselves in that coarse vehicle can only rarely and with great difficulty speak their own thoughts and keep their own memory" (87). Such difficulties in expression arise because we "bewilder and overmaster" the spirits inspiring them.

We are close to Jung's formulation of the "contrasexual" elements characterizing each person—the varying degrees of "anima" and "animus" determining every psyche (see Jung 25–41). While such claims also return us to Plato's Aristophanes, a subject touched upon earlier in the context of Hardy's *Tess,* they don't advance our understanding of the role and "locus" of effeminacy in the nineteenth and twentieth centuries, and they preempt important questions about the antagonism between conscious and unconscious systems, transforming these questions into neutralizing concerns about intrapersonal harmony and balance.[52] For the purposes of this book, Yeats's *difficulty* with passivity—registered variously in *Per amica silentia lunæ* and his *Letters*—fosters a more radical connection with his conception of "[t]he other self, the anti-self or the antithetical self, as one may choose to name it, [which] comes but to those who are no longer deceived, whose passion is reality" (*Per amica* 30). Unlike Jung, I am not trying to define this "anti-self" as a form of man's repressed anima; instead, following the train of thought in Yeats's remarkable essay, I am interested in the repercussions of diverse nineteenth-century suggestions that this anti-self is feminine, even effete.

Because of the long and diverse tradition of representing fancy, thought, desire, and caprice as feminine, it seems necessary to stress that my book addresses only the repercussions of this tradition for various structures of masculinity and effeminacy in Victorian literature. Yet while I'm using Yeats to illustrate the nuances of legacy and anticipation, delay and revision that characterize Victorian culture, I suggest that he also sums up a modernist perspective on my earlier claims about asymmetry and homosexuality. Like all the authors examined in this book, Yeats reminds us that we can't attain wisdom, or understand our identities, without reflecting carefully on the price of identification.

Although chapter 4, on Hardy's poetry and novels, is my study's most elaborate reflection on these issues, I have arranged the chapters chronologically to indicate how concepts such as effeminacy, friendship, and sociality altered perceptibly in the course of the nineteenth century. One could easily imagine an alternative, thematic grouping, leading from the volatile ties of Hardy's fiction to the anticommunitarian fantasies of Bulwer-Lytton's, and then on through the effete aspirations of Schreiner's dandy, the messy inconsistencies of James's characters, the strange excesses of Swinburne's, and the erotic betrayals of Forster's. The book would then end with Santayana's faux asceticism and an afterword indicating how all these treacherous concerns belie our sometimes idealistic accounts of same-sex desire in the nineteenth century. The reader will at least grasp from this summary the broad outlines of subsequent chapters. But the outcome of arranging the book in this way seemed to me too chaotic; I opted instead for chronological order, insisting all the while that history itself deprives us of such simple linearity.

Fully aware of this irony, I turn now to Bulwer-Lytton's popular novel *Pelham; or, The Adventures of a Gentleman,* asking how its diverse themes and many revisions point up the identificatory demands of Georgian and early Victorian culture. Subsequent chapters will build on this reading, striving to explain why these and other tensions recur in the fascinating, fraught margins of the nineteenth century.

ONE

The Specter of Effeminacy
in Bulwer-Lytton's Pelham

To write [a] fitting Preface to this work . . . I must myself
become a phantom, with the phantom crowd. It is the ghost of my
youth that I must call up.
—Edward George Bulwer-Lytton, *Pelham* 454–55

I am a type of a system; I expire before the system: my
death is the herald of its fall.
—Bulwer-Lytton, *Godolphin* 461

One of nineteenth-century England's most popular novels, Bulwer-Lytton's *Pelham; or, The Adventures of a Gentleman* gives us a remarkable—and contradictory—account of dandyism and masculine identification in Georgian society.[1] Bulwer-Lytton (hereafter Bulwer) published this novel in 1828, but revised it later that year and again in 1835 and 1840. He was so concerned about Thomas Carlyle's satire of *Pelham*'s status as a "*Fashionable Novel*" (*Sartor* 278) and William Hazlitt's hostility to similar contemporaneous fiction that he slowly excised the novel's most sardonic elements. These revisions were not painless; Bulwer characterized them as "massacres of whole lines, prematurely and timidly ventured forth as forlorn hopes" (*Pelham* 454). Implicitly, then, the novel's editions tell us a great deal about the course of masculine identity in nineteenth-century English literature: We learn from Henry Pelham that marriage is an appropriate—and perhaps the only—means of enforcing a bachelor's self-discipline. He tells us that although marriage "has not cured me of the passion [of ambition and self-advancement] . . . it has concentrated what was scattered, and determined what was vague" (443–44).

If the nineteenth-century novel is burdened with the task of reforming foppish men, is it thereby simply a repressive agent of Victorian culture? Bulwer's recharting of *Pelham*'s narcissism suggests a more complex representational dilemma. For a start, Bulwer lamented revising the novel, as a result charting an intricate resistance to Carlyle's and Hazlitt's criticisms; he certainly was not an unambivalent agent of repression: "Another Preface!," he exclaimed in 1849.

> What for? Two Prefaces to "Pelham" already exist, wherein all that I would say is said! And in going back through that long and crowded interval of twenty years since the first appearance of this work, what shadows rise to beckon me away through the glades and alleys in that dim labyrinth of the Past! Infant Hopes, scarce born ere fated, poor innocents, to die—gazing upon me with reproachful eyes, as if I myself had been their unfeeling butcher. (454)

By invoking "shadows [that] beckon [him] away . . . in that dim labyrinth of the Past," Bulwer reminds us that if repression is *un*successful (and it partly is in his novel), the demand that repression succeed *intensifies* his character's desire by confronting us with each botched attempt to erase it.

The reader may ask: Since *Pelham* repeatedly identifies what its hero and narrative must transform or give up (the "passions" of advancement and self-love), why not adopt Foucault's argument and method, presenting *Pelham* as exemplary of Victorian culture's "incitement to discourse" (*History* 17)? The answer—as we've seen and Foucault partly made clear—is that repression has no obvious or "hydraulic" relation to social structures; rarely is it logical, consistent, or self-evident. Recall Freud's argument, quoted in the introduction: "A repression is something very different from a condemning judgement" (*From the History* 79–80). Since from this perspective repression is involuntary—quite different from the conscious activity of revision—Foucault can tell us only one side of the story: He can't explain why repression fails and passion often belies meaning. Resisting both "hydraulic" and discursive arguments, my reading of *Pelham* tries instead to highlight the *difficulty* that passion and fantasy represent for Bulwer and his readers.

In *Sartor Resartus* (1833–34), as many readers will know, Carlyle satirizes the "Self-worship" accompanying dandyism, arguing with mock "scientific strictness" that dandies are men "whose trade, office and existence . . . , [whose e]very faculty of . . . soul, spirit, purse and person is heroically consecrated to this one object, the wearing of Clothes wisely and well" (276, 272). Carlyle voices his indignation about materialism through a persona "of unequalled learning and acumen" (272), Diogenes Teufels-dröckh (Born of God, Dung for the Devil), a professor at the University of Weissnichtwo (Nobody-Knows-Where), who insists that the "*Fashionable Novels*" of the day are unreadable (278). Accordingly, the periodical *Magazine* "sets out . . . chiefly from a Secular point of view; directing itself, not without asperity, against some to me unknown individual named *Pelham*, who seems to be a Mystagogue [one initiating religious mysteries], and leading Teacher and Preacher of the Sect" (278).

Contemporaneous with *Sartor*'s first publication in book form (1836), Carlyle argued that the England of Bulwer's *Pelham* "lay all puking and sprawling in Werterism [*sic*], Byronism, and other Sentimentalism tearful or spasmodic (fruit of internal *wind*)" ("Sir Walter Scott" [1838], *Critical* 4: 39; original emphasis). His disdain for the work of "many a sickly and sulky Byron, or Byronlet, glooming over the woes of existence" aimed not only to forge a literature able to "do battle against UNREASON without or within," but to produce writers "who can handle both pen and hammer like a man" ("Corn-Law Rhymes" [1832], *Critical* 3: 158, 162, 139).[2] As before, Carlyle is attacking "silver fork" fiction—including *Pelham,* Theodore Hook's *Sayings and Doings* (1824), Robert Plumer Ward's *Tremaine* (1825), T. H. Lister's *Granby* (1826), and Benjamin Disraeli's *Vivian Grey* (1826–27)—which divulged to avid middle-class readers the secrets of the Regency and Georgian aristocracies. In *Sartor,* Carlyle called these novels "infinite, unsufferable [*sic*], Jews-harping and scrannel-piping" (277), writing disgustedly:

> I could liken Dandyism and Drudgism [Paganism] to two bot-tomless boiling Whirlpools that had broken-out on opposite quarters of the firm land: as yet they appear only disquieted, foolishly bubbling wells, which man's art might cover-in; yet mark them, their diameter is daily widening: they are hollow Cones that boil-up from the infinite Deep, over which your firm land is but a thin crust or rind! Thus daily is the interme-diate land crumbling-in, daily the empire of the two Buchan-Bullers extending. (*Sartor* 286)

Carlyle's essay on the "Condition-of-England Question" helps contextual-ize his satire of "The Dandiacal Body." He tell us that "[b]oils on the sur-face are curable or incurable,—small matter which, while the virulent hu-mor festers deep within; poisoning the sources of life; and certain enough to find for itself ever new boils and sore issues; ways of announcing that it continues there, that it would fain not continue there" ("Chartism" [1839], *Critical* 4: 120). Because Carlyle considers dandyism one of these "sore issues," related phenomena such as effeminacy, narcissism, and hedo-nism take on for him the attributes of a malaise depleting men's vigor. "It is the heyday of Imposture," he wrote; "of Semblance recognising itself, and getting itself recognised, for Substance" (4: 151). These issues are "so many symptoms on the surface; you abolish the symptom to no purpose if the disease is left untouched" (4: 120).

Since Carlyle views Bulwer's style of "silver fork" fiction as a "symp-tom" of proper literature, it follows that Bulwer's revising *Pelham* partly underscores what is at stake in the Victorian novel's conceptual and sub-stantive evolution. Put another way, if Carlyle's aversion to the "Dandiacal Body" highlights forms of effeminacy that Victorian writing must discard, Bulwer's embarrassed response confirms the gradual intensification of this aversion, and thus an increasingly repressive dimension of Victorian culture.[3]

A few years before *Sartor's* serialization in *Fraser's Magazine,* Hazlitt also denounced "The Dandy School" (1827) and "Effeminacy of Charac-ter" (1824), but his objections to the former are subtler than Carlyle's. "Literature," he argued, "so far from supplying us with intellectual re-sources to counterbalance immediate privations, is made an instrument to add to our impatience and irritability under them, and to nourish our fe-verish, childish admiration for external show and grandeur" ("Dandy" 148). Hazlitt's criticisms of effeminacy also bear directly on Bulwer's novel. He argues that

> Effeminacy of character arises from a prevalence of the sensibil-ity over the will: or it consists in a want of fortitude to bear pain or to undergo fatigue, however urgent the occasion. . . . [Effeminate people] cannot put themselves out of their way on any account. . . . Instead of voluntarily embracing pain, or la-

bour, or danger, or death, every sensation must be wound up to the highest pitch of voluptuous refinement, every motion must be grace and elegance; they live in a luxurious, endless dream. (248–49)

Peter Graham has since dismissed Carlyle's and Hazlitt's judgments as "jaundiced" and "unfair" ("Pelham" 71). He claims that both men overlook the extent to which Henry Pelham, "Bulwer's ideal aristocrat, manifests the excellence of a Gallic model, the *honnête homme* of Montaigne, La Rochefoucauld, and La Bruyère" (71). "To be sure," wrote Graham in another article on Bulwer, "many of the fashionable novels [of the time] are shabby, shallow productions of poseurs who pandered to folly and pretense. These ephemera merit their consignment to back shelves and dustbins" ("Bulwer" 143). Now this sounds rather hasty, for even "folly and pretense" are worth studying; indeed, to take Hazlitt's essay on dandyism seriously for a moment, we might consider how "poseurs who pandered to folly and pretense" combine with Bulwer's keen interest in reforming his effete protagonist. Rather than idealizing Pelham as an *honnête homme* who is "physically deft, mentally profound, spiritually elevated, . . . the quintessence of cultivation and the pattern of natural simplicity" (Graham, "Pelham" 72), Bulwer gradually points up a profound, even insoluble, tension *between* the dandy and the *honnête homme,* rendering them nonidentical (see Stanton 38–40, 44). By rejecting Carlyle's and Hazlitt's concerns out of hand, we also ignore the aversion prevailing in their critiques. Instead of taking this course, I want to consider *Pelham*'s troubled, uncertain desire to "counterbalance [its readers'] immediate privations" (Hazlitt, "Dandy" 148). Indeed, while investigating the novel's account of pleasure and enjoyment, I shall question whether *Pelham* does not provocatively frustrate its readers' ability to *tolerate* "privations." To illustrate this argument, I'll pursue an interpretive path similar to that of Christopher Clutterbuck, *Pelham*'s eccentric clergyman, who "derive[s] a far greater pleasure from the ingenious amendment of a perverted text, than from all the turn and thought of the sense itself" (276).

Pelham's "tastes ask to be called effeminate," claims Ellen Moers in her classic study, *The Dandy: Brummell to Beerbohm* (1960), "and—in the first edition of the novel only—Bulwer was not afraid of the term. He used it over and over again to characterize Pelham's dandyism" (81). Yet Bulwer excised many of these references and—while himself engaged in "the ingenious amendment of a perverted text"—slowly turned Henry Pelham into a dull married man. Bulwer was so concerned by Hazlitt's and Carlyle's criticisms that he wrote a preface in 1828 to *Pelham*'s second edition, claiming that he had been misunderstood: He was not, as Hazlitt had argued the previous year, encouraging irresolute and immoral behavior, but just the reverse. Initially, Bulwer had called Pelham's dandyism simply a pose. Moers observes, however, that "enough effeminacy stuck to Pelham to make a Carlyle fume and a soberer Bulwer take up a nervous blue pencil" (81).

Since in his prefaces Bulwer draws repeated attention to subtle differences in each edition's tone, he faithfully records the *price* of these revisions. While indicating that the novel's allusions to effeminacy and dandyism are finally incompatible with Pelham's masculine identification, Bulwer's repeated justifications of the novel's earlier editions inadvertently guarantee that discourses on effeminacy haunt his novel's successive drafts: As Hazlitt and Carlyle almost prophesy, effeminacy becomes a symptom of Bulwer's unwillingness to relinquish entirely his character's dandyism.[4] We must therefore retrace the path of these revisions with assiduous care.

In his preface to *Pelham*'s 1828 second edition, Bulwer admitted ruefully and defensively that his eponymous hero was

> a personal combination of antitheses—a fop and a philosopher, a voluptuary and a moralist—a trifler in appearance, but rather one to whom trifles are instructive, than one to whom trifles are natural—an Aristippus on a limited scale, accustomed to draw sage conclusions from the follies he adopts, and while professing himself a votary of Pleasure, [he is] in reality a disciple of Wisdom. Such a character I have found it more difficult to portray than to conceive: *I have found it more difficult still, because I have with it nothing in common,* except the taste for observation. (xxxiii–xxxiv; my emphasis)

"While professing himself a votary of Pleasure, in reality a disciple of Wisdom": Bulwer overextends himself here, almost writing himself into a corner. It is one thing to suggest that Pelham strays briefly from virtue, learning quickly from his mistakes; it is quite another to imply that Pelham's interest in pleasure is disingenuous—that in "professing himself a votary of Pleasure" he's really hiding a deeper maturity.

Such hasty disavowals aimed to curb charges of autobiography, which implicated Bulwer in an inquiry he was keen to disband. However, in such defensive maneuverings, Bulwer asks us to reject his protagonist's intelligent self-judgments: We must disbelieve what Pelham says about "Pleasure," Bulwer implies, in order to grasp that he is *throughout* "a disciple of Wisdom." In this preface, Pelham's devotion to pleasure seems sufficiently superficial that Bulwer can downplay it as a temporary evasion of adulthood; he characterizes Pelham as duping *the reader* into believing he is a fop. Any reader missing this deceit is, he suggests, fooled by his or her ideas about dandyism. In refuting Hazlitt and Carlyle Bulwer nonetheless implicitly rejects the bildungsroman's developmental model of character:[5] Over the course of several editions charting its hero's erratic progress toward marriage and maturity, *Pelham* meditates profoundly on personality and dissimulation, authenticity and masks.[6] "This difficulty in execution, will perhaps be my excuse in failure" (xxxiv), claims Bulwer, but was his cautious reorientation of Pelham's character any easier to conceptualize?

Pelham sold so well that Bulwer was able in 1835 to revise the novel's second edition and, later still, to issue a new preface in 1840. He took the opportunity that year to distance himself still further from the novel's "gayety of tone" and "supposed foibles and levities" (449). Claiming sardonically that he had "rid [his] bosom of its 'perilous stuff,' . . . confessed [his] sins, and [been] absolved," Bulwer hoped the novel's additional revisions would "put an end to the Satanic mania" of effete fops and dandies (450, 452), so appeasing the likes of Hazlitt and Carlyle. Yet he also admitted that before starting to write *Pelham* at eighteen, he had completed a story entitled "Mortimer, or the Memoirs of a Gentleman," whose

> commencement was almost word for word the same as that of "Pelham"; but the design was exactly opposite to that of the latter and later work. "Mortimer" was intended to show the manner in which the world deteriorates its votary, and "Pelham," on the contrary, conveys the newer, and I believe, sounder moral, of showing how a man of sense can subject the usages of the world to himself instead of being conquered

by them, and gradually grow wise by the very foibles of his
youth. (449)[7]

Since pleasure in "Mortimer" leads inevitably to its hero's "deteriorat[ion],"
Pelham strives to turn its protagonist's narcissism into an altruistic desire
to rescue others. Whether we believe Bulwer here or above, the underlying
message is clear: Pelham's redemption consists in his substituting virtue for
cruelty; thereafter, his pleasure may surface only as a fleeting enjoyment of
others' vice and corruption.

We can of course argue that Bulwer was simply disingenuous at these
moments—that he aimed to veil Pelham's interest in dandyism to protect
himself from related charges. However, such arguments ignore where Bulwer takes us in the course of revising his work, and why pleasure itself
precipitates aversion. Bulwer's effort to rewrite Pelham's progress is indeed
complicated: While in 1828 he asks the reader to believe that Pelham's
flirtation with hedonism is merely a prelude to his general redemption,
the story "Mortimer" suggests more honestly that pleasure is sufficiently
compelling to "deteriorate . . . its votary" (449).

Despite Hazlitt's and Carlyle's misgivings, *Pelham* continued to sell
remarkably well: In addition to its many English and American editions,
the novel appeared in French, Italian, German, and Spanish translations
(in France alone, it was reprinted eight times between 1828 and 1840
[Stanton 38]). In 1849, Bulwer decided to "advertise" Chapman and Hall's
reprinting of the novel's 1840 edition, taking yet another opportunity to
reflect on the distance between his "mature manhood" and the "extreme
youth" of *Pelham*'s composition (457). As if realizing that his earlier argument about Pelham's virtue were unconvincing, Bulwer also partly retracts
that his novel advances an unequivocal morality (see Snyder 27–45). Further complicating the developmental logic of much Georgian and Victorian fiction, he focuses this time on his unresolved relation to the past, and
thus on his revisions' *least* successful aspects: "In the inextricable confusion
of old ideas, many that seem of the time we seek to grasp again, but were
not so, seize and distract us [*sic*]. From the clear effort we sink into the
vague revery; the Present hastens to recall and dash us onward, and few,
leaving the actual world around them when they say 'I remember,' do not

wake as from a dream, with a baffled sigh, and murmur 'No, I forget'"
(455).

Conflating two ideas, Bulwer's first sentence is syntactically rather
unclear. He represents himself trying to grasp the past, only to find that he
is "seize[d] and distract[ed]"; he also realizes that the "old ideas" are no
longer "of the time." Despite the unpopularity of "old ideas," however,
they don't disappear. In ways that undermine the declarative style of Bulwer's 1828 and 1840 prefaces, the 1849 advertisement suggests a persistent
difficulty in prioritizing one idea above another. Sir Reginald Glanville,
Pelham's Byronic enigma, voices a similar tension: "Determine not to
think upon what is painful; resolutely turn away from everything that re-
cals [*sic*] it; bend all your attention to some new and engrossing object; do
this, and *you defeat the past*" (222; my emphasis; see Elfenbein 213–14).
In this passage, as before, we see the substantive and conceptual "work"
involved in Bulwer's revisions; he represents the "trace" of earlier ideas
about Henry Pelham—"massacres of whole lines, prematurely and timidly
ventured forth as forlorn hopes" (454)—as "chimeras" haunting his novel's
later incarnation. In this respect, the past is not defeated; it returns unbid-
den as memory and trauma.[8]

Bulwer's 1849 advertisement begins ironically with a statement
about how long his pen has "rested over the virgin surface of this paper,"
then "manfully" declares his "felicitous" difficulty in remembering the past
(454). In contemplating *Pelham*'s first drafts, Bulwer also reflects on the
endurance of memory and composition of subjectivity. He anticipates
Walter Pater's famous conclusion to *The Renaissance: Studies in Art and
Poetry* (1873; 1893), which argues that "what is real in our life fines itself
down" until we are left with only "that continual vanishing away, that
strange, perpetual, weaving and unweaving of ourselves" (188). In 1849
Bulwer also depicts subjectivity as radically at odds with his 1828 statement about Pelham's progressive maturity:

> This our sense of identity, this "I" of ours, which is the single
> thread that continues from first to last—single thread that
> binds flowers changed every day, and withered every night—
> how thin and meagre is it of itself! How difficult to lay hold of!
> When we say, "I remember," how vague a sentiment we utter!

How different it is to say, "I *feel!*" And when in this effort of
memory we travel back all the shadowland of years—when we
say "I remember," what is it we retain but some solitary poor
fibre in the airy mesh of that old gossamer . . . ? (455)

In light of this difficulty in "remembering" *Pelham's* earlier editions, we
begin to grasp why effeminacy in *Pelham* acquires a spectral quality that
impedes the full reformation of Bulwer's hero.[9]

Adapting the story "Mortimer," *Pelham* begins with similar arch
comments on marriage, families, and social protocol. Through Pelham's
eyes, we witness the shallow and vindictive concerns of upper-class Georgian society. We also experience a certain schadenfreude, or glee, in watch-
ing others fail. Pelham represents this society's grasping avidity as wholly
beneath him: He scorns such people, *not* from a stance of moral superiority, but from *disgust at their vulgarity*. Detached but effortlessly judgmental,
Pelham disdains marriage: "Poor O——i! I hear he is just married. He did
not deserve so heavy a calamity!" (33). By contrast, he comments on his
"total deficiency in all romance" (21) and laments that "single men suffer
a plurality of evils and hardships . . . Oh! the hardships of a single man are
beyond conception; and what is worse, the very misfortune of being single
deprives one of all sympathy" (27).[10]

Such quips made the novel an instant authority on dandyism. *Pelham's* epigrammatic style reflects on social etiquette by advancing a set of
maxims—various dos and don'ts—with a "moral" dimension of their own.
In chapter 7 of volume 2, for instance, Pelham gives the reader twenty-two
"maxims," including:

> 3. Always remember that you dress to fascinate others, not
> yourself. . . .
>
> 5. Remember that none but those whose courage is unques-
> tionable, can venture to be effeminate. It was only in the
> field that the Lacedemonians were accustomed to use per-
> fumes and curl their hair. [In the 1840 edition, "Spartans"
> substitutes for "Lacedemonians."]
>
> 6. Never let the finery of chains and rings seem *your own*
> choice; that which naturally belongs to women should ap-
> pear only worn for their sake. We dignify foppery, when
> we invest it with a sentiment. [. . .]

10. The handsome may be shewy in dress; the plain should study to be unexceptionable; just as in great men we look for something to admire—in ordinary men we ask for nothing to forgive. [. . .]

19. A very benevolent man will never shock the feelings of others, by an excess either of inattention or display; you may doubt, therefore, the philanthropy both of a sloven and a fop.

20. There is an indifference to please in a stocking down at heel—but there may be a malevolence in a diamond ring. (177–80; original emphasis)

Since Pelham insists "that none but those whose courage is unquestionable, can venture to be effeminate" (178), a maxim Lady Parvula repeats verbatim in Ronald Firbank's *Valmouth: A Romantic Novel* (1919; *Complete* 406), we cannot but notice that *Pelham*'s initial disregard for masculinity in the first chapter of its first edition dwindles as the novel progresses through chapters and across editions.[11] Although several passages near the novel's conclusion include Pelham's comments on others' folly, these observations are tempered by charity and kindness. Consider, by contrast, this early account of Pelham's reintroduction to Lord George Clinton, an old school friend:

Clinton was on the eve of setting out upon his travels. His intention was to stay a year at Paris, and he was full of the blissful expectations the idea of that city had conjured up. We remained together all the evening, and took a prodigious fancy to one another. Long before I went to bed, he had perfectly inoculated me with his own ardour for continental adventures; and, indeed, I had half promised to accompany him. My mother, when I first told her of my travelling intentions, was in despair, but by degrees she grew reconciled to the idea. (28–29)

Consider too how Pelham cheerfully admits his inability to shoot or hunt game:

The most unaccountable thing was the fatality which attended *me,* and seemed to mark me out, *nolens volens,* for an untimely death. *I,* who had so carefully kept out of the way of gunpow-

der as a *sportsman,* very narrowly escaped being twice shot as a
ghost. . . . [A]ccordingly I resolved to "give up the ghost" in
earnest, rather than in metaphor. (20; original emphases)

This allusion to phantasms is significant: On the night in question, Pelham
meets his closest school friend, Glanville, while walking in the country.
Glanville is beset by "intense anguish" because his fiancée, Gertrude Douglas, died of grief and insanity after she was raped by Sir John Tyrrell, a
wealthy gambler (21, 362). Various people—including Pelham—suspect
that Glanville murdered Tyrrell in revenge (in fact Tom Thornton, another
gambler, stabbed Tyrrell after robbing him; see 426). Morbidly preoccupied by his friend's misery, Pelham can't bring himself to love Ellen, "the
sister of [a possible] assassin!" (293), until Glanville is discharged of all
blame for Tyrrell's death. By elaborating on Glanville's misery, the novel
frees up Pelham's desire—for Glanville's sister. As we'll see, however, none
of these elements is simple, and each warrants careful attention.[12]

Like Bulwer's prefaces, Pelham's account of character gets revised as
the novel progresses chapter by chapter: First supercilious and shallow, Pelham later appears more reflective.[13] The following passage sets the tone for
his early aesthetic education in Paris, as he ruminates on the "character"
of character:[14]

On entering Paris I had resolved to set up "*a character*"; for I
was always of an ambitious nature, and desirous of being distinguished from the ordinary herd. After various cogitations as to
the particular one I should assume, I thought nothing appeared
more likely to be remarkable among men, and therefore pleas-
ing to women, than an egregious coxcomb: accordingly I arranged my hair into ringlets, dressed myself with singular
plainness and simplicity (a low person, by the by, would have
done just the contrary), and putting on an air of exceeding languor, made my maiden appearance at Lord Bennington's. (30;
original emphasis)

This admission—like Pelham's maxims—indicates frivolity. Over time,
however, tensions surface between Pelham's ability to enjoy his "propensities" (262)—socializing, spending money, and being licentious—and others' demands that he renounce these propensities for altruistic concerns.

This brings the novel close to the bildungsroman's interest in conflicts between duty and desire, but *Pelham* notably departs from this convention by exploring the price and failure of duty. The novel grasps this tension without psychic idealism, offering a subtle account of a protagonist torn between his external surroundings and internal will.

This tension underscores a rigid and conservative aspect of dandyism, which critics tend to ignore when proposing that dandyism is socially and sexually transgressive. Arguing that "[d]andies . . . self-consciously played with the construction of gender" (13), Jessica Feldman claims quite ambiguously that writers such as Théophile Gautier, Jules-Amédée Barbey d'Aurevilly, and Charles Baudelaire *"relocate dandyism within the female realm in order to move beyond the male and the female, beyond dichotomous gender itself"* (11; original emphasis; see also 12–14, 72–73). Yet numerous passages in *Pelham* push us beyond suggestions of self-fashioning and gender performativity. When considered alongside Hazlitt's and Carlyle's asperity, Bulwer's many revisions and the novel's multiple editions indicate not only the anxiety accompanying masculine pleasure, but—perhaps more interesting—the novel's and protagonist's limited capacity to *tolerate* pleasure.

Many passages confirm this novel's complex account of subjectivity. When Pelham is ordered back to England to run for Parliament, for instance, he leaves Paris with relief because his "propensities" have already taken him "in some degree from my approach to that character which I wished to become. . . . One never keeps a restraint on the manner when one unbridles the passions" (104). Not surprisingly, this return is symbolic; since *Pelham* largely concerns the trials and tribulations of masculine identification, Pelham notes his psychic reorientation with remarkable clarity: "I was also by this time wearied with my attendance upon women, and eager to exchange it for the ordinary objects of ambition to men . . . On my return to England, with a new scene and a new motive for conduct, I resolved that I would commence a different character to that I had hitherto assumed" (105). That this character "leans" upon psychic drives and finds itself in conflict with social and authorial mores anticipates what Freud would consider, roughly one century later, a profound ontological malaise (see *Civilization* 75–85).

Before leaving Paris, Pelham meets a man who seems temporarily to

trouble his desire to change. Indeed, though Pelham fosters a deliberately
effeminate and asexual "character" in Paris, the chevalier he meets generates a scene of palpable eroticism:

> He came forward with much grace as I approached, and ex-
> pressed his pleasure at seeing me.
> "You were presented, I think, about a month ago," added
> the ———, with a smile of singular fascination; "I remember
> it well."
> I bowed low to his compliment.
> "Do you propose staying long at Paris?" continued the
> ———.
> "I protracted," I replied, "my departure solely for the honour
> this evening affords me. In so doing, pleasure your ———, I
> have followed the wise maxim of keeping the greatest pleasure
> to the last."
> The royal chevalier bowed to my answer with a smile still
> sweeter than before, and began a conversation with me which
> lasted for several minutes. I was much struck with the ———'s
> air and bearing. They possess great dignity, without any affec-
> tation of its assumption. . . . Judge, then, if they charmed me
> in the ———. The upper part of his countenance is prominent
> and handsome, and his eyes have much softness of expression.
> (114–15; original ellipses)

In this section of narrative most preoccupied with appearance and style,
few women are described in comparable detail. Given the apparent import
of this meeting, the chevalier strangely is soon forgotten, but by this time
Pelham has met Russelton in Calais—a character most critics agree is the
fictional counterpart of Beau Brummell (xvi; Favardin and Bouëxière 43).
    Russelton seems to compensate for Pelham's waning interest in dan-
dyism. Like the Parisian chevalier, he is a conduit for elements of effeminacy and narcissism that Bulwer in his revisions must extirpate from Pelham.[15] Here, for instance, is Russelton's hilarious account of falling in love:

> Other fellows, at my age, in such a predicament, would have
> whined—shaved only twice a week, and written verses. I did
> none of the three. . . . [Since] my *forte* was not in the Pierian

line, I redoubled my attention to my dress; I *coated,* and *cra-vated,* and *essenced,* and *oiled,* with all the attention the very inspiration of my rhymes seemed to advise;—in short, I thought the best pledge I could give my Dulcinea of my passion for her person, would be to show her what affectionate venera-tion I could pay to my own. (130–31; original emphasis)

Russelton represents for Pelham something of a beau, though his character is also enigmatic and perhaps finally asexual: "We sat opposite each other for several minutes as abstracted and distracted as if we had been a couple two months married" (133; see also Carassus 145–56).

An obvious cultural argument surfaces here about Pelham and geog-raphy: In returning to England, a country he repeatedly maligns as cold and asexual (10, 26, 37–38, 299), Pelham's erotic focus narrows to his po-litical career and the remaining enigma of Glanville's melancholy. This diminution of interest and affect is so extensive that Pelham's comparison of himself and Russelton to newlyweds ironically anticipates his eventual marriage to Ellen Glanville, in the novel's penultimate chapter, when mat-rimony appears (as before) joyless but inevitable.[16] The irony is unmistak-able—Pelham becomes the type of man he earlier deplored as barely alive: "I hear [poor O——i] is just married. He did not deserve so heavy a calam-ity!" (33). In Samuel Butler's *The Way of All Flesh* (1873; 1903), too, Mr. Overton, godfather to Ernest Pontifex, laments "the great gulf which is fixed between the married and the unmarried." "A man's friendships are," he adds, "like his will, *invalidated* by marriage" (358–59; my emphasis). Overton tells us a little earlier, "I don't know why, but I never have heard that any young man to whom I had become attached was going to get married without hating his intended instinctively, though I had never seen her; I have observed that most bachelors feel the same thing, though we are generally at some pains to hide the fact. Perhaps it is because we know we ought to have got married ourselves" (339).[17]

Pelham's lack of fervor after the marriage is so pronounced that it seems to warrant explanation: "Marriage with me is not that sepulchre of all human hope and energy which it often is with others. . . . If I am less anxious than formerly for the reputation to be acquired in society, . . . I trust yet to be useful to my friends and to mankind" (443–44). So lackluster is this closing chapter that Pelham temporarily forgets his wife when representing his future as a monastic retreat: "Meanwhile, gentle reader, during the two years which I purpose devoting to solitude and study, I shall not be so occupied with my fields and folios, as to become uncourteous to thee" (444). In describing his quiet country life, Ellen surfaces only as an afterthought: "I will compliment thee on thy horses, thou shalt congratulate me upon my wife" (444). However, when Pelham asks an old friend how he enjoys "the *connubiale jugum*" (267), midway through the novel, he wonders if this friend took Socrates' advice and married a difficult woman. Apparently, such difficulty fosters self-discipline in married men (267 n), a quality Bulwer insisted Carlyle and Hazlitt had overlooked in his protagonist.

How exactly does marriage precipitate these changes in Pelham? Questions such as this implicitly surface in the text whenever Pelham notes the dichotomy between Glanville's Byronism and such bachelors as Russelton, Mr. Wormwood, Monsieur Margot, and Lord Guloseton (190, 452 n; see also xii; Graham, "Pelham" 77; Oakley 70–71). At one point, for example, Pelham notes that after Guloseton argues with "a very young man" about admitting "his [own] juvenile companion" to a club, "Guloseton turned to me, for passion makes men open their hearts, . . . [and] overwhelmed me with his thanks. . . . 'A new friend,' said he, as we descended into the dining-room, 'is like a new dish—one must have him all to oneself, thoroughly to enjoy and rightly to understand him'" (237, 238). (Lord Dawton later says to Pelham: "And, do you know . . . that you have quite made a conquest of Lord Guloseton?" [295–96].) This array of masculine types points up identifications that Pelham and Glanville must discard in order to emerge as fully masculine protagonists. Yet Glanville seems unable to complete this transformation. While Pelham *is* therefore "cured of . . . [all] passion" except his mild ambition to retire to "fields and folios" for two years of seclusion (443, 444), Glanville's excessive sensibility makes him susceptible to internal decay, as if passion eventually renders him ontologically "incurable."[18]

Lord Vincent, Pelham's intellectual friend, remarks that Glanville's "disease . . . is indeed . . . *nullâ medicabilis herbâ*" (191). Jerome McGann, recent editor of *Pelham*'s many editions, comments that Bulwer conflates two passages from Ovid here, though it's McGann who prefaces his Latin translation, "the disease for which there is no cure," with the noun "love." Whether Bulwer considers love an incurable disease remains in question, but we can at least comprehend Pelham's indifferent thoughts about marriage in light of Lord Vincent's aphorism. In many respects, *Pelham*'s ending implies that marriage and passion *are* mutually exclusive—that marriage is possible only when a protagonist has rooted out and destroyed his many wayward desires.

At the end of this novel Glanville dies, expiring when it is certain Pelham will marry his sister and legally proven that Glanville could not have murdered Tyrrell for raping Gertrude, Glanville's dead fiancée. This vindication resolves the novel's principal enigma, for Pelham is so troubled by suspicion that Glanville murdered Tyrrell that he can't properly desire Ellen, Glanville's sister. Slowly, the enigma is resolved and all obstacles to Ellen disappear. However, the novel's primary concern throughout is Pelham's fascination with Glanville's mourning. Thus even when Pelham idealizes Ellen, "whose pure and holy love could be at once my recompence and retreat" (377; see also 247, 311–12), we suspect a crucial displacement, in which Pelham's affection for Glanville is rerouted toward his sister.

If this claim seems doubtful, let me confirm Pelham's interest in Glanville, noting that when these men remeet, having been close friends at school, Pelham becomes obsessed with his friend's fate: "Sir Reginald Glanville. The name thrilled through me. . . . I thought, as I looked at him, that I had never seen so perfect a specimen of masculine beauty, at once physical and intellectual" (180, 184). Later, speaking of Glanville's published novel and repeating his spectral motif in this novel, Pelham observes that "every ear was bent to catch the words, which came alike from so beautiful a lip, and so strange and imaginative a mind. . . . He was luxurious and splendid, beyond all men, in his habits, rather than his tastes. . . . He seemed . . . to be, as he himself said, eternally endeavouring to forget, and eternally brought back to remembrance" (190). At other times Pelham remarks that "Glanville was there . . . , looking remarkably handsome" (210), and that "that extraordinary man still continued powerfully to excite my interest" (346). Finally, when Glanville explains with relief why many have suspected him of murder, Pelham throws himself fervently into the task of nursing his ailing friend. After hinting to Ellen that he loves her, Pelham tells Glanville: "I have a proposal to make, to which you must accede: let me accompany you abroad; I will go with you to whatever corner of the world you may select. We will plan together every possible method of concealing our retreat. . . . I will tend upon you, watch over you, bear with you, with more than the love and tenderness of a brother" (379–80).

In Bulwer's paradigm unruly passion is a character's undoing—recall that it "deteriorates its votary" (449): Glanville's excessive beauty and mourning unravel him, and his "countenance" becomes marked by "dark and deep traces of premature decay" (189). Since the novel measures Pelham's maturity against Glanville's decline, it is crucial that Glanville expire before Pelham marries Ellen. Indeed, this death—and all it signifies—represents a conceptual shift, in which various aspects of masculine identification (including narcissism) are sacrificed to allow others (the desire to marry) to prevail. We might be tempted to call Pelham's final identification "normative," but this chiasmatic substitution is neither smooth nor developmental. The novel highlights the price of Pelham's mature identification, as if the text were haunted not only by Glanville but by its residual interest in dandyism and effeminacy.

Midway through this novel, Pelham declares with relief: "In fine, I loved as other men loved" (235). This tautology implies significantly that if Pelham does not love Ellen—that is, as "other men loved"—he simply couldn't be a man. As earlier quotations from this novel attest, this radical doubt is sufficiently threatening for Pelham to qualify his remark: "I loved as other men loved—and I fancied a perfection in her, and vowed an emulation in myself, which it was reserved for Time to ratify or deride. Where did I leave myself?" (235). Where indeed? And which "self" is left?

These oscillations between endorsing and renouncing the self are ongoing. Pelham notes quite early, with chagrin, that narcissism tends to prevent him from introducing new characters to the reader: "Meanwhile suffer me to *get rid of myself,* and to introduce you, dear Reader, to my friend, Monsieur Margot . . . [I]n a man of Monsieur Margot's temper, even interest is a subordinate passion to vanity" (57, 62; original emphasis). Pelham's "self" nonetheless returns, illustrating his difficulty in renouncing dandyism for an "altruistic" career in politics: "Meanwhile, to return to myself—from which dear little person, I very seldom, even in imagination, digress" (77). This is an arch and telling moment of self-deprecation. Later, too, it seems Pelham combines refined arrogance with extensive—even imperialist—ambition: "So true is it that there is no situation which a little tact cannot turn to our own account: manage *yourself* well, and you may manage all the world" (258; original emphasis; see also Moers 76).

In enhancing Pelham's altruism, Bulwer slowly challenges the aim of this statement, but he can't revoke its underlying principle, which "taints" Pelham's development with an interesting, residual narcissism: Bulwer's increasingly coercive desire to give Pelham appropriate moral subjectivity highlights Pelham's hubris when his public self cannot curb his self-centered propensities. Such setbacks and temporary failures challenge Allan Christensen's belief that "Pelham . . . manages at last to control the demonic energy that emanates, as it were, from his own unconscious being" (51). When ruminating on his first political defeat in running for Parliament, for instance, Pelham acknowledges that his psychological "progress" is more precarious: "I had no guide but passion; no rule but the impulse of the moment. . . . I own that . . . , living in the world, I have not separated myself from its errors and its follies: the vortex was too strong—the atmosphere too contagious; but I have at least avoided the crimes into which *my temper would most likely have driven me*. . . . I no longer divorced the interests of other men from my own" (148; my emphasis).

Although this last claim clashes starkly with two earlier pronouncements on pleasure that I'll quote shortly, suffice that we note the secondary meaning of the word *error.* Pelham earlier claims his narrative "treats rather of my attempts at reformation than my success in error" (148), yet his preoccupation with "error" (it is "too strong . . . too contagious") suggests the novel's interest in the world's "vortex" is stronger than its interest in Pelham's "attempts at reformation." The point is simply that while Pelham's former life ("error") in Paris *was* successful, he is not sufficiently "reform[ed]" to "avoid . . . the crimes into which [his] temper would most likely have driven [him]" (148). And because "error" refers here to Pelham's former "contagious" lifestyle, Bulwer's rhetoric comes close to calling hedonism a vice or crime; he turns *dandyism* into an error by depicting excessive pleasure as a moral defect.

Bulwer's emphasis has profound repercussions for nineteenth-century conceptions of enjoyment: Pelham must curb his self-indulgent "propensities" in part to rescind a widespread belief that effeminacy fosters cultural decay, a belief we are far from having resolved (see Sinfield 69, 93–98). Recalling Bulwer's prefaces, we grasp why he labored so hard to sever this conviction, turning dandyism into an ideal form of masculinity: in Graham's terms, the *honnête homme* not only sustained noblesse oblige, but aspired to being "physically deft, mentally profound, spiritually elevated" ("Pelham" 72; see also Stanton 38–40; Weir 98, 111–12). However, Bulwer's prefaces to *Pelham,* combined with the awkward legacy of his substantive revisions, demonstrate in fascinating ways that he couldn't maintain this vision of dandyism. As we'll see, dandyism and ambiguous sexuality tend to coalesce in his fiction and prefaces, rendering dandyism an error that barely resembles his ideal of normative masculinity.

To illustrate this tension, let us note the similar pressure McGann and Graham exert on the word *dandyism* to release it from suggestions of degeneration and pathology. Echoing Baudelaire's argument in "Le Peintre de la vie moderne" (1863), McGann argues that "dandyism . . . is, *in its achieved condition,* a striking symbol of a fundamental human ideal. In this respect, dandyism *is* an unlimited intellectual and emotional responsiveness manipulated with perfect ease and control by a mastering self" (xxiii; my emphases; see also Coblence 33–37). Baudelaire had argued, with a strong hint of imperialism, that the dandy's "interest is the whole world; he wants to know, understand, and appreciate everything that happens on the surface of our globe. . . . To be away from home and yet . . . feel oneself everywhere at home [*se sentir partout chez soi*]; to see the world, to be at the center of the world, and yet [to] remain hidden from the world" (*Painter* 7, 9; *Œuvres* 1160).

Certainly, *Pelham* emphasizes a similar importance in self-mastery (recall Pelham's maxim: "manage *yourself* well, and you may manage all the world" [258]), but at what price? Bulwer's concern that Pelham *maintain* self-mastery guarantees the precise internal antagonism that Graham especially wants dandyism to override. Here is Pelham's remarkable assessment of this conflict: "There is no triumph so *gratifying to the viciousness of human nature,* as the conquest of our fellow beings" (142; my emphasis). Self-mastery fails spectacularly in much literature about dandyism—for only the most obvious examples, consider Des Esseintes's neuroses in J.-K. Huysmans's *A rebours* (1884) and Barbey's astute observations on

Beau Brummell in "Du Dandysme et de G. Brummell" (1845).[19] So when McGann and Graham praise dandyism's "unlimited intellectual and emotional responsiveness," arguing that both elements are "manipulated with perfect ease and control by a mastering self" (*Pelham* xxiii), they downplay Bulwer's *fascination with self-unmaking* and turn *Pelham*'s effete characters into ghosts haunting Pelham's marriage.

To put this more clearly, let us briefly examine Graham's account of dandyism. He not only repeats McGann's idealist notions of self-mastery but aligns self-mastery with masculinity: "[Pelham's] wide range of sympathies and abilities makes it quite clear that his effeminacy and exclusivism are mere camouflage" ("Pelham" 76). Within these terms, effeminacy can only signify failure. By corollary, homosexuality, which in historical terms increasingly connotes this error, must be incompatible with courage, intelligence, and strength. In refusing to combine effeminacy with a "wide range of sympathies and abilities," Graham ends up simplifying Pelham's character and the novel's many revisions:

> This sort of silliness is only a mask that Pelham chooses to adopt. The effete absurdity of his speech has no counterpart in his action. Pelham professes to shudder on joining a company of "masculine-looking youths" but proceeds to trounce the heartiest of the lot in a session with the ticks. When Lord Vincent comes calling on a matter of importance, Pelham lisps, "Let me ring for my poodle and some *eau de Cologne,* and I will hear you as you desire" [p. 215]. All the same, his subsequent rejection of Vincent's political proposals is as vigorously high-minded and intelligent as any reply could be. . . . Pelham's dandified façade may mislead those who take it seriously, his nonchalance may deceive those unaware that "*le vrai honnête homme est celui qui ne se pique de rien.*" . . . He is a man who does everything, and does it with expertise. . . . When daring is called for, he acts courageously and efficiently. Pelham's drawing-room drawl belies the fact that his story contains enough duels and rescues to make any swash-buckling hero's reputation. ("Pelham" 75)

If we accept this account of masculine prowess and depict only normative masculinity as amenable to social "efficien[cy]," as Graham wants, we must also represent effeminate and homosexual men as incapable of honesty and altruism.[20] To put this more stringently, in ways modifying Freud's bold suggestion that sublimated homosexuality fosters the "emotional ties" of groups, homosexuality must oppose the very parameters of sociality (*Group* 124; see also Bersani, *Homos* 76, 122, 168, and chapter 3 below). However, *Pelham* is more ambivalent about this project than Graham implies. Haunted by prior identifications that never "defeat the past" (222), the novel can't *sustain* a simple faith in ingenuousness.

Things get even more complicated when we consider *Pelham*'s perverse interest in documenting social fault lines. These emerge whenever the narrative conceptualizes enjoyment. To appease readers such as Carlyle and Hazlitt, Bulwer (like Graham) tries to make effeminacy responsible for this problem. However, the real difficulty is the reckless enjoyment of *all* his characters. And though the novel rests on Pelham's ability to resolve this problem, when at his most effete and "coxcombical" in Paris he notes significantly that a dandy's pleasure can deprive *others* of enjoyment. This scenario takes us beyond conventional arguments about cultural hostility and social opprobrium. The dandy doesn't intensify the pleasures to which others aim; he manages somehow to rob them of the *capacity* for pleasure, a dynamic we must now interpret.

Numerous passages illustrate the novel's conventional understanding of self-regard. For instance, Pelham's mother issues the following caution against her son's excessive hedonism: "I wish to recal [*sic*] to your mind that pleasure is never an end, but a means" (102; see also Moers 78). This conception of pleasure is close to Freudian accounts of sublimation: In this scenario the drive isn't repressed but impeded; it is "elevated" above sexual interest and rendered of cultural and professional value (see *Group* 115). However, after briefly describing Pelham's growing unpopularity in Paris, owing to his coxcombical "character," the narrative makes "an unforseen [*sic*] digression" (84), formulating something closer to a theory of radical narcissism:

> Why is it . . . that to be pleased with one's-self is the surest way of offending everybody else? If any one, male or female, an evident admirer of his or her own perfections, enter[s] a room, how perturbed, restless, and unhappy every individual of the offender's sex instantly becomes: for them not only enjoyment but tranquillity is over, and *if they could annihilate the uncon-*

scious victim of their spleen, I fully believe no Christian toleration would come in the way of that last extreme of animosity. For a coxcomb there is no mercy—for a coquet no pardon. They are, as it were, the dissenters of society—no crime is too bad to be imputed to them; they do not believe the religion of others— they set up a deity of their own vanity—all the orthodox vanit- ies of others are offended. Then comes the bigotry—the stake—the *auto-da-fé* of scandal. What, alas! is so implacable as the rage of vanity? What so restless as its persecution? (83–84; my emphasis)[21]

In this remarkable passage, judgments about pleasure barely contain the phenomenon they describe. If "the rage of vanity" is "implacable" in a cox- comb or coquette, this vanity's "persecution" by others recurs in a "restless . . . bigotry." Unusually, Bulwer claims that while "persecution" may be incompatible with "tranquillity," it is *not at all incompatible with enjoyment.* Related claims that dandies are "dissenters of society" weren't especially new in Bulwer's time; they are now part of a standard critical discourse on transgression, deviation, and insubordination.[22] But such emphasis takes us only so far in explaining why self-pleasure ends "not only [others'] en- joyment but [their] *tranquillity.*" Most accounts of cultural opprobrium and gender instability can't explain why the dandy's overabundance of self- regard is so intolerable an offense that people of the same sex, if free of legal repercussions, would "*annihilate* the unconscious victim of their spleen."

In Bulwer's scenario, society intervenes between the subject and its "last extreme of animosity." "The tools of our passions cut both ways," comments Glanville later; "we find our treacherous allies less destructive to others than ourselves" (368). Since the "victim of [this] spleen" is "un- conscious," "Christian toleration" isn't a suitable restraint. While "set[ting] up a deity of their own vanity," the coxcomb and coquette "offend . . . all the orthodox vanities of others," but religion is incapable of curbing this rage. Why is this a same-sex drama? And considering the strength of these murderous fantasies, what (except laws) prevents society from unraveling in its pursuit of this vindictive rage? Perhaps the most radical aspect of *Pelham* is its quiet confidence that political reform and self-change are frag- ile bulwarks against the pressure of this "restless . . . persecution."

I dwell on this passage because it illustrates not only the price of repression in *Pelham* but the reason repression becomes necessary, given the vindictive rage that would ensue if it *completely* failed. And since *Pelham* partly represents this rage, indicating that repression does not entirely succeed, the novel's "unforseen digression" gives us remarkable glimpses of the implicit violence in Henry Pelham's education. I mean this less as an indictment of Pelham's powerless relation to Georgian "discursive regimes" than as an observation on the profound stakes of all subjectivities. Pelham does not, as Graham claims, simply "suppress . . . unprofitable and antisocial feelings even when circumstances would justify his indulging them" ("Pelham" 77); he highlights the violent asymmetry marking every subject's relation to society, so demonstrating why the subject's identifications often fail and inadequately defend themselves *against* cultural demands.

This failure has some bearing on Bulwer's intolerance of masculine "error," but its implications are quite different from his claims. As we've seen, the dandy bears the brunt of this accusation because his self-regard shatters a myth of social connection and altruism. *Pelham* often generalizes this accusation by highlighting an intriguing gap between the individual and his or her society, in which others' relations also go awry.[23] Here is Pelham's observation on the psychic repercussions of this generic failure: "Take from a man his fortune, his house, his reputation, but flatter his vanity in each, and he will forgive you. Heap upon him benefits, fill him with blessings: but irritate his self-love, and you have made the very best man an *ingrat*. He will sting you if he can: you cannot blame him; you yourself have instilled the venom" (84).

The novel tirelessly documents this wisdom when Glanville plots his revenge against Tyrrell for raping his fiancée, Gertrude. Glanville is so overwhelmed by a lust to kill—so infatuated by the idea of perfect retribution—that his life's mission devolves entirely on his anticipating Tyrrell's humiliation and death. This psychic economy is remarkably similar to that prevailing in Rudyard Kipling's short story "Dray Wara Yow Dee" (1890), in which the protagonist swears an eternal and homoerotic "lust of vengeance" against his rival:

> I will follow him, as a lover follows the footsteps of his mistress, and coming upon him I will take him tenderly—Aho! so tenderly!—in my arms. . . . What love so deep as hate? . . . There is no madness in my flesh, but only the vehemence of the desire that has eaten me up. . . . Surely my vengeance is safe! . . . for

I would fain kill him quick and whole with the life [*sic*] sticking firm in his body. ("Dray" 9, 14, 15)

Pelham anticipates this passage in Kipling, but with still greater attention to the psychology of revenge:

> The scheme which I resolved upon was . . . *to feast my eyes upon the feverish intensity of his suspence* [*sic*]—to reduce him, step by step, to the lowest abyss of poverty—*to glut my soul with the abjectness and humiliation of his penury*—to strip him of all aid, consolation, sympathy, and friendship . . . The still more bitter treachery of deserting him in his veriest want I reserved till the fittest occasion, and *contemplated with a savage delight. . . . I revelled in the burning hope* of marking the hunger and extremity that must ensue. . . . [I] flattered my heart, that amidst the applause of senators, and the whirlpool of affairs, I could lull to rest the voices of the past, and the spectre of the dead. (365, 367, 369; my emphases; see also Christensen 75)

To this extent, Glanville *does* follow Tyrrell "as a lover follows the footsteps of his mistress." The irony is that his fiancée's footsteps are a phantom tormenting *him;* they foster his abjection: "the awakened thought of vengeance!—but how was it to be gratified?. . . . I was almost suffocated by the violence—*the whirlpool*—of my emotions" (370, 371; original emphasis). As with Pelham's substitution of Ellen Glanville for her brother, Gertrude and Ellen represent only the unseen *cause* of an erotic rivalry between two men. The thrill of this substitution haunts the novel, Gertrude and Ellen becoming the pretext for a passion that changes radically in aim as the novel progresses: "In all these motions I followed the object of my pursuit; and my heart bounded with joy when I, at last, saw him set out alone, and in the advancing twilight" (372).

Bulwer hardly can cordon off this revenge as Byronic excess.[24] Indeed, Glanville's description of passion returns us to Bulwer's unresolved account of character and ontology in his preface and advertisement. And though we can trace this conception of desire and affect from Byron to Bulwer's 1849 advertisement and on to Pater's *Renaissance,* Bulwer cannot integrate this conception without narrative turbulence. By extirpating this passion and its nonidentical trappings (effeminacy, foppery, homosexuality), Bulwer's successive drafts of *Pelham* strive unsuccessfully to forget it.

We might indeed give the novel this epigraph: "Alas! for the instability of human enjoyment" (243). Or summarize its dilemma by the question: "Sir, what is your will?" (381).

Still, the question of effeminacy and passion persists. Why, for instance, should deficiency of will present such problems in a male protagonist? Bulwer clearly was keen to answer this question, for the eponymous hero of his *Godolphin* (1862) displays an intolerable indolence, a *"passive sin"* (480; original emphasis). Like Pelham, Percy Godolphin is fastidious and reflective, but he has little of Pelham's ambition or drive for self-reform. "I could sacrifice my happiness," he reflects, "but not my indolence; I was not ungenerous, I was inert" (480). ("If I speak of love in connection with dandyism," Baudelaire tells us relatedly, "this is because love is the natural occupation of the idle" [*Painter* 27].) Bulwer adds that "the effeminacy and dreaming of [Percy's] life had *banished* much of its early chivalric and earnest expression" (346; my emphasis). Rather than being imbued with the type of stoic indifference Samuel Beckett would later give Murphy, Molloy, and Malone, Godolphin's inertia represents a "failure to realize his potential" (Graham, "Bulwer" 153). For Graham, however, this failure "is more default than defeat" (153)—Godolphin accepts his internal constraints without striving for heroic self-redemption.

I find this resistance to self-transformation—or *refusal to save oneself from oneself*—fascinating, but Graham again seems troubled by "such a passive protagonist" (152). One recalls similar indictments of Fanny Price, Jane Austen's tranquil, even dour protagonist in *Mansfield Park* (1814), but these complaints usually devolve on Fanny's timidity, not her overall passivity. Why then is male passivity so distressing in Regency and Georgian literature? It seems insufficient to claim that male passivity runs counter to the rhetoric of self-advancement and upward mobility that men such as John Ruskin actively promoted in later decades (see "Of Queens' Gardens," 1864, discussed briefly in chapter 3). Nor is it quite enough to argue that Godolphin, like *Pelham*'s Glanville, represents an unacceptable excess of Romantic sensibility. Although both arguments undoubtedly are partly correct, *Godolphin* and *Pelham* ask us to consider the psychic repercussions of masculine inertia and failure: the reason protagonists devoid of ambition begin to challenge an accompanying imperative for self-management. If the ego is conceived as "lax" in a man, for instance, his passion seems hysterical, wayward, or deficient.[25] The point is simply that Regency and Georgian dandies represent both modalities of desire: hyper-self-vigilance (Pelham as the reformed *honnête homme*) and contemplative apathy (Godolphin as a "passive" masculine failure).

Without an understanding of repression and its failure, we can't explain this excision of masculine "error" in *Pelham* and *Godolphin*. To name this operation merely "an incitement to discourse" is to misidentify the source of difficulty, which recurs at the level of fantasy and identification. As Glanville characterizes his traumatic condition, "I was like a man haunted by a dream, and wandering under its influence; or as one whom a spectre pursues, and for whose eye, the breathing and busy world is but as a land of unreal forms and flitting shadows, teeming with the monsters of darkness, and the terrors of the tomb" (374).

Between the publication of *Pelham* and *Godolphin*, Barbey argued in 1845 that dandyism "force[s one] to find a name for what is not; and that is why the word Dandyism . . . will remain foreign, like the thing it represents [*Il restera étranger comme la chose qu'il exprime*]" (*Dandyism* 25; "Dandysme" 670). We might partly attribute dandyism's "foreign" appearance to "aristocratic" notions of noblesse oblige, but the unsolved drama of effeminacy in Georgian and Victorian literature still weighs heavily on this strangeness, fostering duress and perceptions of cultural decline in mid-Victorian society. Thus while arguing in 1863 that dandyism symbolized "the ephemeral, the fugitive, [and] the contingent" essence of modernity, Baudelaire also insisted that dandyism was "the last spark of heroism amid decadence [*le dernier éclat d'héroïsme dans les décadences*]" (*Painter* 13, 28; *Œuvres* 1179). "Like the declining daystar," he added, "dandyism . . . is glorious, without heat and full of melancholy [*superbe, sans chaleur et plein de mélancholie*]" (*Painter* 29; *Œuvres* 1180).

Perhaps we can best explain such emphases on duress and failure by reconsidering effeminacy's apparitional status in Bulwer's novel. The many ghosts that surface in *Pelham* aren't metaphysical; they are persistent and impalpable forces—remnants of identification and desire—that stall cultural progress by returning us to the past. "Ghosts" trouble us because they highlight a remainder, or *remanence,* that we can't assimilate. Glanville's "loathing aversion to whatever seemed likely to *unrip the secret history of the past*" (375; my emphasis) suggests that something about *dandyism* rejects historical causality and political teleology; while the symptomatic return of "buried" and excised elements of *Pelham* and other fiction persists, "[f]orgetfulness of the past," as Glanville tells us, "is purchased by increasing our anxiety for the future" (222).

In the following chapter, we'll see a comparable interest in masculine failure recur in Algernon Charles Swinburne's poetry and prose fiction. Swinburne's fiction and the many other texts examined in this study will put in finer relief some of the psychic issues I have touched on here.

TWO

Love's Vicissitudes in Swinburne's
Lesbia Brandon

I would my love could kill thee; I am satiated
With seeing thee live, and fain would have thee dead.
—Swinburne, "Anactoria" (1866), *Poems* 58

"[A]lmost no one, today, will wish to read the whole of Swinburne," wrote T. S. Eliot in 1920, confirming a trend in literary studies that seems to be coming to an end ("Swinburne" 281). Building on the "undisputed" fact that "Swinburne did make a contribution; that he did something that had not been done before," Eliot considers "diffuseness" the most important quality of Swinburne's poetry (281, 282). "But in Swinburne there is no *pure* beauty—no pure beauty of sound, or of image, or of idea," adds Eliot, who builds on this claim to advance an interesting point:

> [H]is emotion is never particular, never in direct line of vision, never focused; it is emotion reinforced, not by intensification, but by expansion. . . . *It is, in fact, the word that gives him the thrill, not the object.* When you take to pieces any verse of Swinburne, you find always that the object was not there—only the word. (283–84; my emphasis)

"The world of Swinburne does not depend upon some other world which it simulates," Eliot concludes. "[L]ike statements made in our dreams[,] . . . it has the necessary completeness and self-sufficiency for justification and permanence. It is impersonal, and . . . indestructible" (284–85).

Such claims about dreams and impersonality might have invigorated modernists' interest in Swinburne's work, but to this day surprisingly few critics have written about his radical perspective on desire, character, language, and object choice.[1] Eliot's judgment about selecting the best of Swinburne encouraged critical indifference toward the Victorian writer, but his remarks about Swinburnian "reality" are salutary, dispelling any assumption that the latter's work is easily explained and interpreted.

Building on Eliot's claims, this chapter engages Swinburne's prose fiction, arguing that *Love's Cross-Currents: A Year's Letters* (1862–63) and the incomplete *Lesbia Brandon* (1864) advance through dreams and "fancy" a similar interest in "self-sufficient" reality (Swinburne also wrote a farcical novel in French, *La Fille du policeman* [1860–61], which I won't examine here). However, Eliot's claims about Swinburnian impersonality preempt conventional psychobiographical arguments about the latter's well-known interest in algolagnia, compelling us to engage Swinburnian "fancy" in unorthodox and even anti-identitarian ways (W. Wilson 428; Forbes; Rooksby, *Whole* 15).[2] Although he used the statement as a distancing device to defend his *Poems and Ballads,* First Series (1866), Swinburne usefully reminds us in "Notes on Poems and Reviews" (1866) that "no utterance of enjoyment or despair, belief or unbelief, can properly be assumed as the assertion of its author's personal feeling or faith" (*Complete* 16: 354).[3]

Lesbia Brandon's complex history seems curiously entwined with its enigmatic forms of "character." Owing to Randolph Hughes's overlong and vituperative commentary on the manuscript, first published in 1952, and Edmund Wilson's calmer introduction to a 1962 reprinted edition that also included the earlier (and complete) *Love's Cross-Currents,* we know that Swinburne's companion, critic and lawyer Theodore Watts (later, Watts-Dunton), vigorously persuaded him not to publish it as a novel.[4] Edmund Gosse and Thomas J. Wise, self-appointed guardians of Swinburne's literary estate, also impeded the second novel's publication (*Lesbia* iii–xi, 209–18; Rooksby, *Whole* 7), borrowing parts of the manuscript they later refused to return. Swinburne had rejected the counsel of various friends and published *Poems and Ballads,* First Series, seemingly intent on provoking a response from critics and the public (he was of course successful). Watts must therefore have imagined he was acting in his friend's best interests. Critics had found the First Series "utterly revolting," "loathsome and horrible," "nameless and abominable," "unclean for the mere sake of uncleanness," and "prurient trash," its poet "the libidinous laureate of a pack of satyrs" (qtd. in Hyder 35, 24, 24, 31, 32, 29).[5] Writing for the *Saturday Review* on August 4, 1866, John Morley was typical in remarking,

It is of no use . . . to scold Mr. Swinburne for grovelling down
among the nameless shameless abominations which inspire
him with such frenzied delight. . . . He has revealed to the
world a mind all aflame with the feverish carnality of a schoolboy over the dirtiest passages in Lemprière. . . . *[T]here is an
enormous difference between an attempt to revivify among us the
grand old pagan conceptions of Joy, and an attempt to glorify all
the bestial delights that the subtleness of Greek depravity was able
to contrive.* . . . And no language is too strong to condemn the
mixed vileness and childishness of depicting the spurious passion of a putrescent imagination, the unnamed lusts of sated
wantons, as if they were the crown of character and their enjoyment the great glory of human life. (Qtd. in Hyder 23–24; my
emphasis; see also Snodgrass 61–62; J. Adams 101, 202–3)

These and other responses provoked Swinburne to write Richard
Burton on January 11, 1867, claiming *Lesbia Brandon* was "a scheme of
mixed verse and prose—a sort of étude à la Balzac *plus* the poetry—which
I flatter myself will be more offensive and objectionable to Britannia than
anything I have yet done" (*Letters* 1: 224). Given the frequency with which
Swinburne asked that sections of the manuscript be returned, Watts first
ignoring these requests before claiming key passages had been lost, then
selling "all or most of the manuscript to Thomas J. Wise, the bibliographer
and forger," when Swinburne died (E. Wilson 23), Hughes seems correct
in arguing that Watts was too invested in protecting his friend from notori-
ety to recognize the merits of publishing the manuscript as a novel
(215–18).

While it seems clear that Swinburne did not give the manuscript its
present title, we must accept it as a suitable compromise. Most of the
manuscript's chapters remain untitled and some of the passages withheld
are still missing.[6] Yet *Lesbia Brandon* is a remarkable text, shedding light
on not only Swinburne's *Poems and Ballads,* First Series, written almost
concomitantly, but also a number of sexual and identificatory dilemmas in
Victorian literature that the previous chapter highlighted in earlier texts.
Since little has been published on the novel, and its plot is remarkably—
almost parodically—complicated, we can illustrate these dilemmas simply
by recounting its incestuous relationships, its tortuous paths of desire.

Much of the first half of the novel concerns the relationship between Herbert (Bertie) Seyton and his tutor, Mr. Denham. Following a brief (and incomplete) introductory chapter that rhapsodizes about Herbert's sister, Lady Margaret Wariston, we learn that Herbert's father (Frederick Seyton) recently has died; Herbert, aged nine, is raised by his sister and brother-in-law, Lord Wariston. Increasingly concerned about Herbert's running "wild" (11), Lord Wariston asks his maternal uncle, Mr. Linley, for help in finding Herbert a tutor. And Mr. Linley derives a certain Machiavellian pleasure from recommending Mr. Denham, who is hired for the purpose of "licking a cub into schoolboy shape, and breaking a colt into Eton harness" (12). Linley's sadistic glee is enhanced when Denham is given "single and imperial control over the subject of this experiment; the vile body must lie at his mercy" (12–13).

Denham's "office" begins with predictable and unyielding violence: Herbert is flogged on every available opportunity, his tutor devising "elaborate narratives of punishment" (14) that consistently exceed Herbert's "crimes." One of Herbert's joys (the sign of his initial "wildness") is being buffeted by the sea, but Denham curtails this activity, increasing Herbert's yearning until he sneaks off alone to swim naked in the sea. Predictably, he is caught and the cycle of violence recurs with added intensity. Herbert comes to enjoy this violence so much that his "transgressions" become almost a pretext for punishment. In dismissing the idea that punishment is ever corrective, the novel anticipates Freud's claim that "criminals" suffer from "a sense of guilt"—that a belief in having erred precedes and even causes, rather than postdating, misdeeds and criminal acts.[7]

After giving us further descriptions of Herbert's nude swimming and his being flogged by Denham, Swinburne introduces new characters, guests at the Waristons' dinner party. We read about Lady Midhurst, a woman of "venomous old beauty, who had gone all to brain and tongue. . . . She was . . . voluble and virulent with a savour of secret experience" (44). We learn too about Lord Charles Brandon and his daughter, Lesbia, though the real details of this family romance aren't disclosed for several chapters—and then often only implicitly, when Denham and Linley discuss the Seytons', Waristons', and Brandons' intertwined genealogies. The reason for this discussion is simple: Denham is infatuated with

Herbert's sister, his obsession accentuating—rather than curtailing—his punitive relationship with Herbert.

Linley tells Denham that the now deceased Frederick Seyton, who is also Denham's father, had an affair with an unnamed woman he could not marry. "He was very poor and pretty, your good father," Linley avows, "and she ruined him . . . *Elle en avait vu d'autres, votre mère*" (123). Pregnant by Seyton, the woman gives birth to a child (Denham) before marrying Lord Brandon, who presumably knows nothing of the child.

Denham's mother's sister marries Mr. Linley, the couple becoming Denham's guardian to protect him from knowledge of his illegitimacy, a situation anticipating Herbert's adoption by the Waristons. Having married Brandon, who rejects the counsel of friends and family in choosing her, Seyton's mistress (now Lady Brandon) gives birth to Lesbia, who is thus Denham's half-sister. Both children are represented as outcasts in the novel, greatly disturbed by their traumatic origins.

The affective complexities of *Lesbia Brandon* build on this network of illegitimate and suppressed relationships. Since Seyton later marries a woman (also unnamed) who gives birth to Margaret and Herbert, Denham's abuse of Herbert means that he is beating and arousing his half-brother (they share the same father, though Herbert is unaware of this and Denham seems later to suppress this knowledge [124–25]). And though Herbert's initial object of desire is clearly Denham, Herbert later develops an incestuous love for his own sister, yearning for her to mother him while allowing him to serve and worship her. Herbert's violent relationship with Denham thus repeats itself in altered forms, radically determining both Herbert's and Denham's erotic fantasies about Margaret: "I wish you would kill me someday," Herbert insists to his sister. "It would be jolly to feel you killing me. Not like it? Shouldn't I! You just hurt me, and see" (81). Concerning the now thirteen-year-old's relationship with his sister, we read:

> Kneeling with his face lifted to hers, he inhaled the hot fragrance of her face and neck, and trembled with intense and tender delight. Her perfume thrilled and stung him; he bent down and kissed her feet, reached up and kissed her throat. . . .
> "Oh, I should like you to tread me to death! darling!" . . .

[U]nder cover of the massive and luminous locks she drew
up his face against her own and kissed him time after time with
all her strength. . . .

He fell asleep with her kisses burnt into his mind, and the
ineffaceable brand of love upon his thoughts: and dreamed passionately of his passion till he woke; seeing her mixed with all
things, seeming to lose life for her sake, suffering in dreams
under her eyes or saving her from death. (80–82; see Lafourcade 2: 309–10)

As I mentioned above, Denham by this time has established a comparable
passion for Margaret (his other half-sister), not realizing the family connection until it is too late. He displaces this love and infatuation by punishing
Herbert even more; Herbert's and Margaret's close physical resemblance
allows Denham to substitute the former for the latter, complicating his
erotic relationship to both: "[H]e could but punish her through her
brother, hurt her through his skin; but at least to do this was to make her
own flesh and blood suffer for the pain inflicted on himself" (31). "The
likeness infuriated [Denham]," adds the narrator, "but he subdued the
fury; eyes of cold anger and judicial displeasure followed the boy's movements" (31–32). The quotation begins detailing Denham's heterosexual
interest, but it ends by representing the possibility of his finding an alternative abreaction—erotic relief in punishing Margaret's "likeness," her
brother. The narrator concludes that "such mixed passions, the product of
emotions inverted and perverted, were in [Denham] more durable as well
as more vehement than any simple affection" (34).

These quotations illustrate what *Lesbia Brandon*'s narrator calls "the
desperate caprice of . . . immeasurable desire" (38). Complicating Denham's involvement with Herbert, the narrator also reveals that they have
almost identical fantasies. In the following passage, for instance, we see
Denham's thwarted passion—the repercussions of his being "shaken inwardly and throughout by a sense of inevitable pain" (38; see Baird):

Rage rose in him again like a returning sea. Furious fancies
woke up and fought inside him, crying out one upon the other.
He would have given his life for leave to touch her, *his soul for
a chance of dying crushed under her feet:* an emotion of extreme
tenderness, lashed to fierce insanity by the circumstances,

frothed over into a passion of vehement cruelty. *Deeply he desired to die by her,* if that could be. (38; my emphases)

As Denham engages this tension, partly displacing his remaining conflict onto Herbert, the boy does something similar, substituting Lesbia for his sister in ways that implicitly leave the latter for Denham, though she is of course still married to Lord Wariston. As her name suggests, however, Lesbia initially cannot reciprocate Herbert's love; Margot Northey remarks that since Lesbia is "prevented by social strictures from an open sexual response to Lady Warriston [*sic*], she dreams of pushing her off a cliff" (304). In this way, the novel becomes a type of affective round-robin, Herbert developing an intense (though nonphysical) love for Lesbia, who, in Hughes's words, "is in love with his sister, who is the daughter of a man who had been the lover of Lesbia's mother, and is herself loved by (and later becomes the lover of) a man [Denham] who is not only her half-brother but also the half-brother of Lesbia: it is difficult to state the situation without getting into a dreadful tangle!" (334).[8]

The intensity of this "tangle" renders desperate all of *Lesbia Brandon*'s attachments and idealizations. Swinburne enumerates a type of erotic excess (he called this "over-much delight") that makes his characters frantic and then ill.[9] When describing Denham's love for Margaret, for instance, the narrator tells us

the hidden disease in spirit and heart struck inwards, and daily deeper: it pierced him through the flesh to the mind. Silent desire curdled and hardened into poisonous forms; love became acrid in him, and crusted with a bitter stagnant scum of fancies ranker than weeds. Under the mask or under the rose he was passing through quiet stages of perversion.... Fever and tremor came over him because of her; but when these subsided and made way for thought he was angry, and *passed from scorn of the effect to abhorrence of the cause.* Her he did not hate, but he hated his love for her.... He had grown used to a sense of despair; *to give and take pleasure was so far beyond hope that it soon passed beyond desire.* (20–21; my emphases)

"The result is a deadly devotion . . . beyond desire" (21): Such excess recurs in much of Swinburne's poetry, where death seems not only an aesthetic device intensifying before disbanding affective knots, but a logical answer to the extreme psychic duress afflicting Swinburne's lovers.[10] After hinting that Margaret and Denham have had a clandestine affair, the narrator tells us that Denham commits suicide, leaving Margaret bereft and singing rather cruelly of her loss to her frightened children (see Barrett 113–14).

But it is Herbert's erotic interests that *Lesbia Brandon* tracks. We see his passions shift from Denham (his half-brother) to Margaret (his sister) to Lesbia (whose mother was his father's previous lover). And Lesbia is "dying upwards" by a slow poisoning (159); in Hughes's words, "there is an embargo, a strange doom upon her" (335). Though she and Herbert develop a profound love for each other, she dies just before Denham commits suicide, the novel concluding on a melancholy note with Herbert and Margaret bereft of their loves. Preceding Lesbia's death, the following passage best captures Herbert's response to *Denham's* suicide:

> His old friend's death had hurt him for a time; but the blow fell on senses deadened and a hardening skin. Inaction and inadequacy oppressed his conscience, and a profitless repugnance against things that were: he held on to his daily life with loose and empty hands, and looked out over it with tired unhopeful eyes. He did not seem effeminate or dejected, and hoisted no signs of inward defeat; but at heart he was conscious of weakness and waste. (157)

While assuring us that there are no signs of Herbert's "inward defeat," the narrator highlights strong evidence to the contrary. Like the passages above detailing Denham's "quiet stages of perversion" (20), the novel explores these conflicts, its preoccupation with hatred and love producing what Northey calls "sensuous extremism" (306). While attending Lesbia on her deathbed, for instance, Herbert is overcome by a bizarre and "inappropriate" response, which recalls Eliot's emphasis on Swinburnian impersonality: "The morbid and obscure fascination of obscure disease [*sic*] began to tell upon her listener: his nerves trembled in harmony with hers: he felt a cruel impersonal displeasure, compound of fear and pain, in the study of her last symptoms. Then by way of reaction came a warm sudden reflux of tenderness" (163). As Rikky Rooksby notes, "Herbert is profoundly disturbed by being excited by her suffering" ("A. C. Swinburne's" 489; also McGhee 85–86).

Later, the narrator tells us Denham's obsession with Margaret makes him "glitter . . . with passion" (32) and that Denham is "seized with a fierce dumb sense of inner laughter; it was such an absurd relief this, and so slight" (33). Northey elaborates thus on these vicissitudes:

> Where *Love's Cross-Currents* presents an enclosed controlled world, *Lesbia Brandon* presents a closed world which erupts. Where *Love's Cross-Currents* for the most part gives an impression of the rather neo-classical attributes of wit, restraint, and urbanity, *Lesbia Brandon* comes across as a romantic outpouring in which restraint is thrown to the wind and the intrusion of authorial personality breaks through the bonds of artistic control. (300)

In light of these passages and Northey's remarks, it would be tempting to present the latter novel as Swinburne's intimate testimony. Glossing Georges Lafourcade's belief that "*Lesbia Brandon* might better be read not as a novel but as a confession, a disguised intellectual biography" (300), Northey suggests that "there is good reason to link [the novel's] structural disunity . . . with [its] greater autobiographical emphasis" (300; see also Lafourcade, esp. 2: 306).[11] However, the novel interests her more for its suggestion that characters experience as their "common denominator" a repeated confrontation with extremes of pleasure and pain, a "desire for personal sensuous abandon, for the extreme edge of experience beyond conventional norms" (302). According to this reading, *Lesbia Brandon's* "desire to push life into sensuous channels, to understand experience through one's skin, makes even pain an epiphany of awareness" (302). Strangely, however, Northey's closing remarks shy away from these claims, instead generating criticism of the novel's structure and aesthetic merits. "Whereas *Love's Cross-Currents* makes its point indirectly with psychological dramatic and brilliantly witty exposure of conventional attitudes," she tells us, "the looser, and more autobiographical emphasis of *Lesbia Brandon* replaces control with a license which runs to excess, resulting in a disjointed, rambling, and self-indulgent work. In Swinburne's second novel too often the ego and the artist are at odds" (306).

Northey's argument deserves careful consideration. Since *Lesbia Brandon's* "diffus[ion]" (300) and "sensuous extremism" (306) seem mutually involved, the novel fragmenting *because* it encourages a type of affective exploration undermining conventional narratives, its "sensuous extremism" would be curtailed if it achieved the apparent "control" of *Love's Cross-Currents*.[12] Considering Swinburne's interest in Denham's and Herbert's "quiet stages of perversion" (20), we might turn Northey's lament that the novel "breaks into scattered episodes" (300) into a sign of Swinburne's aesthetic and conceptual sophistication: That *Lesbia Brandon* fails to contain its characters' ontological extremes points up Swinburne's interest in radical psychic states that conventional fiction can't adequately represent.[13] We recall Eliot's related suggestion that "[i]t is, in fact, the word that gives him the thrill, not the object. When you take to pieces any verse of Swinburne, you find always that the object was not there—only the word" (284).

Eliot's emphasis on referents in Swinburne's work risks de-specifying crucial links between passion and gender in his novels. Such emphasis would produce a type of polymorphous perversity, in which the object of desire ultimately proves unimportant, the word alone giving Swinburne "the thrill." Certainly, we see aspects of this "perversity" in Swinburne's poetry, which, despite primarily emphasizing heterosexual love, nonetheless explores androgyny, hermaphroditism, and lesbianism, thus retaining the primacy of objects. Swinburne called his "studies of passion or sensation" "dramatic, many faced, multifarious"; "they are to be taken as the first outcome or outburst of foiled and fruitless passion recoiling on itself" (*Complete* 16: 354, 359).[14] But if, following Eliot, we fully uncouple the object and word, we would ignore Swinburne's interest in fantasy, which connects objects and words with Swinburne's "thrill." It is fantasy that creates the remarkable alternation in his work between same- and other-sex desire, in which the former shapes, overdetermines, and even ruins the latter.

Eliot's argument is nonetheless provocative for indicating the potential *damage* an object can wreak on the desiring subject. His broader claims about Swinburnian impersonality seem most apt when we consider the latter's interest in passion's ontological violence. The poetic repercussions of this violence surface when we consider Jacqueline Rose's astute claim that "[s]exuality is the vanishing-point of meaning" (71). When commenting on Herbert's joy in bathing naked in the cold sea, for instance, the narrator declares that "nothing could repress or resist . . . [t]he bright and vigorous delight that broke out at such times" (*Lesbia* 19). Much later, Lady Midhurst remarks to Lady Wariston: "There is always something attractive in failure after a certain time, as strong as there is for the minute in success" (75). Both remarks indicate the novel's interest in overturning marital, familial, and social stability, an interest perhaps accounting for Northey's claim that Swinburne's "license" in *Lesbia Brandon* "runs to excess, resulting in a disjointed, rambling, and self-indulgent work" (306).

Love's Cross-Currents doesn't pursue these extremes so forcefully, it is true, but it probes the repercussions of a potentially explosive situation— Reginald Harewood's infatuation with Mrs. Clara Radworth—assessing the allure and risk of an extramarital affair even as its guiding authority, Lady Helena Midhurst, insists that adultery is unthinkable: "Married ladies, in modern English society, *cannot* fail in their duties to the conjugal relation. Recollect that you are devoted to your husband, and he to you. I assume this when I address you, and you must write accordingly. The other hypothesis is *impossible* to take into account" (86; original emphases).

Love's Cross-Currents also anticipates *Lesbia Brandon* in its fascination with the characters' interconnected desires and genealogies. Emphasizing the serious hazards of Reginald's extreme passion for Mrs. Radworth, the novel partly gives us its characters' prehistory, suggesting that the pleasure Reginald obtains from his father's beatings as a young man partly inflects his subsequent passion for women. The novel oscillates so unpredictably between idealization and degradation that the reader ultimately cannot tell which extreme is more important to its characters.[15] Considering the passage below—which in its discussion of flagellation alludes strongly to the homosexuality informing aspects of public-school "fagging" (younger boys performing menial chores for their seniors)—we are justified in asking if passion in Swinburne's work doesn't derive from this oscillation between idealization and degradation:

> "When I was your age [nine years old; see 23] I used to get swished twice a week regular. The masters spite me. I know one of them does, because he told one of the big fellows he did. . . . I was the fellow's fag that he said it to, and he called me up that night and licked me with a whip; with a whip like this. He was a most awful bully. I don't think I'll tell you what he did once to a boy. You wouldn't sleep well to-night."

"Oh, do!" said Frank, quivering. The terrific interest of Reginald's confidences suspended his heart at his lips; he beheld the
Complete Schoolboy with a breathless reverence. As for pity, he
would as soon have ventured to pity a crowned head.

"No," said the boy of the world, shaking considerate curls;
"I won't tell a little fellow, I think: it's a shame to go and put
them in a funk. Some fellows are always trying it on, for a spree.
I never do. No, my good fellow, you'd better not ask me. You
had really."

Reginald sucked his whip-handle with a relish, and eyed the
universe in a conscious way.

"Do, please," pleaded the younger. "I don't mind; I've heard
of—that is, I've read of—all kinds of awful things. I don't care
about them the least bit."

"Well, young one," said Reginald, "don't blame me then,
that's all, if you have bad dreams. There was one fellow ran
away from schools when he heard of it—on my word." And
Reginald proceeded to recite certain episodes—apocryphal or
canonical—from the life of a lower boy, giving the details with
a dreadful unction. No description can express the full fleshy
sound of certain words in his mouth. (27–28)

Similar passages recur more violently in *Lesbia Brandon,* where Swinburne's interest in "passion" seems almost to unravel his protagonists, generating a level of ontological vulnerability that aids his exploration of algolagnia and homosexuality. And while maternal figures such as Lady
Midhurst, Lady Wariston, and even Mrs. Radworth elicit forms of idealization usually sustaining his male protagonists, perhaps even "repairing" aspects of their vulnerability, overbearing and virile fathers (Captain Harewood) and father figures (Denham and Linley) represent the other side of
this equation—the physical pain and "humiliation" accompanying this
vulnerability.

Swinburne's fascination with psychic instability and death seems to
enhance his interest in the erotic repercussions of same-sex flagellation. By
contrast, his idealization of women and mother figures seems benignly to
reinforce the lover's role. And even when this idealization shifts perceptibly,
partly destabilizing the lover's identity (one thinks of Herbert's brief masochistic obsession with his sister, or Lesbia's love for the same woman), we

see corresponding efforts to resolve this instability: Herbert falls in love with Lesbia, who eventually responds, the two forming a strong, nonsexual bond, while Denham's infatuation with Lady Wariston surpasses in intensity Herbert's erotic love for his sister. This infatuation tends to deplete, rather than sustaining, Denham, it is true, but he "works off" this antagonism by "punish[ing] her through her brother, hurt[ing] her through his skin; . . . at least to do this was to make her own flesh and blood suffer for the pain inflicted on himself" (31); in this respect, the critic John A. Cassidy considers Denham "psychotic" (111).

Scholars of Swinburne's poetry may detect an interesting reversal here, for male homoeroticism is less palpable in the poetry, the erotic charge deriving largely from men's pursuit of women. The oscillation I've identified is not missing in the poetry, but it tends to prevail as aspects of a single relationship, the idealized woman ("l'Innominata," the unnamed) eliciting ardor *and* disgust from her lover, depending on how hopeful he is. In Swinburne's novels, by contrast, we see much stronger links between male homoeroticism and explorations of psychic extremes.[16] In *Lesbia Brandon,* in particular, the "primary" relationship between Denham and young Herbert determines the novel's subsequent love relationships, heterosexual or otherwise. Remarking on Herbert and Margaret, for instance, Frédéric Monneyron notes, "Basically, they are flip sides of the same entity. Given this, wouldn't Denham's desire be for the androgyne?" (60; my trans.).[17]

The relationship between Herbert and Denham is best characterized by Herbert's joyous "wildness"—his swimming in the sea—which Denham is employed to curtail. Before Denham appears, for instance, Herbert loves swimming in "water [that] moved like tired tossing limbs of a goddess, troubled with strength and vexed with love"; "the wind played upon [the sea] wilfully, lashing it with soft strokes, kissing it with rapid kisses, as one amorous and vexatious of the immense beautiful body defiant even of divine embraces and lovers flown from heaven" (6). The waves have both maternal and paternal properties here: They resemble "the tired tossing limbs of a goddess" and "soft fierce bosoms [that] fought for their sharp embraces" (18), but also "lash . . . and caress . . . [Herbert] with all their might and all their foam" (18); and they "enter" Herbert and "fill . . . him with fleshly pleasure and the pride of life; he felt the fierce gladness and glory of living stroke and sting him all over as with soft hands and sharp lips" (9; see also Pittick 124).[18] "It was in this guise," the narrator tells us,

> that [Herbert] first met the man who was to rule and form his life for years to come. Drenched and hot and laughing, salt and blown and tumbled, he was confronted with a tall dark man, pale and strong, with grey hard features and hair already thinned. Mr. Denham had noticeable eyes, clear brown in colour, cold and rapid in their glance; his chest and arms were splendid, the whole build of him pliant and massive, the limbs fleshless and muscular. But for the cold forehead and profound eyes he seemed rather a training athlete than trained student. . . . As his eyes fell on Herbert, the boy felt a sudden tingling in his flesh; his skin was aware of danger, and his nerves winced. He blushed again at his blushes . . . [Herbert's] soft sunburnt hand with feminine fingers lay in [Denham's] almost like a roseleaf taken up and crushed; his grasp was close and retentive by instinct; he kept hold of the boy and read his face sharply over, watching it redden and flinch. (15–16)

After two days, Denham apparently "saw good to open fire upon his pupil, and it was time indeed to apply whip and spur, bit and bridle, to the flanks and mouth of such a colt" (17). At such moments, we see in the narrator's complete approbation of Denham's discipline an eager endorsement of Herbert's punishment. Such "elaborate narratives of punishment" (14) are excessive for Herbert's mild misdemeanors; they advance an economy of justice and reward wholly tangential to Herbert's scholastic errors and general immaturity, the narrative going off in other directions:

> These encounters did both of them some good; Herbert, fearless enough of risk, had a natural fear of pain, which lessened as he grew familiar with it, and a natural weight of indolence which it helped to quicken and lighten; Denham eased himself of much superfluous discomfort and fretful energy by the simple exercise of power upon the mind and body of his pupil. (17–18)

The narrator's claim that Denham "eased himself of much *superfluous* discomfort and fretful energy" interests me here: Such admissions reveal an instructive psychic exchange, the novel trying to explain and enhance erotic fantasies of punishment. It isn't enough to call these fantasies a rich "deployment" of a new sexual "regime," to invoke Foucauldian terms. The regime is quite obvious, but the Foucauldian reading would fail to engage the novel's interest in the *causes* of Herbert's excitement—why, to continue the above passage, "superfluous discomfort and fretful energy . . . excite and *expand*" the mind of another (18). The clearest sign of this punishment's eroticism (and the sudden revelation of its irrelevance for Herbert's swimming alone in the sea) occurs soon after this passage:

> In summer they went daily into the sea together, and the rougher it was the readier they were for it; Herbert wanted no teaching to make him face a heavy sea; he panted and shouted with pleasure among breakers where he could not stand two minutes; the blow of a roller that beat him off his feet made him laugh and cry out in ecstasy: he rioted in the roaring water like a young sea-beast, sprang at the throat of waves that threw him flat, pressed up against their soft fierce bosoms and fought for their sharp embraces; grappled with them as lover with lover, flung himself upon them with limbs that laboured and yielded deliciously, till the scourging of the surf made him red from the shoulders to the knees, and sent him on shore whipped by the sea into a single blush of the whole skin, breathless and untried. . . . Denham had quietly taken a tough and sufficient rod and followed without a superfluous word of alarm. He took well hold of Bertie, still dripping and blinded; grasped him round the waist and shoulders, wet and naked, with the left arm and laid on with the right as long and as hard as he could. (18–19)

Here, as before, the basis for Herbert's punishment is wholly unclear; his misdemeanor is never explained. Almost comically, the narrative looks for ways to provoke Denham's harshness, the boy learning not to chafe at such excesses, but to enjoy and even encourage them. We later read: " 'Will you tie my hands please . . .' quoth Bertie," the narrator adding: "Denham was rather moved for a minute" (32). Herbert and Denham's relationship seems sufficiently profound to frame all subsequent intimacies in the novel: "Except on Fridays," the narrator tells us, Herbert "began even to take delight in hearing his tutor; and early in the week felt sometimes as if strong liking for him were not impossible. Sitting over his work opposite, he let his fancy fill with dreams about the man; how he lived, what he knew, why he was thus and not otherwise" (21). There are indications that Herbert's "strong liking" is reciprocated, the narrator first assuring us that Denham "had a kind of liking for the boy's quaint frank manner" (23) before Denham assures Herbert directly: "'I rather like to hear you'" (24). "Some boys would have collapsed at this," the narrator remarks, but "Bertie expanded. He was still voluble and impulsive, not afraid of [the] remark or ashamed of excitement" (24).

Without downplaying the importance of Denham's (or Herbert's) love for Lady Wariston, several factors indicate the novel's greater interest in the teacher-pupil relationship, and thus my claim that heterosexuality in this novel builds on a foundational homoerotic drama. For example, while Denham and Lady Wariston meet early in the novel, the former's "amorous agonies" surface only after the long passages quoted above detailing his relationship with Herbert ("Anactoria," *Poems* 58). The novel's emotional arc also is very complex: When Herbert is "goaded by a desire to ask Denham if he liked" his sister, he asks Denham in "a soft, clear, musically resolute voice, pretty in women and boys" (22). Finally, the physical resemblance between Herbert and Margaret aids their substitution for each other, the novel pursuing a "singular dubious beauty . . . ; a loveliness that wavers and hovers between female and male" (110). As Denham later remarks to Linley, "male and female coalesce. You won't deny it?" (122).

While Swinburne probably intended to publish *Lesbia Brandon*, only the less risqué novel *Love's Cross-Currents* appeared in print as *A Year's Letters* (1877), in *The Tatler*, and then under the interesting pseudonym "Mrs. Horace Manners" (see Riede 4; Northey 293; Cassidy 107). Thus we cannot know if, in preparing *Lesbia Brandon* for publication, Swinburne might have downplayed its homoeroticism or perhaps agreed to "normalize" its ending by having Herbert marry a woman (an unlikely situation, as he had the manuscript set up in type).[19]

When these conflicts surface in some of Swinburne's poems, accompanied by suggestions of male homoeroticism, at least three factors shape their meaning: The poet's perspective becomes more abstract and less involved; the poems themselves tend entirely to emasculate their *erōmenos* (younger male beloved), substituting androgyny or hermaphroditism for the novels' interest in the origins of virility;[20] and love—generally not reciprocated—seems to diminish in violence, yielding to passivity and internal constancy, which Monneyron has called "in large part a man's abdication of his own virility, . . . highlighting a feebleness of character generally associated with a certain effeminacy" (58; my trans.).[21]

In the first stanza of "Fragoletta," for instance, the poet appears particularly uncertain of his love's significance, his lines ending repeatedly in questions:

> O Love! what shall be said of thee?
> The son of grief begot by joy?
> Being sightless, wilt thou see?
> Being sexless, wilt thou be
> Maiden or boy? (*Poems* 82)

After referring in the next two stanzas to the younger man's "strange lips," "ambiguous blood," and his "mysterious" and "double" qualities, the poet vacillates between questions and exclamations, the latter almost overriding the doubt and equivocation that every question raises (Laity 474):

> O sole desire of my delight!
> O sole delight of my desire! [. . .]
>
> Thy sweet love bosom, thy close hair,
> Thy strait soft flanks and slenderer feet,
> Thy virginal strange air,
> Are these not over fair
> For Love to greet?
>
> How should he greet thee? what new name,
> Fit to move all men's hearts, could move
> Thee . . . ? [. . .]
>
> Ah love, thy mouth too fair
> To kiss and sting! (82, 83, 84)

Here we see a level of restraint missing from *Lesbia Brandon* and such passionate poems as "Anactoria," whose emphasis on ridding oneself of love's torments—killing the thing one loves, to paraphrase Oscar Wilde—appears in my epigraph: "I would my love could kill thee; I am satiated / With seeing thee live, and fain would have thee dead" (58).

In "Hermaphroditus" (1863), too, love is *almost* self-contained. As in "Fragoletta," it arises in the interval between assertion and equivocation, but it also enhances a form of stasis that, while not entirely missing from *Lesbia Brandon, Love's Cross-Currents,* and many of Swinburne's tragic poems, seems more controlled and restrictive than the wild vicissitudes of passion characterizing the final novel[22]—a point that didn't stop John Morley, in 1866, from calling the poem "nameless and abominable . . . fevered folly" (qtd. in Hyder 24). While parts of "Hermaphroditus" may thus resemble the passages I cited above, in which "the light and heat of dumb desire, of desperate admiration, of bitter and painful hatred" typify Denham's obsession with Lady Wariston (*Lesbia* 31), the poem strives for a level of internal constancy that characters in *Lesbia Brandon* rarely achieve. The narrator tells us that Lesbia is "half male" and that she "wanted all her life to be a boy" (53, 54), but the hermaphrodite in Swinburne's poem is advised calmly to

> Choose of two loves and cleave unto the best;
> Two loves at either blossom of thy breast
> Strive until one be under and one above. (*Poems* 79)

The "loves" in question are of course internal, the hermaphrodite posing an enigma about sexual difference that the poem is willing to expatiate upon—and even to tolerate—*because* it is self-contained and passive, lacking a form of "potency" manifesting extrapsychic desires of its own:

> Love stands upon thy left hand and thy right,
>   Yet by no sunset and by no moonrise
>   Shall make thee man and ease a woman's sighs,
> Or make thee woman for a man's delight.
> To what strange end hath some strange god made fair
>   The double blossom of two fruitless flowers? (80)

The final line above repeats the notion, in stanza 2, that a "*fruitful feud* of hers and his" turns inevitably into "the waste wedlock of a sterile kiss" (79; my emphasis). "[S]omething like as fire is shed / That shall not be assuaged till death be dead," the poet tells us, but "neither life nor sleep can find out this" (79): The hermaphrodite folds this "amorous agon[y]" into itself in a quiet *internal* wedding of "[s]ex to sweet sex" (58, 79).

My reading of "Hermaphroditus" differs slightly from approaches to this poem that consider its inmixing of male and female either a precursor to discussions of "sexual dissidence" (that is, homosexuality) or a point of indeterminacy potentially unraveling the heterosexual binary in much of Swinburne's *Poems and Ballads,* First Series.[23] For the heterosexual binary is already tenuous in "Anactoria," "Erotion," and "Sapphics," as well as in "Les Noyades" and "The Leper," which engage forms of necrophilia, and "Phædra" and "Itylus," which deal respectively with incest and rape.[24] And so I am neither isolating "Hermaphroditus" from Victorian Hellenism and similar, later depictions by the Uranian poets, nor minimizing the risk Swinburne took in publishing this poem, which partly precipitated the widespread denunciation of his first series. I am arguing instead that his emphasis on internal wedding in "Fragoletta" and "Hermaphroditus" fosters a type of psychic constancy missing from such erratic and "volatile" texts as *Lesbia Brandon.* Despite that novel's preoccupation with heterosexuality, its homoerotic radicalism exceeds the classical tropes of same-sex desire informing these two poems. As Edmund Wilson declares of the novel, with some justification, "I know of nothing else like this in English fiction" (27).

To underscore Wilson's claim, let me conclude this chapter by revisiting *Lesbia Brandon*'s psychical interest in effeminacy. In Denham's mind, as we've seen, Herbert's beauty is a simple substitute for his sister's. The narrator establishes the basis for this substitution at the beginning of the novel, long before Denham is employed to curtail Herbert's wildness and Denham has become infatuated with his own half-sister. "While yet a boy," the narrator declares, Margaret's "brother was so like her that the description may serve for him with a difference. They had the same complexion and skin so thin and fair that it glittered against the light as white silk does, taking sharper and fainter tones of white that shone and melted into each other" (2). After Herbert has started daydreaming about his tutor, wondering what kind of man he is, the narrator also notes: "There was a strong feminine element in Bertie Seyton; he ought to have been a pretty and rather boyish girl. The contrast would have been greater then: now he looked at times too like a small *replica* of his sister, breeched and cropped" (30).[25]

In ways that crucially stray from the self-contained passivity of the androgyne and hermaphrodite in "Fragoletta" and "Hermaphroditus," however, Herbert establishes strong ties with others, desiring them desperately and yearning for theirs in return. At such moments, we grasp the full psychoanalytic import of Swinburne's writing, learning too why his writing departs from the restrained classicism of contemporaneous and later homoerotic poetry, such as the Uranians'. Thus, without dismissing the importance of such poems as "Fragoletta" and "Hermaphroditus," I suggest that other poems in *Poems and Ballads*, First Series, such as "Triumph of Time," "Anactoria," and "Sapphics," are conceptually more interesting—and closer to *Lesbia Brandon*—because they show why passion fosters extremes of ecstasy and despair, bliss and unbearable unpleasure.[26] As the narrator of *Lesbia Brandon* avows when describing Denham's "amorous agonies": "When these fits were on him he could have taken life to ease his bitter and wrathful despair of delight" (33).

Over and again in *The Burdens of Intimacy*, we'll see writers attributing these qualities to homoerotic desire and specific deficiencies or excesses of masculinity. The next chapter shows how this "wrathful despair of delight" manifests itself perversely in Olive Schreiner's first published novel, *The Story of an African Farm* (1883).

THREE

"Gregory's Womanhood" in Schreiner's The Story of an African Farm

The strength, the healthiness of man consists . . . in this: that as a
woman, he be truly woman; as man, truly man.
—Ludwig Feuerbach, *The Essence of Christianity* 92

But here's the old confusion. I am a man; you are a woman.
—George Gissing, *The Odd Women* 186

"Sometimes it amuses me intensely to trace out the resemblance between
one man and another," declares Lyndall, the feminist protagonist of Olive
Schreiner's first published novel, *The Story of an African Farm* (1883).
"What is microscopic in one is largely developed in another," she continues; "what is a rudimentary [*sic*] in one man is an active organ in another;
but all things are in all men, and one soul is the model of all. We shall find
nothing new in human nature after we have once carefully dissected and
analysed the one being we ever shall truly know—ourself" (164).

Alluding to Plato, Lyndall's statement about self-knowledge and uni-
versality surfaces in a conversation with Waldo, the novel's other protagonist, in which the two discuss knowledge, effeminacy, and then knowledge
in light of effeminacy: "Life is too short to run after mights," Lyndall observes, "we must have certainties." "She tucked the box under her arm,"
the narrator continues,

> and was about to walk on, when Gregory Rose, with shining
> spurs, an ostrich feather in his hat, and a silver-headed whip,
> careered past. He bowed gallantly as he went by. They waited
> till the dust of the horse's hoofs had laid itself.
>
> "There," said Lyndall, "goes a true woman—one born for
> the sphere that some women have to fill without being born
> for it. How happy he would be sewing frills into his little girl's
> frocks, and how pretty he would look sitting in a parlour, with
> a rough man making love to him! Don't you think so?"

"I shall not stay here when he is master," Waldo answered, not able to connect any kind of beauty with Gregory Rose.

"I should imagine not. The rule of a woman is tyranny; but the rule of a man-woman grinds fine." (163–64)

"[A] true woman . . . a man-woman": In a novel so keenly feminist and perceptive about mid-Victorian sexual politics, it would be difficult to find a more significant paradox or pressing dilemma. To grasp this paradox, we need only compare Lyndall's statement with Ludwig Feuerbach's insistence, in *The Essence of Christianity* (1841), that "personality is nothing without distinction of sex; personality is essentially distinguished into masculine and feminine" (92). "[T]he basis of morality is [also] the distinction of sex," he continues. "Repudiate then, before all, thy own horror for the distinction of sex" (92). George Eliot translated Feuerbach's book in 1854, the year before Schreiner was born;[1] and John Ruskin popularized similar claims in his 1864 lecture "Of Queens' Gardens" (see esp. 100–101).[2] In light of this context and Feuerbach's insistence that we uphold "the distinction of sex," what does Lyndall mean by "the rule of a man-woman"?[3] If her statement is central to *African Farm*'s account of sexual difference, as I'll contend, how does it shape the novel's understanding of suffering and emancipation?

Considering its philosophical debt to Darwin and Herbert Spencer, *African Farm* suggests overall that "mights" prevail over "certainties" (163; see Paxton 565). As Joseph Bristow dryly remarks in his fine introduction to the Oxford paperback, "*African Farm* . . . was originally to have been called *Mirage*, followed by the cheerless motto: 'Life Is a Series of Abortions'" (xxv; also Bradford). Acutely aware that life on a remote African farm manifests unbearable disappointments, yet unwilling to proclaim the death of God, Waldo is tormented by religious doubts. "There is no order," the narrator opines for him, invoking a collective lament: "[A]ll things are driven about by a blind chance" (114). The novel endlessly confronts the psychic repercussions of this missing authority: "If you will take the trouble to scratch the surface anywhere," the narrator continues, "you will see under the skin a sentient being writhing in impotent anguish" (114).[4]

When engaging the imbalance of power between men and women, however, the novel tends to reverse this perspective, promoting "certainties" for women over the "mights" that impede them. Schreiner's interest in such visionaries as William Morris and Edward Bellamy enhances this perspective, giving the novel—despite its underlying bleakness—tremulous forms of hope (Bristow, introduction xxii). Alternating between these perspectives, the novel lacks an overarching sense of unity.[5] For many this lack of unity is a sign of its deficiency (Jacobson 17–18; Marquard 44; Zyl, "Rhodes" 86, 90; Krige 1–2); for others it shows the novel's grasp of sexual and colonial contradictions (Pechey esp. 65–71; Lenta 16, 18; Casey 134; Ogede 26, 32; Monsman, "Olive Schreiner's" 49–50). Since the novel hinges on the revelation or the resolution of these sexual and ontological doubts, however, we can argue that Gregory Nazianzen Rose symbolizes its quandary: As the novel's representative of sexual indeterminacy, he is a symptom of its failure to produce lasting political certainty.

Before elaborating on Gregory's symbolic role, let us reflect on Lyndall's statements about sexual difference. If we compare her suggestion that "all things are in all men" with her scornful belief that Gregory is "a true woman . . . born for the sphere that some women have to fill without being born for it," two conflicting approaches to gender and sexual difference surface in Schreiner's novel, complicating her relationship to debates about the New Woman in the 1890s (for elaboration, see Dowling, "Decadent"; Showalter, *Sexual* 52–58; Berkman, *Healing* 140–49; Boone 130–31). Advancing a politics of mutual respect, the first approach ("all things are in all men") puts individual and even group differences under commonality's generous umbrella. Since it reveals "nothing new in human nature," extensive self-analysis disbands the imaginary conflicts separating one person from another, proving for Lyndall and Schreiner that humans are fundamentally identical: "one soul is the model of all" (164).

In Lyndall's second formulation, however, not only are some women *not* born to be women, but certain men prove themselves unable to be men. Since in Lyndall's estimation Gregory is "a true woman" (164), the feminist argument that women not be coerced into roles and identities deemed feminine produces the lament that some men are disposed to unmanliness. Oddly, these men *are* "born for the sphere that some women have to fill," suggesting that while women's relation to feminism is broadly constructivist in Schreiner's novel, men's relation to effeminacy is wholly essentialist.[6]

This accent on sexual difference and inequality anticipates what George Gissing, a decade later, called "an active warfare" between the sexes, resulting potentially in "sexual anarchy" (*The Odd Women* [1893] 154; Gissing, *Letters,* qtd. in Showalter, *Sexual* 3):[7] Such emphasis offsets women's gains by ensuring that they answer to more powerful men; effectively, inequality becomes a prerequisite for women's sexual interest in men. In gaining self-empowerment, Lyndall suggests, women gain psychically by finding men sufficiently virile to *over*power them sexually. Fascinated by the mysterious stranger who tries to seduce and marry her (he's named only RR), Lyndall responds thus to his question:

> "And you loved me—?"
> "Because you are strong. You are the first man I ever was afraid of. And"—a dreamy look came into her face—"because I like to experience, I like to try." (205–6)[8]

Discussing Lyndall's feminism alongside her relationship with RR, Bristow notes astutely: "Lyndall makes the astonishing admission that her sexual desire for this man was based on her fear of him. Her unbending feminist principles would seem, in part, to be counteracting her acknowledged masochism. Here, in its unusual examination of sexual fears and fantasies, the novel is displaying a prescient understanding of the contradictory drives that would become known by the turn of the century as the psychoanalytical unconscious" (xix).

Building on Bristow's important claim, I'll argue that *African Farm's* interest in sexual fantasy and the unconscious is inseparable from its preoccupation with men's virility—what Schreiner's narrator, in *From Man to Man,* calls "the terrible sex-desire of a man" (279). With this claim, I am (like Bristow) departing from the now standard argument that "Gregory Rose represents the novel's attempt at some kind of androgynous resolution to the problem of sexual difference" (First and Scott 106; Berkman, *Olive* 31–37; but also McMurry 441).[9] The novel's interest in Gregory's effeminacy is, I suggest, an aspect of its profound meditation on authority and doubt. By showing that Gregory heralds a type of weakness or deficiency, the novel itself establishes links among its male characters, connecting Gregory Rose—via Lyndall's and Waldo's respective strangers—to Waldo's erotic thoughts about Jesus and the novel's foundational dispute with religious fathers. And because Gregory's effeminacy interrupts and refashions Lyndall's feminism, his "symptomatic" representation illuminates Schreiner's complex engagement with femininity, masculinity, and the unconscious. The inseparability of these phenomena in *African Farm* ultimately jeopardizes men's and women's capacities for mutual intimacy, enhancing the novel's account of ontological frustration and colonial failure (Pechey 66, 73–74; LeFew 304; Monsman, "Olive Schreiner" 585). Overall, then, sexuality and the unconscious complicate Schreiner's political vision, which Lyndall and other female protagonists frequently voice on Schreiner's behalf (Bristow xxiv).[10]

In approaching these sexual and philosophical tensions, it is too easy to argue that Schreiner simply advocated that men and women (born "little plastic beings" [*African* 154]) revise their social and sexual roles, or that she justified gains in women's power by ridiculing effeminate men— that she could represent Lyndall's gains only defensively, by enfeebling men such as Gregory Rose. It is also too easy to dismiss how Schreiner's novel eroticizes power, discounting these moments in her writing by dwelling only on her communitarian vision—one appealing to feminists and radicals alike in its compelling polemic against inequality.[11] Even the most sophisticated critics struggle to unify Schreiner's vision of female empowerment in *African Farm* and *From Man to Man* (begun in 1873, published posthumously in 1926) with her interest in women's "regressive" sexual fantasies;[12] such critics downplay Schreiner's emphasis on Lyndall's "masochism" and Gregory Rose's effeminacy, striving instead to represent "the organic unity of her social, political, and aesthetic impulses" (Casey 125).[13] But claiming that Schreiner's occasional, implicit arguments *for* inequality amount only to bad faith or bad politics desexualizes her narrative, giving us only the *African Farm* critics prefer: an ideal of female autonomy that Lyndall voices *before* her involvement with RR. These arguments ignore the novel's Swinburnian suggestion that erotic power and sexual fantasies share an *incommensurate* relation to communitarianism.[14]

To advance this suggestion, let us juxtapose Lyndall's admission to RR (" [I loved you] because you are strong. You are the first man I ever was afraid of" [206]) with her earlier rejection of men's claims that "when men and women are equals they will love no more" (161). Exasperated by this latter idea and its antifeminist corollary ("Your highly-cultured women will not be lovable, will not love" [161]), Lyndall asks of these men: "Do they see nothing, understand nothing?" (161). There is much justification for arguing that Schreiner is using Lyndall here to overhaul Victorian conceptions of love.[15] Yet Lyndall's subsequent relationship with RR blunts this claim, suggesting that Schreiner's depiction of desire and her overall vision of love is more complicated than many critics allow. Soon after her apparent rejection of antifeminist caricatures, for instance, Lyndall asserts: "Women bore me" (165).[16] While dismissing "the rule of a man-woman," as we've seen, she insists that "the rule of a woman is tyranny" (164). And on her deathbed, much later, she declares, in words modifying the novel's agnosticism and feminism, " 'One day—perhaps it may be far off—I shall find what I have wanted all my life; something nobler, stronger than I, before which I can kneel down. . . . One day I shall find something to worship, and then I shall be—' " (247).[17] The caesura is interesting, voicing a demand that Lyndall cannot complete. Finally, when speaking of her dead child, Lyndall calls herself "a weak, selfish, erring woman" (247); she tells Gregory: "Its father was not my prince" (246; see Monsman, "Idea" 265).

Although these remarks understandably embarrass many Schreiner scholars, we can't downplay or suppress them to redeem the novel's politics and so rescue its feminism from ambiguity. As Carol L. Barash usefully notes, "Lyndall's feminist rhetoric is at odds with the novel's plot. Without explanation, Lyndall destroys herself by capitulating to the unnamed man who wishes only to master her" (272). Arguably, what matters is the meaning we (and Schreiner) attach to this capitulation, the reason such ambiguity emerges, and the purposes both serve. Surely what also matters is less the suggestion that in finding her "prince" Lyndall would have found happiness, and more the idea that *no* character in this novel is ever content or satisfied. Finding happiness seems so unlikely for a woman of Lyndall's intelligence, living on a remote farm, that her comments appear almost a parody of deathbed confessions: *African Farm* maintains that "redemption is from within, and neither from God nor man" (209), while the narrator concludes on a doubtful and defiant note: "Rob me of the thoughts, the feelings, the desires that are my life, and you have left nothing to take. Your immortality is annihilation, your Hereafter is a lie" (258).[18]

In these and other statements, the novel's feminism builds on a remarkably turbulent understanding of ontology and sexual difference. Schreiner certainly is not unique in advancing such troubled representations: *The Mill on the Floss* (1860) is a compelling precedent because George Eliot can't wrest Tom and Maggie Tulliver from their respective gender-based fates.[19] As Dr. Kenn tells Maggie with "an entire absence of effusive benevolence": "'Your inexperience of the world, . . . prevents you from anticipating fully, the very unjust conceptions that will probably be formed concerning your conduct—conceptions which will have a baneful effect even in spite of known evidence to disprove them'" (625).[20] Similar pious assessments of women's "conduct" recur in Charlotte Brontë's and Elizabeth Gaskell's fiction (one thinks especially of St. John's ascetic tyranny in *Jane Eyre* [1847]),[21] but since Gaskell especially prioritizes women's material conditions, her protagonists' happiness largely is contingent on their improving these conditions.[22] To be sure, Gaskell advances an "emergent psychological domain" in *Mary Barton* (1848; Poovey, *Making* 147) and Brontë contrasts Jane Eyre's and Bertha Mason Rochester's fates, also diminishing Rochester's power to "blind ferocity" at the end of *Jane Eyre* (*Jane* 456). But Gaskell's heroines and Brontë's Jane Eyre generally strive for a balance of "perfect concord" and material security (476), producing what Amanda Anderson calls a "reformist aesthetic" that "elaborates through [fictional characters] a form of sympathetic judgment" (119, 111; see also 11–12, 41). While Jane Eyre therefore pointedly resists being Rochester's "slave" and "harem inmate," she ends up "ever more absolutely bone of his bone and flesh of his flesh" (*Jane* 297, 476).

By contrast, *African Farm* interrupts all expectations that material changes bring lasting happiness, Schreiner's narrator rejecting what she calls the "cankered kingdom of the tangible" (260). Relatedly, in March 1895, Schreiner wrote W. T. Stead, arguing: "To me the purity of the sex relation between a man and a woman lies finally in the fact that it is not a matter of material considerations" (*Letters* 219). Such claims don't revoke Schreiner's interest in women's material plight, but they do underscore her fictional interest in men and women's psychic conflicts. "This is not a novel that reaches predictable conclusions," observes Bristow. "Instead, it is replete with unjust outcomes, forestalled ambitions, and . . . utter bathos" (xi). "There is a clear point to this marked imbalance of justice," he adds: "The characters with the greatest moral strengths are the ones who enjoy the least material gain" (xi). With its remarkable uninterest in genealogy, *African Farm* also is pessimistic about women's chances of finding happiness in marriage: It represents many dead-end and exploitative relationships and implies that its characters might be happiest enjoying affairs.

And yet Schreiner was never flippant about marriage—she saw it as a profound spiritual union between men and women, an ideal to which they might aspire.[23] As Lyndall observes, "Marriage for love is the beautifullest external symbol of the union of souls; marriage without it is the uncleanliest [*sic*] traffic that defiles the world" (156). But *African Farm, From Man to Man,* and *Undine* (begun in 1873, but published posthumously in 1928) provide little evidence that men and women can sustain this union. Bristow comments: "Throughout *African Farm,* the bonds between individuals, even in marriage, often have a striking incongruity, absurdity, and precariousness about them. Even Lyndall and Waldo cannot form a lasting partnership. Instead, this young man and woman recognize in one another what it means to be unable to fit into a society based on institutions, such as Christianity, that cannot serve them adequately" (xiii).

Compounding this pessimism about marriage is Schreiner's suggestion that women cannot develop without the culture's examining its varying expectations of women and men, its insistence that women *differ* from men. As Lyndall remarks to Waldo, half contradicting her argument about men's and women's propensities for various roles: " 'To you [the world] says— *Work;* and to us it says— *Seem!* To you it says—As you approximate to man's highest ideal of God, as your arm is strong and your knowledge great, and the power to labour is with you, so you shall gain all that human heart desires. To us it says—Strength shall not help you, nor knowledge, nor labour' " (154–55). In such passages, the novel criticizes Victorian culture's emphasis on men and women's "separate spheres," a criticism implicit in the novel's remote setting, which compels women and men to live in relative proximity. Since men and women must live in this way, the novel implies, why should they also experience different fates? Additionally, Schreiner's emphasis on fantasy and the unconscious exacerbates her characters' unease and insecurity, culminating in such widespread malaise that her female protagonists inevitably ask themselves if they would be happier living as men, and vice versa. Rebekah muses privately in *From*

Man to Man, in a lesbian reverie that seems partly sardonic, given the novel's former title, *Other Men's Sins:*

> How nice it would be to be a man. She fancied she was one till she felt her very body grow strong and hard and shaped like a man's. . . . She was a man, she thought, . . . and beside her lay the woman she loved, fast asleep. . . . The little one beside her moved uneasily, and as it lay so close she felt the little body throb and knew it was the life within it that he had wakened. (She was him now, not herself any more.) And such a great tenderness came over him, and he drew her close and bound his limbs about her so that she was quite wrapped about, but the little wife upon his arms slept on, not knowing how she was loved. (226)[24]

In *African Farm,* Lyndall asks relatedly:

> "Don't you wish you were a woman, Waldo?"
> "No," he answered readily.
> She laughed.
> "I thought not. Even you are too worldly-wise for that. I never met a man who did. . . . It is delightful to be a woman; but every man thanks the Lord devoutly that he isn't one." (153)

Complicating Lyndall's point about "every man," Gregory gallops by in his finery, precipitating the discussion about effeminacy with which this chapter began.

Lyndall's disparaging remarks about effeminacy frame her political argument, contrasting women's emancipation with men's regressive links to infancy. "There are some men," she announces, "whom you never can believe were babies at all; and others you never see without thinking how very nice they must have looked when they wore socks and pink sashes" (149). The remark might usefully puncture men's virile pretensions, but Lyndall is more interested in the fact that certain men have successfully escaped infancy. As she wonders why most men shun femininity—"But I like to see real men," she tells us. "Let them be as disagreeable as they please, they are more interesting to me than flowers, or trees, or stars, or any other thing under the sun" (164)—Gregory Rose makes almost the same point in a letter to his sister, illustrating too in a chapter called "Gregory's Womanhood" that he might almost lament not being a woman. The point about "pink sashes" therefore recalls the narrator's observation that when writing to Jemima, his sister, Gregory rejected "the white, crested sheets; [and] on deeper reflection . . . determined to take a pink one, as more suitable to the state of his feelings" (140). We read the following:

> "Kopje Alone
> "Monday Afternoon.

"MY DEAR JEMIMA,—"

Then he looked up into the little glass opposite. It was a youthful face reflected there, with curling brown beard and hair; but in the dark blue eyes there was a look of languid longing that touched him. He re-dipped his pen and wrote,—

"When I look up into the little glass that hangs opposite me, I wonder if that changed and sad face—"

Here he sat still and reflected. It sounded almost as if he might be conceited or unmanly to be looking at his own face in the glass. No, that would not do. So he looked for another pink sheet and began again. . . .

"You know how cruelly father always used me, calling me a noodle and a milksop, just because he couldn't understand my fine nature. You know how he has made a farmer of me instead of a minister, as I ought to have been; you know it all, Jemima; and how I have borne it all, not as a woman, who whines for every touch, but as a man should—in silence. . . .

"Dear sister, have you ever known what it is to keep wanting and wanting and wanting to kiss someone's mouth, and you may not; to touch someone's hand, and you cannot? I am in love, Jemima. . . .

"Just then, Jemima, in came a fellow, a great, coarse fellow, a German—a ridiculous fellow, with curls right down to his shoulders; it makes one *sick* to look at him. He's only a servant of the Boer-woman's, and a low, vulgar, uneducated thing, that's never been to boarding-school in his life. He had been to the next farm seeking sheep. When he came in she said, 'Good evening, Waldo. Have some coffee!' *and she kissed him.* . . .

"Your disconsolate brother, on what is, in all probability, the last and distracted night of his life,

GREGORY NAZIANZEN ROSE

"P.S.—Tell mother to take care of my pearl studs. I left them in the washhand-stand drawer. Don't let the children get hold of them." (140–42; original emphases)

The hyperbole, melodrama, and narcissism suffusing this passage cast Gregory as a ridiculous figure whose vanity offsets Waldo's and Lyndall's respective searches for meaning and justice. His effeminacy also is a foil for Waldo's and the two strangers' rugged masculinity.[25] Overall, the avidity with which Gregory pursues Em and then Lyndall enables Lyndall (and Schreiner) to satirize heterosexual courtship and show why men and women's relations must change.

Gregory's almost knightly appearance suggests an archaic faith in courtly love (he "career[s] past" with "shining spurs, an ostrich feather in his hat, and a silver-headed whip. . . . He bowed gallantly as he went by" [164]). Yet his anxious mimicking of this tradition—incongruous on a remote African farm in the mid–nineteenth century—clashes starkly with his palpable misogyny: Alternating violently between idealizing and denigrating women, he relates to women only as types. His actions also are forced and pretentious, as if veiling a profound diffidence, even aversion, to the reality of marriage. Commenting on Lyndall's joke that Gregory is a "man-woman" who "would be [happy] . . . with a rough man making love to him!," Bristow remarks: "There is more than a hint of homosexuality in this daring description" (xxi). He reminds us that Labouchère's amendment to Britain's 1885 Criminal Law Amendment Act passed into law two years after *African Farm* appeared in print (see the introduction above for elaboration on the specifics of this act). The 1885 act not only was the basis for Oscar Wilde's two-year imprisonment in Reading gaol for "gross indecency," but influenced medical conceptions of male homosexuality, in turn altering the way writers represented this desire in literature and nonfiction. As Jeffrey Weeks reminds us, Magnus Hirschfeld estimated that over one thousand books were written about (predominantly male) homosexuality between 1898 and 1908 (*Coming Out* 26).

If we take seriously Lyndall's joke that Gregory Rose would prefer "a

rough man making love to him" to courting Em, the suggestion quickly
arises that *he* might desire RR. Contributing to this possibility, the narrator
counterpoises Gregory's poor treatment of Em with revelations indicating
his "natural" affinity, which surface when his heterosexual courtship fails:

> Of late Gregory had grown strangely impervious to the sounds
> and sights about him. His lease had run out, but Em had said,
> "Do not renew it; I need one to help me; just stay on." And
> she had added, "You must not remain in your own little house;
> live with me; you can look after my ostriches better so."
>
> And Gregory did not thank her. What difference did it make
> to him, paying rent or not, living there or not? It was all one.
> But yet he came. Em wished that he would still sometimes talk
> of the strength and master-right of man; but Gregory was as
> one smitten on the cheek-bone. She might do what she pleased,
> he would find no fault, had no word to say. He had forgotten
> that it is man's right to rule. (211–12)

Wholly sardonic, the narrator's observation that "Gregory was as one smit-
ten on the cheek-bone" jars with the impatient question "What difference
did it make to him, paying rent or not, living there or not? It was all one."
Additionally, "still," in the statement "Em wished that he would *still* sometimes talk of the strength and master-right of man," implies comically that
Gregory has dwelled so obsessively on men's "strength and master-right"
that he not only overemphasizes what is foreign to him, but reveals an
intense desire to submit to another man's "right to rule"—an idea for
which Lyndall's joke prepares us. In light of the crude psychological
sketches and admissions that surface in Gregory's letter to his sister ("how
cruelly father always used me, calling me a noodle and a milksop, just
because he couldn't understand my fine nature," et cetera), there's a certain
homoerotic piquancy to Gregory's misogyny, when he insists to his sister,
in another letter: "I don't believe in a man who can't make a woman obey
him. . . . If a man lets a woman do what he doesn't like, *he's a muff*" (174;
original emphasis). Were Gregory not preoccupied by the thought of his
internal failure, why would he be so concerned to *believe* in another man?

Bristow claims usefully that "Schreiner's fiction . . . shows an exceptional responsiveness to changing perceptions of late Victorian masculinity. Although the novel does not take the truly scandalous risk of allowing

Gregory Rose to fall in love with another man, it permits a near equivalent. For during Lyndall's final and pitiful illness, he tends his beloved in the disguise of a female nurse" (xxi). In a novel that belabors Gregory's equivocal role while voicing anxiety and ridicule about all kinds of sexual "mights," the passages in which Gregory "forg[ets] that it is man's right to rule" and disguises himself as a woman have radical implications: They turn Gregory's blurred distinction between identifying as a man and desiring other men into a symptom of wider concerns about ontological failure and doubt. As First and Scott argue, "In no way conventionally masculine, indeed designated as 'effeminate,' Rose is allowed an interior world of feeling and yearning usually denied to men" (106). As I noted above, the precarious, symptomatic basis of Gregory's "interior world" arises from the novel's agnosticism and uncertain negotiation of sexual authority:

> Above his head rose the clear blue African sky; at his side were the saddle-bags full of woman's clothing. Gregory looked up half plaintively into the blue sky.
> "Am I, am I Gregory Nazianzen Rose?" he said. . . .
> He drew from his breast pocket a little sixpenny looking-glass, and hung it on one of the roots that stuck out from the bank. Then he dressed himself in one of the old-fashioned gowns and a great *pinked-out* collar. Then he took out a razor. Tuft by tuft the soft brown beard fell down into the sand, and the little ants took it to line their nests with. Then the glass showed a face surrounded by a frilled cap, white as a woman's, with a little mouth, a very short upper lip, and a receding chin.
> Presently a rather tall woman's figure was making its way across the "veld." [. . .] Like a sinner hiding his deed of sin, the hider started once and looked round, but yet there was no one near save a "meerkat," who had lifted herself out of her hole and sat on her hind legs watching. He did not like that even she should see. (238–39; my emphasis)

"Like a sinner hiding his deed of sin": Gregory's transformation initially gives rise to shame and the passage is earnestly narrated—Clayton calls the scene "vivid and curiously moving" (*Olive* 53; also "Forms" 23); Monsman calls it "grotesque" ("Olive Schreiner" 593).[26] Not only does Gregory "look . . . up half plaintively into the blue sky," but his cross-dressing enhances doubts about his identity: "'Am I, am I Gregory Nazianzen Rose?'" (238).

Many other examples of self- and sexual transformation in Victorian literature convey similar revelations and epiphanies. The following examples differ in scope from Gregory's cross-dressing, but they nonetheless share an emphasis on distress and trauma rather than joy. In Henry James's *The Tragic Muse* (1890, serialized in 1889), as we'll see in chapter 5, the protagonist Nick Dormer announces: "'I don't know what I am—heaven help me! . . . I'm a freak of nature and a sport of the mocking gods! . . . I'm a wanton variation, an unaccountable monster'" (125–26). Three years later, in *Teleny; or, The Reverse of the Medal,* a novel critics generally attribute to Wilde and his friends, Camille des Grieux remarks: "Like Cain, it seemed as if I carried my crime written upon my brow. I saw a sneer upon the face of every man that looked at me. A finger was for ever pointing at me; a voice, loud enough for all to hear, was whispering, 'The Sodomite!'" (134). Nine years later still, A. E. W. Mason published *The Four Feathers* (1902), a novel exploring military cowardice and sexual ambiguity in 1882, in which the protagonist, Harry Feversham, becomes a pariah who can walk around London only after dark. Seen accidentally by his close friend, Feversham's face is "stamped with an extraordinary misery, [it is] the face of a man cast out from among his fellows" (37).[27]

These examples convey profound links among homosexuality, shame, and distress, the quotation from *Teleny* underscoring that stress usually derives from others' accusations (the situation resembles that in Wilde's *The Picture of Dorian Gray* [1890, revised 1891]); indeed, des Grieux emphatically denies any link between loving Teleny and so-called "crimes against nature."[28] Yet none of these examples disturbs our assumptions about sexual difference in quite the way Gregory does, for although the men in these novels desire other men, they aren't wholly effete and remain identifiable as men.[29] Consider, by contrast, that when Mr. Bevis loses all resolve to elope with Monica Widdowson, in Gissing's *The Odd Women,* we see through Monica's eyes the "dreadful . . . disillusion" of his "unmanliness" (264):

> She had expected something so entirely different—swift, virile passion, eagerness even to anticipate her desire of flight, a strength, a courage to which she could abandon herself, body and soul. She broke down utterly, and wept with her hands upon her face.

Bevis, in sympathetic distraction, threw himself on his knees before her, clutching at her waist.

"Don't, don't!" he wailed. "I can't bear that! . . ."

For a time they exchanged mere incoherences. Then passion seized upon both, and they clung together, mute, motionless. (264)

Like Gregory's "womanhood," Bevis's unmanliness underscores that effeminacy is neither an indication of—nor a simple allusion to—homosexuality. Such examples complicate Nancy L. Paxton's claim that "Schreiner is not very sympathetic in her depiction of Rose's guilty transvestism . . . [y]et [ends up] . . . acknowledging the natural existence of the homosexual impulse" (573). Arguably, there's nothing "natural" nor especially obvious about the "existence of [this] homosexual impulse" in Gregory, who cross-dresses to maintain his devotion to Lyndall; and unlike Bevis, in Gissing's novel, his ardor and "devoted nursing" seem virtuous because he sacrifices honor for love (see Clayton, *Olive* 53). Were Gregory's transvestism detected, too, he would endure greater humiliation. So when Lyndall's doctor says of Gregory, four days later, "'She is the most experienced nurse I ever came in contact with,'" the narrator underscores his *dearth* of shame: "Gregory, standing in the passage, heard it, and laughed in his heart" (241). We glimpse here that the ambiguity and doubt first created by Gregory's "womanhood" are partly resolved; the novel shifts in focus from a specific crisis about sexual difference to a more general crisis about life's meaning when "immortality is annihilation, [and the] Hereafter is a lie" (258).

In light of Gregory's cross-dressing, we should add that Olive Schreiner published *African Farm* under a male pseudonym, calling herself "Ralph Iron" (after Ralph Waldo Emerson) to ensure that the novel be taken seriously. And considering our interest here and in the previous chapter in cross-identification, it seems relevant to note Schreiner's remark to Havelock Ellis on October 3, 1888: "I've not been a woman really, though I've seemed like one" (*Letters* 142). (Brandon stresses unambiguously, "One clue to Olive's life is to remember that *she wished she was a man*. She never made any secret of this . . . [and] acted throughout her life as far as possible in the same way as if she had been a man" [83; original emphasis].) While Lyndall jokes in ostensibly a man's novel about the "rule of a man-woman" (164), Swinburne, who adopted the pseudonym "Mrs.

Horace Manners," evokes in *Lesbia Brandon* a "half male" heroine who "wanted all her life to be a boy" (53, 54).

Because writers such as Schreiner and Swinburne used diverse ideas about hermaphroditism and homosexuality alternately to confirm and disband common notions of sexual difference, their fictional representations of sexual indeterminacy are important to assess. As Betty McGinnis Fradkin notes, "The girlish dandy was a familiar literary figure, but Schreiner's dandy is allowed to grow (there is no other way of putting it) into a responsible—woman" ("Havelock" 146). Following Fradkin's lead, we may therefore compare Schreiner's depiction of Gregory Rose with Jules-Amédée Barbey d'Aurevilly's fascinating treatise "Du Dandysme et de G. Brummell" (1845), in which Barbey characterizes the dandy as "a woman on certain sides [*femme par certains côtés*]" (*Dandyism* 70 n; "Dandysme" 710 n), "a monster" (71 n), and "the hermaphrodite . . . of History [*Androgynes de l'Histoire*]" (78; "Dandysme" 718). We might also note that Lucy Snowe's initial reluctance to play the part of a man, in an interesting chapter of Charlotte Brontë's *Villette* (1853; 208), complements the novel's interest in the effeminacy of Alfred de Hamal, who cross-dresses as a nun to win the heart of Ginevra Fanshawe, and "simper[s]" on most other occasions (281): "He was a straight-nosed, very correct-featured, little dandy," Lucy tells us (216). "[H]e was pretty and smooth, and as trim as a doll: so nicely dressed, so nicely curled, so booted and gloved and cravated . . . What a figure, so trim and natty! What womanish feet and hands! How daintily he held a glass to one of his optics!" (216, 281). Such points underscore that the fortunes of male and female Victorian characters are contingent on a set of shared cultural assumptions about the psychic terrain that divides them.[30]

This terrain arguably is one condition enabling men and women to marry and fall in love. It is also what prevents men from *becoming* women, and vice versa. Thus, while female and male characters in *African Farm* imagine having been born a member of the other sex, the novel strives earnestly to regulate such feelings. And while Gregory might seem to be a symptom of men's "impossible" distance from women, the novel overall has little tolerance for men's effeminacy.[31] Placed in the service of devotion to Lyndall, Gregory's "womanhood"—as Schreiner calls it—illustrates a foundational uncertainty at the heart of her novel.

Lyndall—as we've seen—responds ambivalently to Gregory Rose: Initially contemptuous of Gregory's effeminacy, she later tells RR she would prefer marrying Gregory to him because, having no love for Gregory, she could "'shake him off my hand when it suits me. If I remained with him for twelve months he would never have dared to kiss my hand'" (203; also First and Scott 106).[32] However, Schreiner's perspective on homosexuality and social roles was more complicated than Lyndall's.[33] She was a close friend and intellectual ally of Edward Carpenter, the socialist and homosexual radical, confiding in him her doubts about marriage and the men with whom she was involved, and consoling him when one of his lovers (George Hukin) declared his intention to marry (see *Olive Schreiner: Letters* 128–29); later, Schreiner visited Carpenter and his long-term partner, George Merrill, at their Millthorpe home.[34] "She met him," notes Bristow, "through the Fellowship of the New Life, a group propagating ideas of the American visionaries, Henry Thoreau and Walt Whitman, and from which the influential Fabian Society would develop" (viii; see also McCracken). Around this time (1884), Schreiner became involved with the sexologist Havelock Ellis. Their emotional attachment was stronger than their sexual interest in each other, however, and Schreiner ultimately was repulsed by Ellis's desire that she baby him (Fradkin, "Havelock" 148–49; Clayton, *Olive* 76; also Ellis, "Notes").[35]

Schreiner also befriended Cecil Rhodes in 1890, a man whose misogyny partly veiled his homosexuality, and whose ambition may have exceeded both. Schreiner initially may have liked Rhodes because he admired *African Farm*'s grasp of southern Africa's social atmosphere. As she once said of him, clearly flattered by his praise, "He is even higher and nobler than I thought . . . he spoke to me more lovingly and sympathetically of *An African Farm* than anybody had ever done."[36] And though we can't confirm what Schreiner knew of Rhodes's private life, we know she felt "'a mysterious kind of affinity'" with him (qtd. in Zyl, "Liberal" 49 and "Rhodes" 87). She admired his ambition, her fascination temporarily blinding her to his colonial atrocities—particularly the 1894 "Strop Bill" and the 1895 Jameson Raid that he and Chamberlain engineered, an aborted coup against the Transvaal.[37] In 1896, Schreiner could still declare: "My feelings are a strange mixture of intense personal sympathy with Rhodes in his downfall, and an awful sense of relief that the terrible power which was threatening to crush all South Africa is broken" (*Letters* 219). In 1897, however, she published *Trooper Peter Halket of Mashonaland,* a vehement attack on Rhodes's cruelty and expansionist policies that forever altered her relationship to him (for a close reading of this text, see Gray).

If, as I'm arguing, Schreiner's representation of Gregory Rose isn't simply homophobic, why is the novel so preoccupied by—and anxious to resolve—his effeminacy? Schreiner's friendship with progressive thinkers and her intellectual debts to such radical groups as the Men and Women's Club indicate her familiarity with various sexological and libertarian arguments about sexual orientation (Casey 135; Fradkin, "Havelock" 146).[38] My purpose in raising this philosophical context is to avoid the intentional fallacy, while tying the novel's ambiguous depiction of effeminacy to its interest in authority and doubt: This depiction indicates a type of longing arising when the authority traditionally invested in God proves uncertain—even untenable (LeFew 307). Gregory is a convenient figure on which to hang these anxieties (he's partly a symptom of the novel's preoccupation with asymmetry and incommensurability), but Gregory first materializes in part 2, chapter 3, and all of these issues surface at the start of the novel, when the narrator considers the ego's relation to doubt and desire. In reproducing this perspective, we begin to grasp the cultural and psychic repercussions of Lyndall's "trac[ing] out the resemblance between one man and another" (164), the quotation with which this chapter began.

Schreiner's novel adopts as its epigraph the following passage from Alexis de Tocqueville's *Democracy in America* (1835–40): "We must see the first images which the external world casts upon the dark mirror of his mind; or must hear the first words which awaken the sleeping powers of thought, and stand by his earliest efforts, if we would understand the prejudices, the habits, and the passions that will rule his life" (xlii). The epigraph concludes with a famous Wordsworthian—and psychoanalytic—premise: "The entire man is, so to speak, to be found in the cradle of the child" (xlii). Eager to represent these "passions," *African Farm* tries to depict "the dark mirror of [man's] mind," but the novel isn't certain whether the passions it finds are a source of comfort or torment: "One day we sit there and look up at the blue sky, and down at our fat little knees," the narrator tells us, "and suddenly it strikes us, Who are we? This *I,* what is it? We try to look in upon ourself, and ourself beats back upon ourself. Then we get up in great fear and run home as hard as we can. We can't tell anyone what frightened us. We never quite lose that feeling of *self* again" (103).

The quotation concludes section two of "Times and Seasons," a chapter beginning part 2 of the novel, which in rough order introduces Waldo's stranger, followed by Gregory Rose, before elaborating on Lyndall's feminism, Gregory's second letter to Jemima, Gregory's pursuit of Lyndall, Lyndall's relationship with RR, and "Gregory's Womanhood" (his cross-dressing to nurse Lyndall). Lyndall dies soon after this incident, followed by Waldo, and the novel concludes with two short philosophical chapters on dreams and existence.

I offer this brief summary to register *African Farm*'s narrative logic: The arrival of Waldo's stranger implicitly responds to the narrator's meditation on our tormented "self." There are homoerotic moments in both these chapters, as we'll see, but the introduction of Gregory Rose offsets them (he shares only Waldo's melancholy, not his masculinity; see 139). And Gregory's cross-dressing implicitly anticipates narrative oscillations between Gregory's effeminacy and Lyndall's feminism (it signifies his maturity, sacrifice, *and* effeminacy); the novel ends on a broad philosophical note about our capacity to live with longing and meaninglessness. In this summary I allude to neither the novel's accounts of racial difference nor its setting in the Cape Province, and so partly reproduce the book's tendency to eclipse these matters (see Lenta 17; but also 25, and McClintock 272–76). However, I am emphasizing the novel's thematic arc: *African Farm* gives us comparative assessments of desire between two lengthy meditations on selfhood and consciousness. Failing ultimately to sustain selfhood against its characters' yearnings, the novel ends as it begins—suggesting that *desire* ultimately is the cause of our doubt. Let us consider the repercussions of this claim.

Before telling us how we acquire a "feeling of *self* " (103), the narrator says that "a feeling of longing comes over us—unutterable longing, we cannot tell for what. . . . We look at the white earth, and the rainbow, and the blue sky; and oh, we want it, we want—we do not know what. . . . [W]e cannot tell what ails us" (102; see Klevansky 20). The suggestion that we "never quite lose that feeling of *self* again" appears to resolve this "longing" (103), but the resolution is temporary. That we "ail" from "unutterable longing" indicates Waldo's distress and anticipates the introduction of his stranger, for instance, who tells him a lengthy allegory that fosters his yearning: "Alone he must wander down into the Land of Absolute Negation and Denial," the stranger tells Waldo: "he must abide there; he must resist temptation" (126). "He" is a generic hunter searching for truth; the allegory asks Waldo to forgo satisfaction and tolerate frustration (see Gorak; Monsman, "Olive Schreiner" 587; Clayton, *Olive* 74; Haynes 62–63; also Schreiner, *Dreams*).

Who is this stranger and what is his purpose in *African Farm*? The narrator tells us only that Waldo hears the allegory from "a dark, somewhat French-looking little man of eight-and-twenty, rather stout, with heavy, cloudy eyes and pointed moustaches" (120).[39] "The man's hands were gloved," adds the narrator, noting factors that set apart this stranger from Waldo and the others: "he presented the appearance—an appearance rare on that farm—of a well-dressed gentleman" (120). For our purposes it's significant that the stranger's allegory elicits affection and ardor from Waldo: "Ah! that man who believed nothing, hoped nothing, felt nothing; *how he loved him!*," the narrator informs us in a private aside (123; original emphasis). The same affect recurs in dialog:

> "All my life I have longed to see you," the boy said.
> The stranger broke off the end of his cigar, and lit it. . . . Presently the stranger said, whiffing, ". . . I want you to talk to me. Tell me what you have been doing all your life." [. . .]
> "I have never done anything," he said.
> "Then tell me of that nothing." [. . .] "Boy," he said, "you are happy to be here."
> Waldo looked at him. Was his delightful one ridiculing him? (134–35)

Later, when Waldo returns from his travels and writes Lyndall a long letter she'll never read (by this point she has eloped with RR), Waldo reflects on the importance of his "dark, somewhat French-looking little man of eight-and-twenty" (120): "That day on the farm, when we sat on the ground under the thorn-trees, I thought he quite belonged to me; now, I saw he was not mine. But he was still as beautiful. His brown eyes are more beautiful than any one's eyes, except yours" (228).

These thoughts are not exceptional in *African Farm*.[40] Waldo's feelings for the stranger build on the beatitude he experiences whenever God seems warmly disposed to him and others. Such sensations anticipate the narrator's account of selfhood, depicting the egoic comfort resulting from fantasies of a benevolent father. After Waldo reflects, "I felt you near me, my Father. Why do you love me so?" (34), he sees a vision, which involves his lying down beside the Lord's feet. "When he looked up," the narrator tell us,

> the face was over him, and the glorious eyes were loving him; and they two were there alone together.
>
> He laughed a deep laugh; then started up like one suddenly awakened from sleep.
>
> "Oh, God!" he cried, "I cannot wait; I cannot wait! I want to die; I want to see Him; I want to touch Him. Let me die!" He folded his hands, trembling. "How can I wait so long—for long, long years perhaps? I want to die—to see Him. I will die any death. Oh, let me come! (34)

Waldo later has a "delightful consciousness of something bending over him and loving him" (44). Later still, he experiences "suddenly what he called 'The presence of God'; a sense of a good, strong something folding him round. He smiled through his half-shut eyes. 'Ah, Father, my own Father, it is so sweet to feel you, like the warm sunshine. . . .' His muttering sank into inaudible confusion" (64).

This impression of benevolence doesn't last, however; the novel also details the terror arising from fantasies of a malevolent father. Such terror accompanies Waldo's questions about the existence of God, the novel elaborating carefully on the psychic repercussions of this doubt; we note too that the ego is *emasculated* by its fear: "After hours and nights of frenzied fear of the supernatural desire to appease the power above, a fierce quivering excitement in every inch of nerve and blood-vessel, there comes a time when nature cannot endure longer, and the spring long bent recoils. We sink down emasculated. Up creeps the deadly delicious calm" (108).

Why does this submission "emasculate" Waldo? And why does the narrator consider the calm following such "fierce quivering excitement" "deadly" and "delicious," as if this inertia were something Schreiner's characters ardently awaited but were forced to postpone?[41] We recall Waldo seeing life as an irritating impediment to his death: "'Let me die! . . . . I want to die—to see Him. I will die any death. Oh, let me come!'" (34). Yet even if this "deadly delicious calm" is universal, the psychic principles advanced by the narrator are prescient, as Bristow suggests (xix). We see the beginnings of a radical appraisal of life's importance, in which characters yearn for death not out of morbidity or pathology, but (as Lyndall suggests) because "all things are in all men, and one soul is the model of all" (164). Her suggestion that "we are dying already; it is all a dream" (184) is meant to inspire Waldo ("I want your life to be beautiful, to end in something" [185]), but he heeds only the implicit message of this advice: Renounce meaning, ambition, and action; choose death over life. The novel almost concludes that Waldo's inertia is the humblest and wisest path (270).[42] Like a character in one of Beckett's novels or plays, he sits and waits, alternately grave and jocular, before "muttering to himself after his old fashion. Afterwards he folded his arms upon his knees, and rested his forehead on them. And so he sat there in the yellow sunshine, muttering, muttering, muttering to himself" (269–70).

Critics may try to explain Waldo's "frenzied fear of the supernatural desire to appease the power above" by invoking his terror of God, but such accounts ultimately downplay Schreiner's interest in the *eroticism* of his doubt and rebellion as well as the psychic basis of his conflict. As she wrote Ellis on October 21, 1888: "I suppose one never kills out one's personal instincts entirely till death comes and sets one free. The terrible thing will be if death comes, and instead of rest the struggle goes on on the other side" (*Letters* 143). Thus we need to assess why "the spring long bent recoils"—why Waldo experiences a "deadly delicious calm" after "sink[ing] down emasculated" (108). In doing so we grasp some of the novel's underlying psychic arguments.

Freud did not properly assess scenarios resembling Waldo's until the 1920s, when he reappraised man's superego in terms of its erotic origins. This emphasis stems largely from his 1921 book, *Group Psychology and the Analysis of the Ego,* and his 1923 works, "A Seventeenth-Century Demonological Neurosis" and *The Ego and the Id,*[43] texts shedding useful light on Schreiner's novel. In 1921 and 1923, assessing the relevance of bisexuality for masculine identification, Freud posited the coexistence of two Oedipus complexes in every child: The primary Oedipus complex, in which (for a boy) the father is both an object with which to identify and a rival for the boy's sexual demand for the mother. And the "negative Oedipus complex," in which, as Freud starkly explains in *The Ego and the Id,* "a boy . . . behaves like a girl and displays an affectionate feminine attitude to his father and a corresponding jealousy and hostility towards his mother" (33).[44] Rendering these distinctions schematic in *Group Psychology,* Freud argued: "It is easy to state in a formula the distinction between an identification with the father and the choice of the father as an object. In the first case one's father is what one would like to *be,* and in the second he is what one would like to *have*" (106; original emphases).

Many scholars have critiqued these assumptions, arguing that Freud's distinction between identification and desire is conceptually and even *psychically* untenable (see esp. Borch-Jacobsen 75–82; Fuss 21–56; Warner; but also Silverman, *Male* 356–73).[45] My interest concerns Freud's argument about the *outcome* of the boy's "feminine attitude"; we needn't agree entirely with Freud's thesis to see at least the basis of a compelling argument about effeminacy and homophobia.[46]

In a late essay, "Dostoevsky and Parricide" (1928), Freud argued that the repression of homosexual drives following castration (that is, "the demolition of the Oedipus complex" [*Ego* 32]) doesn't resolve the boy's "feminine attitude" toward his father. Instead, the ego—striving for internal harmony at any price—reproduces this attitude in a modified form and adopts a passive relation to the superego, which is "a substitute for a longing for the father" (*Ego* 37). In other words, Freud claims that the ego tries to appease the superego "in a feminine way" ("Dostoevsky" 185)—that is, by submission and apology. This scenario is apposite for our reading of *African Farm* because, according to Freud, the ego's submission to the superego is not only an indication of femininity, but implicitly a punishment for it: the superego administers threats and judgments that respond to the boy's residual sexual interest in his father. "[E]very punishment is ultimately castration," Freud tells us, "and, as such, a fulfillment of the old passive attitude towards the father" (185; see Delaroche).

Freud gives us the basis of a complex psychoanalytic account of homophobia here, in which the boy's renunciation of effeminacy ("the feminine attitude") is an effect of psychic and, to a lesser extent, cultural pressure.[47] His argument illustrates why Waldo's religious and ontological doubts surface as concerns about effeminacy and emasculation—why, in Sandra M. Gilbert and Susan Gubar's words, Waldo "seems to accept the inevitable castration of no-manhood" (57) and why Schreiner's male characters in general "hint at a startling decline in masculine potency" (57). Gilbert and Gubar conclude that "the decline in masculine dominance dramatized throughout *The Story of an African Farm* implies that women can no longer exploit a male race that has already been effectively exhausted" (60). From this perspective, we begin to see why *African Farm's* questions about "unmanliness" necessarily accompany its interest in women's emancipation. However, the basis for this comparison is not only cultural (an argument about men and women's roles, themselves contingent on the logic of "separate spheres"), but psychic, since the novel adopts a perspective on desire in which sexuality is completely at odds with consciousness.

To advance this second argument, let's reconsider the novel's various observations on selfhood. As we have seen, the narrator wistfully records the moment "we never quite lose that feeling of *self*" (103; original emphasis), later telling us that "redemption is from within" (209)—that our best hope of happiness lies in empowering the ego against the prejudices and judgment of others (one thinks, for instance, of Bonaparte Blenkins's gratuitous cruelty toward Waldo; see Banerjee, "Schreiner's"). The allegory about the hunter hopelessly pursuing Truth endorses and complicates Schreiner's conviction that we must "carefully dissect . . . and analyse . . . the one being we shall ever truly know—ourself" (164). And so while pushing for truth, the novel also probes the repressive, constraining *effects* of selfhood. Critics may be tempted to see this argument as a critique of the limited roles and narrow expectations that society offers women, but the novel suggests otherwise, making the counterintuitive point that expanding and strengthening the self actually guarantees, rather than remedying, women's unhappiness. Always a source of honest and controversial observations, Lyndall remarks: "I am so weary of myself! It is eating my soul to its core,—self, self, self! I cannot bear this life! I cannot breathe, I cannot live! Will nothing free me from myself?" (209). Consider also Waldo's unfinished letter to Lyndall, which the latter never reads: "Of all the things I have ever seen, only the sea is like a human being; . . . [it] is always moving, always something deep in itself is stirring it. It never rests;

it is always wanting, wanting, wanting. . . . It is always asking a question, and it never gets the answer" (227).[48]

In these and other passages we see a tension between self-empowerment and self-depletion, perhaps encouraging critics to conclude that if Lyndall "cannot breathe, . . . cannot live!," the reasons obtain from circumstance, social and geographical isolation, limited opportunities, and narrow gender expectations. But other characters (particularly Waldo) experience similar frustration and discontent. Such critical emphasis would also eclipse Lyndall's argument that "self, self, self" is "eating [her] soul to its core"—that contrary to her earlier beliefs, empowering the "self" through greater opportunities *exacerbates* the problem of ontological distress.

In my introduction I called this perspective "anti-identitarian" to indicate moments in Victorian literature in which desire has a conflictual, asymmetrical relationship to identity. Schreiner's novel depicts this conflict on many occasions, her preface asserting that this conflict lies *at the heart of human character*. "Human life may be painted according to two methods," she tells us:

> There is the stage method. According to that each character is duly marshalled at first, and ticketed; we know with an immutable certainty that at the right crises each one will reappear and act his part, and, when the curtain falls, all will stand before it bowing. There is a sense of satisfaction in this, and of completeness. But there is another method—the method of the life we all lead. Here nothing can be prophesied. There is a strange coming and going of feet. Men appear, act and re-act upon each other, and pass away. When the crisis comes the man who would fit it does not return. When the curtain falls no one is ready. When the footlights are brightest they are blown out; and what the name of the play is no one knows. (xxxix)

In "the method of the life we all lead . . . nothing can be prophesied": Crises occur, Schreiner advises, but her characters are never ready and act with no prepared script. The author is no authority, she implies, because the rules of the drama elude us. Additionally, desire torments her characters by filling them with unfathomable longing. While her male characters therefore implicitly connect with each other through fantasies of authority and submission, the basis of their desire remains unknown: Since its constituents are unconscious, desire arises only as the effect of a drama that occurs offstage.

Schreiner's perspective on character and desire returns us to the issue with which this chapter began: why the novel contrasts effeminacy and virility to advance a thesis that "mights" prevail over "certainties" (163). I have argued that Schreiner's interest in error, failure, and deficiency aids this comparison, and that while Gregory Rose's "womanhood" raises important cultural and psychic questions about the fate of all men and women, it is also symptomatic of Schreiner's more fundamental interest in desire and intrapsychic turmoil.

In the following chapter, on Hardy, I return to this argument about turmoil and desire's anticommunitarian properties. Building on many of this chapter's claims, I try to explain why, to quote Schreiner, "Friendship is good, a strong stick; but when the hour comes to lean hard, it gives. In the day of their bitterest need all souls are alone" (69).

FOUR

Hardy and the Claims of Friendship

Human love is a subjective thing . . . it is a joy accompanied by an idea
which we project against any suitable object in the line of our vision.
—Hardy, *The Woodlanders* 165

A man's friendships are, like his will, invalidated by marriage.
—Samuel Butler, *The Way of All Flesh* 358

Friendship is never an obvious matter in Hardy's writing. Beset by the Immanent Will and the strange vicissitudes of human desire, the ties binding
Hardy's couples and communities are peculiarly susceptible to treachery.
Such ties are worth studying because they indicate Hardy's remarkable perspective on love and sociality. In "Hap" (1866), for example, the poet
imagines the laughter of "some vengeful god," which seems sadistically to
augment our misery:

> "Thou suffering thing,
> Know that thy sorrow is my ecstasy,
> That thy love's loss is my hate's profiting!"
>
> (*Collected* 7)

"How arrives it joy lies slain," the poet asks in bitter response, "And why
unblooms the best hope ever sown?" (7). The poem concludes, paradoxically, that we put faith in the world's indifference: "These purblind
Doomsters had as readily strown / Blisses about my pilgrimage as pain" (7).

Hardly a joyous outlook, to be sure, yet these thoughts about "purblind Doomsters" allow us to reframe conventional arguments about Hardy's fatalism; they also generate a more psychologically attuned account of
failure and intimacy in his work.[1] In this chapter I want less to dispute the
role of fatalism in Hardy's poetry and fiction than to show why this and
related issues, such as stoicism and treachery, inform his accounts of passion and intimacy. Without a psychoanalytic understanding of the factors
enabling and impeding intimacy in Hardy's work, we would misunder-

stand why such elements as aversion and envy drive his characters together and apart.

Many critics have written well about Hardy's interest in fate and character, but only a few have considered how both factors circumscribe his notions of friendship and intimacy. When engaging these last two factors, critics tend to detach them from Hardy's philosophical vision. By contrast, I suggest that we cannot understand Hardy's interest in fatalism by attributing all his characters' difficulties to either external impediments or the vagaries of what he called "[t]he Immanent Will that stirs and urges everything" (*Collected* 289).[2] Although Hardy used this term to inveigh against the cruelty of fate and chance, he also often redefined his characters' relation to this Will, noting that this "Will" emanates *from* them as an involuntary hindrance to their progress and happiness.[3] Admittedly, such novels as *The Mayor of Casterbridge* (1886), *Far from the Madding Crowd* (1874), and *Jude the Obscure* (1894; 1895) support this claim more strongly than do *The Return of the Native* (1878) and *Tess of the d'Urbervilles: A Pure Woman* (1891), in which the protagonists seem less equivocal victims of others' cruelty. As Eustacia Vye famously declares in *The Return of the Native*, "How destiny has been against me! . . . . I was capable of much; but I have been injured and blighted and crushed by things beyond my control" (421). However, *Return* also complicates this perspective when Eustacia declares, "in a frenzy of bitter revolt," "Why should I not die if I wish? . . . I have made a bad bargain with life, and I am weary of it—weary" (421, 401).

Here and elsewhere, it is difficult to sustain interpretations of Hardy's work by focusing only on the cruelty of others or Nature. In a detailed reading of *The Life and Death of The Mayor of Casterbridge: A Story of a Man of Character*, I shall soon argue that Hardy's understanding of psychology *enhances* rather than contradicts his notion of the Immanent Will: The novel's interest in the "persistence of the unforeseen" (411)—which, in the novel's closing words, "teach[es us] that happiness was but the occasional episode in a general drama of pain" (411)—corresponds entirely with Hardy's realization that there are unconscious obstacles to love and friendship. Such an approach bears heavily on Hardy's depiction of friendship in this and other novels. Toward the end of *The Mayor of Casterbridge*, for instance, the narrator carefully elaborates on these obstacles, declaring,

"There is an outer chamber of the brain in which thoughts unowned, un-solicited, and of noxious kind, are sometimes allowed to wander for a mo-ment prior to being sent off whence they came. One of these thoughts sailed into Henchard's ken now" (382). This assertion about "noxious" thoughts, here symbolizing Henchard's wish to avenge himself on Farfrae, so rendering his former friend abject and miserable, partly determines the difficulty of *sustaining* relationships in this and other novels. Elaborating on this point, I suggest that the "certain risk in intimacy" (187) of which Lucetta Templeman writes to Henchard in *The Mayor of Casterbridge* pre-vails in Hardy's writing because he anticipates—in addition to social judg-ments and taboos—insurmountable *internal* impediments to reciprocal affection.[4]

Such claims do not ignore the intervention of social factors, which Hardy's critics justifiably emphasize. We need only consider what Sue Bridehead endures for refusing to marry conventionally in *Jude,* Jude Faw-ley's difficulties in entering the university at Christminster, or the abuse and isolation Tess suffers to grasp that Hardy, like Freud, often considers "civilization" less a means of achieving personal aims than the agent pro-tecting subjects from them (Freud, *Civilization* 82–92, 122); there is no doubt, too, that Lucetta's reference above to "risk" outlines her fear of being branded an unscrupulous or "fallen" woman.[5] However, we encounter problems when claiming that these obstacles arise solely from external difficulties—that they are grounded, for instance, in the ruthless prejudice of southern England's rural communities or, as Rosemarie Morgan argued recently of Hardy's female characters, that their private dreams collapse when "the man-made world superimposes upon them its own curbing shape" (58).[6] Morgan's claims about Sue Bridehead imply a less compli-cated "curbing shape" for men such as Henchard, who ultimately exercises some power in defining "the man-made world" (he becomes mayor of Casterbridge). Yet Henchard's and other protagonists' hubris partly derives from the very world they fantasize controlling.[7] One thinks also of Mr. Boldwood and Bathsheba Everdene in *Far from the Madding Crowd,* who complicate gendered readings of Hardy's novels because they both experi-ence a related, albeit asymmetrical, difficulty in controlling their desires—a difficulty, Hardy emphasizes, that is finally independent of their social standing. This may explain Hardy's baleful assessment that "men's minds appear . . . to be moving backwards," and that "experience *un*teaches," because life depletes—without always proving edifying for—his protagonists.[8] Hardy's radicalism, I contend, stems from his rethinking the very idea of amelioration, presenting failure not only as a more likely outcome for his characters, but, perversely, as a more *attractive* option. Thus Henchard's ruin appears on the novel's first page; we realize that his indifference to his wife and his self-disgust will lead him, irrespective of his fleeting social success, *inexorably* toward ruin and abjection.[9]

Like other readers of Hardy, I am sure, I acknowledge a certain morbid entertainment in assuming that "Fate" really says to Hardy's characters, "thy sorrow is my ecstasy, / . . . thy love's loss is my hate's profiting!" Readers of *The Mayor of Casterbridge* may also experience a cruel piquancy in being able to track what its narrator calls "the edge or turn in the incline of Henchard's fortunes. On that day—almost at that minute—he passed the ridge of prosperity and honour, and began to descend rapidly on the other side. . . . [T]he velocity of his descent . . . became accelerated every hour. . . . New events combined to undo him" (291). Whether intended or not, such piquancy in witnessing this "startling fillip downwards" (291) complicates suggestions that Henchard's and others' misery derives simply from the remorseless persistence of their past.[10] Such claims ignore that many of Hardy's characters (with perhaps the exception of Tess), though powerless to control past mistakes, often fostered—even, in the case of Henchard and Boldwood, perversely encouraged—many of the circumstances now conspiring against them. This idea surfaces at the end of Hardy's bleak poem "The Wind Blew Words":

> I moved on in a surging awe
>   Of inarticulateness
> At the pathetic Me I saw
>   In all his huge distress,
> Making self-slaughter of the law
>   To kill, break, or suppress.
>
> (*Collected* 419)

To make sense of this perverse joy in failure ("self-slaughter of the law") and its impact on Hardy's accounts of intimacy, we might consider the justly famous scene in *Far from the Madding Crowd* in which Gabriel Oak's mad sheepdog arranges the death of his entire flock by herding it conscientiously over a steep cliff. Gabriel awakes to the sound of his flock "running . . . with great velocity" (85) (a word that Henchard's plight in the later novel obviously echoes), but he arrives too late, finding "a heap of two hundred mangled carcases" at the bottom of the precipice (86). He surmises accurately that "the young dog . . . [had] collected all the ewes into a corner, driven the timid creatures through the hedge, across the upper field, and by main force of worrying had given them momentum enough to break down a portion of the rotten railing, and so hurled them over the edge" (87).

Hardy's narrator notes carefully—beautifully—that "the attenuated skeleton of a chrome-yellow moon" hung over a nearby pool, making it "glitter . . . like a dead man's eye" (87). Such accounts of the environment generally accentuate human suffering and isolation. Consider too the famous passage in *Tess* in which the heroine, standing still on an immense "expanse of verdant flatness," is likened to a "fly on a billiard-table of indefinite length, and of no more consequence to the surroundings than that fly" (159).[11] Given these analogies, though, it is difficult to attribute all this malignancy to Nature or the Immanent Will. As the narrator of *Far from the Madding Crowd* observes, the dog performs his task "so thoroughly" (87) that he underscores a related human duress, exemplifying why Hardy's characters (such as Henchard) stubbornly arrange their undoing: They are, as Freud remarked of Lady Macbeth and Ibsen's Rebecca Gamvik in a deceptively simple phrase, "wrecked by success" ("Some Character-Types II" 316–31).[12] Many of Hardy's poems underscore this drive toward death and failure alongside the pleasure both elicit. Indeed, at such times Hardy uses poetry with remarkable concision to sum up the effects of this drive. In "Why Do I?," for example, the poet asks:

Why do I go on doing these things?
    Why not cease?
Is it that you are yet in this world of welterings
    And unease,
And that, while so, mechanic repetitions please?
                                            (*Collected* 799)

Without noting the self-antagonistic bliss that this and other Hardy texts illustrate, we would read *Far from the Madding Crowd* and *The Mayor of Casterbridge* with considerable bad faith, ignoring, for instance, Bathsheba's fascination for Sergeant Troy and her bizarre interest in his misogynistic sword exercises, which come within an inch of killing her (Beegel 111). We would also have to exonerate Henchard from selling his wife at the start of *The Mayor of Casterbridge,* attributing his cruel indifference to Susan to the alcohol he drank or the fate he bitterly accepts.[13] I use these examples to illustrate the point at which faith in Hardy's Immanent Will pushes us into awkward complicity with his characters' hardships. Since I am not oblivious to the possible effects of this complicity, I identify its prominence in Gabriel Oak's "pastoral tragedy" and note its general absence in *Tess.* Still, the narrator of this last novel observes of his eponymous protagonist, "Feeling herself in antagonism she was quite in accord" (135). In this and related examples, Hardy shows us why nonpsychological interpretations of his work ignore that his protagonists *sometimes arrange—and often enjoy—their and others' ruin.* Comparable readings of *The Mayor of Casterbridge* not only overlook why Henchard first turned to drink, but simplify the cause of his misogyny, stating baldly that Henchard's cards are stacked against him from the outset.[14] From this perspective, it is easy to downplay Hardy's interest in self-annihilation and the destruction of relationships. Arguably reflecting on these issues, the narrator in *The Mayor of Casterbridge* quotes Novalis to underscore that "*Character* is Fate" (qtd. 185; my emphasis).

In its interest in failure, then, *The Mayor of Casterbridge* (like *Far from the Madding Crowd*) asks us to rethink the claim that Hardy's protagonists fight stoically against social odds and the vagaries of the Immanent Will— for Hardy, the primum mobile of Nature and the universe. Although many Hardy protagonists *are* eventually defeated, as if expiring from the weight of this opposition, internal factors beyond such generic traits as pride, ignorance, and ambition radically promote their depletion. It might seem odd that Hardy critics sometimes rediscover agency—even triumph—at these moments in Hardy's work, alleging, despite his protagonists' defeat and wish for death, that they display a heroic resilience confirming the strength of their will.[15] That these accounts are not entirely wrong stems less from the heroism of Hardy's characters than from the congruence of death and submission in his work.

Time and again, the effort to convey fatalism *and* heroism forces many Hardy critics to fudge quite complicated psychological questions about failure. Greater subtlety is needed to understand this phenomenon in Hardy's work, not least because the Will that appears to explain human defeat often outwardly resembles the will attesting to personal resilience and defeat.[16] As the narrator tells us of Henchard's interest in death, "Part of his wish to wash his hands of life arose from his perception of its contrarious inconsistencies—of Nature's *jaunty readiness* to support unorthodox social principles" (394; my emphasis). Doubtless, the death drive joins forces here with Nature, but *conflating* the two would eclipse the narrator's precise interest in Henchard's "wish" and "perception," which places this novel on quite unfamiliar terrain.

"Personal resilience and defeat": these aspects of Henchard's will aren't mutually exclusive, but conflicting *and* self-enhancing dimensions of the same force. In *The Mayor of Casterbridge,* Hardy often seems to pit this force against Henchard's will without, however, suggesting that will can overcome its affinity for self-destruction. Hardy's narrator also insists, somewhat morbidly, that we note all of Henchard's psychic difficulties, and he indicates how the narrative tries to accomplish this task. "Let us follow the track of Mr. Henchard's thought as if it were a clue line" (221), he declares, noting earlier that Henchard "was the kind of man whom some human object for pouring out his heat upon—were it emotive or were it choleric—was almost a necessity. The craving of his heart for the reestablishment of this tenderest human tie [with Elizabeth-Jane, his adopted daughter] had been great during his wife's lifetime, and now he had submitted to its mastery without reluctance and without fear" (195).[17]

What is at stake in *submitting* fully to the mastery of this craving? We might learn from another's mistakes, the narrator implies, but we also can't discount that another's mistakes are profoundly satisfying to us. When put this way, entertainment in *The Mayor of Casterbridge* may stem from the novel's willingness to leave no part of Henchard's life unjudged. Such claims don't entirely revoke the bildungsroman's rationale, but they ask us to consider whether Hardy's emphasis on psychic "failure" isn't also perversely edifying (292, 296). I wrote earlier of piquancy, but in detailing the Casterbridgeans' wish for a "skimmity ride" (334)—a public humiliation of figures of authority—Hardy's narrator eventually concedes that there is a "tempting prospect of putting to the blush people who stand at the head of affairs—that supreme and piquant enjoyment of those who writhe under the heel of the same" (375; see also Lerner, *Thomas Hardy's* 79).

To advance this point, anticipating our reappraisal of friendship in Hardy's writing, let us revisit a passage from Immanuel Kant's 1793 text, *Religion within the Limits of Reason Alone*. There is, Kant observes, a "secret falsity even in the closest friendship, . . . a propensity to hate him to whom one is indebted, . . . a hearty well-wishing which yet allows of the remark that 'in the misfortunes of our best friends there is something which is not altogether displeasing to us'" (28–29).[18] The ramifications of suggesting that Victorian literature upholds this "hearty well-wishing . . . in misfortune" are obviously extensive, but the remainder of this chapter explores this idea. I invoke as examples Jude's passing impulse, when he and Richard Phillotson meet to discuss Sue's expulsion from the Training-School at Melchester, "to annihilate his rival at all cost" (219). That Jude's "action did not respond for a moment to his animal instinct" does not prevent his "instinct" from influencing the outcome of Hardy's last novel. Indeed, slightly earlier, when he deduces that "Phillotson's suit was not exactly prospering," Jude is said to feel "unreasonably glad" (183).

In *The Mayor of Casterbridge*, too, a similar dynamic prevails. In fact, Henchard bitterly—sometimes blithely—embraces his defeat, as if consecrating it with love.[19] He revokes straightforward accounts of fatalism in Hardy's work by replacing a stale binary between stoicism and "miserabilism" with an altogether different perspective: a love of death in life, which one doctor in *Jude* calls "the beginning of the coming universal wish *not* to live" (411; my emphasis).[20] This perspective cloaks Hardy's accounts of love in his life, poetry, and other novels, allowing us to see Henchard's ambiguous relation to life in a radically new way. At a point of unbearable abjection, for instance, he asks himself why "I, an outcast, an encumberer of the ground, wanted by nobody, and despised by all, live on against my will" (396).[21]

Our difficulty arises from definitions of will that tend to conceive of the subject's interests as united in their antipathy to forces that would override and annihilate them. Often this union does occur, leading to relatively clear signs of resistance, victory, or defeat. When Boldwood begins to confront—but, fatally, not to overcome—his disastrous fascination for Bathsheba in *Far from the Madding Crowd*, for example, Gabriel resists the ensuing storm by protecting Bathsheba's hayricks. And when Jude strives to pursue a degree at Christminster, the sole factors *initially* impeding him seem to be his desire for Arabella, her duplicity in claiming she's pregnant, and his credulity in believing her—in addition to his obstinate faith in duty and the novel's unambiguous morosity about Fate: "Events did not rhyme quite as he had thought," the narrator remarks, interpreting the thoughts of young Jude:

> Nature's logic was too horrid for him to care for. That mercy towards one set of creatures was cruelty towards another sickened his sense of harmony. As you got older, and felt yourself to be at the centre of your time, and not at a point in its circumference, as you had felt when you were little, you were seized with a sort of shuddering, he perceived. All around you there seemed to be something glaring, garish, rattling, and the noises and glares hit upon the little cell called your life, and shook it, and warped it.
>
> If he could only prevent himself growing up! He did not want to be a man. (57)

This resistance to manhood is notable and has, as we'll see, an important bearing on Henchard's propensity to unman himself before those he loves (Showalter, "Unmanning" 102–3). But as *Jude* progresses in ways resembling *The Mayor of Casterbridge* and *Far from the Madding Crowd*, more complex forms of resistance emerge, transforming Jude and Sue's love from a stark (but somehow satisfying) opposition between the couple and their community, into an intrapsychic conflict that inheres in Hardy's very conception of sexuality.[22] This conflict arises in Sue's final and troubled encounter with Jude; more is at stake here than late Victorian constraints on female sexuality or Sue's abiding sense of loyalty to Phillotson.[23] The following passage, which I quote in full to capture its many vicissitudes, may convince critics that Sue's difficulty converges in a horrified recoil from late Victorian demands on women. However, her preceding encounter with Jude shows that her impulse is both in accord *and* at odds with her primary desires:

> "You crush, almost insult me, Jude! Go away from me!" She turned off quickly.
>
> "I will. I would never come to see you again, even if I had the strength to come, which I shall not have any more. Sue, Sue, you are not worth a man's love!"
>
> Her bosom began to go up and down. "I can't endure you to say that!" she burst out, and her eye resting on him a moment, she turned back impulsively. "Don't, don't scorn me! Kiss me, O kiss me lots of times, and say I am not a coward and a contemptible humbug—I can't bear it!" She rushed up to him and, with her mouth on his, continued: "I must tell you—O I must—my darling Love! It has been—only a church marriage—an apparent marriage I mean! He suggested it at the very first!"
>
> "How?"
>
> "I mean it is a nominal marriage only. It hasn't been more than that at all since I came back to him!"
>
> "Sue!" he said. Pressing her to him in his arms he bruised her lips with kisses. "If misery can know happiness, I have a moment's happiness now! Now, in the name of all you hold holy, tell me the truth, and no lie. You do love me still?"
>
> "I do! You know it too well! . . . But I *mustn't* do this!—I mustn't kiss you back as I would!"
>
> "But do!"
>
> "And yet you are so dear!—and you look so ill—" (469; original emphasis and ellipsis; see McGhee 102)

Hardy documents an important vacillation here between the fulfillment and avoidance of impulses that takes us beyond Sue's admission that other people characterize her as "cold-natured—sexless" (203)—beyond also arguments that Hardy, as a male author, is working out his own fantasies about sexually emancipated women.[24] If I seem not to restrict my reading this passage to an analysis of male-female relations, finding Hardy more interested in detailing the internal *and* impersonal consequences of psychic pleasure and resistance, it is because a similar dynamic emerges in

Henchard's close friendship with Donald Farfrae, denaturing the basis of all intimacy in Hardy's writing by illustrating the psychic repercussions of fantasy, seduction, and aversion.

Such internal resistance to satisfaction and identity, which *Jude* represents obliquely as a "shadow on [its protagonist's] mind" (55), usefully contradicts Hardy's characters' assertions that they are beset only by external problems. Farfrae may thus opine, in *The Mayor of Casterbridge,* "See now how it's ourselves that are ruled by the Powers above us!" (316), but he also concedes, in the very next sentence, "We plan this, but we do that." This admission modifies Hardy's fascination with Shelley's account, in *Epipsychidion* (1821; 1822), of "the sightless tyrants of our fate"—a line, according to Hardy, that "beautifully expresses one's consciousness of blind circumstances beating on one, without any feeling for or against" (qtd. in the introduction to *Mayor* 37). Farfrae's statement is closer to Cassius's famous admonition to Brutus, in Shakespeare's *Julius Caesar* (1598), that "[m]en at some time are masters of their fates: / The fault, dear Brutus, is not in our stars, / But in our selves, that we are underlings" (I.ii, 137–39).[25] We must however push back this argument, for *The Mayor of Casterbridge's* philosophical debt is ultimately to Ovid. Elizabeth-Jane, Henchard's adopted daughter, quotes Ovid's *Metamorphoses* to Lucetta when the latter tries to veil her bad faith: "*Video meliora proboque, deteriora sequor*"—"I can see which is the better course to take, and I agree with it; but I follow the worse" (288).

Establishing the degree of choice in Lucetta's decision presents an obvious difficulty for us; it is convenient but unconvincing to represent Hardy's characters' propulsion toward the worse path as a principle of Fate. The "fault" of which Cassius speaks rebounds in Hardy's writing in all the word's semantic richness, emerging as a cause for blame and a dimension of error for which often no conscious explanation can be found. If we can call Hardy "perverse" at these moments, it is because he stubbornly finds opportunities for his protagonists to ruin themselves.

Hardy demonstrates that this fault is integral to subjectivity; it is one dimension of how the Immanent Will influences and generally besets all his characters. Thus while Hardy advances stoicism in most of his work, he views this philosophy's effect upon an already divided subject. Grappling with an internal propensity to join hostile external forces in a joyous bid for self-annihilation, Hardy's protagonists naturally are quite exhausted. Generally at odds with the past, with one another, and with themselves, they seem uncertain whether to strive to survive these conflicts or to allow themselves blissfully to succumb to them, in a yearning for amnesia and an end to years of tortuous guilt. Jude therefore asks himself before Arabella first leaves him, the latter disgusted by his lack of resolve and virility, "What was he reserved for? He supposed he was not a sufficiently dignified person for suicide. Peaceful death abhorred him as a subject, and would not take him. *What could he do of a lower kind than self-extermination;* what was there less noble, more in keeping with his present degraded position? He could get drunk. Of course that was it; he had forgotten" (116–17; my emphasis).

Considering the resilience of such conflicts, in which buried secrets surface after years of studied silence, and the related difficulty of expiating guilt by symbolizing the past, we can appreciate that all these factors weigh heavily on Hardy's characters' capacity for enjoyment and reciprocal affection. Expiating guilt requires a capacity for reflection and wisdom that many of Hardy's protagonists either are denied or perversely deny themselves: Consider the psychic forces binding Jude to Arabella and Sue to Phillotson, for instance, despite (or perhaps because of) Jude's overwhelming desire for Sue. Or again, consider Henchard's stolid aim to "remarry" Susan, despite his attraction to Lucetta and complicated loyalty to Farfrae. These and other examples indicate that Hardy's notion of internal difficulty weighs heavily on his accounts of friendship and love; we can't interpret the latter accounts without placing them in the context of Hardy's philosophy of the former.[26]

J. Hillis Miller notes that Hardy was fascinated by a passage in Proust's work that summarized his own ideas about love: "Every loved person, even to a certain extent every person is to us like Janus, presenting to us the face that pleases us if that person leaves us, the dreary face if we know him to be perpetually at our disposal" (qtd. 177 n). This passage complicates the stale axiom that familiarity breeds contempt; it indicates a structural relation between love and absence, in which an object seems enticing only because it is distant or unavailable. This too may sound familiar, but Hardy inverts the scenario, rendering *intimacy* a burden and potential cause of love's demise. We see this in *The Mayor of Casterbridge* when Lucetta moves to Casterbridge to renew ties with Henchard, and when Farfrae and Henchard become overinvolved as friends; these characters suffer from the effects of proximity rather than of distance. As Hardy declared on July 9, 1889, "Love lives on propinquity, but dies of contact" (qtd. in Florence Emily Hardy 220).

Many of Hardy's novels and poems attest to this somber statement. One thinks of Boldwood pining for Bathsheba in *Far from the Madding Crowd,* and Fanny Robin's bitter refusal to relinquish Troy in the same novel, which leads Troy to abandon Bathsheba and to claim Fanny (in her coffin, no less) as the only woman he ever loved. Perhaps the same maxim allows us to put Sue and Jude's social difficulties in some relief, suggesting that the novel's tortuous account of their intimacy paradoxically *requires* intrapsychic obstacles to assist the couple's "contact." Arguing relatedly about the meaning of desire, Adam Phillips suggests: "It is impossible to imagine desire without obstacles. . . . The desire does not reveal the obstacle; the obstacle reveals the desire" (83, 82).

This argument highlights a tension between conscious wish and unconscious fantasy that recurs throughout Hardy's work, allowing us to see his fiction and poetry as a profound meditation on the vicissitudes of love and friendship. In *The Mayor of Casterbridge,* especially, Hardy dwells at length on the tensions and demands falling clumsily under the rubric of "affinity": He seems intent on discovering why characters attract each other at one moment and repel each other the next, asking his reader to consider what really happens in this interval, and why, despite numerous literary texts and philosophical treatises, we remain so ignorant of the profound subtleties informing a relationship's success and failure. When describing how Farfrae and Elizabeth-Jane once "walked . . . in a delicate poise between love and friendship—that period in the history of a love when alone it can be said to be unalloyed with pain" (246), Hardy's narrator is already describing the moment in retrospect—that is, as Elizabeth-Jane later recalls it—because she can't help comparing his prior interest in her with his current fascination for Lucetta. Since Elizabeth-Jane has to "b[ear] up against the frosty ache of [his] treatment" (246), the "delicate poise between love and friendship" already has passed, its pleasure entirely contingent on fantasy. Her constant pain suggests that this pleasure can't easily be recovered, and indeed, Farfrae and Elizabeth-Jane seem able to reunite only after Lucetta has died.

Let us also consider the basis of another friendship in *The Mayor of Casterbridge*, in some respects the novel's most important: Henchard and Farfrae's. The narrator and other characters tell us repeatedly that the two men's intimacy proceeds from an "impetuous cordiality" on Henchard's part (167). Henchard is said to possess a "tigerish affection for the younger man" (161), due in part to his gratitude to Farfrae for improving his stock of corn and thus, slightly later, his reputation as mayor. But subsidiary factors operate here that render the friendship very complex. As the narrator notes, Farfrae "plainly" has a "strange influence" on Henchard that prompts the mayor to disclose (almost to confess) his secrets (147). Such impulses do exist among close new friends, it's true, but the complication arises not only from the emotional and erotic ambiguity of the men's intimacy, but also because Farfrae establishes for Henchard a capacity for transference, in which he momentarily relives events in a poignant, but impossible, effort to leave behind the past.

We might consider this transference a sign of Henchard's love for Farfrae: "I am the most distant fellow in the world when I don't care for a man," declares Henchard precipitously, "but when a man takes my fancy he takes it strong" (133). The strength and speed of this fancy has drawn the attention of recent scholars keen to interpret Henchard's infatuation with Farfrae as signs of an undeclared physical demand for the younger man (see Ingersoll, "Writing"; T. Jones; Wright; and Langbaum). Yet we seem caught in a difficulty concerning desire, nomenclature, and the demand for evidence. While Showalter declares, "There is nothing homosexual in their intimacy" ("Unmanning" 107), Tod E. Jones insists on the exact opposite, representing Henchard as "Hardy's male homosexual," before interpreting the two men's competing village festivities, which entail "erect[ing] greasy-poles for climbing" (*Mayor* 174), as "a competition of masculinities . . . reveal[ing] . . .[,] in its most primitive form, a comparing of erections" (Jones 12). If Showalter's argument seems profoundly at odds with the novel's exploration of fantasy and desire, Jones's reading exaggerates the novel's homoeroticism and reads the novel only with contemporary eyes, ignoring the wider continuum of late Victorian masculine affection. Additionally, in ways that paradoxically reproduce Showalter's interpretive confidence, Jones's account aims not to explicate, but to resolve, the novel's uncertainties about the line between homophilia and homosexuality, arguing that the first is reducible to the second. Steering a more subtle path between these readings, T. R. Wright argues usefully, "It is in the presentation of Henchard's relationship with Farfrae that Hardy goes furthest in undermining conventional notions of 'manliness,' for there can be little doubt that the love Henchard bears for the slender and delicate Scot has a sexual component" (76; also 78; see also Daleski 128).[27]

The point of Wright's (and my) reading is not to downplay the novel's homoeroticism. It is to stress that Hardy's psychological emphasis impedes interpretive certainty about love objects, highlighting a productive gap between fantasy and objects in which different forms of desire conflict and temporarily prevail. Many passages in *The Mayor of Casterbridge* confirm this interpretive doubt about Henchard's love for Farfrae by showing the characters themselves acknowledging their fascination and interest. When considering whether to introduce Elizabeth-Jane to Henchard as the latter's estranged "daughter," for example, Susan Henchard, Michael's first (and "sold") wife, states acerbically, "Yes; I am thinking of Mr. Henchard's sudden liking for that young man. He was always so. Now, surely, if he takes so warmly to people who are not related to him at all, may he not take as warmly to his own kin" (127). Elizabeth-Jane later observes Henchard and Farfrae discussing business, and her thoughts about her "father's" "impetuous cordiality" blend with the narrator's: "Friendship between man and man; what a rugged strength there was in it, as evinced by these two. And yet the seed that was to lift the foundation of this friendship was at that moment taking root in a chink of its structure" (167).

Susan's observation on the men's affective tie strikes an interesting chord, for in this novel kinship generally isn't successful at fostering love and a sense of obligation. The exception is Henchard's ultimate despair at losing Elizabeth-Jane to Farfrae. Yet even here, his fear of isolation, which predates his love for her, combines with his now established rivalry with Farfrae, the "seed" of enmity having taken "root in a chink" of their friendship. Building also on Elizabeth-Jane's generally enigmatic relation to Henchard, Hardy demonstrates that Henchard's emotional ties are inseparable from other people's use to him. Henchard's selfishness therefore highlights this novel's (and Hardy's) doubts about altruism.[28] Indeed, Henchard's tragedy consists largely in being an exaggerated version of the other characters in this novel (perhaps excepting Newson, Elizabeth-Jane's true father), who consistently manipulate one another for personal and amorous gain.

Susan and Elizabeth-Jane nonetheless comment on Henchard's affection for Farfrae; in this novel of uncertain ties, the men's friendship stands out as particularly meaningful. Just after commenting on Henchard's "liking for that young man," Susan instructs her daughter to tell Henchard "that I fully know I have no claim upon him" (128), a statement referring explicitly to the annulment of their marriage, though it raises an implicit question about Henchard's subsequent claim on Farfrae and vice versa. Susan later iterates to Henchard, "I consider . . . that I have no claim upon you" (143). Significantly, Henchard disbelieves her, responding, "How could you be so simple?" (143). To conceal that he once sold Susan to Newson, in part to protect his name and to dupe Elizabeth-Jane (whom he imagines is his daughter), Henchard decides to remarry Susan, fantasizing that a proper act can substitute for the improper one: "This would leave my shady, headstrong, disgraceful life as a young man absolutely unopened" (144). Calculating the psychological cost of this *renewed* deceit, the narrator tells us that the mayor "seemed to have schooled himself into a course of strict mechanical rightness towards this woman of prior claim, at any expense to the later one and to his own sentiments" (152).[29]

The effect of this novel's stress on the legal and affective dimensions of its characters' "claims" may be grasped by invoking Charles Dickens's fiction, for in this latter work such claims tend to establish the correct lineage and paths of inheritance of families and social classes; I refer to *Little Dorrit* (1855–57), though other novels by Dickens also endorse these claims' material role. Such emphasis isn't missing in *The Mayor of Casterbridge,* but the novel's psychological emphasis on its characters' drives and fantasies hinders it from attributing *more* value to courtship and marriage than to same-sex friendship. In this respect, Henchard *does* seem to court Farfrae, though this courtship doesn't revoke Henchard's interest in reestablishing ties with Susan, and we can't explain this interest merely by suggesting that it socially or psychologically compensates for the effect of pursuing another man.[30] For Henchard, the added attraction—and perhaps

incentive—in pursuing Farfrae is the suggestion of a reprieve from his obli-
gations to three women: Susan, Lucetta, and Elizabeth-Jane. But Henchard nonetheless oscillates from one object to the other, unable or perhaps
unwilling to decide which he should prioritize. Thus, to read Henchard as
"Hardy's male homosexual" is to excise the psychic and conceptual richness
of this oscillation, explaining Henchard's first and second marriages (and
courtship of Lucetta) only as examples of latency and a temporary confusion of object choice. Let us instead consider the complexity of this oscillation.

We witness a type of excitement in Henchard for Farfrae that surpasses the immediate promise of good grain. After insisting that they previously have met, Henchard follows Farfrae to see where he lives: "Very
few people were now in the street," the narrator remarks, "and [Hench-
ard's] eyes, by a sort of attraction, turned and dwelt upon a spot about a
hundred yards further down. It was the house to which the writer of the
note [Farfrae] had gone" (109). Henchard proceeds to visit him, speaking
all the while "with careless geniality" (114). Still the issue of Henchard's
demand won't abate, and this is another aspect of his eventual tragedy,
proving that his conflict with psychic drives is especially meaningful: "I am
under the impression that we have met by accident while waiting for the
morning to keep an appointment with each other. . . . Surely you are the
man . . . who arranged to come and see me?" (114–15). Even twice corrected, Henchard insists, "And yet I could have sworn you were the man!"
(115); "Come to my house; I can find something better for 'ee than cold
ham and ale" (116); "I couldn't believe you were not the man I had engaged!" (116). Later, his demand intensifies: "I have been looking for such
as you these two year, and yet you are not for me. Well, before I go, let me
ask you this: Though you are not the young man I thought you were,
what's the difference? Can't ye stay just the same? Have you really made up
your mind about this American notion? [Farfrae plans to emigrate]. I won't
mince matters. I feel you would be invaluable to me—that needn't be
said" (117).

In the next few pages, we see Henchard unburden himself entirely to
Farfrae, asking if he seems like a married man, and then revealing that he
previously sold his wife and that he's something of a misogynist. All the
while Henchard—rivaling in tenacity only Schomberg's intense homo-

erotic fascination for Heyst in Joseph Conrad's *Victory* (1915)—insists
that Farfrae simply must not leave.[31] As in all good romances, however,
obstacles emerge at this point (chiefly thoughts in Farfrae's mind that he
should in fact proceed to America). As a result, Henchard pursues him all
the more doggedly:

> After leaving the Three Mariners [Henchard] had sauntered up
> and down the empty High Street, passing and repassing the inn
> in his promenade. When the Scotchman sang his voice had
> reached Henchard's ears through the heart-shaped holes in the
> window-shutters, and had led him to pause outside them a
> long while.
>
> "To be sure, to be sure, how that fellow does draw me!" he
> had said to himself. "I suppose 'tis because I'm so lonely. I'd
> have given him a third share in the business to have stayed!"
> (125)[32]

At this point, Henchard's interest seems radically to exceed his professional
claims on Farfrae, who isn't allowed simply to choose between working for
Henchard and moving to America. He must also live with Henchard, as
the latter makes abundantly clear in a passage I again quote at length to
capture all its nuances:

> Still holding the young man's hand [Henchard] paused, and
> then added deliberately: "Now I am not the man to let a cause
> be lost for want of a word. And before ye are gone for ever I'll
> speak. Once more, will you stay? There it is, flat and plain. . . .
> Some selfishness perhaps there is, but there is more: it isn't for
> me to repeat what. Come bide with me—and name your own
> terms. I'll agree to 'em willingly and 'ithout a word of gainsay-
> ing; for, hang it, Farfrae, I like thee well!"
>
> The young man's hand remained steady in Henchard's for a
> moment or two. . . . His face flushed.
>
> "I never expected this—I did not!" he said. "It's Providence!
> Should any one go against it? No; I'll not go to America; I'll
> stay and be your man!" . . .
>
> The face of Mr. Henchard beamed forth a satisfaction that
> was almost fierce in its strength. "Now you are my friend!" he
> exclaimed. "Come back to my house; let's clinch it at once by

clear terms, so as to be comfortable in our minds." Henchard
was all confidence now. . . . [But h]e would not rest satisfied
till Farfrae had written for his luggage from Bristol, and des-
patched the letter to the post-office. When it was done this man
of strong impulses declared that his new friend should take up
his abode in his house—at least till some suitable lodgings
could be found. (132–34)

Lest we begin seeing this novel solely in Henchard's terms—that is,
believing that women really aren't important in this novel—we must again
stress that Henchard's intense bond with Farfrae emerges *alongside* Henchard's renewed sense of obligation to Susan. The novel complicates each
affective and erotic scenario by running them together, refusing to separate
Elizabeth-Jane's interest in Farfrae from her "father's," but also collapsing
conventional distinctions between Henchard's and Elizabeth-Jane's almost
identical fascination with Lucetta. When Henchard pursues Lucetta, for
example, renewing his previous tie as her lover (relations that cast shame on
Lucetta, forcing her to leave her village), Elizabeth-Jane acquires a strong
admiration for the same woman, seeing her father partly as a rival (while
he, in turn, seems later unconsciously to view Elizabeth-Jane as a rival for
Farfrae). When Farfrae arrives on the scene, he splits the women's friendship by inviting Lucetta to drop Henchard (and Elizabeth-Jane) in order to
marry him. The narrator nonetheless remarks of the women's friendship,
"Elizabeth, almost with a lover's feeling, thought she would like to look at
the outside of High-Place Hall [in which Lucetta lives]. She went up the
street in that direction" (210). The act mirrors Henchard's earlier pursuit
of Farfrae, while Elizabeth-Jane "enjoyed standing under an opposite arch-
way merely to think that the charming lady was inside the confronting
walls, and to wonder what she was doing" (211). "[A]larmed at her own
temerity," however, she redresses her behavior (211). But the attraction
nonetheless resumes: "She now simply waited to see the lady again," for
"she was . . . already, in imagination, at the house of the lady whose manner had such charms for her" (213, 216). While the intensity of this friendship abates when Henchard and, later, Farfrae, pursue Lucetta, the magnitude of Henchard's friendship with Farfrae, though altered by their rivalry
for Lucetta, doesn't diminish.

    This intensity provokes a crisis when Henchard fights Farfrae, a scene whose simultaneous abjection and eroticism D. H. Lawrence reproduced in Gerald Crich's and Rupert Birkin's "gladiatorial" wrestle in *Women in Love* (1920), which follows their homoerotic musings in Lawrence's chapter "Man to Man":

> "Your life is in my hands."
>
> "Then take it, take it!" said Farfrae. "Ye've wished to long enough!"
>
> Henchard looked down upon him in silence, and their eyes met. "O Farfrae!—that's not true!" he said bitterly. "God is my witness that no man ever loved another as I did thee at one time . . . And now—though I came here to kill 'ee, I cannot hurt thee! Go and give me in charge—do what you will—I care nothing for what comes of me!" . . .
>
> Henchard took his full measure of shame and self-reproach. The scenes of his first acquaintance with Farfrae rushed back upon him—that time when the curious mixture of romance and thrift in the young man's composition so commanded his heart that Farfrae could play upon him as on an instrument. So thoroughly subdued was he that he remained on the sacks in a crouching attitude, unusual for a man, and for such a man. Its womanliness sat tragically on the figure of so stern a piece of virility. . . .
>
> "He thought highly of me once," he murmured. "Now he'll hate me and despise me for ever!"
>
> He became possessed by an overpowering wish to see Farfrae again that night, and by some desperate pleading to attempt the well-nigh impossible task of winning pardon for his late mad attack. . . . There was no help for it but to wait till his return, though waiting was almost torture to his restless and self-accusing soul. (348–49; first ellipsis in original)

Hardy's depiction of intense same-sex friendships, here and elsewhere, doesn't sustain a clear division between homo- and heterosexuality.[33] For this reason, it seems inadequate to argue, as Showalter has, that *The Mayor of Casterbridge* highlights only the *social* repercussions of an already established tension between homosexual love and same-sex friendship. Claiming that "there is certainly on Henchard's side an open, and, he later feels, incautious embrace of homosocial friendship, an insistent male bonding,"

Showalter adds, as we have seen, "There is nothing homosexual in their intimacy" ("Unmanning" 107). Such claims interpret male relationships in Hardy only in terms of symbolic authority, power, and rivalry, downplaying his effort to represent the drama (and occasional tyranny) of proximity that constitutes *every* relationship. Showalter's social conception of "unmanning" (103) therefore eclipses the psychological drama she highlights two pages earlier: "In *The Mayor of Casterbridge* . . . , Hardy gives the fullest nineteenth-century portrait of a man's inner life—his rebellion and his suffering, his loneliness and jealousy, his paranoia and despair, his uncontrollable unconscious" (101). Although Showalter proceeds in the next sentence to characterize this "uncontrollable unconscious" as a "passional self," thus overturning Hardy's radicalism by casting the drama in egoic terms, we can at least agree that Hardy's psychological perspective *necessarily* represents the conflict between Henchard and Farfrae in affective and sexual terms.[34] Put another way, *The Mayor of Casterbridge* doesn't consider friendship and marital relationships either predetermined or mutually exclusive; instead, the novel probes the conditions making all forms of intimacy possible and impossible.[35] This point distinguishes materialist and historical readings from psychological accounts of Hardy's work, and it seems useful to highlight the repercussions of this distinction.

Hardy realized that the unconscious is one factor promoting and destroying intimacy, given its emphasis on a type of satisfaction lying beyond union, endurance, and reciprocity.[36] As the narrator of *Tess* laments, "Why so often the coarse [pattern] appropriates the finer [feminine tissue] thus, the wrong man the woman, the wrong woman the man, many thousand years of analytical philosophy have failed to explain to our sense of order" (119). This "appropriation," which refers to Alec d'Urberville's preying on Tess, is clearly at odds with coherent identity. In the same novel, but without the suggestion of external violence, the narrator represents sexuality as inimical to selfhood and, perhaps more important, to *pleasure:*

> The air of the sleeping-chamber seemed to palpitate with the hopeless passion of the girls. They writhed feverishly under the oppressiveness of an emotion thrust on them by cruel Nature's law—an emotion which *they had neither expected nor desired.* The incident of the day [Angel Clare's visit] had fanned the flame that was burning the inside of their hearts out, and the

torture was almost more than they could endure. *The differences which distinguished them as individuals were abstracted by this passion,* and each was but portion of one organism called sex. (204; my emphases)

This passage—and my argument—diverges slightly from the narrator's earlier suggestion that Tess and Angel Clare's mutual attraction is primordial and organic—"an almost regnant power" (186). In these passages, Tess and Angel appear in harmony with their surrounding environment, "[a]ll the while . . . converging, under an irresistible law, as surely as two streams in one vale" (185). Even here, though, the "law," being "irresistible," works only in the interests of desire; recognizing no value in discrete ontology, the same law is fundamentally at odds with identity. In this and other circumstances—and *Tess* gives us many—the inability to resist is neither seductive nor pleasurable, but an illustration of identity's antagonistic relation to jouissance—that is, to unpleasure and distress. We recall Jude Fawley's "erotolepsy," or "love-seizure" (*Jude* 146). And the same young milkmaids who "palpitate with . . . hopeless passion" in the earlier novel *Tess* are later described as being "ecstasiz[ed] . . . to a killing joy" (205; see McGhee 91). The connection between this "killing joy" and Tess and Angel's "almost regnant power" is necessary to consider, and I'll conclude this chapter by attempting to do so.[37]

Because it disregards all factors circumscribing friendship and marriage, especially the rituals and taboos by which society aims to give these relations meaning, jouissance is a vital force in Hardy's writing. Leveling human relationships, jouissance gives them neither priority nor respect. While this element "beyond the pleasure principle" is the volatile force disregarding the gender of love objects, it pushes characters together and apart, connecting Hardy's Immanent Will to the often cruel actions of his protagonists. Thus Hardy underscores that Henchard is a man who knows "no moderation in his requests and impulses" (146). Indeed, when preventing Henchard from meeting the "Royal Personage" (Prince Albert) who "was about to pass through [Casterbridge] . . . on his course further west, to inaugurate an immense engineering work out that way" (336), Farfrae, we are told, "observed the fierce light in [Henchard's eyes] despite his excitement and irritation. For a moment Henchard stood his ground rigidly; then by an unaccountable impulse gave way and retired" (340). Such impulses and "fierce[ness]" may be "unaccountable" in Hardy's work, given the resistance of jouissance to meaning, but Hardy nonetheless draws attention to this gap between psychic drives and their representation.

Given the strength of jouissance in Hardy's novels, we should not be surprised to see his characters recoil from intimacy and abstain from desire. In *The Woodlanders* (1886; 1887), for example, the narrator emphasizes that Giles Winterborne suffers only one lapse in propriety—a "long and passionate kiss" with Grace Melbury, who learns to appreciate his "undiluted manliness" only after her ill-advised marriage to the undeserving Edred Fitzpiers (355, 261).[38] Like Grace, we learn to understand Winterborne's "purity of . . . nature, his freedom from the grosser passions, [and] his scrupulous delicacy" (381; see also Federico 71–75).[39] Hardy even acknowledges, in his preface to this novel, that "the immortal puzzle—given the man and woman, how to find a basis for their sexual relation—is left where it stood" (39). This emphasis on sexual asymmetry and unpleasure returns us to my opening quotation from "Hap," in which "sorrow" seems to give another "ecstasy" while "love's loss" apparently is "hate's profiting" (*Collected* 7). Such emphasis also gives us a crucial interpretive clue to Hardy's thoughts on the affective tie—thoughts that readers accepting only his conception of the Immanent Will generally ignore. J. Hillis Miller is one exception, and he argues compellingly, "The only happy love relationship for Hardy is one which is not union but the lovers' acceptance of the gap between them" (154). In ways that illuminate comparable tensions in *The Mayor of Casterbridge*, however, the protagonists of *The Woodlanders* chafe against accepting this gap; indeed, the effort to "reduce his former passion [for Grace] to a docile friendship" seems in part to aid Winterborne's premature death (340). We might indeed advance a similar point about Henchard's "former passion" for Farfrae.

Such points indicate why readings of *The Mayor of Casterbridge* either downplay the eroticism of Henchard and Farfrae's friendship, seeing this eroticism only as tangential or preparatory to Henchard's jealous love for Lucetta, or else insist that Henchard's avowed misogyny must veil his homosexual desire for the younger man (this is Jones's principal claim). Henchard does avow to Farfrae, "being by nature something of a woman-hater, I have found it no hardship to keep mostly at a distance from the sex" (148); slightly later, he also states, "Farfrae, between you and me, as man and man, I solemnly declare that philandering with womankind has neither been my vice nor my virtue" (149).[40] Of course, the phrase "solemnly declare" echoes a conventional marriage vow. Still, our interpretive difficulty concerns the link between misogyny and "latent" homosexuality. While this psychic gap records Hardy's interest in fantasy and identification, it seems incorrect to suggest (as Jones does) that Hardy offers us a putative homosexual relationship between Henchard and Farfrae—incorrect, because such claims conflict with Hardy's philosophical precepts about intimacy and desire. That Hardy profoundly denatures object relations makes homosexuality part of an extensive meditation on the paradoxical resilience of desire *against* love.

Making clear this point about object relations, as well as the role of the death drive in *The Mayor of Casterbridge,* the narrator tells us that "the dependence upon Elizabeth's regard into which [Henchard] had declined (or, in another sense, to which he had advanced)—*denaturalized* him" (380; my emphasis). To what has Henchard *"advanced"* here except his annihilation, which his ferocious will seems stubbornly to have arranged? Miller calls the effect of Hardy's meditation on object relations "a nightmare of frustrated desire" (148). With a similar emphasis, I have argued that Hardy's fascination with the Immanent Will, and with forces pushing characters together and forcing them apart, highlights the psychic and erotic constituents of friendship—constituents evident in his characters' demands to foster intimacy with others.[41] For this reason, I suggest that *The Mayor of Casterbridge* ceaselessly probes its characters' uncertain demands for—and equal recoil from—intimacy. As Henchard remarks of Farfrae, raising doubts about their relationship that his subsequent question seems unable to resolve, "Well, he's a friend of mine, and I'm a friend of his—or if we are not, what are we?" (183).

FIVE

The Impossibility of Seduction in James's
Roderick Hudson *and* The Tragic Muse

> If on a rare occasion one of these couples might be divided, so, by as
> uncommon a chance, the other might be joined; the only difference
> being in the gravity of the violated law. For which
> pair was the betrayal greatest?
> —Henry James, *The Sacred Fount* 117

How could Henry James represent individuality in novels that stress his
characters' shared traits? Applying this question to James's somewhat
"stolid" novel *The Tragic Muse* (1889; 1890) highlights two related problems. According to its narrator, the novel's characters fail to resolve "the
opposition of [their] interest and desire"; in "a torment of unrest" they
confront "the impossibility of being consistent" (382). When James tried
to explain these problems in his preface to *The Tragic Muse,* he confirmed
that the novel inadvertently raises profound questions about the nature
and stability of character. The initial object of James's complaint is Miriam
Rooth; allegedly, her "theatrical" personality is inauthentic. However,
James raises an important, if less severe, charge against masculinity that is
only partly veiled by his preoccupation with femininity's ability to ensnare
its masculine admirers.

This chapter interprets the tension between individuality and desire
in *The Tragic Muse.* It asks why James conflates Miriam's theatrical personality with femininity, and why the novel's aesthetic failure exceeds James's
difficulties with his characters' credibility and sexuality.[1] I contend that
James's conventional association of femininity with instability is only the
most symptomatic "problem" of this novel; the narrative confronts another
challenge in trying to unify its central "object," for its attention shifts from
the vagaries of a female character (Miriam Rooth) to the thoughts and
desires of her closest male friend (Gabriel Nash). We'll see the consequence
of this shift by assessing the widespread gap between desire and meaning

in fin-de-siècle British literature. Arguing that James finally was unable to distinguish among artistry, masquerade, and interpersonal deceit, I'll approach the meaning of sexual dissimulation in his fiction in terms of the significance his narratives attach to physical desire and same-gender intimacy.

By keeping these textual and contextual questions in play and avoiding the assumption that homosexual desire is simply the "truth" of *The Tragic Muse*—or that its protagonists, Nick Dormer and Gabriel Nash, would have been lovers had James the courage to write otherwise—I will examine the pressure shaping this novel's ending and the reason Nash's disappearance at the end of the novel can't rescind its conflicting economies of desire or "correct" its oscillation between female and male desires. Contrary to James's claim that the novel's difficulties stem from its theatricality, I'll approach *The Tragic Muse* with the premise that failure is its strongest weakness; failure indicates both the novel's inconsistency about sexual difference and its turbulent symbolization of masculinity.

Before addressing the novel's convoluted plot and James's rueful misgivings about its structure, let me make clear my proposition about failure, which recurs throughout James's fiction as a pressing concern. It is now commonplace to argue that James focuses on individual and social duplicity and superficiality; that his heroines (such as Miriam Rooth) often betray a scandalous absence of "deep substance." These heroines invest so much energy in constructing their appearance and sustaining illusions that many relationships collapse when their lovers realize that these women's characters are merely the result of their artful manipulation of roles. But despite the urgency informing this realization—and in novels such as *The Bostonians* (1885–86) and *The Awkward Age* (1899), puncturing feminine "masquerade" seems close to a masculine imperative—the character of each woman endures. What is redefined in interesting ways is the idealizing consciousness that formerly passed between subjects as an elaborate projection of intrigue and fascination (Bersani, *Future* 129–30). As Sharon Cameron brilliantly suggests, James struggled to reorient this consciousness, rendering it less "false" by circumscribing his characters' intentions (47–53). This reorientation produces startling results that, as James sometimes concedes, form an unwanted union of interests and a traumatic merging of identities. The drive informing James's urgent bid for his characters' ontological integrity is thus important; it highlights a crisis of proximity among his male characters.

Although James and his male protagonists usually indict femininity for "betraying" the limits of personality, the drama of differentiation and stability that James explores isn't unique to his fiction; the same charge against women can be found in many turn-of-the-century texts. Consider the undoing of Undine Spragg in Edith Wharton's *The Custom of the Country* (1913), Lena's alleged manipulation of Axel Heyst and Schomberg in Joseph Conrad's *Victory* (1915), and Mildred Rogers's egregious mistreatment of Philip Carey in W. Somerset Maugham's *Of Human Bondage* (1915). Yet although James does examine the "character" of women in *The Tragic Muse* (1889; 1890) and *Roderick Hudson* (1874; 1875), his indictment is not of women alone. He similarly accuses his male protagonists in these novels.

To advance this proposition, let me turn briefly to a contemporaneous text—Oscar Wilde's *The Picture of Dorian Gray* (1890, revised 1891). In Wilde's novel, the "character" and consistency of femininity and masculinity are discussed and finally elided. Connecting James's and Wilde's texts is also worthwhile because Wilde's debt to *The Tragic Muse* is often unrecognized, and because the actress in Wilde's book, Sibyl Vane, proves a disappointment to Dorian Gray when her role points too obviously to her impoverished identity; this occurs, significantly, when she falls in love with Dorian. His complaint about Sibyl's identity assumes in part that Dorian and the reader notice when Sibyl ceases to act—the moment, that is, when her character appears most "true." Attention to such issues downplays the emphasis Wilde placed on the art of successfully exchanging roles. The point is that Sibyl's deficient acting, in her move from offstage to onstage performances, renders the transition apparent; the broken illusion is what galls Dorian. As the narrator of *Dorian Gray* remarks, "[T]he staginess of her acting was unbearable, and grew worse as she went on. Her gestures became absurdly artificial. She over-emphasized everything that she had to say. . . . It was simply bad art. She was a complete failure" (95–96). Although Dorian's proficient offstage acting goes by another name and generates different crises about credibility and passing, the end of Wilde's novel indicates that masculinity possesses an equal, or greater, capacity for dissimulation. We can attribute this capacity, in part, to masculinity's ability to draw on a greater number of social roles (if not desires), and to the other characters' ignorance of Dorian's disguise; they assume his gender signifies ontological integrity and that his appearance denotes sincerity and youth.

In James's "baggy" and less elegant novel, *The Tragic Muse*—which the *Atlantic Monthly* serialized throughout 1889, one year before *Dorian Gray* first appeared in *Lippincott's Monthly Magazine*—a similar drama about integrity arises when the narrative's bid to establish the true character of Miriam Rooth merges with a related question about the intentions of her male entourage: Peter Sherringham, Basil Dashwood, Nick Dormer, and Gabriel Nash. Adopting the perspective of Peter Sherringham, Miriam's suitor, the first half of the novel tries in vain to determine what Miriam's character would be if she left the theater and stopped acting, that is, if she endorsed Sherringham's career as a diplomat by becoming his wife (a role, apparently, in which women can be guileless). *The Tragic Muse* illustrates Sherringham's dilemma about his future by juxtaposing his interest in Miriam Rooth with Nick Dormer's comparable interest in Gabriel Nash—a man who acts in many ways, and whose character ultimately proves more elusive (Gunter 85). The narrative's oscillation between Sherringham and Dormer, its two "centres of consciousness," initially seems deliberate. As James later acknowledged, however, the novel's focus shifts disproportionately onto the ties binding the two men, which generates a discussion about intimacy that James seemed unwilling—but later compelled—to pursue in the book. Following the logic of this novel, I'll begin with Sherringham's investigation of Miriam to accentuate the subsidiary relationship between Dormer and Nash. This second relationship, as James ruefully acknowledged, almost succeeded in displacing the novel's precarious interest in heterosexuality.

Exhibiting the anxious pursuit of self-knowledge and the narcissism characterizing many of James's short stories about desire (for instance, "The Beast in the Jungle" [1903] and "The Jolly Corner" [1908]), Peter Sherringham tries in vain to discover the true personality of Miriam Rooth in order to explain *his* fascination. Sherringham's realization that Miriam never ceases to "act"—that her beauty is "elastic," her character "plastic," and her entire personality an elaborate "embroidery" (230, 131, 146, 145)—is a joyous epiphany to him because it resolves her enigma: She is nothing *more* than an enigma. This limits her appeal and his transference because Sherringham has invested financially and emotionally in her career: He thought he had wanted her acting to improve. When Miriam later displaces this support (she no longer needs to hide her act), Sherringham's courtship of her wavers between annoyance at her role-playing and admiration of her performance. But he is appalled by the ease with which she shifts from one role to another: "she was already in a few weeks an actress who could act even at not acting" (279). As Miriam becomes more adept at managing her career, her ambition becomes voracious while her fame partly hides her lack of "character" and "integrity."[2] Sherringham later decides that Miriam has neither quality; her subjectivity consists of parts and roles whose center is fundamentally hollow.

Considering James's overall remarks about this situation, to which I'll soon turn, Sherringham's bid to expose Miriam's "fraudulence" partly displaces his own identity crisis and those of other male characters.[3] Sherringham reacts cynically to Miriam's "exposure" by rationalizing his interest as a test. Despite his repeated disavowals, however, Sherringham confronts similar, if less intense, questions about his own psychic instability and future in his profession. The narrator answers some of these questions by claiming that men's doubts about their careers shouldn't trouble their identities: Sherringham is merely torn between assisting Miriam and promoting his own career by taking another, more "amenable" woman—Biddy—to the colonies. His problem is thus existential and momentary; it isn't the kind of crisis that threatens many of James's women, whose pleasure hinges on finding vicarious fulfillment in their spouses and whose professional and "private" identities are entirely overdetermined. In this respect, Miriam chooses between the relative stability of marriage and the likely (and, for James, moral) annihilation of her "character" in a series of transient acts. The Tragic Muse wants to imply that men are too stable to experience such conflict; nevertheless, Sherringham's claims of autonomy are implausible and disingenuous. As the narrator declares, "Poor Sherringham . . . was much troubled these last days; he was ravaged by contending passions; he paid, every hour, in a torment of unrest, for what was false in his position, the impossibility of being consistent, the opposition of interest and desire" (382).

The Tragic Muse repeatedly makes and withdraws the suggestion that its male and female characters face comparable ontological crises. Without overlooking the difference in magnitude between Sherringham's and Miriam's dilemmas, I claim that the narrative represents Miriam as the most extreme example of a crisis that hinges, for women and men, on exactly this "impossibility of being consistent, the opposition of interest and desire." In this way, the novel's account of men's impossible consistency generates questions about the conflicts determining "interest and desire" among Sherringham, Dashwood, Dormer, and Nash; indeed, the structure of *The Tragic Muse* renders inevitable this comparison among the men.

The novel implies that Sherringham identifies in Miriam's subjectivity the indeterminacy he finds deplorable in himself. Thus the narrator observes that "Sherringham's reserve might by the ill-natured have been termed dissimulation" (147), though this remark is apparently redeemed several pages later by Sherringham's joke: "'Well, after all I'm not an actor myself.'" Miriam responds adroitly, "'You might be one if you were serious'" (153). It seems that Sherringham's laughter negates an embarrassing contiguity between his and Miriam's "dissimulation[s]." The joke masks his own unstated problems: If he is flippant about his professional rigidity (153), she is paradoxically rigid about her ontological "elastic[ity]" (131).

The "opposition between interest and desire" in Sherringham proves easy to "resolve": The women he pursues (Miriam and Biddy) "correspond" exactly to specific vocations (Miriam to the theater, Biddy to his career as a diplomat); his choice of one or the other will thwart his professional goal or satisfy it. However, the same conflict is hopelessly confused for the novel's other "centre of consciousness," Nick Dormer. The relations among Sherringham, Dormer, and their mediating "object" (initially Miriam, later Gabriel Nash) indicate *The Tragic Muse*'s intent to unify its characters' interests and desires, despite their opposition. As I argued earlier, the narrative's shift from Sherringham's to Nick Dormer's point of view allows it to exchange the latter's insoluble existential dilemma (Nick can't decide whom he wants or what he wishes to be) for the former's problem of courtship: By rejecting Miriam and choosing Biddy, Sherringham "resolves" one half of the novel.

The narrative repeatedly highlights the similarity between Sherringham's and Dormer's dilemmas before substituting the latter for the former. This comparison requires a mediator to offset the novel's preoccupation with masculine similarity. We might consider this preoccupation an effect of James's concern to maintain individual consistency, for consistency raises questions about resemblance and difference. How then can identities in this novel remain discrete and reliable? Invariably, Miriam Rooth is a symptom of this problem. At one point the narrator describes her as "a beautiful, actual, fictive, impossible young woman, of a past age and undiscoverable country, who spoke in blank verse and overflowed with metaphor" (457). Poorly executed, the role Miriam assumes "bleeds" into other identificatory possibilities. By displaying excessive artistry, her performance ruins the fragile link that James and his characters try hopelessly to sustain between a role and the illusion it creates (Litvak, *Caught* 243, 264).[4]

If we extend this notion of roles "overflow[ing] with metaphor" to all forms of illusion and characterization in *The Tragic Muse*, "character" seems unable to prevent the condensed weight of metaphor from dissipating into erratic metonymy: "something monstrously definite kept surging out" (457). Indeed, the problem of relation is so extensive in this novel that any attempt to control it is liable to produce volatile effects. We've already seen this propensity in Miriam Rooth, and we'll encounter it again in the figure of Gabriel Nash. Let us temporarily suspend this account of *The Tragic Muse*'s overproduction of meaning, however, and compare this novel with an earlier one by James that presents similar identificatory and sexual dilemmas: *Roderick Hudson*.

In his preface to *Roderick Hudson*, James acknowledges that his characters' identities threaten to merge: "[R]elations stop nowhere, and the exquisite problem of the artist is eternally but to draw, by a geometry of his own, the circle within which they shall happily *appear* to do so" (preface to *Roderick* 37; original emphasis). James later conceded that he couldn't resolve this "perpetual predicament" (37); it persisted as an aesthetic problem, complicating

> the plain moral that a young embroiderer of the canvas of life
> . . . began to work in terror, fairly, of the vast expanse of that
> surface, of the boundless number of its distinct perforations for
> the needle, and of the tendency inherent in his many-coloured
> flowers and figures to cover and consume as many as possible
> of the little holes. The development of the flower, of the figure,
> involved thus an immense counting of holes and a careful selec-

tion among them. That would have been, it seemed to him, a brave enough process, were it not the very nature of the holes so to invite, to solicit, to persuade, to practise positively a thousand lures and deceits. The prime effect of so sustained a system, so prepared a surface, is to lead on and on; while the fascination of following resides, by the same token, in the presumability *somewhere* of a convenient, or a visibly-appointed stopping-place. (37; original emphasis)

In the ensuing alignments among characters in *Roderick Hudson,* and in the complex erotic configuration that governs (or seems to govern) relations among men and women, James's "problem" emerges from the lack of an agent capable of securing these relations and of thus preventing a "marriage" between its male protagonists—Roderick Hudson and his mentor and confidant, Rowland Mallet. Only Roderick's violent suicide seems able to foster a reciprocal desire between Rowland and Mary Garland, who mourn the same lost object. Without this shared grief over Roderick's death, the metonymy governing *Roderick Hudson* would impede reciprocity; as the narrator reveals, Rowland "desires" Mary, who desires Roderick, who "desires" Christina Light, who desires, perhaps, to be desired.

I put both men's desire for women in quotation marks because—in addition to these structural displacements, which Freud once called the "aim" of desire, as distinct from the "object" representing it ("Instincts" 122)—the novel renders masculine desire inseparable from artistic and ontological deceit. Nothing short of death can prevent the formation of an erotic relation between men in *Roderick Hudson.* The narrative overemphasis on Rowland's improbable attachment to Mary and his jealousy of Roderick for achieving but never clearly returning Mary's interest creates an obsessive, anxious intimacy between Rowland and Roderick. This is a problem for James that exceeds the basic "erotics" of masculine tutelage: Rowland was seduced by Roderick's art when he examined his sculpture. In return, Roderick admitted that the "young Water-drinker," his sculpture, is "thirsty [for] . . . knowledge, pleasure, experience. Anything of that kind!" (66). Roderick's sculpture seems to displace Rowland's palpable interest in Roderick's body and voice—"a soft and not altogether masculine organ" (63).[5] The heterosexual imperative governing Rowland and Mary's intimacy, which marks and even scars the end of this novel, seems to obscure

Rowland's rivalry with Mary for Roderick; Rowland's conventional (that is, "homosocial") rivalry with Roderick for Mary only partly eclipses his "homosexual" interest in the younger man.

In this narrative of precarious sexual and subjective mastery, James struggles to present the "appearance" of delimiting every relation—a control that the text and its preface subsequently belie (Cameron 48–49). As in other Jamesian narratives—including "The Pupil" (1891), "The Great Good Place" (1900), and *The Ambassadors* (1903)—the "high felicity" of masculine friendship draws here on the discipline of a patron or mentor who oversees the talent and "salvation" of a younger artist (for elaboration see Moon; Cooper; Sedgwick, *Epistemology* 182–212; Freedman 183; R. Martin, "High" 100–102; R. Hall 86–87; and Hartsock 305–11). However, in ways that repeat the problem of Miriam's acting in *The Tragic Muse*, these relations of tutelage "overflow" their assigned meanings, creating a metonymic surplus that is either ambiguously erotic in content or diffused by an aesthetic ideal that cancels the opportunity for physical intimacy. As Roderick insists, "The artist performs great feats in a dream. We must not wake him up lest he should lose his balance" (66). The "dream" in this instance conceals a tradition of mentorship already suffused by homo- and ephebephilia: "Rowland took a great fancy to him, to his personal charm and his probable genius. He had an indefinable attraction—the something tender and divine of unspotted, exuberant, confident youth" (68). This "attraction" generates a profound intimacy: "They talked on these occasions of everything conceivable, and had the air of having no secrets from each other. . . . [Roderick's] unfailing impulse to share every emotion and impression with his friend . . . made comradeship a high felicity, and interfused with a deeper amenity the wanderings and contemplations that beguiled their pilgrimage to Rome" (101, 107). We see links here between this "high felicity" and Michael Henchard's intimate confessions to Donald Farfrae, in Hardy's *The Mayor of Casterbridge,* discussed in the previous chapter.

The peripeteia with which *Roderick Hudson* closes is considerably more violent than is Rudyard Kipling's analogous turn in *Kim* (1901), in which Kim's mentor, the Lama, announces his emotional attachment to the young boy, his "beloved," before dying in his arms (338). James's novel is arguably more violent because Roderick's suicide is the only act that can bring this novel's persistent homo/sexual metonymy to an abrupt halt (even marriage would seem to be an inadequate defense against this desire). *The Tragic Muse* may be more daring than either of these texts, however, because its sexual excess creates a bungled ending with an awkward prominence of homosexual desire. Since the narrative has exposed—and all but excised—Miriam's theatricality as a "monstrous" aberration, the figure *necessarily* most contiguous to Miriam is the puzzling Gabriel Nash.

Miriam and Nash share a symbolic function. Yet as several critics have noted, Nash's ability to connect characters renders him more convincing than is Miriam as a narrative "object" (see Funston; Goetz 160–62; W. Hall 167–70; Macnaughton 7). Indeed, as James remarked in his preface to *The Tragic Muse*, the novel's conflicting aims derive from the stubborn indeterminacy of its principal object:

> The influence of *The Tragic Muse* was . . . exactly other than what I had all earnestly (if of course privately enough) invoked for it, and I remember well the particular chill, at last, of the sense of my having launched it in a great grey void from which no echo or message whatever would come back. . . . [P]erversely, incurably, the centre of my structure would insist on placing itself *not*, so to speak, in the middle. . . . [T]he terminational terror was none the less certain to break in and my work threaten to masquerade for me as an active figure condemned to the disgrace of legs too short, ever so much too short, for its body. I urge myself to the candid confession that in very few of my productions, to my eye, *has* the organic centre succeeded in getting into proper position. (Preface to *Tragic* 80, 85; original emphases)

James's difficulty in stabilizing the center of *The Tragic Muse* suggests that the novel eventually loses its focus; it has at least two protagonists and pursues several themes, including art, politics, drama, and representation. To James, the novel's division between two protagonists signified an "incurab[le]" collapse of order because it allowed another term to masquerade in the position he had designated for "good art"; there's no limit to dissimulation or acting in this novel. James considered *The Tragic Muse* disappointing also because its unruly center defied the position he'd assigned it: "In several of my compositions this displacement has so succeeded, at the crisis, in defying and resisting me, has appeared so fraught with probable dishonour, that I still turn upon them, in spite of the greater or less [*sic*] success of final dissimulation, a rueful and wondering eye" (86). James acknowledged that one of his disappointments was Nick Dormer (96); the other, whose "defiance" relates to his "usurpation" of the novel's implied object (Miriam), appears to have been Gabriel Nash.[6]

Despite Nash's important symbolic function in *The Tragic Muse*, he is curiously not named in the novel's preface. Nash also is "unmanned" by the novel's split between Sherringham and Nick because the novel offers no other path to masculinity. When James refers to his intention to make Miriam the "object" of this novel (89)—and his failure to achieve this end—he signals the vigilance necessary *not* to structure the novel around Nash, apparently admitting the failure and even the effort required to conceal it without alighting on its possible solution. Though he deplores Miriam's duplicity, James himself confronts "the question of artfully, of consummately masking the fault and conferring on the false quantity the brave appearance of the true" (86). The irony of his being compelled to adopt artifice while condemning it in his characters is itself "artfully . . . mask[ed]"; James tries to consider artifice the unhappy consequence of *this* novel, not a problem endemic to all representation.

James's conviction that the aesthetic failure of *The Tragic Muse* derives from the poverty of its supports—"legs . . . ever so much too short, for its body"—suggests that his novel's difficulty lies where its "legs," or protagonists, meet. The site of anxiety and contraction is arguably the novel's distended midriff, for it is here that the text's sublime "body" contains a genital region that James tried alternately to hide and "elevate." Thus the "perverse . . . centre" of his novel has an important function: It demonstrates the weight of sexual meaning that must fall outside the narrative's purview. Nash embodies all the difficulties informing this novel's sexual and marital relations; the narrator observes with uncharacteristic precision that Nash's body is overweight and physically incongruous: "[T]his young man was fair and fat and of the middle stature; he had a round face and a short beard, and on his crown a mere reminiscence of hair. . . . Bridget Dormer, who was quick, estimated him immediately as a gentleman, but a gentleman unlike any other gentleman she had ever seen" (20).

Like Maria Gostrey in *The Ambassadors*, Nash is a *ficelle*, or narrative "thread": He encourages intimacy among others, making clear their intentions without seeming to possess any of his own (see Bellringer 75–76). In this respect, he is a vanishing mediator for the novel's heterosexual couples. The narrator poorly explains Nash's motives, but he is an important influence on Nick Dormer because he represents a man who lives entirely for art and pleasure—that is, the pleasurable art of appearing artless.

How does this embodiment of masculine pleasure influence the novel's conclusion and engender its author's bitter disappointment? Several critics have noted that the novel's simplicity lies in its allegorical rigidity: Julia Dallow is its "political" representative, while Sherringham stands for diplomacy and Miriam embodies drama (Goetz; W. Hall; Macnaughton). Considering this economy, Nick Dormer is significant because he doesn't choose between the two options before him—politics or painting. As I argued earlier, a character's vocational aim in *The Tragic Muse* determines his choice of object: Sherringham chooses between Miriam/the theater and Biddy/colonial diplomacy. Since Nick faces a comparable choice between politics and painting, James can't give Nash a specific vocation because Nick would then be deciding between a female and male partner (that is, between Julia/politics and Nash/"art"). Although Nick's family pressures him to commit to Julia, his heterosexual complacency grants Nash an influence that verges on seduction. James seems to obviate this problem by assigning Nash an intangible—if no less constitutive—role as Nick's "imagination"; the narrator's suggestion that Nash has an internal influence alleviates some of James's misgivings about Nick's physical intimacy with Nash. Nick is, as it were, already penetrated by this absent presence.

From the start of the novel, when the narrator and Biddy Dormer observe a reunion between Nick and Gabriel that is by Jamesian standards palpably erotic,[7] Nash shapes Nick's interest in aesthetics. Mrs. Dormer later characterizes British aestheticism as effeminate and irresolute—"a horrible insidious foreign disease . . . eating the healthy core out of English life (dear old English life!)" (385). Indeed, aestheticism represents a counterforce that diminishes the influence of Julia's political and marital ambition for Nick. Mrs. Dormer has reason for concern: Nash's influence on Nick and the legacy of their former friendship at Oxford are so extensive that the "opposition of interest and desire" within Nick seriously jeopardizes his future. Given the burden of these competing demands and his family's panic, it isn't surprising that Nick suffers from indecision. What is surprising is the narrator's inability to name his difficulty: "The explanation . . . consist[ed] . . . of the simple formula that he had at last come to a crisis. Why a crisis—what was it, and why had he not come to it before? The reader shall learn these things in time, if he cares enough for them" (19).

The factors causing this "crisis" remain vague, and the promised explanation never comes. Of course, Nick's crisis has certain obvious, identifiable causes: the overbearing demands of his benefactor, Mr. Carteret; the relentless expectations of his mother and those she attributes to his dead father; and Nick's own disinclination to conform. He poignantly summarizes these factors as "my family, my blood, my heredity, my traditions, my promises, my circumstances, my prejudices, my little past, such as it is; my great future, such as it has been supposed it may be" (125). All these factors resurface with Nick's intended marriage to Julia, though he repeatedly confuses affection for Julia with gratitude for her continued professional support. Nash asks bluntly,

> "Are you in love with her?"
> "Not in the least."
> "Well, she is with you—so I perceived."
> "Don't say that," said Nick Dormer, with sudden sternness.
> (125)

Nash poses this question in a chapter that takes up how the two men might negotiate Nick's marital and professional future: "the more they said the more the unsaid came up" (122). The "unsaid" is ambiguous here, referring either to Nick's marriage as an unspeakable obstacle to their friendship, or to their friendship as an "unsaid" means of averting all other claims to intimacy. Nash implies the second possibility by adopting an antagonistic stance toward Julia, offering to rescue Nick from her: "'It's her place; she'll put me in,' Nick said. 'Baleful woman! But I'll pull you out!'" (127).

Whatever meaning the narrative attributes to Nick's "salvation" (both men consider Julia's appetite for Nick's success—as Sherringham considered Miriam's—voracious and unappeasable), Nick's uninterest in Julia suggests to his family and friends that he cannot love. As in *The Picture of Dorian Gray,* in which desire and convention are split between incompatible demands, Nick's dilemma produces an acute crisis: "'I don't know what I am—heaven help me!' [he] broke out . . . 'I'm a freak of nature and a sport of the mocking gods! . . . I'm a wanton variation, an unaccountable monster'" (125–26). Though the question of monstrosity surfaced much earlier in *The Tragic Muse,* with Miriam's "elastic" disposition, Nick's claim is significant because it is "unaccountable" and unaccounted for. Despite the narrator's promise to explain it, Nick's problem remains an enigma.[8] The reader can connect Nick's crisis with this novel's conflict between marriage and masculine friendship only by accepting a generic tension between men's vocations and their unacceptable desires.

Although this novel is concerned with Nick Dormer's relation to marriage, Nick's problem doesn't resurface with much force. When the subject of marriage arises for Gabriel Nash, however—and it does so repeatedly—the narrator is much less cautious: The novel's association of decadence with "irresponsible" pleasure is sufficient to mark Nash as one of James's most persistent bachelors. The narrator also describes Nash as "the mysterious personage," "an anomaly," "a strange man," "Nick's queer comrade," "cheerfully helpless and socially indifferent," "unregenerate . . . the merman wandering free," "a little affected," "this whimsical personage . . . a slippery subject," "the recreant comrade," "romantically allusive," and generally "different" (22, 23, 37, 44, 53, 117, 120, 262, 263, 263, 326). The idea that Nash would ever marry seems not only unlikely, but a source of poignant mirth: "This was a law [of courtship and desire] from which Gabriel Nash was condemned to suffer, if suffering could on any occasion be predicated of Gabriel Nash. His pretension was, in truth, that he had purged his life of such incongruities, though probably he would have admitted that if a sore spot remained the hand of a woman would be sure to touch it" (104). Nash later volunteers, "Oh, I'm never another man . . . I'm more the wrong one than the man himself" (372). The narrator describes Nick and Nash's friendship so soon after this remark that the following statement seems intimately connected to his observation: "one of them [was] as dissimulative in passion as the other was paradoxical in the absence of it" (374).

The narrator consistently declares Nash to be "outside" the novel's circuit of suitors and possible partners; Nash is the overseer of others' relationships. Since James's fiction never entirely detaches his observers from their surrounding dramas, however, the observers become implicated in the very scenes they evaluate (see Kappeler 118; Silverman, *Male* esp. 167–74).[9] The central problem of *The Ambassadors* therefore hinges less on the rescue of Chad Newsome (the principal "object" Strether must redeem from Europe's vices) than on Strether's vicarious participation in the younger man's passions and follies. While Nash also confirms that James's observers perform a crucial task of detection, Nash's role as narrative *ficelle* and his replacement of Miriam Rooth as the novel's mediating "object" destroy his capacity for detachment. After this substitution, most of the remaining characters represent Nash as a perverse muse with growing influence on Nick. When the two men reminisce about their undergraduate days at Oxford, for example—a university that spawned both aestheticism and the homoerotic underpinnings of Victorian Neo-Hellenism in Britain (see Dowling, *Hellenism* esp. chap. 3)—Nick invokes Nash as "'very bad company for me, my evil genius; you opened my eyes, you communicated the poison. Since then, little by little, it has been working within me; vaguely, covertly, insensibly at first, but during the last year or two with violence, pertinacity, cruelty. I have taken every antidote in life; but it's no use—I'm stricken. It tears me to pieces, as I may say'" (126). In other words, by detailing the prehistory of the two men's friendship, the novel slyly invokes homoerotic aspects of the Oxford Movement.

Although much of the novel's melodrama and humor derive from Nick's mock-heroic attempt to rid himself of Nash, we can't discount these remarks as banter. A serious, redemptive expectation underlines this melodrama, which raises pressing questions about Nick's ontology and his unsettled relation to male and female objects. At this juncture the reader may discover—in the "cruelty" of Nash's influence, the impatience of Nick's family, and the agony of his indecision—partial reasons for Nick's crisis. One might ask, too, whether "stricken" implies seduced.

I argued earlier that Miriam personifies a split in Sherringham's character that he resolves by breaking off their intimacy. Nick can't resolve his dilemma by comparable action. He circumvents the dilemma by seeing the demand for resolution as a reason for his dual identity: "He was conscious of a double nature; there were two men in him, quite separate, whose leading features had little in common and each of whom insisted on having an independent turn at life" (176). The text later aligns this "double nature" with the public and private division of his character. When Nick decides to run for a seat in Britain's Parliament, he becomes fascinated with employing political rhetoric, which convinces others of an integrity he doesn't possess. He finds he must decide whether to stand for his constituency as its political representative or remain "true" to his own volition and maintain his "private" and creative desire without the symbolic legitimacy of public office: "The difficulty is that I'm two men; it's the strangest thing that ever was. . . . One man wins the seat—but it's the other fellow who sits in it" (166).

The question of Nick's nomination and election to Parliament doesn't resolve his earlier struggle to align every impulse with an acceptable object; it repeats this struggle in an urgent, public form. Although the problem of sexuality seems to fall outside this conflict, the success of Nick's political career still hinges on his dissimulating a "private" self ("He had . . . above all to pretend" [161]). This masquerade creates such distress that Nick declines the nomination; were he to take up public office, he would begin a career as a hypocrite. By exposing politics as another form of acting, however, Nick not only indicts the hypocrisy of British (and perhaps all) political representatives, but covertly declares his preference for "the other fellow" whose career lies in painting, and whose constitutive desire is now remarkably *legible*.[10] "The other fellow" refers to aspects of Nick's character he hasn't explored (that is, painting), as well as to Nash, the signifier of his "imagination," who inspires and later displaces this pursuit by making it tangible. Within this field of ambition and partly realized desire, Nash regains some of his former influence by representing Nick's aesthetic fantasies: "There were two voices which told him that all this [marriage and political career] was not really action at all, but only a pusillanimous imitation of it: one of them made itself fitfully audible in the depths of his own spirit and the other spoke, in the equivocal accents of a very crabbed hand, from a letter of four pages by Gabriel Nash" (177). When Nash is later meant to "interpose" for Nick by preventing his fall into marital "perdition" (according to the narrator, Nash "was to have dragged [Nick] in the opposite sense from Mrs. Dallow" [262]), Nash materializes in the place of both of Nick's dissenting "voices," as if to embody Nick's redemption from politics and heterosexuality: "[Nick] had stayed in town to be alone with his imagination, and suddenly, paradoxically, the sense of that result had arrived with Gabriel Nash" (265).

We should note the consequence of substituting Nash for the conventionally feminine muse. The narrator earlier described Nash as an ontological—perhaps sexual—"paradox"; his sudden appearance at this point interrupts conventional behavior, expectations, and marriage. Besides the obvious fact that Nick is inspired—and partly seduced—by this aesthetic embodiment, Nash is provocative because he compels Nick to question all his assumptions and demands. Nash, however, never embodies *more* than a fantasy; as James suggests in the preface to this novel, the removal of Nash's body represents the novel's frantic erasure of homosexual meaning. Nash disturbs the marital arrangements of this novel by intruding, facilitating, and then vanishing. When other characters reflect on Nash's aesthetic and hedonistic pursuits, however, they indicate his enigmatic relation to Nick: "[T]his contemplative genius seemed to take the words out of [Nick's] mouth, to utter for him, better and more completely, *the very things he was on the point of saying*" (282–83; my emphasis).

Given Nash's "paradoxical" status, and the enduringly "tragic" dimension of Nick's muse, Nash seems to embody James's title more completely than Miriam can. At the beginning of the novel, and with considerable irony, Nash describes Miriam as a muse because her performance lacks immanence. However, the narrative can't detach Nash's power to inspire from his ability to perplex. Thus Nash and Miriam are initially related because her "haunting" of Nick resembles Nash's (see Freedman 190–91). And Sherringham describes Miriam as "an angel" (272, 229) who evokes the ethereal qualities and eventual vanishing of *Gabriel* Nash.[11] Later, however, the tragic aspects of James's muse recur more consistently in Nash. Although early in the novel Nick calls Nash "my evil genius" (126) and "the merman wandering free" (117), he later calls him "Mephistopheles" (372), the spirit of seductive evil to whom Faust sold his soul.

The most significant impediments to representing Nash surface when Nick tries to paint him. Although Nick's portrait of Miriam confirms her strength as a muse, Nash proves an unwilling and finally impossible subject. As in such related James texts as "The Madonna of the Future" (1873) and "The Liar" (1888), portraiture seems to frame its subjects' psychic history (see Lane, *Ruling* 81–82). Nick's attempt to paint Nash consequently reveals how little he knows of him. The place where he lives, the people with whom he associates, and the terms of his privacy constitute an enigma that consistently evades representation:

> Nick . . . never caught, from the impenetrable background of [Nash's] life, the least reverberation of flitting or flirting, the smallest aesthetic ululation. . . . [I]t qualified with thinness the mystery he could never wholly dissociate from him, the sense of the transient and occasional, the likeness to vapour or murmuring wind or shifting light. It was for instance *a symbol of this unclassified condition, the lack of all position* as a name in well-kept books, that Nick in point of fact had no idea where he lived. (505; my emphasis)

The narrative adopts metaphors evoking the ethereal (vapor, wind, light) here because a signifier seems incapable of representing Nash; his name designates an "unclassified condition" for which there is no corresponding signified. Here, we could compare James's novel with Wilde's *The Picture of Dorian Gray*, since Dorian's secret indicates a gap between his "actual" identity (the picture of unsullied youth) and his "painted" identity (the grotesque image of an unrepentant "sinner"). While Dorian widens an already palpable split between his utterance and the place from which he has symbolically spoken, Nash seems to repress his private life and identity; his relations to others consistently flounder when they request more information. Nick knows only that Nash belongs to a club without a name—a club whose obvious importance to this text can't sustain specification: "Nash had a club, the Anonymous, in some improbable square, of which Nick suspected him of being the only member" (505). What escapes definition in lexical terms guarantees speculation among other characters; Nash's meaning as a composite of others' fantasies and projections eclipses his probable banality and the vague, conjectural images accompanying his hedonism. As Nick remarks to Julia about his family's judgments, "Excuse my possibly priggish tone, but they really attribute to Nash a part he's quite incapable of playing" (516). With poignant relevance for both contemporary homophobia and the narrative's obsession with "parts" (roles, arbitrary divisions, and discrete elements of anatomy), Nash himself observes that others represent him according to their own projections: "Ah, for what do they take one, with *their* presumptions?" (119).

Questions about the painter's "desire" surface at this point, anticipating Wilde's novel by forcing us to ask, What does Nick Dormer *want*? While Dorian Gray's portrait generates concern about the desire the painter "put . . . into it" (*Dorian* 8), horror at its exhibition (35), and the drama surrounding its eventual recovery (245), Nash's unsuccessful portrait in *The Tragic Muse* comes close to erasing not only the meaning of painting in this novel but the "truth" of the portrait's avatar. The image of Nash is not simply "killed" (as in James's "The Liar") or brutally returned to its source (as in Wilde's novel); the narrative deprives it of authority by compelling it to fade. Nash vanishes "without a trace" (511) when he can't "interpose" between the novel's heterosexual partners: "Nick had the . . . diversion . . . of imagining that the picture he had begun had a singular air of gradually fading from the canvas. He couldn't catch it in the act, but he could have a suspicion, when he glanced at it, that the hand of time was rubbing it away little by little . . . making the surface indistinct and bare—bare of all resemblance to the model" (511–12).

William Hall usefully notes that this sense of fading or *aphanisis* is somewhat delusive, because Nick's "diversion" allows him to forget his sudden loss of Nash and to relive Nash's departure in a more bearable form: "He's only dead to me. He has gone away" (*Tragic* 515; see also W. Hall 180). In this respect, Nick's projection of loss onto the painting relinquishes the object he formerly incorporated as his "Imagination." While the "fading" of Nash's portrait overdetermines his mysterious departure, Nash's portrait still betrays the novel's inability to close upon his absence.[12]

This conflict between representation and sexual fantasy suggests that Nash's disappearance is the precondition for marriage in this text; his disappearance binds characters who no longer depend on their *ficelle*. Nash's departure also releases meanings that are unwritable in this text because they constitute the enigma that supports all previous identifications (especially Nick's). Miriam makes this explicit when she proposes Nash as a substitute for herself. According to Miriam, Nick's decision to externalize Nash would allow Nick—and presumably the text—to abreact an obsessional fantasy:

> "You'll find other models; paint Gabriel Nash."
> "Gabriel Nash—as a substitute for you?"
> "It will be a good way to get rid of him. Paint Mrs. Dallow too . . . if you wish to eradicate the last possibility of a throb." (502–3)[13]

The advice proves correct insofar as the painting of Nash hastens his literal and figurative departure. However, the consequences for Julia, Nick's fiancée, are anticipated but never shown. This advice is intimately connected with the anxiety surrounding the novel's heterosexual conclusion. Thus the novel ends with a mild resurgence of interest between Nick and Julia; he promises to begin a full-length portrait of her. From this indication alone, we see that *The Tragic Muse* connects painting with seduction. Nick's wavering consent implies both his promise to seduce Julia (and, by implication, Nash) and the unstable meanings that circulate from the impossibility of either event. Although these developments confirm relations among painting, acting, and seduction, painting exacerbates the novel's problem of courtship by producing a visible "scar"; by contrast, Miriam's acting seems indistinguishable from most behavior in this text.

Nash's incomplete painting seems to haunt Nick as a visible reminder of their unfinished business; the painting clearly fails to "eradicate . . . the last possibility of a throb." Unlike the picture of Dorian Gray, Nash's painting denotes neither "homosexual" duplicity nor the "sin" of an illicit desire (none is ever avowed); it represents a powerful "resentment" and irrational shame: "[Nick] seized it and turned it about; he jammed it back into its corner, with its face against the wall. . . . The embarrassment however was all his own" (518).

As in Wilde's novel, the "homosexual" meaning of Nash's painting remains enigmatic; the subject's haunting look is defaced similarly to Dorian's portrait. The drama of masculine desire in *The Tragic Muse* is also paradoxically revealed when Nash "disappears" from his canvas. While Miriam was an "embroidery" without genuine form, the significance of Nash *supersedes* the narrative's "overflow" of "metaphor." By generating more meanings than Miriam's acting, Nash's painting reproduces—and then disfigures—the drama of identification in James's novel. Every protagonist in *The Tragic Muse* is propelled by a volatile set of drives and fantasies that painting seems to "realize" with remarkable accuracy (see Rose 226–27; Silverman, *Subject* 162–67).

What makes the fading of Nash's portrait so poignant, finally, is that the character most supportive of others' identifications ultimately is shorn of his own. Having established a tenuous intimacy between Sherringham and Biddy, and between Nick and Julia, Nash is expelled from the novel as a trope of psychic instability. In his preface James explains that in his perversity as this novel's muse, Nash's "fading" cancels its awkward expression of desire by reshaping others' fantasies into acceptable form.

By leaving the text, Nash relieves the group of its surplus member: the confirmed bachelor whom the novel couldn't pair off. His departure conveniently arrests the novel's sexual metonymy by allowing the tentative formation of a partnership between Nick and Julia. The narrator alludes to their marriage, but it is unclear whether Nash's residual influence will finally make Nick's career in politics—and thus in heterosexuality—intolerable. More obviously, *The Tragic Muse*'s conclusion demonstrates that painting's meanings surpass the delineations of its subjects. If the painting of Nash expresses Nick's "spiritual" seduction, it also exhibits a putative identification that its artist and subject find impossible to express. Put another way, Nash's painting illustrates a relation that exceeds masculinity's existing boundaries and that is unrepresentable for Nick or Nash *because of* this excess.

Given the obvious danger here of men painting and seducing other men, *The Tragic Muse* and *Dorian Gray* engage the limits and possibilities of "pleasure." Considering the legal constraints that Britain imposed on pleasure at the turn of the last century, it is perhaps unsurprising that the erotic project of painting fails in James's and Wilde's texts, and that *The Tragic Muse* and *Dorian Gray* find no answer to this failure, reaching instead for violence and death to destroy their homoerotic "interest and desire." Without a referent more specific than "pleasure" to signify seduction and the aesthetic practice of Gabriel Nash and Dorian Gray, these men's "interest" can't signify more than a generic "opposition" to their cultural and symbolic structures. Unable to represent "pleasure" in detail or at length, these novels have no alternative but to excise it in the interests of narrative consistency and resolution. One recalls this startling observation, made by the narrator of *The Tragic Muse,* about portraiture: "[U]nlike most other forms, it was a revelation of two realities, the man whom it was the artist's conscious effort to reveal and the man (the interpreter) expressed in the very quality and temper of that effort. It offered a double vision, the strongest dose of life that art could give, *the strongest dose of art that life could give*" (282; my emphasis). Since its "vision [is] double," painting indicates why desire is constantly at odds with itself. To put this another way, *The Tragic Muse* and *The Picture of Dorian Gray* offer the "strongest dose of art that life"—at least in 1890s Britain—seemed able to tolerate.

SIX

Santayana and the Problem of Beauty

There is a mystery . . . [to the] union of one whole man
with another whole man. . . .
—George Santayana, "Friendships" 56

It's a popular error to suppose that Puritanism has anything
to do with purity.
—Santayana, *The Last Puritan* 13

1. SPIRITUAL PROCREANCY REVISITED

George Santayana was not the first writer or philosopher to reflect on the
sexual constituents of aesthetics and creativity. An elaborate history of this
reflection would return us—via Arnold, Pater, Ruskin, Newman, and Carlyle, to name only the most obvious Victorian aestheticians—to Aristotle's
Poetics and Plato's *Symposium*. Santayana's literary and philosophical work
is notable, however, for highlighting sexuality's turbulent relationship with
aesthetics. Despite his immense intellectual effort to the contrary, Santayana displays for us a profound conceptual difficulty about desire and eroticism that not only influenced late-Victorian debates about aesthetics and
sexuality—including those discussed in the previous chapter—but anticipated Freud's earliest discussions of creativity and sublimation.[1] In his recent study *George Santayana: A Biography,* John McCormick confirms this
reading: "Santayana applied certain findings of recent psychology to aesthetics, a novel and even startling procedure in 1896, particularly in his
suggestion that sex and aesthetics are allied. . . . Santayana's argument derived in part from Stendhal's *De l'amour,* but it also anticipated Freudian
theory" (124).[2]

Santayana's lectures on aesthetics, given at Harvard at the cusp of the
last century and published in 1896 under the title *The Sense of Beauty,* also
partially bridge a transatlantic gap among scholars and writers in Boston,
Oxford, and London. Writing to Thomas Munro from Rome on December 13, 1928, for example, Santayana insisted retrospectively that he was

not very much later than Ruskin, Pater, Swinburne, and Matthew Arnold: our atmosphere was that of poets and persons touched with religious enthusiasm or religious sadness. Beauty (which mustn't be mentioned now) was then a living presence, or an aching absence, day and night: history was always singing in our ears: and not even psychology or the analysis of works of art could take away from art its human implications. (*Letters* 238–39)

"But now," Santayana laments, "analysis and psychology seem to stand alone: there is no spiritual interest, no spiritual need. The mind, in this direction, has been *desiccated*" (239; original emphasis). Elaborating on Santayana's inadvertent contribution to this psychic "desiccat[ion]," I offer in this chapter a reading of the impact—both violent and strangely conducive—of sexuality on Santayana's life and theories of artistic pleasure. Departing from standard approaches to Santayana's work claiming that he successfully transvalued sexuality into art or, related, that sexuality was irrelevant to his philosophy and life (J. Epstein, Porte), I contend that for Santayana the relations among art, desire, and object choice ironically became troubled, even antagonistic, when he sought in art a redemptive and desexualizing power. This chapter is thus partly a philosophical reflection on my reading of Jamesian aesthetics. Like Henry James, Santayana occasionally sexualized beauty and creativity, but what interests me more is the conceptual labor informing his aesthetic theory—a type of philosophical overreach deriving in part from Santayana's desire to bridge the work of such diverse influences as Plato, Keats, Schopenhauer, Lotze, Emerson, William James, and Pater. One effect of this overreach, I contend, is a fascinating oscillation between passion and asceticism, which fosters in *The Last Puritan* (1935; 1936) what Mario Van de Weyer, Santayana's friend, calls "Puritanism Self-condemned" (11). Santayana concurs, somewhat tautologically: "Puritanism is a natural reaction against nature" (11). Building on these and related suggestions in Santayana's love sonnets, *The Sense of Beauty,* and *The Last Puritan,* I think it's appropriate—if slightly anachronistic—to consider these works an inadvertent contribution to late Victorian accounts of sexual desire.

Santayana's precise willingness to conflate persons and things assists our interpretive aims; he frequently sees people as works of art and art as the study of people.[3] Santayana certainly doesn't consider art and life homologous, but as susceptible to the influence of comparable passions.[4] In *Persons and Places* (1944), he argues that similitude between persons and things arises when the subject binds itself too closely to an object, an argument building on related claims in Plato's *Phaedrus* and Arthur Schopenhauer's *The World as Will and Idea* (1818).[5] Santayana remarks, "To possess things and persons in idea is the only pure good to be got out of them; to possess them physically or legally is a burden and a snare. . . . A perfect love is founded on despair" (*Persons* 428).[6] Underscoring this burden's psychic implications, *The Sense of Beauty* argues that "the human mind is a turbulent commonwealth" (22).

In claiming that Santayana's philosophy assisted contemporaneous theories of art and sexuality, I want to distinguish the type of generic, objectless love and pleasure recurring in Santayana's work from what is often called "self-love" or "narcissism." I take this distinction from Santayana himself, who argued: "The *perfect* lover must renounce pursuit and the hope of possession. His person and life must, in his own eyes, fall altogether out of the picture. . . . It is therefore psychologically not only possible but normal for the passion of love to be self-forgetful, and to live on in the very act of sacrifice and personal despair. So transformed, the great passion becomes worship" (*Persons* 428–29; original emphasis).

How close is this argument to suggestions of self-annihilation and even of passion's ability to destroy us? After all, while Santayana tries to distance his argument about passion from Stendhal's accounts of *"l'amour-physique"* and *"l'amour de vanité"*—terms that Santayana rejects as "obviously imperfect and impure" (428)—he nonetheless wants to conceptualize a type of "passion of love, sublimated, [that] does not become bloodless, or free from bodily trepidation" (429). The fundamental *difficulty* he attributes to sexual desire is thus distinct from the relative calm he finds in creativity and oblation: "Falling in love is often fatal and involuntary," he warns,

> although it can sometimes be headed off; but then reason and duty come in, in a strong soul, to suppress or sacrifice the pas-

sion. But what is reason or duty? Either another passion—the passion for harmony and integrity in the soul—or social conventions, expediencies, and taboos. Against everything of the latter kind a transcendental free spirit rebels; and there I see the secret of tragic strength being often mixed with an extraordinary fatalistic weakness. (473)

Let us consider the implications of this "extraordinary . . . weakness," asking too how the ensuing psychic hemorrhage affects Santayana's ideas of beauty, particularly beauty in another person—and even in another man. *The Sense of Beauty* aims, in McCormick's words, "to define aesthetics and to explain its naturalistic base in psychology" (123); it strives initially to distinguish object love from love of people, arguing that "sex is not the *only* object of sexual passion" (*Sense* 40; my emphasis). Here Santayana implies and withholds a claim—which Socrates and Phaedrus debate extensively in Plato's *Phaedrus,* and which Freud, Santayana's contemporary, later refined—that oblation, narcissism, and creativity all obtain from "sexual passion" (see Freud, *Three* 217–19). It may shock Santayana scholars to link the apparently asexual philosopher with Plato *and* Freud, but Santayana tells us clearly in 1896 that "passion . . . overflows and visibly floods those neighbouring regions which it had always secretly watered" (40).[7] And all three thinkers concur, in Santayana's words, that "halfway between vital and social functions, lies the sexual instinct" (37). In Freud's work, however, this "halfway" point is not sexuality detached from an object, but a modified form of homosexuality he calls "sensuous" same-sex attachments. In *Group Psychology and the Analysis of the Ego* (1921), as we saw in chapter 3, Freud claims that the "emotional tie" is the "successor to a completely 'sensual' object-tie with the person in question or rather with that person's prototype (or *imago*)" (138), and the "person in question" for Freud—given his focus here and elsewhere on masculine identification—is invariably male.

Although Santayana did not formulate the same claim unequivocally, his work on beauty represents subjects, society, and sexuality as similarly fraught with problems of "connexion" (*Sense* 37). Ostensibly, these are connections between men and women in which beauty seems to bind an otherwise fraught social and psychic gap. Later in *The Sense of Beauty*, though, the distinction first sought between persons and things shifts to one between procreation and sexual beauty, and here things get complicated. "Beauty," Santayana writes, "borrows warmth . . . precisely from the waste, from the radiation of the sexual passion" (38). Here he differs slightly from Freud, who tried initially to give sublimated drives a type of purity untarnished by psychic waste—untarnished, that is, by the homoerotic factor making sublimation possible (*Three* 178; *Group* 138);[8] like Santayana's, Freud's conception of sublimation failed entirely in this regard (see James Strachey's introduction to Freud's *Papers on Metapsychology*, *Standard* 14: 106). Santayana's notion that beauty emerges from a depletion or *wasting* of desire nonetheless points up his complicated relation to late-nineteenth-century arguments about passion and asceticism.[9]

McCormick notes that toward the end of 1887, when Santayana (then twenty-four) was alone in Berlin studying the philosophy of Rudolf Hermann Lotze, he wrote William Morton Fullerton, a friend from Harvard and an "exquisite rakehell, probably both homo- and heterosexual, . . . [later] the lover of the Ranee of Sarawak and of Edith Wharton, among others" (37), asking: "What is one to do with one's amatory instincts?" Santayana expatiates at length on this problem, claiming that after

a boy lives to his twelfth or fifteenth year . . . in a state of mental innocence, . . . [h]e grows more and more uncomfortable, his imagination is more and more occupied with obscene things. Every scrap of medical or other knowledge he hears on the subject he remembers. Some day he tries experiments with some girl, or with some other boy. This is, I say, supposing he has not been corrupted intentionally and taken to whorehouses in his boyhood as some are, or fallen a victim to paiderastia, as is the lot of others. But in some way or other, sooner or later, the boy gets his first experience in the art of love. Now, I say, what is a man to do about it? It is no use saying that he should be an angel, because he isn't. Even if he holds himself in, and only wet dreams violate his virginity, he is not an angel because angels don't have wet dreams. He must choose among the following:

Amatory attitudes
1. Wet dreams and the fidgets.
2. Mastibation [*sic,* written in Boston dialect].
3. Paiderastia.
4. Whoring.
5. Seductions or a mistress.
6. Matrimony.

I don't put a mistress as a separate heading because it really comes under 4, 5, or 6, as the case may be. A man who takes a mistress from among prostitutes, shares her with others, and leaves her soon, is practically whoring. A man whose mistress is supposed to be respectable is practically seducing her. A man who lives openly with his mistress and moves in her sphere is practically married. Now I see fearful objections to every one of these six amatory attitudes. 1 and 6 have the merit of being virtuous, but it is their only one. 2 has nothing in its favor. The discussion is therefore confined to 3, 4, and 5. 4 has the disadvantage of ruining the health. 5 has the disadvantage of scenes and bad social complications—children, husbands at law, etc. One hardly wants to spend one's youth in acting French dramas. 3 has therefore been often preferred by impartial judges, like the ancients and orientals, yet *our prejudices against it are so strong that it hardly comes under the possibilities for us.* What shall we do? Oh matrimony, truly thou art an inevitable evil!

As you perceive, I do not consider sentimental love at all in my pros and cons. It is only a disturbing force, as far as the true amatory instincts are concerned. Of course it has the same origin, but just as insanity may spring from religion, so sentimental love may spring from the sexual instinct. (Qtd. in McCormick 70–71; my emphasis)

McCormick adds, "No answer from Fullerton to Santayana's unusual letter survives. Homosexuality is absent from the list of amatory attitudes, an irony of omission, perhaps" (71). He refers here to the fact that in 1887 Benjamin Jowett suspended Santayana's close friend and perhaps subsequent lover,[10] John Francis Stanley, second Earl Russell (Bertrand Russell's older brother), from Balliol College, Oxford, because "a scandalous letter of Russell's had come to light" acknowledging that Lionel Johnson (Santayana's and Russell's mutual friend) "had spent a night in R[ussell]'s room" (qtd. 65). Refusing to admit that he and Johnson had spent a night together, Russell later belabored his "innocence" so extensively in his autobiography that even Santayana, reading Russell's patently absurd claim—"I was entirely possessed by that white virginal flame of innocence which I think is even stronger in adolescent boys than in girls"—acknowledged, in a private note to himself, "This is true as regards Lionel Johnson and Russell, but it is a lie if applied to R. in his general habits—a cheeky lie, when so many of his readers know the facts" (qtd. in McCormick 65).[11] Yet while Santayana's October 20, 1929, letter to Russell overall is quite revealing of the two men's intimacy,[12] in *Persons and Places* Santayana speaks only elliptically of Russell's "petty vices[,] which gave him infinite trouble and no pleasure" (309). In another interesting aside, however, he does admit that "what damned [Russell] was not the things of which he was accused . . . , but his own perverse way of *wasting* his opportunities" (309; my emphasis). In other words—and with embarrassing practical and conceptual consequences for Santayana—the ideal of sublimation again surfaced as a failed imperative.

Santayana's letter to Fullerton and subsequent remarks about Russell aid us greatly in determining his own critical relation to sexual drives. Many other examples illustrate this relative crisis. When recalling the poet A. E. Housman in 1929, Santayana remarked to Daniel Cory, his friend and confidant: "I suppose Housman was really what people nowadays call 'homosexual.'" According to Cory, Santayana added, "as if he were primarily speaking to himself: 'I think I must have been that way in my Harvard days—although I was unconscious of it at the time'" (Cory 40). Much later, on August 17, 1945, Santayana wrote Cyril Clemens, claiming that when dining with Housman many years earlier, the poet "was amiably silent. However, I had meantime read *The Shropshire Lad,* and *Last Poems,* and now *More Poems,* always with tears. There is not much else than tears in them, but they are perfect of their kind" (qtd. in McCormick 118). Given this and similar preoccupations, McCormick notes of Santayana's 1929 conversation with Cory,

Santayana may have consciously misled the young man who might become his Boswell; or Cory, always at pains to present his subject in the best light, may have edited Santayana's words. It is hardly credible that a man of Santayana's education, urbanity, and circle of acquaintance could have remained unconscious of his own tendencies until sixty-five. He knew enough Greek to gather that not all love in Plato's circle was Platonic; he knew Tacitus on the later Roman emperors; and he lived through Oscar Wilde's trial[s] in 1895, his imprisonment and exile. Nor could the house guest of Howard Sturgis at Windsor and the classmate and friend of William Fullerton be unaware of homosexuality as a word or as a fact of many men's lives. (51)

To repeat: "What is one to do with one's amatory instincts?" (qtd. in McCormick 70). Nine years after asking Fullerton this question, Santayana engaged it philosophically in *The Sense of Beauty* when, to quote a line from one of his 1896 "sublimated love sonnets," he tried to explain why "[t]he spirit [must] purge away its proper dross" (*Complete* 95). The "purge" wasn't always successful; indeed, it remained something of an ongoing disturbance in Santayana's literary and philosophical work. Many years later, for instance, in *Realms of Being* (1927–38), Santayana avowed, "Carnal pleasures . . . , which are but welcome pains, draw the spirit inwards into primal darkness and indistinction" (706). Despite his subsequent claims about the mind's "desiccat[ion]," Santayana represents the unconscious here not as a benign influence, but as a cause of internal havoc: "The chained dogs below keep on barking in their kennels" (689).

Numerous cultural and philosophical influences converge in these statements. In striving to account for the erotic hinge between subjects and groups, however, Santayana and his contemporaries turned more often to Plato than to Marx and Engels. In August 1896, Santayana wrote Conrad Slade from Oxford, noting, "My idea is to go on with my writing, but at the same time to see something of people, and if possible to read a little Plato, and see what the aesthetic religious and philosophical atmosphere in England is now-a-days" (*Letters* 45). The following year, he wrote Guy Murchie from Cambridge, England, noting, "I am now at work on an exposition and defence of Plato's bad treatment of poets, whom, as you may know, he banished from his republic as trivial and demoralizing persons"; he added that he would teach a course primarily on Plato when he returned to Harvard (57, 56). In approaching Santayana's work on object choice and creativity, we must therefore briefly revisit Plato's arguments about love and desire.[13]

In the *Symposium,* Plato has Diotima tell Socrates that love arises as a power "between [the] divine and mortal" (202E). Diotima adds, in a speech directly influencing how Santayana's protagonist in *The Last Puritan* defines his own passions (527–28; 695), that love's power lies in "[i]nterpreting and transporting human things to the gods and divine things to men; entreaties and sacrifices from below, and ordinances and requitals from above: being *midway* (ἐν μέσῳ) between, it makes each to supplement the other, so that the whole is combined in one" (202E; my emphasis). By representing love as a go-between, transporting (διαπορθ-μεῦον—literally, "carrying across") "entreaties and sacrifices" from men to gods, and "ordinances and requitals" from gods to men, Plato uses Diotima to suggest not that love rescinds—or leaves behind—the erotic, but just the reverse: Love exists in addition to the erotic, she insists, arguing later that previous and "lesser" loves should be "used as steps" (ὥσπερ ἐπαναβαθ-μοῖς χρώμενον; 211C) to attaining a greater—and still physical—form of love.[14] Thus it would be wrong to claim that love and the erotic are mutually exclusive in Plato's philosophy.[15]

By reproducing this argument alongside Diotima's related claim that "procreation in the beautiful" (τόκος ἐν καλῷ, 206C; or, as other translations put it, "giving birth in beauty" and "begetting on a beautiful thing by means of both the body and the soul") is more alluring than biological procreation,[16] Santayana molded Plato's aesthetic arguments to late-Victorian Hellenistic conceptions of art and masculine beauty. For this reason, however, Santayana's conception of love and beauty is not devoid of tension. Indeed, in reproducing Diotima's depiction of love as a *dynamic* intermediary between "gods . . . and men," Santayana grasps that love rarely forms a stable "supplement" between gods and men, such that "the whole is combined in one" (202E). He finds instead that love arises as a volatile excess, pushing the lover (*erastēs*) *beyond* the beloved (*erōmenos*) in ways that point up both parties' mutual deficiencies.

Although I'll later analyze Santayana's 1896 sonnets in some detail, it seems useful to illustrate two examples of his poetry's affective turbulence. In Sonnet XVI, Santayana tells us,

> A thousand beauties that have never been
> Haunt me with hope and tempt me to pursue;
> The gods, methinks, dwell just behind the blue;
> The satyrs at my coming fled the green.
> The flitting shadows of the grove between
> The dryads' eyes were winking, and I knew
> The wings of sacred Eros as he flew
> And left me to the love of things not seen.
> 'T is a sad love, like an eternal prayer,
> And knows no keen delight, no faint surcease. (*Complete* 98)

Perhaps the first thing we note in this poem is that beauty isn't singular. That Santayana invokes a thousand haunting beauties here suggests that no single vision of beauty—and thus desire for a single object—is possible. To put this slightly differently, Santayana's poetic vision engages part objects—imagoes—that surface as recollections belying immediacy and reciprocity; their distorting character *removes* Santayana and his reader from immediate contact with the beloved.

This sonnet counters in tone and substance a number of Santayana's related poems in which his faith in a redemptive deity is strongly pronounced. Whereas in Sonnet XVI, the poet likens "sacred Eros" to "an eternal prayer, / . . . [that] knows no keen delight, no faint surcease," in Sonnet XVIII he seems to withdraw this Hellenistic pronouncement: "My angel is come back," he now declares, "Oh, trust in God, and banish rash despair, / That, feigning evil, is itself the curse!" (98, 99). Before we attain this "trust in God," however, we read an ever bleaker, more ironic account of beauty's ability to ensnare the *erōmenos:*

> O subtle Beauty, sweet persuasive worth
> That didst the love of being first inspire,
> We do thee homage both in death and birth.
> Thirsting for thee, we die in thy great dearth,
> Or borrow breath of infinite desire
> To chase thine image through the haunted earth. (99)

If "Beauty" in this sonnet represents the cause of desire (it "did[] the love of being first inspire"), it doesn't appease desire but exacerbates it, generating a craving precisely from its failure properly to materialize or impose limits on the poet's erotic demands. In despair, the poet finds himself taunted by a vision whose perfection is unrealizable. Refusing to question the validity or degree of idealization informing this vision, he has no option but "[t]o chase thine image through the haunted earth." In this and similar sonnets, as I'll soon show, Santayana's conception of desire and beauty does indeed corroborate McCormick's claims that he "applied certain findings of recent psychology to aesthetics" (124).

That Santayana's aesthetic vision oscillates between Victorian and "modern" conceptions of art and beauty may derive from his dissatisfaction with the traditional—or phenomenological—school of aesthetics. As Kailash Chandra Baral claims, this school aimed at "discriminating the aesthetic from the moral and cognitive dimensions of human experience" (59).[17] Yet Santayana also was ill at ease with the "so-called modern school" of aesthetics, which, Baral argues, "put emphasis on [the] psychological interpretation of beauty" (59). In *The Sense of Beauty*, Santayana argues that our understanding of beauty "must be nothing less than the exposition of the origin, place, and elements of beauty as an object of human experience," and he elaborates: "We must learn from [this definition], as far as possible, why, when, and how beauty appears, what conditions an object must fulfill to be beautiful, what elements of our nature make us sensible of beauty[,] and what the relation is between the constitution of the object and the excitement of our susceptibility" (11).

We are clearly some distance here from Arnold's famous dictum that we "see the object as in itself it really is" ("Function" 258), a demand that generally bored Santayana, whose curiosity about "the relation . . . between the constitution of the object and the excitement of our susceptibility" is more amenable to Freud's contemporaneous interest in explaining how fantasy defines external meaning and events (*Sense* 11). In 1897, the year after Santayana gave his lectures on beauty, Freud revised his theory of seduction, placing greater emphasis on the internal apprehension of sexual meaning. Santayana, however, would not, and could not, follow Freud in pursuing the implications of this conceptual reorientation. Some of this resistance is attributable to his limited (and generally desexualized) conception of the unconscious.[18] *The Sense of Beauty* remains precisely that—an endeavor to locate beauty's "sense," its moral and cognitive dimension. Yet as we'll see, Santayana's perspective on beauty differs only slightly from what Freud would later consider a type of cognitive *disorder*, in which the *object* is understood to elicit fantasy and cause desire.

The gap emerging here between the object and the subject's fantasy of it arises in Santayana's reflections on beauty as the turbulent sensations an object can evoke in its viewer or lover. In his section on "Aesthetic and Physical Pleasure," Santayana calls these sensations "a complication" (23), after noting the "imagination['s ability to] invade . . . the sober and practical domain of morals" (23; for a useful elaboration, see Lentricchia 790–92). Partly for this reason, he rejects Arnold's and others' faith in the object's immanent beauty as "radically absurd and contradictory" (29), insisting instead that beauty is a "value . . . which affects our senses and which we consequently perceive" (29). At the same time, Santayana acknowledges that the subject's sensations about an object, which are "compacted of all the impressions, feelings, and memories, [and] which offer themselves for association, . . . fall within the vortex of the amalgamating imagination" (29).

Here and elsewhere, we see Santayana grappling with the vagaries of fantasy in his wish to theorize not only beauty but the aesthetic basis of sexual attraction. And it's here that *The Sense of Beauty* appears to suffer its greatest (and most interesting) conceptual problem. Santayana introduces aesthetics to biological accounts of sex attraction to illustrate how fantasy pushes us beyond biology and how our interest in objects arises as a compromised choice. The logical result of this argument is an emphasis on heterosexuality's *noninevitability;* in enhancing biological attraction, beauty paradoxically projects it into a different ontological register. Thus we read in *The Sense of Beauty,* "The attraction of sex could not become efficient unless the senses were first attracted. The eye must be fascinated and the ear charmed by the object which nature intends should be pursued" (38). Two paragraphs earlier, we see Santayana pushing to improve the "precision" of biology's influence on human procreation to ensure that a man can quickly find "the one female best fitted to bear [his] offspring . . . , leaving *his* energy and attention free at all other times to exercise the other faculties of his nature" (38; my emphasis).

What precisely is Santayana trying to formulate here? Without aesthetics, he declares, "there is a great deal of groping and waste; and the force and constancy of the [procreative] instinct must make up for its lack of precision" (38)—an idea echoed in Sonnet XIII: "Why this inane curiosity to grope / In the dim dust for gems' unmeaning ray?" (*Complete* 97). In the next paragraph of *The Sense of Beauty,* Santayana states that if we could somehow perfect biology, the procreative instinct, "like all those perfectly adjusted, would tend to become unconscious" (38). Santayana then reveals, as we've seen, the basis of his thesis: "It is *precisely from the waste,* from the radiation of the sexual passion, that beauty borrows warmth" (38; my emphasis). Santayana has already told us that the aesthetic, while necessary to perfect human procreation, ultimately is superfluous to it. Put another way, he tells us that the aesthetic is not reducible to sex attraction for reproductive ends; it is instead contingent on what *escapes* this economy as "waste"—that is, as the beauty and passion informing poetry. In ways that Freud would formulate more succinctly twenty-five years later, in *Group Psychology,* Santayana theorized for beauty in 1896 what many decadent artists and writers in Europe and Britain struggled to convey in their fiction and poetry: a profound rapport among creativity, beauty, and same-sex desire.[19] Of course, Victorian Hellenists had advanced similar claims nearly five decades before Santayana; his role was to aid the Hellenists' *philosophical* claims, providing theoretical weight to their "spiritual procreancy" precisely when their related emphasis on male love was attacked and legally challenged in Britain (see Dowling, *Hellenism* 67–103; Dellamora, *Masculine* 33, 169–71, 196–99; also DeLaura, *Hebrew* 171–81; Jenkyns esp. 140–53).

Santayana represents objects as "organiz[ing]" and "classif[ying] the diffused experiences of life"; they "frame . . . the world . . . out of [a] chaos of impressions" (*Sense* 29). Objects give the subject a reprieve from formlessness and anxiety, and so are susceptible to idealization, a condition, as we'll see below, on which Santayana frequently expatiates. When the subject invests a specific object with erotic longing, however, the object acquires a different type of "power," combining in the subject "exquisiteness and breathlessness with awe" (37). And by exacerbating the subject's demand still further, the object and the "dumb and powerful [sex] instinct" it elicits "join . . . to possession the keenest pleasure, to rivalry the fiercest rage, and to solitude an eternal melancholy" (39); one might call these passions the vicissitudes of the transference.

Our discussion could widen immeasurably at this point, highlighting parallels with Walter Pater's related discussion of subjectivity and diffusion in *The Renaissance: Studies in Art and Poetry* (1873; 1893; see 455 and chapter 1 above). We could also enumerate links between Santayana and William James (a mentor he didn't entirely admire) on the issue of autonomy and subjective defenses ("Apologia" 499, 503; Ruddick 347). To avoid oversimplifying these complex and nonidentical antecedents, however, I want to limit my argument to two claims. First, Santayana's discussion—in *The Sense of Beauty*, his sonnets, and other texts—of the subject's internal ambivalence about love and longing modifies the prevalent claim in Santayana studies that his interests were as ascetic as the philosophy he seemed consistently to espouse.[20] Second (and related), Santayana's misogynistic reduction of women to procreation (the flip side of his and his characters' chaste idealization of them) by inference leaves aesthetics and sexuality—the "surplus" constituency of everyday life—entirely to men.

In light of Santayana's extensive meditations on sex attraction in *The Sense of Beauty* and elsewhere—as well as our discussion of Santayana's erotic passions and McCormick's speculation that in 1896 Santayana may have had "an intense physical affair" with the second Earl Russell (119), Joseph Epstein's impatient response to McCormick's suggestion that Santayana may have had a "homosexual temperament" seems wrong. (For additional elaboration on Santayana's homophilic attachments in Boston and England, see Posnock 58–62, 67–70; Woodward 11–12; Holleran; and Shand-Tucci 168–250.) Insisting that "homosexual temperament" is itself an "unfortunate phrase," Epstein writes that any attention to Santayana's erotic interests is "the sheerest twaddle," for it involves a type of speculation "worthy of Barbara Walters" (18). Such chastening reminders about the intentional fallacy and the potential abuses of psychobiography may be useful. But Epstein's point, phrased as *incredulity* about same-sex attraction, not only taints homoeroticism with a type of shame Santayana never simply endorsed in his writing, but ignores in his philosophy, fiction, and poetry Santayana's profound meditation on the vagaries and psychic complexity of *every* erotic object's "turbulent" impact on the subject.

Let us therefore consider in greater detail how Santayana's philosophy informs his poetry. The importance—and the difficulty—of such consideration is suggested by a letter Santayana wrote Henry Ward Abbot on January 16, 1924, calling his "sublimated love sonnets" "an evasion of experience, on the presumption . . . that experience would be a ghastly failure" (*Letters* 208). Such "evasion" and dread of failure didn't prevent Santayana from reflecting on love and desire, but no doubt contributed to his difficulty in candidly representing this desire. Thus William G. Holzberger, editor of *The Complete Poems of George Santayana,* notes that the "quest to determine whether a real woman, loved by the poet, generated the Lady of the Sonnets may prove futile in light of an aspect of Santayana's personality ['a tendency toward homosexuality'] that became public recently and that had long been suspected" (52). Santayana partly corroborates this reading: "The lady of the sonnets, far from being the one you absurdly mention [Cory's edition doesn't enlighten us here], is a myth, a symbol: certainly she stands for Somebody, not always for the same Somebody, and generally for a hint or suggestion drawn from reality rather than for any specific passion; but the enthusiasm is speculative, not erotic" (*Letters* 208).

Such admissions relieve us of one interpretive dilemma concerning attribution and the type of authority we might invest in biography. But the problem doesn't end here. Santayana's sonnets are such an insistent account of "prolonged sexual conflict," in McCormick's words (49), that we might gently dispute Santayana's claim that

> love has never made me long unhappy, nor sexual impulse uncomfortable: on the contrary in the comparatively manageable form in which they have visited me, they have been *great fun,* because they have given me an interest in people and (by a natural extension of emotion) in things, places, and stories, such as religion, *which otherwise would have failed me altogether.* (*Letters* 208; final emphasis mine)

Engaging these remarkable admissions—particularly the subsequent claim that a "golden light of diffused erotic feeling fall[s] upon . . . the world"—I suggest that Santayana doesn't sustain simple assumptions of homosexual latency or stable object choice. Instead, he indicates a related—and perhaps conceptually more interesting—issue: an inability to desexualize aesthetics and creativity. Here I am reengaging my earlier thesis that Santayana's effort to *limit* desire generated a type of philosophical overreach in his work: The effort to absorb only partially congruent theories of desire and beauty exacerbated his loss of control over these elements.

Between 1885 and 1904, Santayana regularly contributed poetry to the *Harvard Monthly,* publishing a collection of these poems in 1894 as *Sonnets and Other Verses.* Holzberger notes that while Sonnets I—XX were written between 1882 and 1893, Sonnets XXI—L were written exclusively in 1895, the year Oscar Wilde was convicted for "gross indecency" and sentenced to two years' imprisonment with hard labor in Reading Gaol (*Complete* 720–22). In 1896, Santayana was on leave in Cambridge, England, and may have had a sexual affair with the second Earl Russell. Of course, we need accept neither McCormick's suggestion here—nor the mounting evidence that Santayana, aged twenty, had already written a number of passionate sonnets for Ward Thoron, then seventeen, and Warwick Potter, then roughly twenty-one—to observe a fascinating tension in Santayana's poetry (McCormick 49; R. Martin, *Homosexual* esp. 110–12).[21] This tension arises as an identificatory conflict between Christianity—which enhances Santayana's interest in repose, contemplation, and serenity—and Hellenism, which usually generates in his poetry greater unrest than satisfaction. In the opening sonnet, for instance—particularly its third and fourth lines—we see Santayana torn between Christian and classical precepts:

> I sought on earth a garden of delight,
> Or island altar to the Sea and Air,
> Where gentle music were accounted prayer,
> And reason, veiled, performed the happy rite.
> My sad youth worshipped at the piteous height
> Where God vouchsafed the death of man to share;
> His love made mortal sorrow light to bear,
> But his deep wounds put joy to shamèd flight.
> And though his arms, outstretched upon the tree,
> Were beautiful, and pleaded my embrace,
> My sins were loth [*sic*] to look upon his face.
> So came I down from Golgotha to thee,

Eternal Mother; let the sun and sea
Heal me, and keep me in thy dwelling-place. (*Complete* 91)

One effect of this poetic turbulence is that Christ, who incarnates in "deep wounds" the love that God "vouchsafe[s]" in line 6, begins to acquire an erotic significance for the poet. We are told that "his arms . . . / Were beautiful, and pleaded my embrace."[22] In "c[oming] down from Golgotha," the mount on which Christ was crucified,[23] we see the poet—despite his longing to recover Eden—turn not to Christ or God but, out of shame, to "Eternal Mother," perhaps an invocation of Nature gesturing to a more pagan conception of beauty and desire.[24]

In Sonnet II, this brief turn from Christianity, granting Santayana space to advance pagan and classical motifs, recurs with more insistence than confidence. The transition seems the result of a deliberate *pursuit* of temptation rather than an inadvertent effect of his shame before Christ:

Slow and reluctant was the long descent,
With many farewell pious looks behind,
And dumb misgivings where the path might wind,
And questionings of nature, as I went.
The greener branches that above me bent,
The broadening valleys, quieted my mind,
To the fair reasons of the Spring inclined
And to the Summer's tender argument.
But sometimes, as revolving night descended,
And in my childish heart the new song ended,
I lay down, full of longing, on the steep;
And, haunting still the lonely way I wended,
Into my dreams the ancient sorrow blended,
And with these holy echoes charmed my sleep. (91)

To what does the poet descend here? While his "slow and reluctant" task resembles Orpheus's "descent" into Hades to rescue Eurydice, Santayana's "dumb misgivings" are more tentative than Orpheus's, and they entail besides—"With many farewell pious looks behind"—"questionings of nature."[25] Such questioning recalls the phrase *against* nature,[26] used in Santayana's day to represent sodomy as *peccatum illud horribile, inter Christianos non nominandum*—"the sin so horrible that is must not be mentioned among Christians." Highlighting an awkward affiliation to Christian *and* classical precepts, the poet concludes: "Into my dreams the ancient sorrow blended, / And with these holy echoes charmed my sleep." These and other lines demonstrate that Santayana's conflict isn't solved: He remains "full of longing," haunted by a desire perhaps exacerbated by his earlier "descent," possibly an allusion to sodomy. Certainly, the "dumb misgivings" and "questionings of nature" persist in his sleep, "haunting still the lonely way I wended," as if the final "blend[ing]" of "longing" and "ancient sorrow" can "charm" Santayana's sleep only because longing itself is tolerable as a wish informing dreams.[27]

With this turbulent and only partial transition between Christian and classical precepts, Santayana advances a related proposition—that love, in failing to identify God as its exclusive object, pushes the lover toward narcissism or abjection. In the poetic schema of Santayana's sonnets (as in Swinburne's poetry), the object is often denounced as cruel and inaccessible. By emphasizing this outcome in Sonnet VI, Santayana argues that love engenders blindness and self-deceit—that the inspiration it generates isn't altruistic, as the lover wants to believe, but entirely self-serving. (This is so even if, as in Sonnet VII, the poet uses love to attempt to disband his identity and to forget himself. "I would I might forget that I am I" [94], he writes, but the very expression of the wish makes the result impossible and the statement a tautology.) Further, by abandoning the claim that love generates wisdom, Santayana urges us in Sonnet VI to refuse love's snares:

> Love not as do the flesh-imprisoned men
> Whose dreams are of a bitter bought caress,
> Or even of a maiden's tenderness
> Whom they love only that she loves again.
> For it is but thyself thou lovest then,
> Or what thy thoughts would glory to possess; (93)

The voice we read here arguably is the Santayana contemporary readers know best—the poet and philosopher bound upon an ascetic course, wisely rejecting the snares of passion and deliberately choosing solitude and skepticism over the folly of infatuation. Doubtless, this is the poetic and philosophical voice Santayana preferred, capturing a strength he struggled privately to maintain. Yet it's not the only voice we hear in his poetry. In Sonnet XXIV, to be sure, this disenchantment and self-questioning seem more pronounced, the poet's persona striving to expose a certain fraudulence in his belief that marriage will make him happy. However, if the drive toward solitude in these poems smothers an impulse to connect, the very urgency of desire radically undermines his anticipation of serene autonomy:

> Although I decked a chamber for my bride,
> And found a moonlit garden for the tryst
> Wherein all flowers looked happy as we kissed,
> Hath the deep heart of me been satisfied?
> The chasm 'twixt our spirits yawns as wide
> Though our lips meet, and clasp thee as I list,
> The something perfect that I love is missed,
> And my warm worship freezes into pride.
> But why—O waywardness of nature!—why
> Seek farther in the world? I had my choice,
> And we said we were happy, you and I.
> Why in the forest should I hear a cry,
> Or in the sea an unavailing voice,
> Or feel a pang to look upon the sky? (106)

The "chasm" invoked in line 5 bears heavily on my immediate argument about Santayana's work as well as my wider thesis about propinquity and asymmetry in the Victorian era. If, as the poet ruefully insists, this "chasm 'twixt our spirits yawns as wide / *Though* our lips meet, and clasp thee as I list," the yearning bid for completion that Santayana announces ("The something perfect that I love is missed") may exist not only despite physical intimacy, but crucially *because* of it. Perhaps for this reason, oblation seems to lapse in these sonnets into sterility, even boredom: "And my warm worship freezes into pride." Pride about what? Acknowledging, perhaps, that such "worship" leans on nothing more than a rigid idea of the beloved's perfection.

Resembling key moments in *The Sense of Beauty*, Santayana's frustration with oblation here seems not only to question object choice (and thus the inevitability of heterosexuality), but to clear a path for the expression of another kind of love. In Sonnet XIV, Santayana writes of wanting to protect "my nature's shell . . . / Where now, perchance, some new-born Eros flies . . ." (97). In Sonnet XXXI, too, he ruminates in detail on the affective states informing brotherhood, friendship, love, and religious worship:

> A brother's love, but that I chose thee out
> From all the world, not by the chance of birth,
> But in the risen splendour of thy worth,
> Which, like the sun, put all my stars to rout.
> A lover's love, but that it bred no doubt
> Of love returned, no heats of flood and dearth,
> But, asking nothing, found in all the earth
> The consolation of a heart devout.
> A votary's love, though with no pale and wild
> Imaginations did I stretch the might
> Of a sweet friendship and a mortal light.
> Thus in my love all loves are reconciled
> That purest be, and in my prayer the right
> Of brother, lover, friend, and eremite. (110)

Endorsing these claims, McCormick tells us that Santayana's "prolonged sexual conflict . . . dates from early in his Harvard career, when he met Ward Thoron, seventeen, and thus three years younger than he was. . . . The intimacy of the two young men produced the 'Sonnet' which Santayana later indicated was 'Ward's' and dated as 1884 or 1885" (49):

> Pale friends you wish us ever to remain:
> The thriftless seasons no new hope must bring
> To tempt our thoughts on more adventurous wing?
> Must we the pulses of a heart restrain
> Or rob the prelude of its sweet refrain,—
> That subtle music each entrancèd spring
> Hath heard anew its captive lovers sing
> And in the buzz of summer lost again?
>
> I have been guileless long: angels and you
> And beauty in my dreams together played.
> The sunshine and your smile my heaven made

Laden with some great joy that I half knew.
That holy happiness did mortal prove;
A wind blew, and dim worship flamed to love. (*Complete* 396)

"Angels and you / And beauty in my dreams together played": These words
again combine Christian and classical motifs, blending the ethereal with
the corporeal (McCormick 50). Indeed, frustration with the ethereal seems
to inspire this sonnet, the poet longing for a reciprocal passion that will
invigorate the relationship with lust: "The thriftless seasons no new hope
must bring / To tempt our thoughts on more adventurous wing?" From
this perspective, "pale friends" implies weakness and lack of resolve, perhaps even cowardice in refusing to undertake this "adventure." Considering this material, there *is* some justification for arguing that when Santayana writes, in Sonnet XXXII, "Be mine, be mine in God and in the
grave, / Since naught but chance and the insensate wave / Divides us, and
the wagging tongue of men" (*Complete* 110), he is representing social dis-
approval, or homophobia, as the sole hindrance to same-sex passion.

However, if Santayana's ambivalence about desire renders heterosexuality noninevitable, as I've argued, it also preempts the possibility of a
purely gay-affirmative reading. Put another way, that Santayana aspires to
an autonomy *releasing* him from the burden of objects makes it difficult to
see how his involvement with another man could resolve this conflict. Indeed, if we bear in mind Santayana's elaborate meditation on *internal* resistances to love and desire, it is near impossible to argue convincingly that
he is expatiating only on Victorian society's hostility toward same-sex love.
Instead, Santayana gives us a powerful account of the extremities of longing. In Sonnet XXIII, for example, he asks:

But is this love, that in my hollow breast
Gnaws like a silent poison, till I faint?
Is this the vision that the haggard saint
Fed with his vigils, till he found his rest?
Is this the hope that piloted thy quest,
Knight of the Grail, and kept thy heart from taint?
Is this the heaven, poets, that ye paint?
Oh, then, how like damnation to be blest!
This is not love: it is that worser thing—
Hunger for love, while love is yet to learn.

Thy peace is gone, my soul; thou long must yearn.
Long is thy winter's pilgrimage, till spring
And late home-coming; long ere thou return
To where the seraphs covet not, and burn. (*Complete* 106)

"This is not love: it is that worser thing— / Hunger for love . . .": Santayana returns us here to the idea that desire depletes, rather than enhances, identity—that pursuing beauty leads the lover not toward the "whole," as Diotima contends in the *Symposium* (202E) and Santayana urges in Sonnet VI ("Love but the formless and eternal Whole"; *Complete* 93), but toward his own ontological unraveling. Santayana returns us, in other words, to the idea that desire is the very element fostering a "waywardness of nature" (Sonnet XXIV; 106). Searching for love and beauty, the poet finds neither when, intimate with his beloved, he logically should find both: "The chasm 'twixt our spirits yawns as wide / Though our lips meet, and clasp thee as I list, / The something perfect that I love is missed" (106).

2. Lost Purity in Santayana's Novel

This conception of desire prevails in Santayana's *The Last Puritan*, a "memoir in the form of a novel" advancing similar arguments about sex attraction, creativity, abstention, and homoeroticism in a way that paradoxically illustrates the *unreliability* of fantasy in Santayana's philosophy, where it manifests as "chaos" (*Sense* 29), a "vortex" (29), the "irrational" (13), "vanity" (25), "inva[sion]" (23), "turbulen[ce]" (22), and "pain" (12).

Published in London in 1935 (and by Scribner's of New York in 1936), *The Last Puritan* actually derives from the mid-1890s, when Santayana was completing his first collection of love sonnets. As McCormick notes, justifying our study of this novel among these fin-de-siècle texts, "Already [in 1893–94] *The Last Puritan* was beginning to take shape in his mind" (110): While working briefly at Oxford in 1896, Santayana "no doubt [was] making notes, if only mental ones, for *The Last Puritan*" (117); apparently, he was also "at work on *The Last Puritan* in 1923" (41), many years before its publication.

Santayana's letters confirm these origins of his novel. Writing Henry Ward Abbot from Rome on January 16, 1924 (roughly eleven years before

the novel's publication), Santayana declared: "My hero (in the novel) . . .
is a *natural* Puritan, and it is not his sexual suppressions that make the
thread of the story, at least not on the surface, but his general discovery
that it is *wrong* not to live naturally, not to tell the truth about important
things" (*Letters* 207; original emphases; see also T. Armstrong 350–52).
Drawing on this statement and our previous discussion, we can now explain why Oliver Alden invokes Plato to understand his desire and friendships. The narrator tells us that Oliver, as an undergraduate at Harvard,
composes a "thesis" on Plato "in a moment of intellectual euphoria" (*Last*
526): He realizes with joy that "it was not the spirit of Plato . . . that now
descended on Oliver: it was his own spirit that inspired him" (527). The
following extract from this thesis reveals much about Oliver's aversion to
all sexual intimacy and his ascetic wish to sustain only friendships:

> A beastly consequence of Plato's confusing love with desire is
> that *he allows desire to pollute friendship.* In friendship there may
> be love, perhaps the highest and most intense love, *but there is
> not a bit of desire;* or if desire ever creeps in, it is by the intrusion
> of mere sensuality, which has nothing to do with friendship
> and is at once driven out by friendship, when friendship be-
> comes clear and strong. (527–28; my emphases)

Oliver asserts here that friendship and sexual desire are nonidentical, and
he faults Plato for "allow[ing]" the first "to pollute" the second. However,
the verb *allow* demonstrates that this pollution is a powerful propensity
and not an exception. From this perspective, Plato's error lies only in failing
to separate two phenomena that, Oliver later admits, are impossible entirely to differentiate: "In friendship . . . there is not a bit of desire; *or if
desire ever creeps in,* it is by the intrusion of mere sensuality, which has
nothing to do with friendship" (my emphasis). If in this example friendship lies uneasily between "love" and "sensuality," how can love and sexual
desire combine? Perhaps the narrator's point is that Oliver can't let these
elements coalesce, but we nonetheless see repeatedly that he also can't isolate the "superior passions" informing the "Absolute Idea of the Beautiful"
from the "swoon of pleasure" accompanying "a kind of orgasm" (528,
527). In other words, despite Plato's apparent ease in distinguishing *agape*

from *eros* and *philia,* Oliver inadvertently shows why these forms of love (oblation or religious love, physical love, and friendship, respectively) endlessly converge.

As if Oliver's argument with Plato ran a secret course throughout this novel, we later see Oliver realizing "why [he] was wrong in [his] old thesis about Plato . . . Plato was talking poetry about a love that is an inspiration, a divine madness" (695). Most of Oliver's self-appointed task—the psychological training informing this bildungsroman—is to distance himself from "divine madness," to see why "[a]t bottom it ['the thing (he) needed, . . . the thing (he) must find'] can't be any one woman or any one thing. It must be all perfections and all beauties and all happiness" (695). In this way, Oliver tries to emulate his eventual rival, Edgar Thornton, in whom "perfect manliness [was] consciously reconciled with supreme consecration" (591). In practice, however, as the passage above pointedly attests, such distance from women highlights Oliver's profoundly "sensuous" interest in male friendship and his corresponding disenchantment with marriage; he concludes that men marry "to deaden the itch of sense in them, and to [have women] stew their dinner" (588).

If the final section of Santayana's novel interests me most here, it's because it tirelessly enumerates Oliver's affective response to women, marital commitment, and several forms of love (philia, eros, and agape). When courting Edith, for instance, Oliver maintains a ridiculous image of himself as a lover: "Something precious seemed essential to a beautiful woman, something slightly mysterious and slightly absurd. [Oliver] was confirmed by this in his masculine poise, in his sense of holding the reins, and of being right in holding them. He felt himself already the husband, the master, the affectionate father. It was just a bird of this plumage that he wished to attract and to tame" (579). It is difficult to avoid comparing this passage, with its strange emphasis on "holding the reins," to Socrates' suggestion that the soul is analogous "to the composite nature of a pair of winged horses and a charioteer" (*Phaedrus* 246B).

And where is Santayana in all of this? Just before this passage, the narrator tells us—in a scene that would make the most detached reader wince—that Oliver tries clumsily to seduce Edith. The narrator's account of this scene oscillates between morbid horror at Oliver's apparent interest in Edith and a strange, paternalistic endorsement of his nervous endeavor:

He had put his arm round her and drawn her up very close with a gentle but quite irresistible strength, and now he proceeded to kiss her. It wasn't easy, or very satisfying, as little but her nose peeped out between her hat and her fur boa; but he managed it after a fashion. The action, however, was far from advancing his wooing. Not that Edith resented the liberty or attempted to deny the allegation that she liked him well enough. He tempted her, he almost overcame her in his crude capacity of awkward lover, of casual male, almost dumbly begging and asserting his primeval privilege. (574)[28]

Although this passage appears to support Oliver's perspective, more devastating sentences follow it. Three pages later, at the end of the chapter, we finally see Edith's perspective: "As a lover the boy was ridiculous, at once oldish and green. As a husband the man would be insupportable, a biting critic, a frigid tyrant, methodically making love" (577)!

After Edith successfully convinces Oliver that they don't, after all, have much in common, the narrator invokes certain ideas prevailing in Santayana's sonnets: "For some moments Oliver did not speak. He felt a great wave of desolation passing over him, an abyss separating him not only from Edith but from everybody and from everything. How could this most intelligent, most perceptive of women, fail so utterly to understand him?" (587). One might respond here that Edith has understood him only too well, but such rejoinders would overlook Oliver's *perception* that no affective tie is in fact adequate to his need ("*Desire,* indeed! Could there be a more ignorant guide?" [613]); that the best way to avoid disappointment—and the wisest way to tolerate solitude—is to follow Schopenhauer as close as is bearable and find consolation in pain. "[E]ssentially we have to live alone. In different degrees we are all put to that test," Edith advises Oliver (589), appearing to iterate Schopenhauer on stoicism and misery: "[Man] discovers adversaries everywhere, lives in continual conflict and dies with sword in hand. . . . [T]he world is Hell, and men are on the one hand the tormented souls and on the other the devils in it" (Schopenhauer, *Essays* 42, 48).

Schopenhauer's vision of life clearly is more bleakly anticommunitarian than Santayana's, but the latter's novel does insist that a person's *gender* and *sexual identity* in large measure are responsible for their suffering (for an excellent reading of this, see Posnock 61, 78–84). *The Last Puritan* is not a novel to read if one's looking for reassurance that relationships can succeed. At some point in the novel almost every relationship and friendship fails, often from the outward projection of internal antagonisms, such as the inability either to sustain psychic ideals or to protect consciousness from desire. For Santayana, it seems, people's inconsistency is responsible for a profound misunderstanding between men and women, as well as their peculiar joy in destroying what might otherwise have offered them comfort and consolation. Musing sadly on "the fleshly and criminal impulses which are in every man's heart," for example, Oliver thinks "almost enviously": "What power there is . . . in that unregenerate human nature, how it survives, how fertile it is, how all our admired refinements and heroisms hang upon it!" (677).

Oliver's despair—obtaining from his anticipating the death in combat of his close friend, Mario Van de Weyer, as well as a creeping nihilism, for which the First World War is largely responsible—characterizes the novel's tone. *The Last Puritan* perversely engages what its narrator calls "a kind of vindictive joy" (602)—a form of schadenfreude that Santayana is adept at describing. When characterizing the old Calvinists, for instance, the narrator tells us that they expressed "vengeance against everybody who was happier and better than themselves . . . They had perched at a certain height on the tree of knowledge, had stuck fast at a certain point up the greased pole of virtue. They would climb no farther; and from there they had turned and pecked ferociously at everybody below them and screeched ferociously at everybody above"; the result is an impossibly "cruel morality" (385–86). Such attention to—and suspicion of—"joy" makes *The Last Puritan* extraordinarily attentive to the wild vicissitudes of internal life: "Was there anything here [i.e., in what he was thinking] but chaos and a welter of impulses . . . ?," asks Oliver, one page later. "[A] truth composed of illusions, a home all perpetual unrest? If the spirit of life was really free and infinite, what difference could there be between freedom and madness? The whole adventure of existence became no less horrible than enticing" (387). Other statements expressing Oliver's solitude are equally declarative: "I hate pleasure. . . . When its over, there's just emptiness. . . . I remain unhappy, I remain desolate" (449). And from this bleak summary, which links Schopenhauer and Freud, we read alternately poignant and comical reflections on the apparent banality of desire: "What is love-making but a recurring decimal, always identical in form and always diminishing in value? True; yet it's a part of life, and it's no use trying to live on principles contrary to nature" (452).

The point is that Santayana cannot isolate beauty or identity from these internal conflicts; despite his many attempts, he can't sustain an image of masculine identity exempt from aspects of *Sturm und Drang.* Instead, *The Last Puritan* seems committed to expounding these weaknesses, as if in bringing them to light it might finally surpass them, eliminating the strange crises of desire that stymie even the most aloof man. In an astonishing passage aiming to depict Oliver's prehistory, for instance, the narrator describes Oliver's embryonic struggle with femininity thus:

> His little organism, long before birth, had put aside the soft and drowsy temptation to be female. It would have been so simple for the last pair of chromosomes to have doubled up like the rest, and turned out every cell in the future body complete, well-balanced, serene, and feminine. Instead, one intrepid particle decided to live alone, unmated, unsatisfied, restless, and masculine; and it imposed this unstable romantic equilibrium on every atom of the man-child's flesh, and of the man-child's sinews. To be a male means to have chosen the more arduous, though perhaps the less painful adventure, more remote from home, less deeply rooted in one soil and one morality. . . . Mysterious influences may cross and pervade the system, and send through it, as it were, a nostalgia for femininity, for that placid, motherly, comfortable fulness of life proper to the generous female.
>
> Had the unborn Oliver decided to be a girl, he—or rather she—could hardly have been blamed. Such a result would have been equally involuntary, equally normal, equally useful; yet somehow it would have been disappointing. (95)

There is no mistaking the misogynistic assumption here that nature bestows on women an easier social and biological fate than it exacts of men. As before in *The Sense of Beauty,* Santayana reduces women to procreation, granting men alone the challenge (and exhilaration) of freedom, self-responsibility, and cultural creativity. One could elaborate at length on this single aspect of his thought, yet such emphasis would ignore the precise "nostalgia for femininity" besetting boys and men such as Oliver. What interests me is the way Santayana's narrator conflates effeminacy in boys with the ego's wish to destroy itself, relinquishing the responsibility of freedom and self-autonomy in a luxurious disbanding of identity. The male chromosome, choosing already in utero to "put aside the soft and drowsy temptation to be female," aims "intrepid[ly] . . . to live alone, unmated, unsatisfied, restless, and masculine"—we note the narrator's insistence that Oliver will not find a mate, female or male. (Although Edith and Rose reject his marriage proposals, he does in fact establish comparable male friendships with Jim Darnley and Mario; and Tom Piper seems to be in love with him [see 595–604].) But while this "arduous" decision seems honorable to the narrator (and surely to Santayana), it exacts a tremendous psychic cost, producing an "unstable romantic equilibrium" precisely because "[m]ysterious influences . . . cross and pervade the system." As the narrator later tells us about Oliver, "He seemed a perfectly conventional, model young man; yet under this commonplace mask, a secret drama was always being played in his mind" (457).

The temptation to choose luxury and "effeminacy" apparently is so pressing in Oliver and other male characters in *The Last Puritan* that to overcome it requires a counterforce of formidable strength. Anticipating the passages above in which he praises Oliver's ridiculous "impersonat[ions]" of virility (565, 579), the narrator insists that a boy aged five "wants only machines expertly workable" with "stops and springs to be controlled by his little master-ego, so that the immense foreign force may seem all his own, and may carry him sky-high. . . . His instinct is masculine, perhaps a premonition of woman: yet he is not thinking of woman. Indeed, his women may refuse to satisfy his instinct for domination, because they share it: machines can be more exactly and more prodigiously obedient" (124–25).

The logic here is severe and prescriptive, but the reader would be pressed to fit this account to a male character in *The Last Puritan*. Jim Darnley may be the sole exception, but Oliver later dismisses him as dishonest and opportunistic—too eager to "seduce" Oliver's father in order to inherit his wealth. And what of those boys, like Oliver, who fail to sustain this ideal—whose "little master-ego," chafing at the expectation that he would want to keep this "immense force in reserve," prefers an "unstable romantic equilibrium"? Santayana seems loath to imagine an "effete" alternative to their distress. He wants his hero to be austere and resolute in his solitude. The logical result is that failure—which the unconscious, with its contrary "[m]ysterious influences," consistently represents in this novel—seems inseparable from effeminacy and death, from the hysterical, "vindictive joy" often puncturing Oliver's bland stoicism. As the narrator explains, echoing Oliver's thoughts: "Existence was a complication, a commitment, a pose. . . . There seemed to be two selves or two natures within him" (424–25).[29] And as Santayana bleakly iterates, in Sonnet XXV, "So in this great disaster of our birth / We can be happy, and forget our doom" (*Complete* 107).

A good deal more could be said of these passages and the novel as a whole. We could elaborate on Santayana's claims about identity, which are neither essentialist in the strict sense nor amenable to performative explanations of self-invention.[30] We could also expatiate on the novel's preoccupation with rigidly maintaining a distinction between the inside and outside—a distinction that repeatedly fails whenever desire surfaces. I'll conclude, however, by introducing a passage that serves as Oliver's sexual epiphany—a scene inaugurating the desire that thereafter leaves him perplexed, unable to do more than reproduce a virile ideal he only "half-consciously impersonat[es]" (*Last* 565). In this passage, I contend, we see why desire creates the need for "a mask for internal and incessant war" (187)—why the "hidden springs and unexpected affinities" lead the narrator to exclaim, "How many problems in one brain . . . !" (187).

Jim Darnley—alias Lord Jim—is Oliver's father's companion, a man whom others call "a bodily man, [one who] has bodily virtues" (335). Halfway through the novel, we discover that Jim has kept secret his marriage to Rose for fear that Oliver would view it as a betrayal of their intimacy. (Oliver's father, Peter, who later commits suicide [401, 413], tries also to forget that *he* is married, wanting only to take sailing trips with Jim.) To understand the passage, we must state in advance that Oliver has strong feelings for Jim. "When we are together he is happy, just as I am happy" (428), Oliver reflects, later musing on a return boat trip with Jim to the

States: "Not only was he beautifully shaved, shorn, and ruddy this morning, but radiant as a village bridegroom in an immaculate white silk shirt and skyblue knitted silk tie" (438).

But the observation pales beside this description of Oliver's response to Jim's masculine beauty: "Oliver felt like a stripling matched against a man's strength; and something feminine in him found pleasure in prolonging a resistance which he knew would be overborne. The big dog might throw him but wouldn't bite him" (439–40). Later, Jim tells Oliver, "Well, if you prefer, I could jolly well slip into your quarters, at night I mean" (440). Oliver then reflects excitedly (and erroneously): "He doesn't like women as women" (453).

As my epigraph from "Friendships" attests, Santayana endorsed this conception of homophilia. "The friendship I have in mind," he wrote, "is a sense of . . . initial harmony between two natures, a union of one whole man with another whole man, a sympathy between the centres of their being, radiating from those centres on occasion in unanimous thoughts, but not essentially needing to radiate. Trust here is inwardly grounded; likes and dislikes run together without harness, like the steeds of Aurora; . . . affection is generously independent of all tests or external bonds" (55–56). In *The Last Puritan,* however, this "affection" is *not* "generously independent of all tests or external bonds": We recall Oliver's observation that "[a] beastly consequence of Plato's confusing love with desire is that he allows desire to pollute friendship" (527). Indeed, although we see traces in this novel of Santayana's homophilic ideal, whenever *The Last Puritan* represents Oliver and Jim's intimacy it is strikingly unable to avoid meditating on this inward "pollut[ion]." The passage I have in mind concerns an earlier episode, also on a boat (Oliver's father's), during which Jim invites Oliver to swim naked with him while Peter Alden is ill inside his cabin:

> Lord Jim had called a sailor and given some orders; had touched the cabin bell; had himself unhooked a span of the deck rail, had undressed in an instant—for to Oliver's surprise he wore no underclothes—and was vigorously swinging his arms and expanding his chest, evidently in preparation for diving. What a chest, and what arms! While in his clothes he looked like any ordinary young man of medium height, only

rather broad-shouldered, stripped he resembled, if not a professional strong man, at least a middle-weight prize-fighter in tip-top condition, with a deep line down the middle of his chest and back, and every muscle showing under the tight skin. By contrast, Oliver felt very slim, rather awkward, and a trifle unsteady on his long colt-like legs. (190)

The palpable eroticism of this scene—which reminds us of Bertie's loving account of Mr. Denham in Swinburne's *Lesbia Brandon*—apparently is offset by Oliver's concern that Jim may have drowned; after Jim's dive "describ[es] a magnificent parabola" (191), he doesn't surface for "[a] long time." But this delay merely accentuates Oliver's admiration for Jim, and he later reflects carefully on their physical differences. Losing his inhibitions, Oliver dives in "and for the moment escaped observation," but the two naked men soon retire to a nearby float, staying there long enough for Oliver to observe Jim's hair and body closely (192) before they decide, four pages later, "[a]mid laughter and mock imprecations," to "scramble . . . [back] on deck" (196). "Why should he have shivered on such a sultry evening?," the narrator asks. "And the shyness of an hour before seemed a ridiculous dream, the experience of some silly baby who had ceased to exist years ago" (196).

Unlike most of Santayana's sonnets, *The Last Puritan* seems temporarily disposed to tolerating sexual desire between two men. We even glimpse a suggestion that Santayana was imagining for Jim and Oliver the type of "happiness" that Forster insisted was "imperative" for the conclusion of *Maurice* (1913–14; 1971). "I shouldn't have bothered to write otherwise," Forster tells us in that novel's terminal note, an idea to which we'll return in the next chapter. "I was determined that in fiction anyway two men should fall in love and remain in it for the ever and ever that fiction allows" (236). But we know *The Last Puritan* cannot end this way: The revelation of Jim's marriage to Rose not only precipitates in Oliver a period of acute mourning, but encourages him "half-consciously" to "impersonat[e]" the man he emulates and admires (565), culminating in the ridiculous courtship scenes with Edith we witnessed above.

Ultimately, Santayana's "memoir in the form of a novel" seems almost to enjoy overruling its protagonist's desires, protecting Oliver from the painful vulnerability entailed by wanting another. The novel tries instead to shore up Oliver's fantasies of autonomy and self-regulated pleasure. As Santayana insists in his essay "Literary Psychology," "The universe is a novel of which the ego is the hero" (395). However, Oliver's emphasis on control and self-management necessarily blunts his sensitivity to the outside world, making him suspicious, rigid, and somewhat immature. As a consequence, too, the outside world acquires a menacing potential in this novel, seemingly capable of violating, even obliterating Oliver's fragile defenses at any moment. It shouldn't surprise us that the outside would thus appear "[b]eyond the pale," as "nothing but outer darkness—an alien, heathen, unintelligible world, to be kept as remote as possible" (*Last* 112). Nor is it remarkable that the novel can't limit its conception of this "unintelligible world" to the elitism and solitude it proffers as a sublime alternative. What is surprising, though, is the unmistakable sense of pride—almost conceit—pervading work on Santayana that claims his philosophy and fiction successfully achieved this goal.

SEVEN

Betrayal and Its Consolations
in Forster's Writing

Eros is a great leveler.
—Edward Carpenter, *The Intermediate Sex* 114

Physical love means reaction, being panic in essence.
—E. M. Forster, *Maurice* 211

If we apply Forster's famous maxim in *Howards End* (1910)—"only connect the prose and the passion" (174)—to his *Life to Come and Other Stories* (1972), the latter text is bound to disappoint us. Although Forster's posthumous collection contains his most explicit accounts of love and sex between men, thus documenting a series of fantasies that Forster refused to publish in his lifetime, the majority of these stories have extremely volatile endings: "The Life to Come" and "The Other Boat" conclude in violent murder; "Arthur Snatchfold" in possible treachery and ethical compromise; "What Does It Matter? A Morality" in political banishment; and "Dr. Woolacott" in likely delirium, even psychosis. Considering these amorous failures, how seriously can we take Forster's 1928 observation that "[love] needs must come, but I am against lending it any prestige. I am all for affection and lust"? (*Commonplace* 39). Later the same year, for instance, Forster offered a perspective on Ibsen that alters our understanding of his own work: "This time sex is the villain" (42).

June Perry Levine usefully observes that "in the serious homosexual stories, one pair suffer[s] no violence, three pairs share death, and only one pair meet[s] separate fates, with the lower-class member the sole victim" (81). For Levine, however, this basic list of failures doesn't revoke Forster's "vision of eternal love" (81);[1] allegedly, it modifies Wilfred Stone's observation that "some infuriating inequality" usually stymies Forster's works (393; Stone is quoting here from *Maurice*).[2] In this chapter, I qualify Levine's and others' remarks by arguing that we can't wholly explain this dis-

197

tress by social opprobrium or cultural homophobia. Nor can we simply conclude, as Stone does, that Forster's characters are manifestations of his self-hatred (389).[3] Without ignoring biographical or material registers, I contend that the sexual turmoil prevailing in *The Life to Come* collection warrants serious interpretation on its own terms. As Stone once remarked, "If one feels that violence is alien to the gentle Forster, one needs to reread his fiction" (390).

Having carefully shown how Forster transformed John Addington Symonds's account of Greek love and Carpenter's model of homophilia,[4] critics such as Levine and Judith Scherer Herz argue that "The Life to Come" (1922) and "The Other Boat" (1913; 1957–58) conclude in redemptive passion. According to Levine, the first story's "romantically triumphant ending . . . moves beyond personal vengeance against the white man and into a vision of redemption through action" (85; see also Herz 47). If we place such "romantic triumph" alongside Levine's prior emphasis on the lovers' material and racial inequality, however, we must ask whether one man murdering the other before committing suicide is really "mov[ing] beyond personal vengeance." (Levine writes: "In 'The Other Boat,' it is a white man . . . who jumps to his death. He has just strangled his dusky lover" [85].) Recalling the turmoil of Forster's stories' bizarre conclusions renders unpersuasive such claims of "romantically triumphant ending[s]," yet critics nonetheless face a dilemma in explaining the precise stakes of these narrative resolutions. Although Forster's vision of sexual love scarcely appears redemptive—perhaps especially in stories that magnify the heroism of love and passion—critics who stress only his lovers' material and structural inequality ignore an important point: Forsterian passion partly derives from what is irregular and incompatible about his characters' material conditions (*Commonplace* 34). While this suggests that *inequality* can cause desire, the resulting fantasies push Forster's narratives beyond such explanations as discrepancies of wealth and racial oppression. Forster's stress on material incompatibility illustrates why in *Maurice* (1913–14; 1971) love and friendship coexist between Maurice Hall and Clive Durham without an overwhelming sexual frisson: Since for Forster "there can be no passion . . . [b]etween two tamed creatures" (*Commonplace* 50), the prerequisite for Forsterian desire is a form of "wildness" that not only destabilizes "tameness" but implicitly shatters it (50; see also Bersani, *Freudian* 38; Silverman, *Male* 200).

To assess how these material and psychic tensions inform Forster's statements on nationalism, colonialism, and comradeship, we must revisit a passage from the manuscript of *Maurice* that Forster excised from the novel's final draft; Levine cites this passage quite early in her article, later to ignore it: "During passion, [Alec Scudder] would have died for his friend, but there had been some time since to reflect that a gentleman lay in his power" (77). Scudder's reflection anticipates *Maurice*'s scene of bungled blackmail, which Forster downplayed at the novel's end to confirm Maurice and Scudder's lasting union. As he acknowledged in the novel's terminal note, "A happy ending was imperative. I shouldn't have bothered to write otherwise. I was determined that in fiction anyway two men should fall in love and remain in it for the ever and ever that fiction allows" (*Maurice* 236).

By reminding us why Scudder "would [*not*] have died for his friend," Forster's excised passage disproves existing readings of the novel's benign comradeship and "imperative" sexual happiness. Indeed, Scudder's reflection asks us to consider not only class privilege and cultural homophobia, but the peculiar eroticism of betrayal that unexpectedly recurs in Forster's writing.[5] Scudder's conflict of interest suggests not that Forster was lying when he made these claims about the novel's "happy ending," but that unconscious elements of his fictional relationships eluded his narrative control. These elements underpin and often ruin—through ambivalence and retribution—the fraternal idealism prevailing in many of Forster's novels, at least two of which he wrote concomitantly with the *Life to Come* stories (Lane, *Ruling* 149–50). And since Forster repeatedly, if inadvertently, shows that the "fraternal" and "sexual" are nonidentical—perhaps mutually exclusive—categories, we need to assess this sexual difficulty in his *Life to Come and Other Stories*. In this way, we can gauge the conceptual distance between the politics at which Forster aimed and the desire that his stories actually foster. We can also question whether Forster's narratives confirm his professed belief that "two people pulling each other into salvation is the only theme I find worthwhile" (*Commonplace* 55). *The Life to Come* reveals characters torn in directions that not only preclude salvation but fundamentally question its possibility.

Considering Forster's repeated failure to attain his political ideals and his stories' astonishing turbulence at the level of sexual demand, I want first to examine several political essays that Forster reprinted in *Two Cheers for Democracy* (1951). Written in the late 1930s, these essays engage profound questions about racial prejudice, anti-Semitism, and the possibility of sustaining "tolerance" in times of extreme social hatred. "Racial Exercise" and "Jew-Consciousness," both published in 1939, also display inadvertent turns in Forster's argument that betray unconscious elements of racism precisely when Forster attempts to diminish it in others. These essays highlight the limits of Forster's liberalism by detailing his and our unexamined phobia and malice; they also profoundly affect how we read Forster's fiction.[6]

Perhaps the most striking example of Forster's analysis of racial intolerance is his brief essay "The Menace to Freedom" (1935), in which he claims we can't reduce tyranny and prejudice to external forces or material conditions. The essay concedes that prejudice combines with external and internal forms of violence in a cycle we can't eradicate by political will or material change:

> The menace to freedom is usually conceived in terms of political or social interference—Communism, Fascism, Grundyism, bureaucratic encroachment, censorship, conscription, and so forth. And it is usually personified as a tyrant who has escaped from a bottomless pit, his proper home, and is stalking the earth by some mysterious dispensation, in order to persecute God's elect, the electorate. But this is too lively a view of our present troubles, and too shallow a one. We must peer deeper if we want to understand them, deep into the abyss of our own characters. For politics are based on human nature; even a tyrant is a man, and our freedom is really menaced today because a million years ago Man was born in chains. (*Two* 9)

Juxtaposing this passage with *Howards End*'s maxim—"[o]nly connect the prose and the passion" (174)—indicates why Forster's idea of "connection" can rarely succeed; internal impediments often ruin the hope of complete interpersonal understanding and cross-cultural harmony.

Since psychic conflict surpasses external violence, in "The Menace to Freedom," Forster argues that we can't reason violence into harmony: "That unfortunate event ['Man's origins'] lies too far back for retrospective legislation; no declarations of independence touch it; no League of Nations can abolish it" (9). Additionally, Forster's stress on internal conflict and hostility implies that both exist irrespective of external harmony. Like Ernest Jones's claims in his essays on war and sublimation, Forster suggests that the pressure to achieve "peace" may precipitate fresh outbreaks of military conflict, for "peace" compels every subject—regardless of its conscious desire—to renounce whatever aspects of unconscious conflict a war can represent or abreact (see E. Jones, "War and Individual" and "War and Sublimation"; Lane, "Thoughts" 6–7). To put this contentiously, subjects may receive announcements of peace with conscious relief, but the announcements themselves may not bring lasting happiness or unconscious satisfaction; often the reverse, as Jones, Freud, and even Forster radically imply (see Freud, "Thoughts," "Why?," and *Civilization*).

As in "Jew-Consciousness" and "Racial Exercise," Forster's argument in "Menace" makes several unforeseen turns concerning the unconscious. Toward the end of this paper, for instance, when Forster considers that love can assuage an excess of fear and hatred, he modifies the unconscious's previous intractable quality in a hope that it will eventually disappear:

> It is difficult not to get mushy as soon as one mentions love, but it is a tendency that must be reckoned with, and it takes as many forms as fear. The desire to devote oneself to another person or persons seems to be as innate as the desire for personal liberty. If the two desires could combine, the menace to freedom from within, the fundamental menace, might disappear, and the political evils now filling all the foreground of our lives would be deprived of the poison which nourishes them. They will not wilt in our time, we can hope for no immediate relief. But it is a good thing, once in a way, to speculate on the remoter future. (11)

"If the two desires could combine": Forster's political philosophy hinges on this outcome. Like Forster, we might want to "speculate on the remoter future," but "The Menace to Freedom" insists that "we can hope for no immediate relief." This conclusion recalls the narrator's famous pronouncement in *A Passage to India* (1924) that Aziz and Fielding must defer a full and open friendship: "No, not yet . . . not there" (316). However, the narrator of *Passage* renders *external* the impediments disrupting two otherwise willing friends: "[T]he horses didn't want it . . . ; the earth didn't

want it . . . ; the temples, the tank, the jail, the palace, the birds, the car-
rion, the Guest House . . . : they didn't want it" (316). This projection of
hostility differs radically from Forster's understanding in "The Menace to
Freedom" that if devotion to another is "innate," so is the "poison which
nourishes" the possibility of a different outcome: "We must peer deeper
. . . deep into the abyss of our own characters. . . . [E]ven a tyrant is a
man." Put differently, "The Menace to Freedom" carefully probes whether
characters such as Aziz and Fielding really want to be friends; it examines
their desire for and ambivalence about intimacy. And so "Menace" prevents us and Forster from defining hostility solely as a cultural or political
phenomenon; the essay asks us instead to consider the subtle pleasure a
person may experience in his or her hostility to another, a pleasure that
complicates—but doesn't entirely jeopardize—Forster's characters' professions of desire and companionship.

How does this difficulty affect Forster's vision of "connection"? How,
moreover, does it alter materialist readings of his work, in which prejudice
is historically specific and Forster's "Menace" a clear indictment of mid-
1930s European fascism? If Forster could not envisage "personal liberty"
combining with "devotion to another person or persons" in 1935, should
we interpret his fiction's precarious combination of these factors as a wider
indictment of society, or was he also grappling with the possibility that if
"even a tyrant is a man," so can a man (or woman) easily become tyran-
nical?

It doesn't seem adequate to claim that Forster's understanding of political hostility wholly explains the turbulence of his short stories, most of
which were written "not to express myself but to excite myself . . . [and]
they were the wrong channel for my pen" (Diary, April 8, 1922). As Forster
remarked of such materialist emphasis, "this is too lively a view of our
present troubles, and too shallow a one" (*Two* 9). Beyond improbability,
such attribution ignores moments in Forster's writing when outcomes
differ extensively from what Forster and his narrators anticipate or intend:
interpersonal connection. For instance, if the materialist reading is correct
and Forster struggled to represent human tragedy and incompatibility in
his fiction, why did he also cling (despite all odds) to a vision of connection
and not take the more radical path of such contemporaries as Auden, Isher-
wood, and Spender? At the same time, if Forster struggled to portray cross-

class and cross-cultural harmony in his fiction in liberal ways, as other critics maintain, why does this harmony repeatedly fail if the fiction was not written for the general public? Neither approach seems able to address unconscious pressures and difficulties in Forster's work and life. I think Forster was torn between the hope of achieving "connection" and the realization, undoubtedly magnified by historical circumstances, that in describing "the menace to freedom from within, the fundamental menace," he had alighted on a more extensive ontological difficulty about human relations.

Careful readings of Forster's essays and fiction demonstrate Forster's vacillation between explaining and downplaying this ontological problem. My aim is not to dehistoricize Forster's dilemma, but to demonstrate what history and the unconscious partially taught him about human relations. That Forster professed a fierce belief in "connection" lies in interesting tension with his realization that altruism and misanthropy are coeval propensities. This chapter therefore interprets the conceptual and substantive pressure informing Forster's belief that "connection" must avoid the possibility—and attraction—of human treachery.

Forster's admission in "Menace" that he (and we) often "get mushy" when discussing love is invaluable at least in capturing his short stories' apparent discrepancy between their objective of reconciliation and their violent displays of passion and cruelty. Far from transcending or displacing these informing tensions, as Levine, Herz, Norman Page, and Jeffrey Meyers contend,[7] these eruptions of violence seem structurally inevitable; they detail the pressure Forster exerted to remove temporarily these eruptions from psychic and textual vision.

Without a psychoanalytic understanding of unconscious fantasy and the death drive, we gain only a limited understanding of Forster's characters in his posthumously published fiction. The following statement by Meyers is a useful example: "These men overcome racial, social and sexual prejudices, and achieve temporary liberation by sodomizing an obliging and acquiescent farmer, milkman, Indian, soldier, sailor, policeman and even an animated statue, before lapsing back into their 'apparatus of decay' or plunging to a violent death" (108). Meyers's claim isn't in any simple sense untrue, but it fails to grasp the connection between Forster's characters' "temporary liberation" in sex and their resultant "laps[e] back into their 'apparatus of decay.'" And so while the last phrase is Forster's, Meyers ignores Forster's link between sexual liberation and sexual decay; he implies that the relations among sex, liberation, and death are contingent for Forster. For psychoanalysis, however—and at moments for Forster too—these factors are mutually involved, if not causal.

Forster explains this involvement in "The Menace to Freedom" by acknowledging that our obstacles to union, peace, and happiness are chiefly internal. He claims these obstacles have a "primaeval" (9) influence on our character. Considering our "evol[ution] among taboos," Forster writes, cultures from ancient Greece to the present are deceptively civilized; they are "abortive morally because of those primaeval chains. The ghosts of chains, the chains of ghosts, but they are strong enough, literally stronger than death, generation after generation hands them on" (9–10).

"The Life to Come" and "The Other Boat" point up this implicit equation in Forster's writing between the unconscious and a state of savagery. Based on this argument, which I advance elsewhere (*Ruling* 172–73), I suggest that Forster's hopes of interracial union and intimacy stumble on elements of distrust and the assumption that every fault line in Western consciousness is "racially" significant. These assumptions add to Kipling's notorious complaints about "the White Man's burden" (1899): By eluding Forster's attempts at symbolization, this "burden" surfaces in all his discussions of self-strangeness and weakness. Hence Forster's belief in "Menace" that *if* "the two desires [for personal liberty and devotion for another] could combine, . . . the political evils now filling all the foreground of our lives would be deprived of the[ir] . . . poison" (11). He formulates an implicit connection between error and "race" here that turns failure into a self-fulfilling prophecy: If the unconscious—our "error"—is primitive and racial, according to Forster, history traps us in a psychic deadlock and blind repetition of prejudice and pleasure, for race and the unconscious persist.

Considering this repetition, we must return to the terminal note of *Maurice*. We've seen Forster insist that "two men should fall in love and remain in it for the ever and ever that fiction allows" (236). Later in the same paragraph he explains that such a "happy . . . imperative" responds to the British government's delay in decriminalizing male homosexuality by waiting to render as law the recommendations of the 1957 Wolfenden Report.[8] This admission fosters speculation about the implications of publishing the novel without legal protection: "If [the novel] ended unhappily, with a lad dangling from a noose or with a suicide pact, all would be well, for there is no pornography or seduction of minors" (236).[9]

While true in principle, this statement displays an odd disregard for his characters' plight—a notable emphasis on self-interest. If we suspend disbelief here and treat Forster's characters with the degree of reality with which he apparently invests them, we'd note a concern for self-survival that is not only complacently at odds with "a lad dangling from a noose" or with "a suicide pact," but substantively in conflict with Forster's now infamous claim in "What I Believe" that friendship outweighs the value of national loyalty: "I hate the idea of causes, and if I had to choose between betraying my country and betraying my friend, I hope I should have the guts to betray my country" (Two 68; see also Herz 120).

Since Forster wrote Maurice without the legal support of Wolfenden, Maurice and Alec Scudder inevitably become "criminals" (this is Forster's word and it confirms his stress on realism). Forster explains: "[T]he lovers get away unpunished and consequently recommend crime. Mr. Borenius is too incompetent to catch them, and the only penalty society exacts is an exile they gladly embrace" (236). Forster's posthumously published story "Arthur Snatchfold," written in 1928, many years after Forster had completed Maurice, describes a similar scenario, but though this story's eponymous hero has the same initials as Alec Scudder, he suffers a quite different fate.

Arthur Snatchfold is as bisexual in temperament as Alec Scudder; both protagonists hail from working-class backgrounds and are symbolically associated with nature (Alec is a gamekeeper, Arthur a milkman). Resembling Maurice as an upper-middle-class stockbroker (although he's bisexual in temperament while Maurice is not), Sir Richard Conway is bored and sexually restless one weekend while staying with Trevor Donaldson and his family. Conway has several daughters (106, 112) and is said to enjoy "an intrigue with a cultivated woman, which was gradually ripening" (108). Nonetheless, the narrator informs us, "The female sex was all very well and he was addicted to it, but [he] permitted himself an occasional deviation . . . [for h]e believed in pleasure; he had a free mind and an active body" (101).

Arthur and Conway have sex in a wood on Donaldson's grounds

(Maurice and Scudder only eloped to the boathouse together): "Thus, exactly thus, should the smaller pleasures of life be approached. They understood one another with a precision impossible for lovers" (103). However, Conway hears much later from Donaldson that the police caught Arthur and were able to convict him because of "abundant evidence of a medical character" (110). Since the police and Donaldson can't trace Conway, Conway is secretly relieved he can resume his career and former life: "He was safe, safe, he could go forward with his career as planned. But waves of shame came over him. . . . For a moment he considered giving himself up and standing his trial, however what possible good would that do?" (112).

Critics have responded in various ways to "Arthur Snatchfold." Meyers endorses the narrator's meditation that the affair was "trivial and crude" (104; Meyers 110), while George Steiner sees this and other Forster stories as the attempted reparation or sublimation of elements of "self-condemnation . . . , as if [Forster] could never shake off the secrecies, the aura of shame that a prudish, vengeful society had sought to instill in him" (165). Forster's interest in working-class men resembles that of his friend, novelist J. R. Ackerley, who acknowledged that "guilt in sex obliged me to work it off on my social inferiors" (qtd. in Salter 25). And all these statements endorse Stephen Adams's objection to *Maurice:* "[Forster's] nostalgia for a simpler way of life . . . invests the physicality of the working man with redemptive power" (127; see also Malek). Yet despite capturing the magnificent untruth of Forster's claims in "What I Believe," Adams's reading of "Arthur Snatchfold" ignores various elements of treachery and sexual disloyalty.

Forster represents Conway as pleasure seeking and eager to have sex with Arthur, to be sure, but he also represents Conway's passing impulse to give himself up to the police. Such an act, Conway realizes, "would ruin himself and his daughters, . . . would *delight* his enemies, and . . . *would not save his saviour*" (112; my emphases). This last phrase clearly represents Arthur as a redemptive figure whose social position and lack of power are woefully at variance with his imaginary stature. Compare this fantasy to Adams's characterization of Conway as "a smug, well-to-do business man [of] . . . selfish cunning . . . [who] schemes to encounter the milkman in a nearby wood . . . [and who is so] well practised in the art, he is able to bluff his way out of danger" (122). This condemnation of Conway asks us to consider what Adams would deem an appropriate prelude to cross-class sexual intimacy. Adams writes: "[Conway's] selfish cunning contrasts with the naïve courage that the milkman had shown by stubbornly protecting Conway's identity and by refusing to show any shame in court" (122). He's referring to an exchange between Conway and Donaldson during which Conway realizes that Arthur consistently misled the police:

> "Tell me," [Conway] said, taking his enemy's [Donaldson's] arm and conducting him to the door, "this old man in the mackintosh [Conway, viewed from behind by the police]— how was it the fellow you caught [Arthur] never put you on his track?"
> "He tried to."
> "Oh, did he?"
> "Yes indeed, and he was all the more anxious to do so, because we made it clear that he would be let off if he helped us to make the major arrest. But all he could say was what we knew already—that it was someone from the hotel."
> "Oh, he said that, did he? From the hotel."
> "Said it again and again. Scarcely said anything else, indeed almost went into a sort of fit." (111)

Taking sole responsibility for his and Conway's shared pleasure renders Arthur entirely honorable, but how would we read this scene if Arthur were to cede the correct information to the police? (The blackmail scene in *Maurice,* quoted below, suggests we must at least consider this outcome.) An obvious rejoinder might be that Forster's narrator, by emphasizing Arthur's loyalty, intends us not to read the story in this way. However, Adams implies that Conway's "selfish cunning" makes him legally responsible for his and Arthur's alleged "crime"; that Conway fails to substitute himself for Arthur renders him, in Adams's eyes, a traitor. Stone too insists that Conway "*was* up to sacrificing his friend and lover in order to avoid his own 'ruin'" (396–97; original emphasis), and he claims that "Forster was intent on making Conway morally disgusting" (397). Yet Conway *does* contemplate giving himself up for "his saviour" (112; see also Page 47). That he finally decides not to stems from his understanding that such action would have no political impact, and perhaps from his realization that Arthur was in fact caught when returning to the scene with someone else (see below). Forster's narrator also goes to great lengths to convince us not only of Arthur's willing participation, and thus shared responsibility, but that *pleasure in this legal context renders justice impossible:* "It was a cruel stupid world" (109).

How does Arthur's emphatic loyalty square with Forster's briefly de-idealizing account of Maurice and Scudder's relationship in *Maurice's* blackmail scene? If we recall the excised passage from this novel, in which Alec Scudder realizes that "a gentleman lay in his power," Arthur's insistent derailing of the police investigation suggests an overemphasis—"a sort of fit"—that aims to smother and render obsolete *Scudder's* passing impulse to betray his friend for financial gain in *Maurice.* At these moments, we see Forster struggling to fit several economic *and* psychic conflicts into his vision of love-without-betrayal. We risk downplaying—even trivializing—the fraught, political significance of these conflicts when claiming that Forster was being ironic at these moments, or that he "seeks to disrupt the economy of the normal" (Martin and Piggford 4). Forster's dilemma arises from his awareness that comparable "disruptions" arise in "queer" scenarios too—that love and sex between men aren't exempt from the power struggles informing all sexual and social relations.

In light of these psychic disruptions, let's consider other aspects of "Arthur Snatchfold" that Adams seems to miss. Although a policeman sees Arthur and Conway having sex and Conway escapes undetected while Arthur's distinctive yellow shirt makes him easy to trace, the policeman, horrified and disbelieving of what he's witnessed, waits before arresting Arthur, who is arrested when he later *returns* to the scene with someone else. The narrator corroborates: "Alas, alas, there could be no doubt about it. [Conway] felt deeply distressed, and rather guilty. The young man must have decided *after* their successful encounter to use the wood as a rendezvous. It was a cruel stupid world, and he was countenancing it more than he should. Wretched, wretched . . . betrayed by the shirt he was so proud of . . ." (109; my emphasis; final ellipsis in text).

Considering this narrative turn, Conway's behavior may be unheroic, but it's neither treacherous nor "smug." To avow his role in what we imagine is the critical—but what is actually in the story, and for legal purposes, a quite different—sexual scene would offer Conway no guarantee that the police would release Arthur, or, indeed, that Conway would not face similar or greater public humiliation. Adams and Stone are surely correct to allude to the wider ramifications of class and self-interest, however, and this rebounds on Forster's statement about *Maurice*'s "happy . . . imperative" and the terminal note's concluding remarks:

> We [Edward Carpenter and Forster] had not realized that what the public really loathes in homosexuality is not the thing itself but having to think about it. . . . Unfortunately [homosexuality] can only be legalized by Parliament, and Members of Parliament are obliged to think or to appear to think. Consequently the Wolfenden recommendations will be indefinitely rejected, police prosecutions will continue and Clive on the bench will continue to sentence Alec in the dock. Maurice may get off. (240–41)

The note is dated "September 1960" (the British government partly decriminalized male homosexuality in 1967). Following this prophecy's realization in "Arthur Snatchfold," we could reframe the scenario as "Donaldson on the bench will continue to sentence Arthur in the dock. Conway may get off." Adams and Stone almost imply that *Conway* on the bench would try Arthur in the dock. While this suggestion is substantively incorrect, I think there are still grounds for suspecting elements of treachery in Forster's work; let me explain why.

Forster's terminal note implies that "Arthur Snatchfold" is the realistic conclusion to *Maurice*'s sexual idealism. All the same, we can't elide Forster's concern in this novel to show Alec Scudder blackmailing Maurice in the British Museum: "You've had your fun and you've got to pay up" (207). Whatever fantasy this conveys about the implied treachery or opportunism of working-class lovers, we can ignore neither the historical frequency of this scenario[10] nor, more pressing for us here, the attempt's internal impact on Forster's accounts of love and friendship. (The narrator tells us, "[Scudder] looked handsome as he threatened—including the pupils of his eyes, which were evil" [207].) The attempted blackmail belies Forster's subsequent wish to ignore internal obstacles to homosexual love; hence the "happy . . . imperative" conflicts with the general tenor of the terminal note.

To illustrate this point, we should consider how Maurice and Scudder resolve their different class interests. In the following passage, which I quote at length to capture its emphasis on treachery, Scudder tries to blackmail Maurice and to rebuke him in front of his former teacher:

"... I've a serious charge to bring against this gentleman."

"Yes, awfully serious," remarked Maurice, and rested his hand on Alec's shoulder, so that the fingers touched the back of the neck, doing this merely because he wished to do it, not for another reason.

Mr. Ducie did not take notice. An unsuspicious man, he assumed some uncouth joke.... Alec jerked away and muttered, "That's all right.... I won't trouble you now."

"Where are you going with your serious charge?" said Maurice, suddenly formidable.

"Couldn't say." He looked back, his colouring stood out against the heroes [in the British Museum], perfect but bloodless, who had never known bewilderment or infamy. "Don't you worry—I'll never harm you now, you've too much pluck."

"Pluck be damned," said Maurice, with a plunge into anger.

"It'll all go no further—" He struck his own mouth. "I don't know what came over me, Mr. Hall; *I* don't want to harm you, I never did."

"You blackmailed me."

"No, sir, no ..."

"You did."

"Maurice, listen, I only ..."

"Maurice am I?"

"You called me Alec.... I'm as good as you."

"I don't find you are!" There was a pause; before the storm; then he burst out: "By God, if you'd split on me to Mr. Ducie, I'd have broken you. It might have cost me hundreds, but I've got them, and the police always back my sort against yours. You don't know. We'd have got you into quod, for blackmail, after which—I'd have blown out my brains."

"Killed yourself? Death?"

"I should have known by that time that I loved you. Too late ... everything's always too late." The rows of old statues tottered, and he heard himself add, "I don't mean anything, but come outside, we can't talk here." .... On the portico Maurice stopped and said bitterly, "I forgot. Your brother?"

"He's down at father's—doesn't know a word—I was but threatening—"

"—for blackmail."

"Could you but understand . . ." He pulled out Maurice's note [suggesting that they meet at the British Museum]. "Take it if you like. . . . I don't want it . . . never did. . . . I suppose this is the end."

Assuredly it wasn't that. Unable to part yet ignorant of what could next come, they strode raging through the last glimmering of the sordid day; night, ever one in her quality, came finally, and Maurice recovered his self-control and could look at the new material that passion had gained for him. In a deserted square, against railings that encircled some trees, they came to a halt, and he began to discuss their crisis. (208–10; original emphasis and ellipses)

What *has* "passion . . . gained" for Maurice? As he and Scudder try to resolve their dispute, Scudder conveys that he was angry because Maurice failed to meet him at the boathouse at Penge, and implied his social inferiority at an earlier cricket match. The novel suggests that Scudder wants largely to confront Maurice about these humiliating moments ("Maurice, listen, I only . . ."; "Could you but understand . . . [?]").

This public confrontation is meant to help Maurice recognize his love for Scudder. But in arguing that Scudder's approach is simply misguided—that his anger and passion make him desperate rather than opportunistic—we'd miss important observations on the two men's "infuriating inequality" (210). Consider Scudder's admission: "I'll never harm you *now,* you've too much pluck," which suggests he *did* originally intend harm, however fleeting or misdirected; somehow "pluck" is enough of a deterrent. Consider too the partial contradiction of this statement: "I don't know what came over me, Mr. Hall; *I* don't want to harm you, I never did" (original emphasis), as well as the narrator's remark that Scudder "struck his own mouth." Certainly, other characters in Forster's novel *are* capable of harming Maurice Hall, but Scudder's admission seems instead to point up the satisfaction he'd derive from harming a man he *also* loves and esteems. As the narrator partly corroborates, "They know too little about each other—and too much. Hence fear. Hence cruelty" (211).

We can't resolve these tensions by invoking competing economic and social interests; these factors explain only one side of the story. The other side is best grasped by Forster's admission that the public's homosexual "loath[ing]" concerns less the act of sex than the *thought* of it—its perception by others and their ensuing fascination or disgust. Again, it would be tempting to accept Forster's word here and believe the problem is merely someone else's: the Other's, the homophobe's, et cetera. But as Steiner and Meyers observe, Forster represents sex as a profound hermeneutic and psychic difficulty.[11] Steiner claims Forster "had found no sensuous enactment adequate to his vision of sex. Gesture recedes in a cloying mist" (166). He continues: "In the light of an intensely spiritualized yet nervous and partly embittered homosexuality, a number of Forster's most famous dicta—it is better to betray one's country than a friend, 'only connect'—take on a more restricted, shriller ambiance" (169).

Partly corroborating Steiner's reading, Forster avowed to Siegfried Sassoon on October 11, 1920: "Nothing is more obdurate to artistic treatment than the carnal" (*Selected* 316). This statement sheds light on the subtle enigmas of "Arthur Snatchfold" and "The Menace to Freedom," yet it also powerfully conflicts with Forster's haunting rhetorical question in "The Beauty of Life" (1911): "Why don't we trust ourselves more and the conventions less?" (*Albergo* 173). The conceptual tension here between his declaration to Sassoon and his earlier rhetorical question informs Forster's story "What Does It Matter? A Morality," written in the 1930s, which also appears in the *Life to Come* collection. This story brings to the fore a number of volatile issues concerning sexual and social harmony. As we'll see, Forster's hope of integrating sexual conflict into fraternal happiness proves elusive and impossible, though in the process the story raises a fascinating question about sublimation's relation to utopia, and desire's violent impact on Forster's liberalism.

"What Does It Matter?" is a Forsterian "morality" insofar as it rejects conventional religious and political assumptions that homosexuality is a crime, pathology, or evil; the story imagines with humor and intelligence a political scenario in which homosexuality—and, indeed, all sexual relations—bears no stigma. Dr. Bonifaz Schpiltz is president of Pottibakia, an imaginary republic that resembles the Balkans or Eastern Europe (the narrator tells us that Pottibakia's "capital city could easily be mistaken for Bucharest or Warsaw, and often was" [130]). President Schpiltz is married, but he's sexually involved with Mme. Sonia Rodoconduco. Count Waghaghren (Pottibakia "retained her aristocracy" [130]) is the president's rival, and seeks to depose him, being "perhaps . . . a royalist, perhaps a traitor or patriot. . . . It is hopeless to inquire" (130–31). The count aims to exploit dissension between the president and his wife by creating a political scandal over the president's mistress; the plot backfires because Mme. Schpiltz is too urbane or indifferent to mind her husband's sexual affair: "She watched the lovers without animosity and without amusement, occasionally showing concern when they struck one another but not caring to intervene" (131).

Rueful of his failure, the count later believes the president winked at a handsome gendarme on duty at his quarters, so the count contrives to arrange a homosexual scandal. The narrator carefully emphasizes, however, that all of this is "based on a misconception. It is true that the President had winked as he drove away, but only because some dust blew in his eye. His thoughts were with the ladies at their *goûter*, not of gendarmes at all" (132). Thus the planned scandal does not easily materialize, for the president is basically oblivious to all his male guards, who now wink at him regularly on the count's orders. The narrator corroborates: "We do not see what we do not seek" (132).

Mme. Schpiltz detects this unusual mannerism in the guards and points it out to her husband. But while the "roguish smile" on many of the guards' faces (133) secretly amuses the president, he is sexually uninterested: "I am a man, aha, no danger in that quarter for *me!*" (133; original emphasis). When strolling alone in a public park, however, the president "suddenly encountered an incredibly good-looking mounted gendarme, and before he could stop himself had winked back" (133).

Unable to find privacy in the park, the two men reluctantly forgo having sex there. Soon after, the president resumes his affair with Mme. Rodoconduco. On his way to one tryst with her, however, he again meets Mirko Bolnovitch, the gendarme from the park, who we are told is "a model of Pottibakian manhood" (135). Captivated by the man's beauty, the president agrees that Mirko should join him in Mme. Rodoconduco's bathing room, knowing his mistress isn't there:

> The science of the barrackroom, the passions of the stables, the
> primitive instincts of the peasantry, the accident of the parallel
> bars [the bathing room is also a gymnasium, and Mirko a gym-

nast] and Dr. Schpiltz's quaint physique—all combined into
something quite out of the way, and as it did so the door
opened and Mme. Rodoconduco came into room, followed by
the Bessarabian Minister.

"We have here . . ." she was saying.

Neither of them heard her.

"We have here . . . we have . . ." (137)

The news breaks and a political scandal ensues, but Mme. Rodoconduco "remain[s] in a sort of frenzied equilibrium" (138). The count turns
out to have been instrumental in getting the president and Mirko together,
but when the president asks Mirko of his role in the scandal, the latter
remains "half a-dreaming, drowsy with delight. He had carried out the
instructions of his superior officer, gratified a nice old gentleman and had
a lovely time himself" (139). By partially rewriting Forster's axiom of national betrayal, Mirko (like Scudder) considers betraying his *lover* for his
country before alighting on an altogether different ruse. He asks: "What
does it matter?" (139). This rhetorical question provides Forster's narrator
with an apparent solution to such comparable dilemmas in *Maurice* and
"Arthur Snatchfold," yet other questions of loyalty and sexual intimacy
remain. Stone's remarks about Forster's conception of love are useful to
recall: "Forster's favorite medium for connection is *love*. No word in his
work gets higher marks—unless it is 'art'—than love. Democracy gets only
two cheers, but 'Love the Beloved Republic' gets three" (392).

Perhaps conscious of his self-contradiction (Mirko's betrayal clearly
undermines the trust informing Forster's vision of love), Forster emphasizes that Mirko's behavior is ingenuous because it is commensurate with
his background's sexual honesty: "I am a peasant, and we peasants never
think a little fun matters. You [Mme. Rodoconduco] and His Excellency
and the head of the police know better, but we peasants have a proverb:
'Poking doesn't count'" (140). When it turns out that the count secretly
installed a microphone and taped the encounter, Mirko pushes aside that
he was acting on orders by insisting: "Still, what does it matter? It was fun.
Oh, some things matter, of course, the crops, and the vintage matters very
much, and our glorious Army, Navy and Air Force, and fighting for our
friends, and baiting the Jews, but isn't that all?" (141). Following Mirko's
rather frivolous question, we are quietly invited to forget that he betrayed

his lover and precipitated a national scandal. Such an outcome puts in context Sir Richard Conway's comparable question in "Arthur Snatch-fold": "What can it matter to anyone else if you and I don't mind?" (104). Alongside the "fun" of serving "our glorious Army, Navy and Air Force . . . and baiting the Jews," the pleasures of sex in "What Does It Matter?" apparently compensate for the president's lost respect and subsequent humiliation. As the narrator quickly reminds us, however, the president is *not* entirely humiliated, because everyone soon learns to laugh at their folly and prejudice.

This reading partially downplays the story's valuable comedy; there is clearly a dimension in which the affair does not—and should not—matter, a dimension too in which we appreciate the tale is fiction. With considerable humor, Forster wants us to imagine legal and social indifference to homosexuality, and he seems to draw our attention to other factors, such as anti-Semitism and ethnic warfare, in order to parody them. But when does social indifference to homosexuality become a generic indifference to *sexuality?* Later pronouncements about the president's renewed career also ring hollow after Forster's concern to avoid the "humiliation" of publishing *Maurice.* Such concern appeared to outweigh the relative literary victory of his and others' defense of D. H. Lawrence's *Lady Chatterley's Lover* in 1960 and Forster's serving, with T. S. Eliot, as literary representatives on the 1958 Select Committee on Obscene Publications (some of whose recommendations were formalized by an Act of Parliament one year later; see Page 7–20). For important political reasons, then, Forster spent a good deal of time urging us to believe that such issues *do* matter to the public—that sexual honesty carries a price, however heinous or unjustified, *and that this price exceeds political ignorance and superficial bigotry.* Forster implies that the price inheres in every sexual dynamic as an inevitable accompaniment to what is tempting and seductive about physical intimacy.

This price overrides distinctions between realpolitik and Forster's virtual world, making it impossible for us to suspend disbelief and imagine a country with no sexual intolerance. For how do we square Mirko's betrayal with the narrator's quiet insistence that Pottibakia hasn't yet learned its lesson? (Apparently, Mirko's repeated question "was soon to rend the nation asunder" [142].) In attempting to avert a scandal and because "[i]t's essential to a stable society" (143), the president and his lovers issue a public statement:

> Fellow Citizens! Since all of you are interested in the private lives of the great, we desire to inform you that we have all three of us had carnal intercourse with the President of the Republic, and are hoping to repeat it.
>
> > Charlotte Schpiltz (housewife)
> > Sonia Rodoconduco (artiste)
> > Mirko Bolnovitch (gendarme)
> > (143)

This is obviously amusing, but what is the precise referent for "it" in the statement "It's essential to a stable society"? Considering the ensuing scandal, which culminates in Pottibakia's (somewhat fantastic) diplomatic isolation from the rest of the world for failing to condemn the president's sexual infraction (144), we might conclude that by "it" the president is referring to sexual honesty. Yet we alight on a paradox here: Although such "honesty" eventually works in Pottibakia (the president's declaration of his various passions is so remarkable that no one wishes to succeed him), the Pottibakians' initial response is as predictable as the outside world's: "The Chamber of Deputies kept a stiffer upper lip, and there were cries of 'Flogging's too good!' and faint counter-cries of 'Flog me!' No one dared to take office, owing to the President's unmeasured eulogy of the police, and he continued to govern as dictator until the outbreak of the civil war" (144).

The paradox is that sexual honesty initially doesn't appear as "the only way" or, indeed, as "essential to a stable society" (143). On the contrary, the narrator admits that Mirko's disclosure "was soon to rend the nation asunder" (142). Were the count neither envious of the president's power nor sexually voyeuristic, Forster's narrative developments might lead us to consider that *hypocrisy* is in fact "essential to a stable society." This reading would confirm Freud's argument in *Civilization and Its Discontents* (1930) and elsewhere that society is contingent on its subjects' partial renunciation of sexual pleasure. Freud writes: "It is impossible to overlook the extent to which civilization is built up upon a renunciation of instinct, how much it presupposes precisely the non-satisfaction . . . of powerful instincts" (97). Maurice Hall faces this quandary when he ruminates on his "lustful . . . yearn[ing]" for Alec Scudder: "He called it lustful, a word easily uttered, and opposed to it his work, his family, his friends, his position in society. In that coalition must surely be included his will. *For if the will can overleap class, civilization as we have made it will go to pieces.* But his body would not be convinced. Chance had mated it too perfectly" (191; my emphasis).

When read alongside plot complications in "What Does It Matter?," this passage from *Maurice* highlights Forster's profound difficulty in accepting the strength and radicalism of "will" (sexual and otherwise): "Will" generates sexual pleasure and intellectual excitement; it also destroys civilization and "rend[s] . . . nation[s] asunder" by combining communal distress with ontological unpleasure. An entry in Forster's *Commonplace Book* confirms this dilemma: "Until we are tamed we cannot be civilised, and as soon as we are civilised we revolt from civilisation" (50).[12] In this respect, it shouldn't surprise us that a character in Forster's story "The Point of It" realizes, when ruminating on his life's "elusive joy," "It was part of the jest that he should . . . oscillate eternally between disgust and desire" (*Collected* 162).

Given this paradox about sexual instability, "What Does It Matter?" produces a conceptual twist of which I don't think Forster is fully aware. Certainly, his narrator gives us a shrewd reading of the effects of sexual intolerance. After the president makes his speech, for instance, various government officials empathize so entirely (or fear such widespread reprisals) that they confess all of their sexual indiscretions in an abreactive—or preemptive—gesture: "The scenes at the conclusion of [the president's] speech were indescribable, particularly in the Senate, where old men got up and poured out their confessions for hours, and could not be stopped" (144). These scenes portray a joyous unburdening and freedom that render Pottibakia threatening—and attractive—to its neighbors. As the narrator archly remarks, Pottibakia is soon isolated from the rest of the world because its "surrounding powers . . . hold—and perhaps rightly—that the country has become so infectious that if it were annexed it would merely get larger" (144).

Despite these claims of sexual freedom, we can't overlook that the president "continued to govern [after his speech] as dictator until the outbreak of the civil war" (144). This suggests, quite interestingly, that the

Pottibakians may have been sexually content while lacking political democracy. The next sentence corroborates: "He [the president] is now dictator again" (144). This suggests that although "the civil war," which the narrator barely mentions, fails as a *social* revolution, it apparently succeeds in making the Pottibakians happy. In this respect, Forster's story details a persistent—perhaps even prerequisite—gap between sexual happiness and social harmony that reminds us of his related dilemmas in "The Menace to Freedom."

Although Forster tries to integrate sexuality into social life without prejudice, hypocrisy, or phobia, his story concludes with a bizarre picture of Pottibakians as socially content under a politically "benign" dictatorship and sexually happy because their desire is no longer repressed *or* expressed. Allegedly, their desire is so perspicuous, it is annulled of all social difficulty—which is to say, it is magnificently "sublimated" so that no one in Pottibakia seems to want or have sex anymore. This outcome is obviously contentious, but it's interesting for detailing both a blind spot in Forster's liberalism and a failure in the scope of related sexual utopias that try to excise pleasure—or jouissance, which is beyond pleasure—from society in the interests of class harmony and cultural equanimity. These sexual utopias reproduce the dictates of the ego as the agent most hostile to difference and desire (Bersani, *Freudian* 93, Dean, "Eve" 126; for a different account, see B. Martin).

Following Forster's stubborn ambivalence about sexual desire at moments of its apparent emancipation, the outcome of "What Does It Matter?" isn't surprising. Forster's vision of sexual liberation may appear emancipatory, but it is actually closer to what the philosopher Herbert Marcuse called "repressive tolerance" (see *One-Dimensional* 76–78). Indeed, to the disbelief and perhaps horror of many Forster scholars, we could read Mirko's titular question as a complacent remark about Forster's difficult relation to unconscious prejudice and hostility. I base this polemical claim on extraordinary moments in Forster's autobiographical writing, such as "Kanaya" (c. 1922), in which he describes how he had violent sex with an Indian boy: "[The] sexual intercourse . . . was . . . mixed with the desire to inflict pain. It didn't hurt him to speak of, but it was bad for me, and new in me, my temperament not being that way. . . . I wasn't trying to punish him—I knew his silly little soul was incurable. I just felt he was a slave, without rights, and I a despot whom no one could call to account" (324).

In this fragment, Forster expresses genuine surprise at finding power over another sexually arousing. By invoking this incident, I don't wish simply to indict Forster for racial intolerance. Forster admitted, for instance, that the incident didn't recur. Such reproachful readings are anyway of limited value: By distancing Forster's readers from ambivalent involvement, they leave the text "tarnished" and the critic magically exonerated of racism. Rather, "Kanaya" displays a conceptual and substantive gap between Forster's vision of "acceptable" and "unacceptable" politics. Against Forster's implicit claim that Mirko's question, "What does it matter?," gives us a lasting sexual morality, I therefore propose that Forster's "gap" is actually a stronger ethical guide. It reminds us that prejudice can surface in the most unexpected and politically embarrassing moments; that issues concerning psychic enjoyment don't sit easily with mandates for sexual and political tolerance.

To support these claims about Forster and the unconscious, let me cite the penultimate paragraph of "What Does It Matter?," which captures several conceptual shifts in Forster's argument; it also reminds us of the history of East Germany and the splitting of Berlin:

> He [President Schpiltz] is now dictator again, but since all the states, led by Bessarabia, have broken off diplomatic relations it is extremely difficult to get Pottibakian news. Visas are refused, and the international express traverses the territory behind frosted glass. Now and then a postcard of the Bolnovitch Monument falls out of an aeroplane, but unlike most patriotic people the Pottibakians appear to be self-contained. They till the earth and have become artistic, and are said to have developed a fine literature *which deals very little with sex.* This is puzzling, as is the indissolubility of marriage—a measure for which the Church has vainly striven elsewhere. Gratified by her triumph, she is now heart and soul with the nation, and the Archimandrite of Praz has reinterpreted certain passages of scripture, or has pronounced them corrupt. Much here is obscure, links in the argument have been denied to us, nor, since

we cannot have access to the novels of Alekko, can we trace *the steps by which natural impulses were converted into national assets.* There seem, however, to have been three stages: first the Pottibakians were ashamed of doing what they liked, then they were aggressive over it, and now they do as they like. There I must leave them. (144; my emphases)

The story's final paragraph details the fate of the hypocritical count, who is not banished (as most initially desire) but left to repeat what he's done. In this way, the Pottibakians amuse themselves by recalling their repressive history: "On public holidays his private cabinet (now his cell) is thrown open, and is visited by an endless queue of smiling Pottibakians, who try to imagine the old days when that sort of thing mattered, and emerge laughing" (145).

In our present times of increasing sexual repression, it is tempting to accept Forster's morality and identify with the Pottibakians, as if we could smile and laugh with similar relief on the demise of homophobia and related forms of sexual antipathy. Yet much is questionable about Forster's myth of sexual integration. The Pottibakians have become such adept, compliant citizens that all or most of their "natural impulses [have been] converted into national assets" (144). In other words—and Forster's narrator puts this in illiberal terms—they have rescinded not only privacy but sexual pleasure by offering up both as "national assets." The narrator also suggests that Pottibakia's "self-contain[ment]" derives from its uninterest in empires; by corollary, Forster usefully critiques the myth that empires were built on sublimated desire, arguing instead that sexual conflict and distress informed nineteenth-century imperialism. But what of Pottibakian literature? Forster's narrator suggests that creativity requires a measure of sexual discomfort (see also "Literature as Compensation," *Commonplace* 47–48). If Pottibakian literature "deals very little with sex," it is ostensibly because the Pottibakians' interpersonal and intrapsychic conflicts have dissolved and they have displaced their passion outward or upward in a magnificent display of esprit de corps.

Given this story's unfortunate aim to foreclose on desire at the precise moment of its apparent social integration, where would we locate pleasure or jouissance in this text? The answer, I think, lies in the final paragraph, when the Pottibakians laugh at the count for his folly. In the suggestion that they line up "smiling" to see the count "and emerge laughing," Forster's narrator tries to temper the magnitude of this jouissance by making it part of a ritual; but why, otherwise, would the Pottibakians concern themselves with this act? And why would it focus on one object that can serve as their mirth's *cause*? The point is surely that this annual ritual functions—like related forms of commemoration on public holidays—to remind us of what cannot pass, of what we haven't processed, and of what we cannot, or must not, forget.

Thus far, I have written only on betrayal's recurrence in Forster's stories—whether in interpersonal, group, or social forms—and on this phenomenon's inconsistency with Forster's belief in "connection." I now want briefly to consider how betrayal *consoles*. My reading of "What Does It Matter?" gives some indication of what is consoling for Forster (and, allegedly, for the Pottibakians) in such fantasies of controlled sexual pleasure, malice, and mirth. To engage this phenomenon more fully, however, we must resist reading Forster's stories at a level of conscious understanding and narrative enunciation; the satisfaction of betrayal emerges when we address an economy of unconscious pleasure of which Forster was aware but never entirely at ease.

As I earlier described, this economy surfaces in "The Menace to Freedom"; it also returns in a brief fragment that Forster wrote in 1939 on "Jew-Consciousness," which I discuss more fully elsewhere (*Psychoanalysis* 16–18). In this second fragment, Forster speaks of Londoners "sniggering" at Jewish misfortune when discussing pogroms. He admits that this response is shocking, but argues that we must acknowledge our "enjoy[ment] in others'] misfortunes" (*Two* 13). What makes these essays more distressing, though, is Forster's understanding of mass hatred and genocide only as instances of personal "silliness"—that is, as setbacks to an otherwise ongoing interpersonal dynamic (14). According to Forster, we can "stop . . . [prejudice only by] . . . cool reasonableness" and periodic acts of bravery (14). Such phenomena as mass hatred and genocide spiral beyond Forster's comprehension, leaving him without understanding, and his reader amazed—given the overwhelming historical evidence to the contrary—at Forster's naive faith in humanity's concern for individual well-being.

Despite Forster's effort to mitigate these political crises, we see their interpersonal constituents recur in such stories as "Arthur Snatchfold,"

"The Life to Come," and "The Other Boat," allegories about a wider default in human relations. This explains why Adams and Stone find Sir Richard Conway reprehensible in "Arthur Snatchfold," but to read the story only in this way is to misrecognize a drama about sexual interest and non-reciprocity that Forster inadvertently—but I think invaluably—represents in his writing. Stories such as "The Obelisk" (1939) seem to integrate homosexuality into their protagonists' consciousness, but these stories nonetheless reveal other fault lines in human contact and understanding. Despite the humor of "The Obelisk," for instance, in which two sailors separately seduce a bored husband and wife (Ernest and Hilda), who later infer each other's passions through instructive lapses of circumspection, the story ultimately is a cynical account of marriage and heterosexual monogamy. Such readings may be useful in themselves, but related issues about the terms, endurance, or fiction of this marriage never surface in Forster's text. In his concern to emphasize that Hilda's sexual pleasure with her sailor equals Ernest's pleasure with his, Forster elides the type of complicated scenario that David Leavitt, for one, finely elaborated in *The Lost Language of Cranes* (1986) concerning a gay son and his closeted gay father.

"The Obelisk" downplays provocative suggestions of marital betrayal: Its stress on the "consolation" of sexual pleasure offsets any difficulty about infidelity, or sexual interest in anyone other than one's spouse. This is not the case in "Arthur Snatchfold," "The Life to Come," and "The Other Boat," whose respective accounts of sexuality precipitate a difficulty about human relationships that Forster can't resolve by praising sexual pleasure. These stories bind enjoyment to attempts at *divesting* others of pleasure and, in the case of these last two stories, of life. They represent an economy of pleasure whose source and intensity is contingent on what one subject can *deny* another. This dynamic jeopardizes Forster's already awkward project of combining sexual enjoyment with interpersonal harmony. We've seen, for instance, that sexual enjoyment derives for Forster largely from the material *dis*harmony of two (or more) lovers. Those aspects of enjoyment's "theft" that we glimpse from the count in "What Does It Matter?," the concluding remarks of "Arthur Snatchfold," and the blackmail scene in *Maurice* add to this disharmony, rendering such "theft" almost a precondition for sexual happiness. This takes Forster perilously close to the scenes of racism and anti-Semitism that he denounced in *Two Cheers for Democracy;* it also turns his idea of betraying one's country for a friend into an unlikely, even impossible, proposition. Given these psychic determinants, it's no wonder Forster's accounts of friendship support an improbable idealism. His stories buckle under the pressure, making his characters more complex and selfish than I think he initially envisaged.

By emphasizing the difficult undercurrents of "Arthur Snatchfold" and "What Does It Matter?," I have tried to show why unconscious hostility and aversion inform Forster's narratives of sexual desire. I have no doubt that Forster understood Freudian conceptions of the unconscious. In "What I Believe" and "Anonymity: An Enquiry" (1925), for instance, he addressed the consequences of a split and shattered conception of the mind;[13] in "Inspiration" (1912), he argued too that in the act of writing, "a queer catastrophe happens inside [the writer]. The mind, as it were, turns turtle, sometimes with rapidity, and a hidden part of it comes to the top and controls the pen" (*Albergo* 118–19).

Unlike Levine's, Adams's, Meyers's, and Herz's readings of *The Life to Come* collection, I have tried to explore the ramifications of this "queer catastrophe" for homosexual desire. In the final paragraphs of "What Does It Matter?," for instance, Forster redefines community, sublimation, and the relations between art and sexuality, only to conclude that sexual desire has no manifest role to play in his social utopias. Put this way, Forster demonstrates that certain utopias by definition foreclose on sexual desire to advance their vision of social equanimity. This conclusion may be politically unfortunate and conceptually embarrassing, particularly when we recall Forster's desire to represent homosexuality in his "morality" without prejudice, but the story culminates in neither a "vision of eternal love" nor a trope of "romantic . . . triumph." If anything, and despite its contrary conception, this and other stories attribute a nonredemptive dimension to human sexuality and social interaction, in which desire gleefully emerges from the manifest failure of ordinary connection (see Bersani and Dutoit 1–9). This disparity between Forster's political and fictional ideals is surely the "queerest" aspect of his work and thought, where "queer" is a dimension of unconscious fantasy rather than a politics or performance of the ego. We would do well to remember this disparity when next we feel inclined to rhapsodize on Forster's art of connection. Indeed, Forster gives us ample warning of this dilemma in his *Commonplace Book:* "In a world where so little is known, how shouldn't we, how should we happen to be friends?" (46).

Afterword

The Homosexual in the Text

[T]o characterize sex is immediately to make it deviant; until its
disclosure, the enigma will therefore be subject
only to snares, equivocations.
—Roland Barthes, *S/Z* 107

1. Opacity and Sexuality

Can we "queer" our relationship to history without also defining the past
as a record of contemporary conflicts? The question presents us quickly
with another: Although queer theory aims to advance a notion of sexual
dissent, can the search for sexual resemblance in former times and other
cultures avoid being inherently normalizing?

Historian and cultural critic Lisa Duggan partly addresses these questions in her essay "Making It Perfectly Queer" (1992). She states that
"[q]ueer theories do their ghetto-busting work by placing the production
and circulation of sexualities at the core of Western cultures, defining the
emergence of the homosexual/heterosexual dyad as an issue that *no* cultural
theory can afford to ignore" (23). Duggan adds that critics such as Eve
Kosofsky Sedgwick are "now performing the work of legitimation and de-
ghettoization" (24). But while Duggan intends this last statement as "a
criticism . . . of the conditions of reception for [Sedgwick's] work," the
tension surrounding "legitimation and de-ghettoization" extends beyond
Sedgwick's arguments, raising concerns about affirmation that haunt queer
literary studies.

How does queer theory combine "legitimation and de-ghettoization"
with its emphasis on dissidence? And does the "legitimation" of queer sexuality end up confirming untenable, even naive assumptions about homosexuality's historical consistency? Such questions could quickly expand into
impossibly large debates about the relationship between sexuality and
meaning, asking too whether we can suspend our present sexual conditions
to recover those of other times. My focus here will be more modest, inter-

224

preting a specific tendency in recent studies of sexuality and narrative—
that of treating opacity in literary and cultural material as a sign of an
author's or protagonist's homosexual secret. Sounding a caution against
this tendency, I contend that literature and history can't be read merely as
coded records of sexual desires. And while many queer theorists support
this argument, even claiming that it is self-evident, I suggest there are hidden, affirming strategies of queer critique that push for resemblance and
similarity—even "gay hagiography"—while insisting on conflict, rigor,
and historical differences (Halperin, *Saint Foucault* 6, 31).[1] In light of my
contention, and contrary to various claims that "disclosure" *resolves* the
"snares [and] equivocations" of sexual enigmas, I'll argue that literature
and history by definition frustrate the desire for sexual clarity—indeed,
that narrative represents the *failure*—and not merely the construction—
of sexual meaning.[2]

We've become quite adept at downplaying the extent to which lesbian and gay studies and queer theory rely on enigmatic narrative moments for their conceptual vigor and political strength. In the process,
we're reaching a point where no such moment can appear without "queer"
significance. In a wide range of critical studies, as we'll see, textual opacity
has become exclusively a queer issue, and every instance of narrative
difficulty a site of undeclared sexual deviance. Within these terms, the critic's task is simply to render visible what was formerly veiled or partially
silenced. Numerous critics would dispute this claim, arguing that queer
theory has surpassed these naive expectations, but the idea of sexual fixed-
ness and transparency nonetheless remains the hidden expectation of
much of this work. How indeed could this idea fail to motivate when such
theory requires that queer issues be *recognized textually* before they can be
put to cultural and political use?

Let me voice an immediate caveat: I am not unaware of the prepon-
derance of secrets, particularly in late-nineteenth-century fiction; nor am
I blind to this fiction's recurrent interest in sexual difficulty and difference.
My concern is that we ask what model of subjectivity and desire our assumptions advance, particularly when representing homosexuality as a secret or not-yet-palpable enigma. I want also to consider the conceptual
blind spots and historical idealism accompanying demands that we retrieve
and "out" people in the past in order to render them our own. Proposing

that we rethink the assumed relations among textual opacity, the closet, and lesbian and gay studies/queer theory, this afterword examines the "work" of conjecture and interpretation, asking whether such relations finally assist or hinder our search for homosexual meaning in literature.[3]

One of the ironies of eclipsing historical difference is that we easily can forget that these interpretive problems aren't new. When various characters in Oscar Wilde's *The Portrait of Mr. W. H.* (1889) try to appropriate Shakespeare's *Sonnets* for a homoerotic reading, for instance, they soon realize the futility of the task. The radically different meaning of homosexual desire in Britain only three centuries earlier defeats their search for exact resemblance or even partial correspondence. Toward the end of this novella, the character Erskine remarks to the narrator:

> "My dear fellow, . . . you believe in Cyril Graham's theory, you believe in Willie Hughes, you know that the Sonnets are addressed to an actor, but for some reason or other you won't acknowledge it."
>
> "I wish I could believe it," I rejoined. "I would give anything to be able to do so. But I can't. It is a sort of moonbeam theory, very lovely, very fascinating, but intangible. When one thinks that one has got hold of it, it escapes one. No: Shakespeare's heart is still to us 'a closet never pierc'd with crystal eyes,' as he calls it in one of the sonnets. We shall never know the true secret of the passion of his life." (251)

There's no epistemology of this "closet"; nor can the narrator or Wilde provide one (see Dowling, "Imposture" 27; Danson 979–81).[4] Ignoring Wilde's characters' interpretive difficulties, however, and thus the crux of this novella, Claude Summers has called *Mr. W. H.* "a foiled coming-out story" (35). In this way, he erases Wilde's concerns by redefining same-sex desire as a history of certainty and positive identification. Summers's chapter on Wilde begins: "Modern gay fiction in English begins with Oscar Wilde" (29). Although it's unclear whether this assertion refers to Wilde's writing or to the figure he came to represent, Summers's statement expresses a desire for origins and stability that the history of homosexuality poignantly cannot sustain (see Weeks, "Discourse"). When Summers therefore writes of "the novelette's emphasis on the continuity of homosexual feeling from the past to the present" (38), he announces the theoretical premise of his own book but misrepresents the dream of homosexual similarity that Wilde ultimately dispelled.

These issues recur in lesbian, gay, and queer criticism when critics use contemporary sexual terms to eclipse the medical, legal, and sexual nomenclature of former times. The irony is that queer theory increasingly *assists*—rather than avoiding—this eclipse of historical difference by substituting terms such as "deviance" and "perversion" for the dissimilarities, aporias, and discontinuities they only partially represent.[5] Addressing the normalizing effects of this substitution, David Halperin usefully cautions: "The moment has come to suspend our projects of identification (or disavowal, as the case may be) long enough to devise an interpretation of erotic experiences in classical antiquity that foregrounds the historical and cultural specificity of those experiences" (*One* 2). Because it seems to impede comparisons with contemporary sexual movements, to depoliticize our relation to the past, and to jeopardize our self-evident relation to the present, "suspend[ing] ... identification" is crucially at issue here. As Halperin observes, our difficulty lies in engaging "sexual practices [that] ... do not merely confirm current cherished assumptions about 'us' or legitimate some of 'our' favorite practices" (2; see also J. Scott 776).

What is the result of *failing* to heed Halperin's advice—a failure that arguably is widespread despite (or perhaps because of) the recent efflorescence of "queer" approaches to literature and culture? When critics such as Summers credit nebulous elements of sexuality in other times and other cultures with the apparent definitional stability of modern times and Western terms, at least two things happen: historical differences immediately get lost and sexual meaning buckles under a demand for interpretive certainty. Instead of usefully pointing up similarity *and* discontinuity, identification in this guise serves only to bolster homosexual positivism. The wager of this afterword is that claims about sexual truth and historical consistency are not only misleading, but fundamentally disabling—ironically when the psychic and political constituents of identification require careful elaboration. Highlighting the ramifications of these assumptions in literary criticism, this afterword tries to explain why certain assumptions in lesbian and gay studies are paradoxically limiting our understanding of sexual difference and diversity.

Although it is now possible in most "developed" countries to advance an identity more or less commensurate with sexual preference, the meaning we attribute to these identities is nonetheless contested from without and within—that is, by politics and the unconscious. The "character" of sexuality ensures that this contest will remain. While we can of course justify more equitable policies and more extensive social representation of lesbians and gay men, the unconscious reminds us that the desires, acts, and relationships we invoke as elements of our *sexual identity* are never quite the same as the contradictory psychic impulses of which this identity consists. Indeed, the discrepancy between psychic drives and sexuality's social representation undermines the idea that there is sexual *consistency* across historical periods, cultures, and—perhaps above all—between different subjects.

Elaborating on this discrepancy, this afterword tries to explain why aspects of sexual identity remain ineffable. Given the problems that inconsistency poses for lesbian and gay studies (as examples will soon demonstrate), it doesn't seem useful to dismiss what is psychically doubtful about sexual identity because one must otherwise engage with psychoanalytic theory.[6] My claims here are conceptual and specific, based on the premise that interpreting the gap between the ego's precarious control of psychic drives and our culture's symbolizations of sexual desire yields important— if rarely predictable—political results. Although I revisit this point at the end of this afterword, I'd add that claims that the *ego* is often defeated by sexual drives, due to the antagonism prevailing between conscious and unconscious systems, don't exclude objections that we need more prominent and varied symbolizations of same-sex desire. We clearly can advance the second argument while still presupposing the first (see Bersani, *Freudian* 36–38; Silverman, *Male* 3–8).[7]

If sexuality has an intractable conflict with identity and an unreliable relation to meaning, *every* identity must struggle with *internal constraints*. It isn't difficult to see why this emphasis is a neglected aspect of lesbian and gay studies—why emphasizing the "performative" basis of gender and sexual identity seems more productive and satisfying. Indeed, arguing that subjectivity has internal limits that necessarily *curtail* performativity strikes critics and activists as "degaying"; it also precludes political and interpretive certainty. While aspects of this concern may be justified, emphasizing the alternative not only represses homosexuality's historical inconsistency and its internal—or psychic—unreliability, but aligns queer theory and lesbian and gay studies with the ego, which desexualizes both fields because the ego is the enemy—rather than the ally—of desire (Dean, "Eve" 126; see also section 1 of the introduction to this book, "Foucault and Psychoanalysis"). For all these reasons it seems vital to revisit these debates, if only to register the gap separating homosexual desire from our current political and identitarian concerns.

By acknowledging the complex drives and resistances that determine "sexual identity"—a phrase we might henceforth consider an oxymoron—we'd approach the idea of "successful" identity with skepticism; an identity built on the vicissitudes of sexual drives is notoriously unstable and subject to change. How, then, does this variance between the public and the private influence desire's elaboration in writing—specifically, the formidable and sometimes treacherous task of representing homosexuality in literature?

Homosexuality's *meaning* is overdetermined and improperly assumed. To many, this statement will seem self-evident, but the argument that public and psychic fields constantly reformulate homosexual meaning is further-reaching than it may at first seem. This statement doesn't deny the oppressive consequences arising from homogenous ("degaying") assumptions about sexual meaning, or the relentless endeavor by social and cultural forces to give homosexuality one description—as contrary, wayward, or unnatural. Instead, that no signifier can fully capture the diversity of homosexual desire asks lesbian and gay studies to stress this desire's *disparity* with our culture's insistence that it holds one, perverse meaning.

This proposition gets complicated when we consider homosexuality's cultural and historical discontinuities, which many examples of literary criticism ignore. They presume a homology among homosexuality's elaborate variables, whose resemblance to present terms we can't rule out—if only for the sake of expediency—but whose connection to modern times seems unreliable and impossible to assume. By ignoring these nonidentical problems, critical interpretation often tries to produce certainty from what's ineffable by uncovering a text's or author's sexual difficulty. Yet as David Savran notes, these attempts to "translate" texts by writers whom we now consider homosexual produces "an unintelligible clutter whose only coherence becomes the ill-concealed homosexuality of its author" (115). David Van Leer takes us even further, arguing that such moves also simplify and falsely homogenize homosexuality: "Not only does the notion of the mysterious effectively silence homosexuality, but the implication that all silences are homosexual reduces homosexual meaning to a single thing, a 'We Know What That Means'" (592).

We face still greater problems: Even critics reminding us of these conceptual difficulties reproduce them in their work. On the opening page of *The Wilde Century: Effeminacy, Oscar Wilde, and the Queer Moment*, for instance, Alan Sinfield cites Savran's precaution, only to conclude his book by noting the resemblance between Wilde's "sexual dissidence" and our own: "'Oscar Wilde' has been a shorthand notation for one way of apprehending and living *our* sexual and emotional potential" (176; my emphasis). Given Sinfield's emphasis on "dissident potential" in twentieth-century Britain from Wilde to us (203), how indeed could he avoid attributing this political force to one progenitor?

2. The Challenge of the Past

Historical accounts of Wilde's 1895 trials demonstrate that Wilde's influence as a symbol of national decline and cultural "depravity" far exceeded his passions. Wilde himself avowed in *De Profundis* (1905), "I was a man who stood in symbolic relations to the art and culture of my age. . . . I awoke the imagination of my century so that it created myth and legend around me" (77). The difficulty arises in the type of "shorthand notation" that Sinfield wants Wilde to represent, for it begs as many conceptual and political questions as it allows. To name only one, when Sinfield invokes Wilde as a founder of Britain's "queer moment," he radically downplays Wilde's marriage and complex relation to fatherhood. Unlike many related studies of Wilde, Sinfield does cite Wilde's eldest son's vow to avoid his father's taint of effeminacy; remarkably, Ed Cohen and Neil Bartlett ultimately ignore Wilde's family, despite their concern to study growing political and conceptual distinctions between heterosexual and homosexual men. After usefully asking, "How are we to read, for instance, 'Oscar Wilde'?" (31), Bartlett responds two pages later: "We often assume (rightly) that homosexuality must be hidden, that it has to be found. But what are we free to search for if the author's sexuality is common knowledge—as, in this case, it is—if the 'homosexual meaning' of his texts is well-known, obvious, taken for granted, unconcealed?" (33).

Bartlett's question oddly implies that once we have grasped "the" secret of an author's sexual preference, there's nothing left to discover, little interpretive work to do, almost nothing left to interest us. Clearly, Bartlett's fascinating book *Who Was That Man?* consistently demonstrates otherwise, but his question uncannily reminds me of the conservative lament that gay and lesbian liberation has radically demystified homosexuality in literature, to the point that we can only read (and write) grotesque accounts of desublimated desire.

Bartlett's question still troubles me. Is homosexuality in Wilde's *writing* truly "well-known, obvious, taken for granted, unconcealed"? While Christopher Craft has noted many homosexual nuances and possible subtexts in *The Importance of Being Earnest* (1895), Sinfield prefaces his own book on Wilde by stating: "Yet the place of homosexuality in his plays is by no means plain. Many commentators assume that queerness, like murder, *will out,* so there must be a gay scenario lurking somewhere in the depths of *The Importance of Being Earnest.* But it doesn't really work. It might be nice to think of Algernon and Jack as a gay couple, but most of their dialogue is bickering about property and women; or of Bunburying as cruising for rough trade, but it is an upper-class young heiress that we see Algernon visiting, and they want to marry" (vi).

Sinfield's book usefully begins by stating the difficulty of *reading* effeminacy and male homosexuality in twentieth-century Britain. His next paragraph partially retracts this admission, rendering doubtful the aim and principle of his opening words: "All that said, Wilde's principal male characters do look and sound like the mid-twentieth-century stereotype of the queer man (I am using 'queer' to evoke this historical figure)" (vi). This statement asks us to consider more carefully how men and women adopt, parody, or discard stereotype, and then how mid-twentieth-century "queer men" patterned their symbols and understanding of desire after Wilde's trials and imprisonment. Clearly, it's much harder to claim in Wilde a prospective understanding of how the "queer" moment would unfold in twentieth-century Britain.

Having cited Cyril Wilde's difficulties after his father's public humiliation, imprisonment, and premature death, Sinfield—like Bartlett—assumes that Wilde's fatherhood requires no comment and has no bearing on Britain's queer history beyond its difficulty for Wilde's sons.[8] In its omissions, then, Sinfield's "dissident" reading is quite conservative; Sinfield would likely find Marjorie Garber's reading of Wilde's sexual politics and "bisexuality" as politically inefficacious, if not "degaying" and neutralizing (see Garber 20, 28, 486). Sinfield also ignores that Wilde himself complicated his family and sexual politics by writing his sons into his "gay" canon: He gave the interlocutors in *The Decay of Lying* (1891 [1885–90]) the names Cyril and Vivian. The ease with which Sinfield downplays Wilde's marriage and fatherhood indicates what is at stake in such acts of reclamation: While Sinfield, Cohen, and Bartlett pattern Wilde as the precursor to (and "father" of) contemporary British gay men, Garber's attention to Wilde's historical figure alights on a quite "dissident" aspect of Wilde's character concerning the institution of marriage (see also Craft 139).

Why does lesbian and gay studies consistently "forget" Wilde's marriage and fatherhood? We could highlight many similar blind spots or deliberate reformulations, such as Terry Castle's desire to name Greta Garbo "as a lesbian" immediately after acknowledging that Garbo sometimes had sex with men (15). Castle is quite honest in stating her reasons: "While Garbo sometimes makes love to men, she would rather make love to women. . . . [so] I think it is more *meaningful* to refer to her as a lesbian" (15; original emphasis). This may be so, but what does it mean that Garbo nonetheless continued to sleep with men? Should we gloss this point as a political embarrassment, or infer that we understand Garbo's passion better than she did? Certainly, we must consider other factors here—not least, the unremitting pressure on lesbians and gay men to turn straight, and on women in general to sleep with men—but are these adequate explanations or simply expedient answers to Garbo's sexual complexity? What is perhaps most unsettling here is Castle's insistence that her certainty can dispel what, because it relies on inference, can only be doubtful: "She *would rather* make love to women." Even accepting that Garbo's sleeping with men could have been part of a conscious strategy to complicate assumptions about her sexual identity, how would this "queer" strategy blend with Castle's political insistence that we call Garbo a lesbian? In our concern to explain the terms and vicissitudes of other people's sexuality (much less our own), don't we almost imply that Garbo's bisexuality was simply bad faith—that with sufficient courage and opportunity, she'd have desired only women?

These examples show that declarations about an author's, character's, or actor's homosexuality often result from a type of interpretation that minimizes uncertainty and ambiguity, while political assertion in turn seems to answer all sexual and textual enigmas. Although this pattern of connotation and declaration dominated lesbian and gay criticism in the 1970s and early 1980s, its influence still prevails when sexual indeterminacy and narrative inconclusion seem either inadequate or unfortunate to critics intent on disclosing the "full" meaning of an author's desires. To these critics, textual opacity signifies a partial homosexual revelation provocatively veiled by *preterition*—that is, by proscription, indictment, and taboo. This claim forgets that modernism addressed a similar—if less obviously sexual—*resistance to meaning,* and that psychoanalysis was central to modernism's interest in the limits and difficulties of human ontology (see Bersani, "Representation"; Poirier, "Difficulties" and "Writing"). Instead, contemporary lesbian and gay critics often transform homosexuality into the privileged site of unknowing on which all difficulties turn and all coherence appears to founder (see Sedgwick, "Privilege" 104).[9] I'll refine this point by engaging more examples.

In *Closet Writing/Gay Reading: The Case of Melville's "Pierre,"* James Creech strives to amplify what Herman Melville apparently could express only in limited ways:

> It is not a question of reducing Melville's writing to homoerotic ciphers and tracts which, once decoded, can be discarded as empty containers of a now-consumed erotic content. Rather, the task is to augment Melville's work by retrieving content he had only the option of either encoding or omitting, as we shall see. We must make it speak where it is silenced, and we must answer back where it manages, despite everything, to speak. (45)

This and other passages in Creech's book might divide us between admiration at his desire to engage homoeroticism in Melville's work ("giv[ing] homosexuality . . . its place in these works" [45]), and concern about how we actually "*retriev[e the]* content [that Melville] had only the option of either encoding or omitting." To aid this retrieval, we might distinguish between truth and truth-effects in literature, hoping thereby to settle, once and for all, the meaning that Melville and others intended to convey. Yet in doing so we risk forgetting that "literary truth" is an oxymoron with a complex relation to historical events. We also might downplay that forms of desire in Melville's and others' literary texts are by definition fictional— meaning not that they are invalid, spurious, or even artificial, but that they have a complicated relation to fantasy, wish, and facticity. If they aren't simple emblems of history, then, neither are they unequivocal revelations of a hitherto veiled biography.

Such distinctions between truth and truth-effect inform Eve Sedgwick's work, and she uses them to analyze cultural homophobia. Initially, Sedgwick seems to complicate Creech's expectation that literary characters can simply yield homosexual meaning. Her interest lies instead in demonstrating the erotic and sometimes violent repercussions of structural distinctions among men. Yet Sedgwick's difficulty in separating truth from literary truth-effects—given these terms' virtual and oxymoronic relation—eventually leads her also to assume that literature is a repository for homosexual meaning. At such points, Creech and Sedgwick advance quite similar expectations about literature: Before representing narrative aporias as sites of homosexual fantasy, they strive to make literature, history, and politics equivalent statements about same-sex oppression. And so while her reading of Melville's *Billy Budd, Sailor* (1891) differs radically in strategy from Creech's reading of Melville's *Pierre* (1852), Sedgwick nonetheless concludes: "There is *a homosexual* in this text. . . . That person is John Claggart" (*Epistemology* 92; original emphasis).

These remarks about Claggart are I think synecdochic of an interpretive dilemma in Sedgwick's work. On the one hand, her assertion about Claggart's homosexuality bolsters the suggestion that late-nineteenth-century Western culture tried repeatedly to establish discrete sexual categories. On the other hand, Sedgwick's interest in identifying a single homosexual seems to be a prerequisite to her *complicating* this period's turbulent sexual relations. My point is that Sedgwick can't complicate sexual categories without first identifying their fictional representatives, and at these moments any distinction between truth and truth-effect becomes impossible to sustain.

Arguing that narrative riddles convey homosexual secrets gives opacity a tortuous—and tautologous—relationship to sexual enigmas. Sedgwick suggests, for instance, that the resistance to homosexual meaning in Proust's writing is an "obdurate transparency" and a "transparent obduracy" (248). Making Proust's obduracy transparent not only occludes this proposition's noninevitability, however, but characterizes any approach to Proust that is hesitant about this link as homophobic in its blindness. In this way, doubting elements of Sedgwick's procedure implies calumny, an assumption we need to surpass.

"One particular sexuality [homosexuality] . . . was distinctively constituted *as* secrecy," argues Sedgwick (73). At such moments—and despite its theoretical sophistication—*Epistemology of the Closet* (1990) comes close to the gay literary criticism of the 1970s and 1980s that troped on latency and disclosure. But since nineteenth-century literature is replete with hetero- and nonsexual secrets, we can't accept Sedgwick's claim.[10] And as soon as we refute such foundational arguments in *Epistemology*, we can't accept Sedgwick's belief that the closet is the privileged *episteme* of modern subjectivity (1–2). Related questions also arise: Do the dense and oblique circumlocutions of James's fiction necessarily or even indicatively veil a "beast" in Victorian masculinity's closet that in turn masks James's homosexual crisis? In her account of "homosexual panic" in "The Beast in the Jungle" (1903), Sedgwick moves in one paragraph from usefully proposing that "the possibility of an embodied male-homosexual thematics has [in this story] . . . a precisely liminal presence" to insisting, in ways that echo her pronouncement on *Billy Budd*'s Claggart, that "to the extent that Marcher's secret has *a* content, that content is homosexual" (201). By tying such substantive claims to James's alleged sexual crisis (195), Sedgwick risks repeating not only the intentional fallacy, but psychobiography's egregious mistakes, in which every textual attribute holds an apparently obvious relation to its author's repressions.

Since Sedgwick's earlier book, *Between Men: English Literature and Male Homosocial Desire* (1985), emphasizes homosocial exchange more than antihomophobic reading, identifying homosexual characters probably would jeopardize—rather than bolster—its argument. Thus *Between Men* is concerned *not* to fall into a "minoritizing" trap: Sedgwick contends that the "premature recuperation . . . of a thematic array that might in the first place have a special meaning for homosexual men as a distinctively oppressed group . . . would risk cultural imperialism" (115). At the same time, in a classic volte-face allowing her to accept two contradictory positions, Sedgwick admits a possible "danger" in dismissing this "special meaning" by trying to avoid the "potential blurring, the premature 'universalization,' of what might prove to be a distinctly homosexual, minority literary heritage" (115). Finally unwilling to choose between these perspectives, Sedgwick rejects this "heritage" in *Between Men* to distance herself from "cultural imperialism." Yet this "minoritizing" perspective haunts all her work, resurfacing with insistence in *Epistemology*'s "rehabilitative readings" (154); given Sedgwick's political concerns, such haunting is structurally inevitable. Her pattern of particularizing homosexuality in some characters and diffusing it among others recurs in *Tendencies,* too, in which *queer* describes what is ontologically deviant in so many desires and acts that the word loses conceptual *and* political value (7–8). Adopting the word *queer* cannot alleviate this "minoritizing" problem if those using the word aim generously to expand—and eventually to rescind—the category of "perversion" (8; see also Dean, "Eve" 130–31). Indeed, it seems unrealistic to expect the word *queer* to include all sexual "deviance" and *still oppose a notion of norms.*

Since critics and historians can't renounce inherited terms of sexual identity without idealism or naïveté, applying the word *queer* to late-Victorian and even contemporary culture poses still greater substantive and conceptual difficulties. Let's interpret two: First, the mistake of assuming that the desire of literary characters corresponds exactly with historical changes—for instance, the discursive "invention" of the homosexual in 1869 (Halperin, *One* 155 n. 2). This simple point highlights the limits of New Historicist readings attempting to explain the meaning of desire by invoking proximate historical events. Second, the conceptual tension for critics such as Sedgwick, who are torn between a theoretical desire to disband "the homosexual" as a category, given its oppressive origins, and a political need to recover and defend this category because the alternative seems to them politically ineffective or "degaying" (see *Epistemology* 16).

In advancing these criticisms of Sedgwick's and others' work, let me reemphasize that I'm not ignoring the social and sexual difficulties that many nineteenth-century texts adumbrate. Nor am I deaf to what Sedgwick calls the "whoosh of relief" of readers eager to displace pressing questions about homosexual meaning onto sexually nebulous claims (*Epistemology* 247). Jeffrey Meyers illustrates this second approach by confirming what's at stake for many heterosexual readers in *retaining* such assumptions about homosexual opacity. Meyers insists we critique and discard "direct" sexual writing because unequivocal representations of homosexuality create for him an immediate loss of aesthetic appeal. For Meyers, Britain's partial decriminalization of male homosexuality in 1967 was responsible for a lamentable decline in literary achievement: "When the laws of obscenity were changed and homosexuality became legal, apologies seemed inappropriate [!], the theme surfaced defiantly and sexual acts were grossly described. The emancipation of the homosexual has led, paradoxically, to the decline of his [*sic*] art" (3).[11]

Despite this argument's appalling logic, which redeems bigotry as a precondition for art, we should ask what "unequivocal" literature and, by implication, graphic desire signify for Meyers and other conservatives. These factors highlight our political *and* conceptual difficulty in integrating homosexual desire into modern fiction and society. Indeed, these factors implicitly question whether sexuality *can* be "integrated" into society, or whether its purpose isn't precisely to remind us of our *failure* in representing psychic pleasure and difficulty—to remind us, in Jacqueline Rose's astute formulation, that "[s]exuality is the *vanishing-point* of meaning" (71; my emphasis).[12] And though this argument tells us nothing precise about a writer's specific relation to sexual acts and cultural fantasies, it indicates that sexual representations have no necessary relation to social liberation, a point taking us back to Foucault (see *History* 7 and "Sexual" 286–303). This in turn may help us reflect critically on progressivist notions of lesbian and gay history, based as they are on the idea that sexual clarity is our primary antecedent to political change.

3. SEXUALITY AND THE INEFFABLE

These arguments about sexuality's complex relation to representation pose difficulties about the meaning of homosexual desire for contemporary politics and culture. If we aim to "integrate" homosexuality into society, for instance, must we disband the "minoritizing" perspective and return to former conditions of relative indifference? Is it a mistake to seek out, in a "reverse discourse," the particular identity of a desire whose meaning Western cultures have overdetermined for roughly the past one hundred years, often in irredeemable forms? And if, following queer activists, we aim not to integrate homosexuality and to resist assimilation, can we avoid idealizing this desire's propensity for insubordination, even sidestepping such questions altogether by redefining homosexual desire as simply "queer"? Finally, what happens to queer literary studies, when the "reverse discourse" becomes an inevitable—if inadequate—hermeneutic device?

All these concerns affect our ability to interpret homosexuality in literature. We have seen conservative, gay, and pro-gay critics alternately praise and revoke the opacity of many homosexual writers, with conservatives generally silencing questions about literary taboos and public censure, and gay and pro-gay critics using these questions to shape their critical readings (see R. Hall, Kellog, McClary, Richardson, Stockinger; for a critique, see Acocella 68–71). My point is not that sexuality has no relation to creativity or representation. I am saying instead that for these gay and pro-gay critics, sexuality has become such a forceful determinant of meaning that when heterosexuality surfaces in the work of lesbian, gay, or bisexual writers, it is treated with embarrassment, even disdain, as if the presence of two orientations in an author or narrative is mutually exclusive.

In Western cultures, the burden of alterity now falls on homosexuality, leaving readers to assume that a character or author is heterosexual unless desires and acts prove otherwise (Beaver 100, 109). But while this burden presents us with hermeneutic difficulties, criticism arguably must find ways of responding to this cultural bias without suggesting that every enigma in literature or film "mak[es] things perfectly queer" (Doty). We can, that is, address homosexuality's conceptual and substantive conflict with other sexualities without assuming that homosexuality has a content we must retrieve and reown. If we don't, criticism becomes merely an exercise in veracity, culminating in intolerance about sexual doubt and interpretive uncertainty. This uncertainty surely is what lesbian and gay studies must thoroughly engage.

Although lesbian and gay critics are justifiably suspicious of conservative critics' attempts at subjecting "homosexual writing" to often moralistic readings, many of the precepts underlying even complex gay and lesbian readings can alert us to the damaging effects of declarative criticism.[13]

What, then, does it mean to interpret an author's work as a transparent—
or even opaque—record of his or her sexuality? And what does it mean not
to do so? If it is—according to Halperin—homophobic of James Miller to
read the philosophy of Michel Foucault through the lens of his death, isn't
it complicated that D. A. Miller aims to interpret the philosophy of Roland Barthes largely through the lens of his desire? I ask this provocatively,
but not disingenuously, realizing the extent of Barthes's autobiographical
investment in *Roland Barthes, A Lover's Discourse, Camera Lucida,* and
many of his other works. For despite the two Millers' political differences,
there's an uncanny critical resemblance between the recuperative strategies
of *Bringing Out Roland Barthes* and the attributive logic of *The Passion of
Michel Foucault.*[14] Had D. A. Miller represented Barthes's *Writing Degree
Zero* as projective of what it means to be hit by a laundry truck, we would
question his critical precepts. Considering his biographical readings of
S/Z and *A Lover's Discourse,* why wouldn't we do so? The answers may return: Miller gives us an amenable reading and saves Barthes from the
shame of closetry; and Barthes's sexuality is anyway relevant to *S/Z*
and *A Lover's Discourse,* but not to, say, *Writing Degree Zero.* But where
does this leave lesbian, gay, or bisexual writers whose work depicts relationships quite different from their orientation? Are we really "degaying" these
writers by suggesting their work isn't always a foil for their desires?

Recent debates over Barthes and Foucault reveal instructive tensions
between both philosophers' aims of suspending, even *dissolving,* the authority traditionally invested in literary writers, and the attempt by North
American gay theorists to read this putative dissolution as politically inadequate and even sexually evasive. In engaging these debates, I want to highlight some conceptual and political differences between French and North
American accounts of gay identity and homosexuality, as well as a significant paradox: How can we engage with Barthes's and Foucault's lives, desires, and relationships without reinscribing their philosophy or criticism
in a tradition they were both loath, for *conceptual* reasons, to conserve?
D. A. Miller partly tackles this point when writing, "To refuse to bring
Barthes out consents to a homophobic reception of his work. But to accept
the task? . . . [T]here is hardly a procedure for bringing out this [homosex-
ual] meaning that doesn't itself look or feel like just more police entrapment" (17–18).

Ultimately, Miller considers the political need to "bring out" Barthes sufficient justification to risk this scenario. But if *Bringing Out Roland Barthes* manages to avoid "entrapment" (and I'm not convinced it does or can), it also downplays a number of vital questions about sexual identity that Miller rejects as "consent[ing] to a homophobic reception of [Barthes's] work" (17).

Elizabeth Weed puts this problem well: "What is at stake here for Miller is [homosexuality's] symptomatic diminishment. . . . [T]he encounter between Miller and Barthes is a confrontation between two theories of writing and two theories of desire" (261). Weed reminds Miller that part of his recuperative desire is a self-acknowledged "fantasy . . . of alleviating *an erotic pessimism* by producing with [Barthes], against him, a sexuality that had become 'ours'" (262, quoting Miller 7, original emphasis). Again the problem with this possessive pronoun. The fantasy of similarity produces what Miller recognizes are all the "usual vicissitudes of adulation, aggression, ambivalence" (8). For Miller and Halperin, however, the political rationale for "bringing out" Barthes rescinds any suggestion that there *could* be a *conceptual* rapport between outing Barthes and "police entrapment" (see *Saint Foucault* 182–84). When the interests of the lesbian and gay community are invoked, any resemblance between outing and entrapment seems too quickly to disappear (see Dean, "Sex").

We might recall that in *Roland Barthes* (1975), Barthes writes at length about the need to advance "homosexualities" (69). "[S]ex," he proposed utopically, "will be taken into no typology (there will be, for example, only *homosexualities,* whose plural will baffle any constituted, centered discourse, to the point where it seems . . . virtually pointless to talk about it)" (69). This statement iterates Barthes's published claim in 1971: "What is difficult is not to liberate sexuality according to a more or less libertarian project but to release it from meaning, *including from transgression as meaning*" (133; my emphasis). Why does Miller ignore these passages, quoting only Barthes thoughts on "The goddess H."? "The pleasure potential of a perversion," Barthes observes, "(in this case, that of the two H.'s: homosexuality and hashish) is always underestimated. Law, Science, the *Doxa* refuse to understand that perversion, quite simply, *makes happy;* or to be more specific, it produces a *more*" (63–64, original emphases; also qtd. in Miller 22). Perhaps Miller quotes neither Barthes's thoughts on sexuality and transgression nor his famous claim about "homosexualities" because Barthes repeated attention to the subject of homosexuality in his 1975 memoir diminishes the political and interpretive urgency of Miller's book. The above quotations render doubtful Miller's claims that "Barthes falters" when discussing homosexuality (44), that this subject was an "Open Secret" in his work, and that "[h]owever intimately Barthes's writing proved its connection with gay sexuality, the link was so discreet that it seemed to emerge only in the coy or hapless intermittences of what under the circumstances I could hardly pretend to reduce to just his repression" (16, 6). Do the above statements really stem from "coy or hapless intermittences"? Are they even "so discreet"?

"To refuse to bring Barthes out consents to a homophobic reception of his work" (17): Miller simplifies the process of reception here in suggesting that if lesbian and gay critics don't "bring [someone] out" they are *necessarily* homophobic, promoting "a mass denial" (17). His contention ignores that for French readers, as Kevin Kopelson observes, Barthes's sexuality was already known; for them, the project of outing Barthes was either misframed or redundant (150; see also R. Martin, "Roland" 294–95). This doesn't mean that French "urbanity" has no elements of sexual blindness or intolerance. The point is rather to consider what "bringing out" entails and achieves when it claims an interpretive clarity and political rigidity that *sexuality*—quite aside from Barthes's and Foucault's philosophies—can't sustain.

If we ignore the assumptions that shape our interest in "restoring" sexual agency to hitherto "repressed" sites of sexual activity, we might fail to heed those deconstructive principles advanced by Barthes and Foucault that determine our current interpretive theories. Paradoxically, we might also push queer theory toward a philosophy of the ego that has consistently repressed sexual difference and the unconscious by championing normative patterns of gender. This philosophy underpins the widespread assumption that humanity is contingent on heterosexuality; the obvious corollary to this argument, which the Christian Right to date has successfully advanced, is that homosexuality renders a person inhuman. This corollary is a long shot from critical readings of Barthes's and Foucault's sexuality—or is it? In the second half of *Saint Foucault,* Halperin thinks not, for he worries that the ease with which James Miller conflates Foucault's philosophy with his death reduces the latter's concepts to the circumstances of his life, trivializing both. Foucault himself nonetheless proposed connections between his work and life—connections James Miller exploits that Halperin is careful to downplay.

Although conservative critics sometimes use sexual indeterminacy to confirm a neutralizing (or phobic) heterosexual consensus, we should ask if sexual clarity is the only means of forestalling this emphasis. Above all, has such a counterstrategy any chance of succeeding? A detailed critique of biography's reliance on sexual secrets as apparent instances of subjective "truth" might offer us a more engaging—if precarious—account of the gap between sexuality and "the character of 'character'" (Cixous). In this respect, following certain moves in D. A. Miller's account of Barthes, we could use biography to explore subjective instability, not ontological veracity (see *Bringing Out* 28, 48–49).

Is lesbian and gay studies willing to countenance such apparently cautious or lackluster approaches to our new "great tradition"? Considering that sexual and textual ambiguity is amenable to political manipulation, Sedgwick may be right to indicate the danger of

> a momentarily specific pluralizing of [gay issues and homophobia] to—with a whoosh of relief—the terminus of a magnetic, almost religiously numinous insistence on a notional "undecidability" or "infinite plurality" of "difference" into whose vast and shadowy spaces the machinery of heterosexist presumption and homophobic projection will already, undetected, have had ample time to creep. (*Epistemology* 247)

However, her rejection of "notional 'undecidability'" is curious when this principle informs much of her book. Concluding her chapter "Epistemology of the Closet," for instance, Sedgwick writes:

> I have no optimism at all about the availability of a standpoint of thought from which [the minoritizing/universalizing impasse] could be intelligibly, never mind efficaciously, adjudicated, given that the same yoking of contradictions has presided over all the thought on the subject, and all its violent and pregnant modern history, that has gone to form our own

thought. Instead, *the more promising project would seem to be a study of the incoherent dispensation itself,* the indisseverable girdle of incongruities under whose discomfiting span, for most of the century, have unfolded both the most generative and the most murderous plots of our culture. (90; my emphasis)

This argument seems correct: studying "the incoherent dispensation" of meaning informing male and female homosexuality *would* seem "more promising" than trying to adjudicate between diffuse minoritizing and universalizing claims. For this reason, Sedgwick *is* willing to advance "notional 'undecidability'" in *Epistemology of the Closet,* insisting twice that the "presumptuous, worldly implication 'We Know What That Means' happens to be . . . the particular lie that animates and perpetuates the mechanism of [modern] homophobic male self-ignorance and violence and manipulability" (45 and 204).[15]

If "We Know What That Means" is a "lie," "notional 'undecidability'" ironically must be a critical prerequisite for interpreting literature, an argument I am stating here. Sedgwick, as we've seen, rejects this last point as degaying (247). How then do we *resist* assuming "We Know What That Means"—a belief Sedgwick advances in her literary readings before denouncing it, in my estimation correctly, as a "presumptuous, worldly implication"? Critics would be pressed to resolve these contradictions, especially since Sedgwick is quick to criticize those endorsing her own doubts about interpretive certainty. The argument gets so complicated here because Sedgwick's own readings of Melville, James, and Proust tend to reduce all silences to veiled forms of homosexual meaning.

We can't annul the distance between implicit homosexual meanings and contemporary gay issues to reduce either our political discomfort or the possibility that such meanings will go awry. Besides, perspectives of "notional 'undecidability'" don't elide the question of homosexuality's meaning; they simply dislodge the certainty that much of our criticism and culture would like to invest in homosexuality.[16] When faced with the conservative suggestion that the critic should fetishize authorial silence, the political insistence by lesbian and gay studies and queer theory that we must "out" the author tacitly demands that we also resolve textual ambivalence by providing the missing "answer" (sexual repression, inhibition, or displacement) to narrative and sexual uncertainty: We absolve the author's reticence by trying to speak on his or her behalf.

4. Anti-Essentialism and Critical Reading

These arguments about sexual indeterminacy ask lesbian and gay studies to relinquish the attraction of critical certainty. In the place of stable procedures and diagnostic confidence, we would find a level of unreliability that is disconcerting for a field already beset with external questions about its validity and conceptual rigor. In other words, we would need to consider the role and prevalence of *doubt* that informs and sometimes bedevils lesbian and gay studies. If we refuse to conflate each author with his or her text (refusing also the conservative assumption that, concerning sexuality, the two are quite unrelated), and if we take seriously the predicate that sexuality lies beyond stable reference and knowledge, then we can't produce a criticism that promotes conditions of certainty. We would also challenge our culture's often appealing contrary insistence that sexuality is something we can know, master, and consciously manipulate.

This paradoxical approach illustrates the stakes informing modern theories of gay and lesbian identity. Engendering discomfort and anxiety, always engendering uncertainty, this approach prevents us from representing homosexuality and heterosexuality as stable and separate phenomena. Such emphasis denies that external impositions of discourse and power alone create homosexuality's structure—denying too that individuals internalize, briefly mediate, and then—if they are writers—simply transcribe this sexual meaning into literature. Beyond the obvious point that sexual difficulty does not correlate simply or inevitably with textual obscurity, we can't understand past forms of identification in history and literature without accepting the gap between cultural representations of sexuality and unconscious patterns of fantasy and self-definition. Another factor insists on being heard in all these discussions, though it is notoriously difficult to talk about: the unconscious.

If there's a lesson to learn here, it is surely that we can't assume that interpretation will master the enigmas of sexuality. If psychoanalysis has taught us anything, it is to recognize that our identities "lean" on absence, enigma, and doubt. This gap between the subject and its symbolic register is a space allowing identity to function and turn awry; without this gap, we would indeed be locked in determinism, having no chance of psychic or political transformation. To consider the performative a path to freedom and emancipation is thus to misunderstand a crucial point: This gap returns individuals and "sexual communities" to their fragile consistency; there is no psychic guarantee of their stability. And to ignore this difficult truth is ultimately to misrepresent a crucial—and invigorating—aspect of lesbian and gay history. Isn't it time to give the ineffable the role it deserves in all our reflections?

Notes

1. Although *From Man to Man; or, Perhaps Only . . .* concerns the repercussions, for women, of men's selfishness (the book originally was entitled *Other Men's Sins*) and Schreiner's protagonist Rebekah "scribbl[es] on to show how the new attitude [about religion and life] influenced the emotional relations between man and woman," the same character nonetheless asks, in words that appear to endorse Schreiner's perspective, "Might not [a man's] very attempts to bring men and women into freer and more equal fellowship in themselves seem to produce more evil than they remedied, simply because they were not ready for it?" (184, 194).

2. Swinburne was primarily a poet, Hardy wrote excellent poetry, and Santayana's love sonnets are discussed in chapter 6. However, this study primarily examines these writers' prose fiction; I discuss their poetry when it endorses a set of concerns that their prose fiction represents.

3. For an excellent account of early psychological theories—including phrenology and associationist psychology—as well as of sensorimotor physiology, physiognomy, and the influence of evolutionary theories on studies of the mind, see Robert M. Young esp. 9–53. Young's book gives a fine account of the work of Franz Joseph Gall, Pierre Flourens, François Magendie, Johannes Mueller, Alexander Bain, Herbert Spencer, and Hughlings Jackson. For a clear summary of later nineteenth-century psychologists, such as Ernst Mach, and of the early theories of William James, see Ryan 1–22. And for a detailed account of the historical emergence of dynamic psychiatry, see Ellenberger 53–109.

4. Randolph Hughes is "infamous" among readers of Swinburne's novels for denouncing the work of other Swinburne scholars. However, his edition of *Lesbia Brandon* is not without errors of its own (see Lang for an extensive list of them), and I have silently corrected these when quoting from his edition.

5. See Robert M. Polhemus: "What often stirs erotic love is a drive for the most intimate kind of communication with another person and one that cannot be shared by anyone else. Before Freud, novelists did a good job of showing how this drive grows up in the smoldering emotional life of familial groups" (37). For useful elaboration on the unconscious before Freud, see Whyte x, 10–11, 169, 177–82. See also Carter 142; Shaw 21–33. And D. A. Miller makes a similar point about prescience for altogether different purposes in *The Novel and the Police* 190.

6. My account of homoeroticism in Disraeli's work here differs from Andrew Elfenbein's account of Disraeli and Bulwer's close friendship and their "homosexual performativity" (216; see also 217–19 and chapter 1 below).

7. For an excellent reading of the *Phaedrus*'s importance for Victorian Hellenism, see Linda Dowling, *Hellenism*, chapter 3: "The Socratic Eros."

8. See Freud, *Three* 136, 149n; *Beyond* 57–58. The second reference to Freud's *Three Essays* is sufficiently important to quote in full: "The most striking distinction between the erotic life of antiquity and our own no doubt lies in the fact that the ancients laid the stress upon the instinct itself, whereas we emphasize its object. The ancients glorified the instinct and were prepared on its account to honour even an inferior object; while we despise the instinctual activity in itself, and find excuses for it only in the merits of the object" (*Three* 149 n). See also Foucault's comparable observation in *The Use of Pleasure* (1984; 1985), esp. 19, 35–62, and 125. The importance of Freud's observation for this book properly emerges in my chapters on Schreiner and Santayana.

9. Although his book primarily concerns medieval and Renaissance conceptions of passion, dealing only briefly with nineteenth- and twentieth-century definitions of love, de Rougemont's *Love in the Western World* usefully underscores some of my arguments. See esp. books 6 and 7 of his study.

10. See Richards esp. 92–94, 100; Dowling, *Hellenism* esp. 67–103; Jenkyns 140–53; Dellamora, *Masculine* 24–25, 33; and DeLaura, *Hebrew* 165–81.

11. "The author," states Judith Butler's blurb for *The Psychic Life of Power*, "considers the way in which *psychic life is generated by the social operation of power,* and how that social operation of power is concealed and fortified by *the psyche that it produces*" (my emphases). And so while Butler modifies the starker claims about psychic causality of her earlier works, such as *Gender Trouble* (1990), her latest book nonetheless displays at the outset a visible ambivalence about the psychoanalytic argument that only a *non*social factor—the drive— is fully capable of *determining* psychic life (see, for instance, her two formulations of death: 27, 142). See also Joan Copjec's astute summary of Freud's argument in *Civilization and Its Discontents* (1929, 1930), quoted below in note 5 of chapter 4.

12. I have scaled down the overwhelming number of authors and issues I might have included by engaging texts displaying a prescient understanding of the unconscious. Several recent studies examine the work of writers such as Carlyle, Tennyson, Dickens, Patmore, Trollope, Newman, Arnold, Kingsley, Robert Browning, Pater, and Stoker (obvious candidates for this book). See notes 12 and 39 to the introduction for related publications on this period and phenomenon.

INTRODUCTION

1. Perhaps the most eloquent and accessible book to date on these differences is Copjec's *Read My Desire: Lacan against the Historicists* (1994). Copjec's account of Jacques Lacan's rereading of Freud informs many of my arguments in this book. She writes, "We are calling historicist the reduction of society to its indwelling network of relations of power and knowledge" (6). Such a reduction, she notes, fails to consider "a surplus existence that cannot be caught up in the positivity of the social" (4).

2. In her influential study, *Epistemology of the Closet* (1990), Eve Kosofsky Sedgwick summarizes her thoughts on psychoanalysis with the following claim: "It was in the period of the so-called 'invention of the homosexual' that Freud gave psychological texture and credi-

bility to the countervalent, universalizing mapping of this territory, based on the supposed protean mobility of sexual desire and on the potential bisexuality of every human creature; a mapping that implies no presumption that one's sexual penchant will always incline toward persons of a single gender, and that offers, additionally, a richly denaturalizing description of the psychological motives and mechanisms of male paranoid, projective homophobic definition and enforcement. Freud's antiminoritizing account only gained, moreover, in influence by being articulated through a developmental narrative in which heterosexist and masculinist ethical sanctions found ready camouflage" (84). One need only glance at Freud's *Three Essays on the Theory of Sexuality* (1905) to reveal the inaccuracy of these claims. Here Freud argues cogently: "Psycho-analytic research . . . has found that all human beings are capable of making a homosexual object-choice and have in fact made one in their unconscious" (145 n). This and other arguments indicate that Freud's theory of sexuality is profoundly antidevelopmental and antiheterosexist: "Thus from the point of view of psycho-analysis," he continues, "the exclusive sexual interest felt by men for women is also a problem that needs elucidating and is not a self-evident fact based upon an attraction that is ultimately of a chemical nature" (146 n). By corollary, as Tim Dean has shown, Sedgwick's refusal to consider any aspect of sexuality as unconscious renders her own account of sexuality, despite her professions to the contrary, entirely developmental (see "Eve" 122–26).

3. For an account of the reasons for Foucault's uncharacteristic vagueness here, see Spivak 34–37. I thank Jeff King for bringing Spivak's essay to my attention.

4. However, the most significant revisions occurred after Freud's death in 1939. For elaboration on this death's consequences for psychoanalytic theories of homosexuality, see Abelove (I return to related points in section 2 below). Although Reich's analysis of the relations among society, libido, and orgasm date from the mid-1920s, his work became famous only in subsequent decades.

5. Ann Laura Stoler usefully suggests why in "The Education of Desire and the Repressive Hypothesis," *Race* 165–95. Although Stoler's assessment of psychoanalysis differs from mine, her account of *Foucault's* doubts about psychoanalysis is very useful. See also J. Butler, *Subjects of Desire* 217–29 and Rajchman 88–93.

6. See for instance Nancy Armstrong's *Desire and Domestic Fiction* (1987): "The first volume of [Foucault's] *History of Sexuality* makes sex a function of sexuality and considers sexuality as a purely semiotic process. Sexuality includes not only all those representations of sex that appear to be sex itself—in modern culture, for example, the gendered body— but also those myriad representations that are meaningful in relation to sex, namely, all the various masculine or feminine attributes that saturate our world of objects" (11). But which body—including the transsexual's and perhaps even the hermaphrodite's—is not gendered, and when did Foucault ever consider sexuality "a purely semiotic process"?

7. To the extent that Lacan debunked many of the arguments of Freud's followers, considering his own work—especially on repression, as we'll see—a faithful "return" to Freud's arguments, we cannot implicate him in Foucault's thoughts about the "repressive hypothe-

sis" (see section 2 below for elaboration). As David Macey has shown, Foucault's relationship to Lacan's work is extremely complex; see esp. 215, 245, 422, 513 n. 26; also James Miller 62.

8. See F. Smith, "Sexuality"; Barret-Ducrocq, *Love in the Time of Victoria* esp. 1–4; and Mason's two volumes, *The Making of Victorian Sexuality* and *The Making of Victorian Sexual Attitudes* (see esp. 6–8 in the first volume). For an interesting meditation on this conceptual dilemma, see Weeks, "Discourse," and Goldfarb, "The Problem of Intention," *Sexual Repression and Victorian Literature* 59–65; also Marcus, *The Other Victorians* (1966) and *Freud and the Culture of Psychoanalysis* (1984). For historical evidence demonstrating Victorian society's repressive effects—despite its proliferation of discourses about sexuality—see Pearsall, *Worm* 421–30 and *Public* esp. 95–110; Goldfarb 20–21, 24–58; and Houghton 355, 408–9. Literary examples supporting these assertions will soon appear from the works of Thackeray, Hardy, Schreiner, Swinburne, Meredith, and Gaskell. But for an example of repression and psychoanalytic prescience, consider the narrator's representation of Maggie Tulliver's internal strife, in George Eliot's *The Mill on the Floss* (1860), which I quoted in my preface. Later, the narrator adds these thoughts about quiescence and resistance: "All yielding is attended with a less vivid consciousness than resistance—it is the partial sleep of thought—it is the submergence of our own personality by another" (592).

9. Jacoby interprets a different tradition of psychoanalysis in his important book *The Repression of Psychoanalysis.* By corollary, since Thomas's study of psychoanalysis demonstrates little tolerance for Freud's doubts, speculations, and revisions, the manifestation of these qualities in Freud's work is apparent grounds for a wholesale rejection of psychoanalytic practice and theory; see esp. 1–15.

10. For examples of this tension, see Sedgwick, *Epistemology* 3, 9, 23–35, 60–62, 84; and Jonathan Dollimore, *Sexual* 27–35, 216–17, 253–60. See also Stoler esp. 165–69 for a lucid overview of the problems resulting from this false opposition.

11. The statement is not fortuitous, and we don't need to represent Hardy as a historian in order to understand it as such: Hardy published these words in January 1890, partly because of the difficulties he was having with Tillotson and Son of Bolton. Having accepted for serialization the manuscript of *Tess of the d'Urbervilles,* these publishers "turned it down on moral grounds, alarmed that they had contracted for a story involving seduction and illegitimate birth" (*Tess* 497). Rewriting part of the manuscript for "a family paper, the *Graphic,* in which it finally appeared in 1891, [Hardy] 'carried out this unceremonious concession to conventionality with cynical amusement'" (qtd. 497). "The seduction scene was omitted," adds critic David Skilton, "all references to Tess's child expunged, and at the editor's request, Angel Clare was made to wheel the milkmaids through a flood in a wheelbarrow to avoid close physical contact" (497). For details about the public's reaction to the publication of *Tess,* see Hardy's "Preface to the Fifth and Later Editions" (*Tess* 37). Hardy experienced similar difficulties in depicting Jude Fawley and Sue Bridehead's relationship when *Jude the Obscure* was serialized from December 1894 to November 1895 in *Harper's New Monthly Magazine.*

12. Studies of Victorian culture both applying and extending Foucault's insights include

Judith Halberstam, *Skin Shows: Gothic Horror and the Technology of Monsters* (1995); Dennis Allen, *Sexuality in Victorian Fiction* (1993); Armstrong, *Desire and Domestic Fiction: A Political History of the Novel;* and, famously, D. A. Miller, *The Novel and the Police* (1988). Related historical studies include Frank Mort, *Dangerous Sexualities: Medico-Moral Politics in England since 1830* (1987); Catherine Gallagher, *The Industrial Reformation of English Fiction, 1832–1867* (1985); and Weeks, *Sex, Politics, and Society: The Regulation of Sexuality since 1800* (1981). See also the following collections: Miller and Adams (ed.), *Sexualities in Victorian Britain* (1996); Parker (ed.), *Gender Roles and Sexuality in Victorian Literature* (1995); Harrison and Taylor (ed.), *Gender and Discourse in Victorian Literature and Art* (1992); Shires (ed.), *Rewriting the Victorians: Theory, History, and the Politics of Gender* (1992); and Morgan (ed.), *Victorian Sages and Cultural Discourse* (1990). For an important overview of theoretical blind spots in related historical approaches, see Joseph Litvak, "Back to the Future: A Review-Article on the New Historicism, Deconstruction, and Nineteenth-Century Fiction" (1988), which argues that "a certain metahistorical or utopian fantasy quietly impels much new historicist discourse" (138). Joseph Childers's *Novel Possibilities: Fiction and the Formation of Early Victorian Culture* (1995) usefully complicates existing materialist and historicist perspectives on social change and individual choice (2–10), and Mary Poovey's *Uneven Developments: The Ideological Work of Gender in Mid-Victorian Britain* (1988) also refines several New Historicist precepts, arguing that "the middle-class ideology we most often associate with the Victorian period was both contested and always under construction; because it was always in the making, it was always open to revision, dispute, and the emergence of oppositional formulations" (3). Although Poovey's argument informs my study, I would add that engaging signs of contestation within ideological formations does not in itself address psychic structures and conflicts. Poovey's *Making a Social Body* is more attentive to these conflicts; see esp. her chapter 7, "Homosociality and the Psychological: Disraeli, Gaskell, and the Condition-of-England Debate" (132–54).

13. I am also interested in Carpenter's lyrical argument, which strongly resembles Freud's: "Love and death move through this world of ours like things apart—underrunning it truly, and everywhere present, yet seeming to belong to some other mode of existence. When Death comes, breaking into our circle of friends, words fail us, our mental machinery ceases to operate, all our little stores of wit and wisdom, our maxims, our mottoes, accumulated from daily experience, evaporate and are of no avail. . . . And with Love, though in an opposite sense, it is the same. Words are of no use, all our philosophy fails" (*Drama* 1).

14. See Lacan's remarks on Darwin, particularly in *Seminar I* 177.

15. Theodor Adorno seemed also to invoke Aristophanes' fable when, commenting to Walter Benjamin about the relation of high art to popular culture in 1936, he famously observed: "Both are torn halves of an integral freedom, to which however they do not add up. It would be romantic to sacrifice one to the other" (Bloch 123).

16. While emphasizing the psychic repercussions of this "impassable mental chasm," I am not eclipsing that Victorian society was itself riven by internal conflicts such as class differences. In *The Way of All Flesh*, for instance, Samuel Butler's narrator observes that "between the upper and lower classes there was a gulf which amounted practically to an

impassable barrier" (278). However, we cannot simply add the "chasm" of which Schreiner and others write to the existing social "gulf" in order to form an accurate picture of Victorian life. The repercussions of this "impassable *mental* chasm" are sufficiently complex and autonomous to need examination on their own terms. The narrator of Arnold Bennett's *Old Wives' Tale* (1908) underscores this last point when noting that soon after Constance and Samuel Povey's marriage: "Both of them suddenly saw that they were standing on the edge of a chasm, and drew back. They had imagined themselves to be wandering safely in a flowered meadow, and here was this bottomless chasm! It was most disconcerting" (178). When the couple resolves its immediate difficulties, "the chasm . . . disappear[s]" (178), only to resurface as an "unspeakable horror"—an "obscene form between them"—when Samuel violently chastises their son, Cyril, for stealing from them (242).

17. See Carpenter, "Exfoliation," *Civilisation* 129–47, esp. 130.

18. Diana Fuss's recent book is a notable exception that usefully outlines Freud's conceptual difficulties with identification. In *Group Psychology and the Analysis of the Ego* (1921), Freud argued that identification hinges on a binary distinction between "being" and "having" the object: "It is easy to state in a formula the distinction between an identification with the father and the choice of the father as an object. In the first case one's father is what one would like to *be,* and in the second he is what one would like to *have*" (*Group* 106; original emphases). As we'll see in chapter 3, however, Freud later complicated this argument. In his 1961–62 *séminaire* on identification, Lacan also reframed this binary by distinguishing between symbolic and imaginary identification. For elaboration on Freud's concept of identification, see Fuss 21–51; and Wollheim esp. 175–76.

19. In addition to Robert M. Young's important book (see preface note 3 above), an interesting study examining this prescience is Judith Ryan's *The Vanishing Subject: Early Psychology and Literary Modernism* (1991), esp. 1–22. Whereas Ryan examines the influence of such early psychologists as Ernst Mach, Franz Brentano, and William James on European modernism, the present study details the conceptual prescience of nineteenth-century British literature. Similar excellent studies on related topics include Garrett Stewart's *Death Sentences: Styles of Dying in British Fiction* (1984), Robert M. Polhemus's *Erotic Faith: Being in Love from Jane Austen to D. H. Lawrence* (1990), and Vincent P. Pecora's *Households of the Soul* (1997). Concerning prescience, I adopt Shoshana Felman's crucial distinction between "applying" psychoanalysis to literature and "implicating" each element with its other (8–9). Spurning "application," *The Burdens of Intimacy* tries, like Felman, to show instead the textual repercussions of this "implication."

20. D. A. Miller advances an identical claim about nineteenth-century novels: "power can scarcely be exercised *except* on what resists it, and—shifting Bersani's perspective somewhat [in *A Future for Astyanax*]—one might claim that the novel rather than fearing desire *solicits* it" (*Novel* 27; original emphases).

21. For examples see Dollimore, "The Perverse Centre: Freud versus Foucault," *Sexual* 105–6; Sedgwick, *Epistemology* 83, 90; John D'Emilio 104–6; and Weeks, "Discourse" 100–103.

22. See David M. Halperin, *Saint* 120–23; Sedgwick, "Queer and Now," *Tendencies* 7–8; and Dollimore, *Sexual* 105–6.

23. See Leo Bersani, *Homos* 101–2; Tim Dean, "Eve" 126, "Sex" 74–75.

24. See John Brenkman 226; Halperin, *Saint* 121; and J. Butler, *Gender* esp. 64–65: "Far from foundational, these dispositions are the result of a process whose aim is to disguise its own genealogy. . . . What precisely does it mean to reverse Freud's causal narrative and to think of primary dispositions as effects of the law?" See also Sedgwick, *Epistemology:* "Psychoanalytic theory, if only through the almost astrologically lush plurality of its overlapping taxonomies of physical zones, developmental stages, representational mechanisms, and levels of consciousness, seemed to promise to introduce a certain becoming amplitude into discussions of what different people are like—only to turn, in its streamlined trajectory across so many institutional boundaries, into the sveltest of metatheoretical disciplines, sleeked down to such elegant operational entities as *the* mother, *the* father, *the* preoedipal, *the* oedipal, *the* other or Other" (23–24).

25. For an illustration of Foucault's suggestion, see Sedgwick's argument about psychoanalysis in *Epistemology,* qtd. in note 2 above.

26. See Reich, "Gaps in Psychology and in the Theory of Sex," *The Function of the Orgasm* 51–83.

27. See Marcuse, *One-Dimensional Man* 72; see also 73–78; and Marcuse, *Eros and Civilization* 208–11. Concerning Marcuse's understanding of repression, see *Eros and Civilization* 8: "'Repression,' and 'repressive' [in this text] are used in the nontechnical sense to designate both conscious and unconscious, external and internal processes of restraint, constraint, and suppression. 'Instinct,' in accordance with Freud's notion of *Trieb,* refers to primary 'drives' of the human organism which are subject to *historical* modification; they find mental as well as somatic representation" (original emphasis). Marcuse's definition of *Trieb* is *not* Freud's notion, however, a point emerging precisely in the former's hydraulic theory of repression: "Freud's individual psychology is in its very essence social psychology. Repression is a historical phenomenon. The effective subjugation of the instincts to repressive controls is imposed not by nature but by man" (16).

28. Dean usefully underscores these confusions and contradictions in "Eve"; see especially 126–27, 132–33.

29. Partly misconstruing Foucault's arguments about sexuality, Sedgwick and J. Butler have advanced questionable claims about gender performativity, Butler maintaining all the while that her related arguments about contingency and sexual desire do not lead to voluntarism. See Sedgwick, *Epistemology* 3; Butler, "Imitation" 18, 24–29, and *Bodies That Matter,* in which, after extensive criticism of her work's psychic voluntarism, Butler finally concedes that "sexuality cannot be summarily made or unmade" (94). While Butler's latest book, *The Psychic Life of Power: Theories in Subjection* (1997), modifies some of her earlier claims, reminding Foucauldians that they can't successfully theorize sexual and other politics without also engaging their psychic constituents (12–30, 94, 97, 104–5), N. Armstrong shows us just how entrenched the "Foucault-effect" is in gender studies, an "effect" we can

now define as *the persistent notion that gender is only an egoic response to social demands:* "Sexuality is . . . the cultural dimension of sex, which, to my way of thinking, includes as its most essential and powerful component the form or representation we take to be nature itself. Thus we can regard gender as one function of sexuality that must have a history" (11).

30. As Weeks notes in *Sex, Politics, and Society*, "there appears to have been an increase in prosecutions in the first third of the nineteenth century when more than 50 men were hanged for sodomy in England. In one year, 1806, there were more executions for sodomy than for murder, while in 1810 four out of five convicted sodomists were hanged. . . . As late as 1817 a man was sentenced to death under the sodomy laws for oral sex with a boy (he was later pardoned)" (100). In no other Western country was the law so severe. Adds Weeks: "no executions elsewhere have been documented after 1784. And the policy of *sentencing* to death continued to the eve of repeal. In the years 1856–59, 54 men were sentenced to death for sodomy, though the capital punishment was not carried through" (119).

31. The purity movement is an obvious example of this demand for the stricter social control of homosexuality, prostitution, vagrancy, abortion, and contraception. For analyses of this movement, see Mort, *Dangerous* 109–50; Jeffreys 6–85; Weeks, *Sex* 81–95.

32. Thus N. Armstrong concedes, after a paragraph detailing repressive elements of mid- and late-nineteenth-century society, "In all fairness, as Foucault notes, the middle classes rarely imposed institutional constraints upon others without first trying them out on themselves" (20). Although ultimately Foucauldian, Armstrong's point nonetheless begs a question: How does the imposition of "institutional constraints" upon *either* class *not* constitute repression? The only debate here concerning my example, homosexuality, would be whether the 1885 act's specific definitions of male homosexuality did not paradoxically release those engaging in lesbian sex and heterosexual sodomy (that is, oral and anal sex) from the law's purview. Unlike many U.S. laws that prohibit "sodomy" by technically including heterosexual oral and anal sex in this term's definition, the 1861 Offences Against the Person Act refers to (among its other concerns) buggery, and not sodomy. As Alan Bray has argued at length, however, Henry VIII's 1533 statute was less specific in this regard, often punishing from allegations of bestiality and even witchcraft; see esp. 25, 27–28, 62–63.

33. See Mort, *Dangerous* 104–5, 126, 128–36. See also Weeks, *Sex, Politics, and Society*, which complicates Foucault's argument by observing that "discourses [are not] the only contact with the real" (10–11). To endorse my point about the law's increasing power, consider that the Latin "*reprimere*," from which "repression" derives, when transformed into the plural noun of its gerundive, "*reprimenda*," produces "reprimand," the word we use to designate an official or legal rebuke.

34. See Lacan, *Four* 34–35. See also *The Order of Things* 374–78, where Foucault summarizes the importance of "Desire, Law, and Death" for both psychoanalysis and the human sciences. For different readings of Foucault's claims, with which I slightly disagree, see J. Butler, *Subjects* 218 and Stoler 165.

35. Such characterizations of the ego are—at least in Freudian terms—wildly inaccurate.

In *The Ego and the Id* (1923), Freud tells us that the ego, a "sycophantic, opportunist and lying . . . frontier-creature," has a "cap of hearing (*Hörkappe*)" worn haphazardly "on one side only. . . . It might be said to wear it awry" (56, 25). I elaborate on the way Freud's claim is revoked by elements of Nicolas Abraham and Maria Torok's theory of consciousness, fantasy, and "encryptment," in "Testament."

36. For this reason, I disagree with Butler's and Dollimore's suggestions that psychoanalysis is ultimately coercive in manipulating the subject's desire (J. Butler, *Gender* esp. 56–57; Dollimore, *Sexual* 202–4). Such arguments ignore psychoanalytic critiques of social manipulation and psychoanalysis's concern to assist the subject in symbolizing the distress and trauma of this manipulation.

37. See translator's note to Lacan's *Four* 281: "'Pleasure' obeys the law of homeostasis that Freud evokes in *Beyond the Pleasure Principle,* whereby, through discharge, the psyche seeks the lowest possible level of tension. '*Jouissance*' transgresses this law and, in that respect, it is *beyond* the pleasure principle."

38. Charles Baudelaire advanced a similar set of assumptions in 1863 when he argued that the dandy "is an 'I' with an insatiable appetite for the 'non-I,' at every instant rendering and explaining it in pictures more living than life itself [*un* moi *insatiable du* non-moi, *qui, à chaque instant, le rend et l'exprime en images plus vivantes que la vie elle-même*]" (*Painter* 9; *Œuvres* 1161; original emphases); in *Mon cœur mis à nu* (1861–63), he tied this interest in the "non-I" to "*la vaporisation et de la centralisation du* Moi [the vaporization and centralization of the Self]" (*Œuvres* 1271; original emphasis).

39. Studies attesting to a remarkable recent interest in Victorian masculinity include: Donald E. Hall, *Fixing Patriarchy: Feminism and Mid-Victorian Male Novelists* (1996); Paul Hammond, *Love between Men in English Literature* (1996); George L. Mosse, *The Image of Man: The Creation of Modern Masculinity* (1996); James Eli Adams, *Dandies and Desert Saints: Styles of Victorian Manhood* (1995); Herbert Sussman, *Victorian Masculinities: Manhood and Masculine Poetics in Early Victorian Literature and Art* (1995); Joseph Bristow, *Effeminate England: Homoerotic Writing after 1885* (1995); Christopher Craft, *Another Kind of Love: Male Homosexual Desire in English Discourse, 1850–1920* (1994); D. Hall (ed.), *Muscular Christianity: Embodying the Victorian Age* (1994); Alan Sinfield, *The Wilde Century: Effeminacy, Oscar Wilde, and the Queer Moment* (1994); Dennis Allen, *Sexuality in Victorian Fiction* (1993); Kaja Silverman, *Male Subjectivity at the Margins* (1992); Eve Kosofsky Sedgwick, *Epistemology of the Closet* (1990); Richard Dellamora, *Masculine Desire: The Sexual Politics of Victorian Aestheticism* (1990); Elaine Showalter, *Sexual Anarchy: Gender and Culture at the Fin de Siècle* (1990); J. A. Mangan and James Walvin (ed.), *Manliness and Morality: Middle-Class Masculinity in Britain and America, 1800–1940* (1987); Sedgwick, *Between Men: English Literature and Male Homosocial Desire* (1985); Norman Vance, *The Sinews of the Spirit* (1985); and Don Richard Cox (ed.), *Sexuality and Victorian Literature* (1984). Notable essays on Victorian literature include Oliver Buckton's essay on Newman; Carol T. Christ's essays on Carlyle ("Hero") and on Patmore, Tennyson, Ruskin, and Newman ("Victorian Masculinity"); Linda Dowling's essay on Pater and homosexuality

("Ruskin's"); David J. DeLaura's essay on Billy Andrew Inman's biography of Pater ("Reading"); Thaïs E. Morgan's essay on Victorian criticism ("Reimagining"); and Adrienne Donald's reading of Romanticism and Browning's poetry (esp. 249–51).

40. In *Woman and the Demon*, Nina Auerbach argues that "the social restrictions that crippled women's lives, the physical weaknesses wished on them, were fearful attempts to exorcise a mysterious strength" (8).

41. In *The Way of All Flesh* (1873; 1903), Samuel Butler makes a similar point in mock-serious concern. The "wicked inner self" of young Ernest Pontifex apparently insists on telling him: "the self of which you are conscious, your reasoning and reflecting self, will believe [the] lies [that surround you constantly] and bid you act in accordance with them. This conscious self of yours, Ernest, is a prig begotten of prigs and trained in priggishness" (159).

42. Freud, "On Narcissism" 91 n, as Tim Dean has argued in "Eve" 132. See also Lane, *The Ruling Passion* 11.

43. This is N. Armstrong's characterization: "In the name of her health and liberation, Freud views the mother's domesticity as an unhealthy sign and installs an eternally desirous woman in her place. His ideal is a woman who feels herself lacking as such and, in order to fill the lack, desires nothing so much as the male organ" (235–36).

44. For various readings of Freud's theories of self-negation and repression, all opposed to psychoanalysis, see Thomas 1–15; J. Cohen 1, 30; Crews, et al., *Memory;* and Crews, "Beyond" 1, 10–11.

45. See Dellamora, *Masculine* 193–217; Dowling, *Hellenism* esp. 27–31; Richards esp. 92–94, 100; Showalter, *Sexual* 172–77; J. Adams esp. 229–31; Sussman esp. 1–7, 13–15. For essays on Tractarian faith, see Chadwick.

46. See also Sedgwick, *Between Men* 1–27; *Epistemology* 27–35; and Rubin's "The Traffic in Women: Notes toward a Political Economy of Sex," an essay that greatly influenced Sedgwick's *Between Men*.

47. See also Carpenter, *Intermediate* 16–38. And Havelock Ellis's thoughts on "Sexual Selection in Man" challenge assumptions informing the "vertical" model of virility/effeminacy. "The perfection of the body of man," he wrote, "is not behind that of woman in beauty, but the study of it only appeals to the artist or the aesthetician; it arouses sexual enthusiasm almost exclusively in the male sexual invert" (*Studies* 189).

48. Brenkman overlooks this point when arguing, "Psychoanalysis affirms this imaginary heterosexual couple by placing it at the heart of the Oedipus complex, at the origin of desire and law, sexuality and identity. Psychoanalysis's complicity with compulsory heterosexuality has affected its intellectual habits, its conceptual style and its therapeutic strategies" (226).

49. I am most indebted to Laity's essay for elaborating on a set of modernist assumptions about nineteenth-century aestheticism. For other critical accounts of modernist revisionism, see B. Scott and Carol T. Christ, whose excellent chapter on "Modernism and Anti-Victorianism" appears in the latter's *Victorian and Modern Poetics* 142–58.

50. Eliot's, Pound's, Hulme's, and Yeats's perspectives on the psychic are, of course, not representative of British or European modernism; they merely underscore an interesting

antipathy for "effete" forms of sensibility. Regarding modernist writers and psychoanalysis, one might as easily substitute Virginia Woolf's perspective for Eliot's and H. D.'s for Pound's. I elaborate below on some of the conceptual repercussions of Yeats's reflections on passivity and ingenuousness, but the reader may also consider Yeats's perspective alongside the "dissociation of sensibility" that Eliot discusses in "The Metaphysical Poets" (1921)— a dissociation illustrating "the difference between the intellectual poet [Donne, Herbert] and the reflective poet [Tennyson, Browning]" (247). For an overview of the relationship between modernism and Freud's work, see Frederick J. Hoffman, *Freudianism and the Literary Mind.*

51. I am grateful to Tim Dean for referring me to Yeats's essay, the pagination of which follows Macmillan's special New York limited edition.

52. In *The Archetypes and the Collective Unconscious,* Jung argues: "As civilization develops, the bisexual primordial being turns into a symbol of the unity of personality, a symbol of the self, where the war of opposites finds peace. In this way the primordial being becomes the distant goal of man's self-development, having been from the very beginning a projection of his unconscious wholeness. Wholeness consists in the union of the conscious and the unconscious personality" (175; see also 178). Jung's muddled conception of wholeness is completely antipathetic to not only the grain of Freud's thought but the most basic tenets of psychoanalysis.

CHAPTER 1

1. Since George IV was crowned in 1820, *Pelham* (1828) technically is a Georgian novel (William IV reigned from 1830 until 1837, and Queen Victoria's reign began in 1837 and ended in 1901). However, in light of Bulwer-Lytton's extensive revisions to the novel, which continued into Victoria's reign, this chapter also considers early Victorian prose fiction and literary criticism.

2. I am adding the essays' titles here because various editions of Carlyle's *Critical and Miscellaneous Essays* divide the volumes' contents quite differently, some placing the essay "Sir Walter Scott" in volume 4, others in volume 3. To avoid confusion, I have also followed the Scribner's edition. For important elaborations on Carlyle's argument and work, see J. Adams 21–60; Sussman 16–72; Vanden Bossche esp. chap. 3; and DeLaura, "Ishmael."

3. I thank Jerome Beaty for helping me see the full implications of this claim.

4. The words *effeminacy* and *dandyism* were not synonymous in Georgian and early Victorian British culture. And though they occasionally implied homosexuality—sometimes with phobic undertones—the word *homosexuality* was not coined until 1869 (see Halperin, *One* 155 n. 2, 158–59 n. 17). For an account of "Georgian homophobia" containing invaluable material on Edward Gibbon, Jeremy Bentham, William Beckford, and Matthew Bacon, see Crompton 12–62.

5. Much of this chapter voices my disagreement with Oakley's claim that *Pelham*'s "view of character is . . . Aristotelian and teleological—not existential or emotivist—and this again gives any idea of mask a different inflection from what it might currently have. . . . Behind the variety of masks is required a moral consistency that has to be reconciled with

the development of the self" (56, 59). I also disagree with Graham's account in "Bulwer," which faithfully reproduces Bulwer's 1828 premise without asking whether it is *credible,* and thus why Bulwer later contradicts it in 1849: "Secure in his wide-ranging competence, Pelham makes artful use of apparent frailties to test his fellow men and to distract inferiors from envying his real excellence. His most obvious characteristics—effeminacy, languor, pedantry—are misleading gestures" (146). This claim ignores that for Bulwer, as *Pelham's* revisions attest, these "frailties" became *substantive* concerns. See also Lane, *Ruling* 74–75, 92; Christensen 26.

6. Compare Oakley's opening claim—"Essentially dandyism provides the mask behind which the character formation takes place; it constructs a *reserve* that forestalls intrusion or premature judgment" (51)—with his later, more interesting suggestion: "Dandyism is both disguise and active agency in that it provides a de-ontological ethic that gives an appearance of consistency to a teleological one" (64). I would want to advance this "de-ontological ethic" even further than Oakley does (see 56 and 59 cited above in note 5).

7. Bulwer reprinted the story "Mortimer" in his 1835 edition of *Pelham* (449 n); it seems he chose not to include the story in the 1840 edition. Elfenbein usefully observes that during his "conservative middle age," Bulwer frequently "whitewashe[d]" himself by selectively recounting his past. The example on which Elfenbein draws is Bulwer's affair with Lady Caroline Lamb; he argues that the affair "is a vivid example of how Bulwer-Lytton performed his life as an echo of Byron's" (214)—an echo necessarily resonant of Byron's *sexuality.* For elaboration on Bulwer's relationship to Byron and Byronism, see Buckley 20.

8. Moers argues famously that the dandy, "in all his ghostly elegance, . . . haunted the Victorian imagination" (13).

9. See Castle (esp. 28–65) for an interesting account of lesbianism's "apparitional" status in both eighteenth-century fiction and modern culture.

10. See Barbey; D. A. Miller, "Austen's" 1, 3; Sedgwick, *Epistemology:* "The bachelor hero can only be mock-heroic; not merely diminished and parodic himself, he symbolizes the diminution and undermining of certain heroic and totalizing possibilities of generic embodiment" (189).

11. For evidence of these excisions, see McGann's detailed "Textual Notes," *Pelham* 459–76, esp. 465, which provides an elaborate passage on tailors and men's clothes that Bulwer cut from the 1828 edition. See also Oakley 59–61, 65; Moers 81. For general elaboration, see Dowling, *Hellenism* 6–9; J. Adams 17, 98–99; Bristow, *Effeminate* 5–6; and especially Coblence 146–48.

12. Although Elfenbein similarly examines the homoerotic basis of Pelham's interest in Glanville, he doesn't emphasize so strongly the *legacy* of this friendship, which manifests itself in Pelham's marriage to Ellen Glanville. Elfenbein's and my readings of *Pelham* differ also in their approach to Bulwer's account of passion—particularly its effects on ontology. My overall concern is to bind Bulwer's interest in passion's *difficulty* to his numerous revisions of the novel.

13. The following citations from the novel will I hope demonstrate that McGann is only partly correct when arguing in his introduction to *Pelham:* "If we observe the novel closely

we cannot fail to see that none of the characters, not even Pelham, is alive by any realistic standards. They are all morality figures of one sort or another" (xx).

14. I am alluding to Cixous's important essay, "Character," but see also Reed 65–66, 76–79. In *Pelham,* the narrator (Pelham) states that he does not wish to "render . . . great injustice to the character [of Lord Vincent]. . . . Buried deep beneath the surface of his character, was a hidden, yet a restless ambition: but this was perhaps, at present, a secret even to himself. We know not our own characters till time teaches us self-knowledge" (42, 43). See also Christensen 49–50.

15. See *Pelham* 334–35; also Oakley 57–58; Graham, "Bulwer" 146. For interesting accounts of dandyism, narcissism, and narration, see Moers 76–79; Zima esp. 213–20.

16. See McGann: "of course in one sense Ellen Glanville is *not* alive. As a realistic character she is hopelessly dead" (*Pelham* xx; original emphasis). Considering Graham's defense of *Pelham,* it is striking that he admits: "Even Ellen Glanville, the woman Pelham finds worthy of playing Millamant to his Mirabel, is limited by her sex to so passive a role that we must take Pelham's word for her superiority" ("Bulwer" 146). As I underscore in this chapter, taking Pelham's or Bulwer's word for anything generates radically unpredictable repercussions.

17. Overton later caustically remarks: "As soon as I found that [Ernest] no longer liked his wife I forgave him at once and was as much interested in him as ever. There is nothing an old bachelor likes better than to find a married man who wishes he had not got married" (359). In *Samuel Butler Revalued,* Thomas L. Jeffers considers Butler "a latent or confused homosexual" (5).

18. The extent to which Graham accepts this metaphor about degeneration is striking proof of its ongoing power. He writes, in ways that endorse Bulwer's conservatism without understanding its rationale: "Lack of self-restraint separates these Byronic misanthropes from the serene Pelham. Tyrrell, the villain of the piece, embodies mental and physical disorder. Badly ruled passions intensify the brilliant Glanville's morbidity. Ultimately, the unmanaged characters of these men bring about their downfalls" ("Pelham" 77).

19. In Huysmans's novel, Des Esseintes's thoughts are reproduced thus: "Could it be that this slime would go on spreading until it covered with its pestilential filth this old world where now only seeds of iniquity sprang up and only harvests of shame were gathered? . . . Well, it is all over now. Like a tide-race, the waves of human mediocrity are rising to the heavens and will engulf this refuge, for *I am opening the flood-gates myself, against my will*" (219–20; my emphasis).

20. It is worth comparing Graham's remarks on masculinity with Hazlitt's: "There is nothing more to be esteemed than a manly firmness and decision of character. I like a person who knows his own mind and sticks to it; who sees at once what is to be done in given circumstances and does it. . . . There is stuff in him, and it is of the right practicable sort" ("Effeminacy" 253).

21. For useful elaboration on Bulwer, will, and self-love, see Reed 18, 226–44. Consider also Hazlitt's assessment of narcissism in his essay on the effeminate: "They are completely wrapped up in themselves; but then all their self-love is concentrated in the present minute.

They have worked up their effeminate and fastidious appetite of enjoyment to such a pitch, that the whole of their existence, every moment of it, must be made up of these exquisite indulgences; or they will fling it all away, with indifference and scorn. They stake their entire welfare on the gratification of the passing instant" ("Effeminacy" 249). Such comments seem to have influenced Pater's discussion of temporality and subjectivity in *The Renaissance*. And compare Hazlitt's remarks with Bulwer's 1849 advertisement, cited above.

22. For valuable readings of decadence that complicate simplistic understandings of transgression, see Calinescu; Gilman; Bernheimer: "Decadence provides evidence of an arrest and regression on what is assumed to be a path of progressive cultural development" (Bernheimer 53). Compare Pelham's above account of coxcombs and coquets with Oakley's claims: "Dandyism thus becomes an aspect of an inner-directed honor that dandyism itself is not. . . . The persona is not the reality of the subject but indeed a mask behind which a range of languages and faculties can be mastered" (52).

23. See Pelham's observation: "[Lady Roseville] possessed great sensibility, and even romance of temper, strong passions, and still stronger imagination; but over all these deeper recesses of her character, the extreme softness and languor of her manners, threw a veil which no superficial observer could penetrate. There were times when I could believe that she was inwardly restless and unhappy; but she was too well versed in the arts of concealment, to suffer such an appearance to be more than momentary" (19).

24. Consider Hazlitt's judgment here: "Lord Byron is a pampered and aristocratic writer, but he is not effeminate, or we should not have his works with only the printer's name to them! I cannot help thinking that the fault of Mr. Keats's poems was a deficiency in masculine energy of style. He had beauty, tenderness, delicacy, in an uncommon degree, but there was a want of strength and substance. . . . All is soft and fleshy, without bone or muscle. We see in him the youth, without the manhood of poetry" ("Effeminacy" 254, 255).

25. The etymology of *lax* gives the Latin *laxus,* meaning "slack, not strict, . . . loose" (Hoad 261).

CHAPTER 2

1. My argument about T. S. Eliot and impersonality owes much to Dean, "Sex" esp. 82–84. For illustrations of T. E. Hulme's and Ezra Pound's antipathy for Swinburne's poetry, see the preface of this book. The best work addressing Swinburne's radical perspective is by Harrison, Morgan, and Rooksby.

2. Concerning algolagnia in Swinburne's writing, Lafourcade remarked: "le sadisme de Swinburne dépasse de beaucoup une simple théorie de l'amour; de purement instinctif et sensuel, il devient bientôt raisonné et intellectuel. Eclairé par les doctrines du Marquis de Sade, et jusqu'à un certain point poussé par une conviction personnelle, Swinburne découvre dans la nature cette même loi de souffrance universelle et de mort qui lui était apparue dans le mécanisme des passions [Swinburne's sadism far surpasses simple theories of love; purely instinctual and sensual, it turns out to be well reasoned and intellectual. Illuminated by the Marquis de Sade's theories, and up to a point impelled by a personal belief, Swinburne discovered in nature the same law about suffering and death that for him manifested

itself in passion]" (2: 431; my trans.). Baird reminds us (50) that Swinburne did not read Sade until August 1862, the year in which he wrote most of *A Year's Letters* (later, *Love's Cross-Currents*). See also Carter 150; McGann, *Swinburne* 276–84.

3. Morgan confirms this perspective: "Even granting that *Poems and Ballads* have some basis in Swinburne's personal experience and his predilection for sado-masochism and homoeroticism, the point remains that Swinburne perceived a general crisis in sexual mores in mid-Victorian England and decided to take public action through the rhetoric of his poetry" ("Swinburne's" 177). Paglia adds that "Swinburne's poetry demolishes the hallowed institutions of Victorian manhood" (220). See also Morgan, "Mixed," but also McSweeney 672–73.

4. From 1879 until Swinburne's death in 1909, Watts and Swinburne lived together in Putney, South-West London, the lawyer and critic nursing Swinburne when he lost his health by taking over his "domestic life and financial affairs" (Jordan 205). Jordan describes the two men as "the Victorian odd couple—aging poet and stolid solicitor, two old codgers walled in behind their books and settled snugly for thirty years in the middle-class suburb of Putney" (206). On July 31, 1891, Swinburne wrote Watts, noting "I feel very thankful to you when I think I have one who is more to me and nearer than a brother" (*Letters* 6: 13). For Jordan, the remark indicates that Watts was for Swinburne "a stabilizing and supportive maternal figure. . . . He gave encouragement, but never became himself the lost object of desire" (212). Max Beerbohm satirized the two men's domestic arrangement in "No. 2 The Pines," writing that Swinburne, even in old age, had "about him something—boyish? girlish? childish, rather; something of a beautifully well-bred child. But he had the eyes of a god, and the smile of an elf" (64–65). For elaboration on Swinburne's love of Mary Gordon, see McGann, *Swinburne* 211–18; Lang, "Swinburne's"; F. Wilson, "Swinburne."

5. Harrison discusses these responses in "Swinburne's Losses" 689, an essay to which I am indebted.

6. As I caution in the preface (n. 3), Hughes's edition contains many errors. By referring often to Lang's valuable list of these errors (see "Lesbia"), and by checking all quotations against the more recent edition of *Lesbia Brandon,* in *The Novels of A. C. Swinburne: Love's Cross-Currents and Lesbia Brandon,* I have silently corrected these mistakes.

7. See Freud, "Some Character-Types (III)": "Paradoxical as it may sound, I must maintain that the sense of guilt was present [in certain patients] before the misdeed, that it did not arise from it, but conversely—the misdeed arose from the sense of guilt" (332). In *The Ego and the Id* (1923), Freud sums up this argument by stating: "Punishment must be exacted even if it does not fall upon the guilty" (45). See also *Civilization and Its Discontents* 137.

8. Mario Praz makes a similar point when comparing Swinburne's second novel with a painting by Gustave Moreau (*Romantic* 290–91).

9. "Over-much delight," wrote Swinburne about Dante Gabriel Rossetti's poetry, is "the passion of overrunning pleasure which quivers and aches on the very edge of heavenly tears—'tears of perfect moan' for excess of unfathomable pleasure and burden of inexpressible things only to be borne by Gods in heaven" (*Complete* 15: 31).

10. See Harrison: "[A]s in most of Swinburne's passion poems, death does not just provide an alternative to sexual gratification: it constitutes the only total consummation to sexual desires that are by definition insatiable" ("Eros" 22; see also Rooksby, "Upon" 137–38).

11. Riede adds: "[P]erhaps *Lesbia Brandon,* designed as a hybrid of poetry and prose, was [Swinburne's] attempt to unify his divided sensibility. If so, the fact that Swinburne cherished it for forty years without finishing it may well suggest that the feat was not possible" (7). While this suggestion is worth pondering, Hughes provides ample proof that Swinburne *did* attempt to complete the second novel: He had it set up in type (*Lesbia* 219–20), but found it increasingly difficult to finish scenes when Watts refused to return crucial passages that he had borrowed.

12. Additionally, some of Northey's claims about the first novel are misleading: Reginald Harewood's pleasure in receiving Captain Harewood's ferocious and "manly" beatings—as well as his Romantic passion for Clara Radworth—are obvious precursors to Herbert's flagellation by Denham and love for Margaret and Lesbia. As many critics observe, the novels are closely related, the latter repeating many of the dynamics, scenarios, and even dialog informing the former (see Hughes 275–76, 285, 290, 314–15; Riede 7; E. Wilson 34; F. Wilson, "Swinburne's Prose Heroines" 250–51).

13. See Harrison, who argues astutely: "Swinburne's personae, although always victims of their love, are not always victims of those they love, masochistic counterparts of Sadian figures. *The very violence of their lust often generates an almost paralyzing equivocation between murderous and suicidal inclinations*—the effect, ultimately, of the persona's awareness that in the pain-pleasure complex, pain triumphs simply by virtue of its indivisibility from pleasure" ("Eros" 23; my emphasis). See also his excellent "Swinburne's" esp. 690, and W. Wilson's psychoanalytic reading of Swinburne's "Before the Mirror" esp. 431–32.

14. For a general overview of Swinburne's, Courbet's, and Baudelaire's interest in lesbianism, which advances important points about "alternative masculinities" in the nineteenth century, such as the idea of "voluntary self-feminization," see Morgan, "Male" esp. 39, 49–53.

15. Connolly (56–58) interprets Swinburne's association of passion with suffering and exaltation. And Harrison's "Swinburnian" is a fine account of the way "Female figures . . . dominate Swinburne's works . . . [as] archetypal representatives . . . whose beauty and often whose love prove fatal to the men who crave union with them" (90; see also 97; Harrison, "Love"; and Fisch). For a Lacanian account of this psychic oscillation, see Salecl.

16. Interpreting *Love's Cross-Currents,* Riede states: "In writing these letters [in the novel] Swinburne displayed a capacity for psychological insight and analysis that never appears in his poetry, and a corresponding ability to write with minute precision and subtle nuance that is hardly characteristic of 'Dolores' or 'Faustine' or even of such masterpieces as 'The Triumph of Time' and 'Ave atque Vale'" (6). I disagree that such "psychological insight and analysis . . . *never* appear in his poetry," but I am arguing that the novels pronounce these factors more strongly than do the poems.

17. The original gives: "Ils ne sont en fait que l'endroit et l'envers d'une même entité. Dès lors le désir de Denham ne serait-il pas le désir de l'androgyne?" (60).

18. In *Lesbia Brandon,* as elsewhere in Swinburne's writing, the sea is overdetermined symbolically. In addition to the passages above, see *Lesbia* 18, 24. For elaboration, see Charlesworth 31–32; McGhee 86.

19. Swinburne was more cautious than this statement implies, however, and unceremoniously dropped Simeon Solomon when the latter was arrested and convicted for immoral behavior in a public urinal. As he wrote Watts on December 1, 1873, "in such a case as this I do think a man is bound to consider the consequence to all his friends and to every one who cares for him in the world of allowing his name to be mixed up with that of a ——— let us say, a Platonist; the term is at once accurate as a definition and unobjectional as a euphemism" (*Letters* 2: 261).

20. While making these claims about Swinburne's emasculation of the male *erōmenos,* I am not discounting that other poems in his First Series, such as "Anactoria," correspondingly "virilize" Sappho (Carter 153).

21. The original gives: "une large mesure de l'abdication par l'homme de sa propre virilité, . . . mettant en valeur une faiblesse de caractère généralement associée avec une certaine effémination" (58). Although I make this claim for the two poems only, Monneyron is referring to Herbert's perverse indolence in *Lesbia Brandon.* Our readings therefore slightly disagree with each other, for mine builds partly on the narrator's insistence, in *Lesbia Brandon,* that after Denham's death, Herbert *"did not seem effeminate* or dejected, and hoisted no signs of inward defeat; but at heart he was conscious of weakness and waste" (157; my emphasis).

22. For details of Swinburne's related argument, see *Swinburne Replies* 23–24. Greenberg observes significantly, "Though a union of sorts occurs in the probing and quizzically tender 'Hermaphroditus,' it . . . is without the authority of love: allegorized—'with veiled eyes'—Love turns away, refusing to participate. The speaker, moreover, remains in the voyeur's role, a third party looking on" (80).

23. For instance, Dellamora argues that Swinburne's "Anactoria" aims "to free desire" by making sexual difference and orientation "indeterminate" (77). Slightly earlier in *Masculine Desire,* he argues relatedly that Swinburne "enjoyed imagining such possibilities" as "male-male genital activity" (69). Sussman makes a similar point in *Victorian Masculinities* 179, 185, but Harrison's reading of Swinburne's "hermaphroditic ideal," in "Aesthetics," is closer to my argument (95). See Busst and Black for excellent accounts of androgyny; also Weil (esp. 17–25).

24. John A. Cassidy crassly explains that these poems are among "the 'shockers' which most clearly express [Swinburne's] abnormal sexuality and his savage rejection of religion" (97–98).

25. Monneyron observes: "Herbert Seyton reçoit une féminisation extrême à laquelle répond, à un degré moindre, la masculinisation de Lesbia Brandon [Herbert Seyton receives/accepts an acute feminization to which Lesbia Brandon's masculinization responds, albeit to a lesser degree]" (55; my trans.).

26. Cassidy fails to consider this point when arguing, "Homosexual proclivities being at variance with nature, the victim [*sic*] is impelled by nature, at various times in his life, to reach for normalcy. If the attempt meets with frustration, he falls back all the more deeply

and hopelessly into abnormality" (112). Invoking Irving Bieber's discredited, homophobic work on homosexuality, Cassidy implies absurdly that any interest in psychic extremes leads a poet "hopelessly into abnormality," a word he uses repeatedly to characterize Swinburne's erotic disposition. As such, Cassidy consistently misunderstands (in ways that Eliot and others did not) that Swinburne's interest in ecstasy and unpleasure bears little relation to the status of objects, real or imagined.

CHAPTER 3

1. Kucich gives a fine account of Feuerbach's *Essence of Christianity* and its impact on George Eliot in *Repression* 123–30.

2. "We are foolish," Ruskin writes, "and without excuse foolish, in speaking of the 'superiority' of one sex to the other, as if they could be compared in similar things. Each has what the other has not: each completes the other, and is completed by the other: they are in nothing alike, and the happiness and perfection of both depends on each asking and receiving from the other what the other only can give" (100–101). Carol Christ's reading of Coventry Patmore's *The Angel in the House* (1854) argues similarly that "[m]an . . . is defined precisely by the desire to achieve." However, cautions Christ, "that desire brings him only anxiety and pain. Failure and success both lead to self-hatred" ("Victorian" 149; see also her essay "Hero"). My reading of Gregory Rose in *The Story of an African Farm* underscores a similar idea.

3. As Joseph Bristow points out, the phrase "woman-man" recurs in Alfred Tennyson's poetry (*Effeminate* 8). That Tennyson published this phrase in 1886 and 1889 suggests a *possible* allusion to Schreiner's novel, published to wide acclaim in 1883. In 1889, for instance, Tennyson published "On One Who Affected an Effeminate Manner," which voices a similar argument about sexual difference:

While man and woman still are incomplete,
I prize that soul where man and woman meet,
Which types all Nature's male and female plan,
but, friend, man-woman is not woman-man. (*Poems* 1424)

And in the earlier "Locksley Hall Sixty Years After" (1886), Tennyson writes: "As our greatest is man-woman, so was she the woman-man" (see *The Poems of Tennyson* 1359–69). Editor Christopher Ricks notes that one of Tennyson's late notebooks contains the jotting: "Men should be androgynous and women gynandrous, but men should not be gynandrous nor women androgynous" (qtd. 1424).

4. See also 113, where the narrator observes: "Now we have no God. We have had two: the old God that our fathers handed down to us, that we hated, and never liked; the new one that we made for ourselves, that we loved; but now he has flitted away from us, and we see what he was made of—the shadow of our highest ideal, crowned and throned. Now we have no God." For general elaboration (engaging George Eliot and Hardy), see Reardon 188–98, 318–50, and Maynard 271–98.

5. However, the novel was very popular: Two editions appeared in 1883 and fifteen editions were published in Schreiner's lifetime (Bristow, introduction xxxiv). By the sum-

mer of 1900, the novel had sold one hundred thousand copies, making Schreiner famous in literary and related circles.

6. My argument here (which builds on Lyndall's) differs slightly from Cherry Clayton's suggestion that "[s]exual identity is revealed as fluid, a point made in many other ways in the novel, whereas gender norms are shown to be rigid" (*Olive* 53). She and Paxton (574) refer here to Lyndall's claim that "[w]e all enter the world little plastic beings, with so much natural force, perhaps, but for the rest—blank" (*African* 154). I agree that there is a rigidity to gender norms in *African Farm,* but will argue that there are internal resistances to sexuality affecting its "fluidity" in Schreiner's work; hence, in part, Lyndall's scorn for Gregory's effeminacy. Finally, it is unconvincing to argue, as Paxton does (573), that "Lyndall's contempt for Rose expresses, in part, her appreciation of the strenuous, productive labour from which she, by her sex, feels excluded." For although Gregory wants little part of this "strenuous, productive labour," Lyndall tends to raise these arguments when Gregory appears, but downplays them in conversation with RR, a character to whom she is drawn out of fear rather than resentment (see *African* 206).

7. Earlier in *The Odd Women,* the narrator blithely invokes what he calls "the marriage war" (76).

8. Berkman quotes one of Schreiner's letters illustrating a similar notion: "When I find a man as much stronger than I am as I am stronger than a child, then I will marry him, no one before" (qtd. in "Nurturant" 11). And on August 1, 1893, Schreiner wrote this to Edward Carpenter: "If I marry it'll be the type of man most removed from our divine Bob [Robert Muirhead], a man compared to whom I shall be a saint!!! A sort of small Napoleon! I don't know why it is *those* natures always draw me. *Not* the man of thought and fine-drawn feelings like Bob and [Havelock] Ellis and Karl Pearson, intensely as I love them" (*Olive Schreiner: Letters* 223; original emphases).

9. However, First and Scott qualify this claim, later arguing: "The novel did not resolve the paradox [because] . . . it resorted to the conventional view of men degenerating to womanhood if they had any human or 'maternal' qualities at all" (107). Although I am closer to agreeing with this latter claim, Schreiner's interest in the unconscious—and thus in the unconscious meanings of sexual difference—seems to offset suggestions that Gregory's "womanhood" signifies only his degeneration in Schreiner's eyes. For elaboration on nineteenth-century definitions of "unmanliness," see Hilliard; Mangan and Walvin; and Bristow, *Effeminate.*

10. Monsman calls Lyndall Schreiner's "persona" ("Patterns" 256).

11. Woolf quotes with interest Schreiner's observation " 'Nothing matters in life but love and a great pity for all our fellows' " ("Olive" 180), though she concludes quite harshly that Schreiner was "one half of a great writer; a diamond marred by a flaw" (183). For a different account of Schreiner, see Fradkin, "Olive."

12. Lerner underscores this point ("Olive" 76–79). For examples of this difficulty, see Gilbert and Gubar 52–53; Parkin-Gounelas 100–101, 118–19; and Showalter, *Literature* 198–99, "Olive," and *Sexual* 53, 55–56. In *Literature,* Showalter argues: "With Schreiner we see a perverse will to fail that rationalizes itself as the artist's superiority and need for self-protection" (198).

13. See also Berkman, "Nurturant" 10–11 and *Healing* 5–8; Parkin-Gounelas 99–119. Bristow, introduction; and Barash are valuable exceptions.

14. One sees various connections with Gissing's *The Odd Women,* a novel I'll invoke periodically in this chapter because it advances a similar interest in feminism, politics, and the unconscious.

15. For instance, Clayton: "[Schreiner's] letters reveal constant reflections on possible ways of combining friendship and passion, but a realization that imbalances within contemporary marriage destroyed the basis for equality and thus for love" (*Olive* 53). See also Toth 647–48.

16. On October 3, 1888, Schreiner wrote Ellis, arguing relatedly: "Oh, it is awful to be a woman. These women are killing me. Give my love to Louie, but I don't want to see her or any other woman. I want to live *alone, alone, alone.* I don't say the fault is not in myself, but they are doing it all the same. . . . Oh, please see that they bury me in a place where there are no women" (*Letters* 142).

17. Earlier in the novel, however, Lyndall scorns Em's engagement to Gregory Rose, adding as an embarrassed remark when Em comments on the "massive" diamond ring that Lyndall is wearing, a gift from RR: "I am not in so great a hurry to put my neck beneath any man's foot; and I do not so greatly admire the crying of babies" (150).

18. See Waldo's remarks about desire and disappointment (227). And, for elaboration on Schreiner and psychic isolation, Horton 60–65.

19. Bristow remarks that "in some respects [Waldo and Lyndall's love for each other] parallels the childhood passion of Tom and Maggie Tulliver" (xii). He adds that "Schreiner informed the sexologist Havelock Ellis that she had read [*The Mill on the Floss*] as a young woman, and 'not cared' for Eliot's writing. But its presence can certainly be felt" (xii; see also Paxton 566–71). For an interesting elaboration on Maggie's "indiscretions," see W. Cohen 130–58. Kucich usefully observes that in Eliot's novels, the "twin themes—excessive egotism and excessive anxiety about the regard of others—are systematically linked" (*Repression* 186).

20. As I point out in the preface and introduction to this book, the narrator of Eliot's novel shows that the "quell[ing]" of Maggie Tulliver's "passionate tumult" is contrary to her independent character. We should add that Bulwer-Lytton criticized Eliot's novel: "The *indulgence* of such a sentiment for the affianced of a friend [Stephen Guest] under whose roof she was, was a treachery and a meanness according to the Ethics of Art." Eliot responded fiercely: "If the ethics of art do not admit the truthful presentation of a character essentially noble but liable to great error—error that is anguish to its own nobleness—*then,* it seems to me, the ethics of art are too narrow, and *must be widened to correspond with a widening psychology*" (both quotations appear in A. S. Byatt's introduction to the Penguin edition 34–35; final emphasis mine).

21. As Jane Eyre recounts at the end of the novel, St. John's "is the ambition of the high master-spirit, which aims to fill a place in the first rank of those who are redeemed from the earth—who stand without fault before the throne of God, who share the last mighty victories of the Lamb, who are called, and chosen, and faithful" (477).

22. In many ways anticipating Schreiner's writing, Eliot advanced a more complicated

notion of discontent than did Gaskell. However, Brontë's *Villette* (1853) has a comparable intensity.

23. In an undated letter to the Rev. J. T. Lloyd, probably written in 1895, Schreiner
remarked: "One thing I always find . . . difficult to understand is how people gather from
any of my writings that I think lightly of marriage. I think it to be the most holy, the most
organic, the most important sacrament in life, and how men and women can enter into it
with the lighthearted indifference they do, has always been, and is, a matter of endless
wonder to me" (*Olive Schreiner: Letters* 259).

24. Monsman considers reveries such as this a "mistake," and in doing so he not only
implicitly rejects Rebekah's (and Schreiner's) fantasies, but overlooks their occasional lesbian significance: "But in a world in which success is defined by men in male terms, the
tragic mistake for a woman is to think that she has to be a man to succeed; that is, to
adopt male values" ("Olive Schreiner" 593). For an interesting account of "the dynamics
of woman-to-woman influence" in Schreiner's work, see Paxton; Berkman, "Nurturant"
12–13; Barash 270, 275–77; and Steele 107.

25. See Gilbert and Gubar 58. As evidence of his effeminacy, consider the following early
description of Gregory's home: "All was scrupulously neat and clean, for Gregory kept a
little duster folded in the corner of his table-drawer, just as he had seen his mother do, and
every morning before he went out he said his prayers, and made his bed, and dusted the
table and the legs of the chairs, and even the pictures on the wall and the gun-rack" (139).

26. It is, Clayton continues, "as if sexual passion itself has to be dismantled before women
and men can approach each other with an understanding of human need" (*Olive* 53). By
contrast, Monsman appears to want the lines of sexual difference restored: "A woman cannot be a man without distortion, any more than Gregory Rose can become a woman except
through a grotesque cross-dressing" ("Olive Schreiner" 593).

27. I interpret the sexual ambiguity of Mason's writing in chapter 2 of *The Ruling Passion:
British Colonial Allegory and the Paradox of Homosexual Desire*. The narrator of Schreiner's
African Farm picks up on this Cain motif: "He walked home behind his flock. His heart
was heavy. He reasoned so: 'God cannot lie. I had faith. No fire came. I am like Cain—I
am not His. He will not hear my prayer. God hates me'" (7).

28. I am thinking of the moment Dorian Gray asks Alan Campbell to assist him in
destroying Basil Hallward's body, and his friend comments: "I don't care what shame comes
on you. You deserve it all. I should not be sorry to see you disgraced, publicly disgraced.
How dare you ask me, of all men in the world, to mix myself up in this horror?" (187).

29. See the descriptions of Teleny and des Grieux on 28, 69, and 131. Concerning
Schreiner's novel, see Bristow, introduction xx, for a credible history of Gregory's name;
also Monsman, "Olive Schreiner" 594.

30. For elaboration, see Feldman esp. 54–142; Felski 1–34; and Howells esp. 136. As
Jacqueline Rose theorized astutely, "Men and women take up positions of symbolic and
polarised opposition against the grain of a multifarious and bisexual disposition . . . The
lines of that division are fragile in exact proportion to the rigid insistence with which our
culture lays them down; they constantly converge and threaten to coalesce" (226–27).

31. Although I have put *impossible* in scare quotes to underscore what Rose calls, in the

note above, "the rigid insistence with which our culture" opposes men's and women's roles (227), I am calling Gregory only a "symptom" of this impossibility, rather than arguing that he shows that men's and women's imaginary and symbolic distance is *fallacious*. Claiming the latter would downplay both the extent of our and Victorian cultures' "rigid insistence" that men and women differ and the psychic repercussions of this insistence. Critical approaches stressing only the performative dimension of gender often entirely ignore the second factor, as a result turning masculine and feminine identification into a type of voluntarism. For an invaluable critique of these approaches, see Dean, "Transsexual."

32. Elsewhere, however, Lyndall downplays the importance of men's virility, indicating that androgyny may be closer to her highest vision of love: "'When I am with you,'" she tells Waldo, "'I never know that I am a woman and you are a man; I only know that we are both things that think. Other men when I am with them, whether I love them or not, they are mere bodies to me; but you are a spirit'" (177).

33. See Paxton 573; also Berkman, *Healing* 149–54. However, concerning the interpretive risks of psychobiography, see Rive, in which Schreiner oddly is quoted as writing: "I make no comment throughout the book [*From Man to Man*], I *never* speak in my own person, the characters simply act and you draw your own conclusions" (qtd. in 44; original emphasis).

34. See *Olive Schreiner: Letters* 221–24; Rowbotham and Weeks 43–44; Buchanan-Gould 70, 72; Hobman 41–43; Brandon 69.

35. Clayton earlier remarks: "Schreiner constantly told Havelock Ellis, during their initial abortive romance, that passion separated her from him" (*Olive* 53).

36. Zyl comments: "She was alternately attracted and repelled by his character, for he seemed to have both the directed drive, and channeled energies of Lyndall, and the unscrupulous potential to corrupt of Blenkins [in *African Farm*]" ("Rhodes" 87). See also Lewis esp. 45–46; Brandon 79–80, 94.

37. Zyl notes that the farmers could invoke the bill to "mete out punishment to their own labourers" and that Schreiner called it the "Every man beat his own kaffir" bill (qtd. in "Rhodes" 87). And yet, he notes, Schreiner "still believed in [Rhodes's] greatness" (87).

38. Schreiner only participated in the Men and Women's Club from 1885 on, however, so the club could have influenced only her later works, such as *Women and Labour*, and her ongoing novels, *From Man to Man* and *Undine*.

39. Haynes notes: "overwhelmingly critics of the novel have proclaimed as a serious defect the arrival of the two different strangers and their failure to return" (69). See below for a reading of Schreiner's preface to the novel.

40. Indeed, their recurrence does justice to Lyndall's claims that "all things are in all men": "We shall find nothing new in human nature after we have once carefully dissected and analysed the one being we shall ever truly know—ourself" (164). Considering the novel's interest in homoeroticism, these remarks anticipate Freud's 1910 and 1915 revisions to his *Three Essays on the Theory of Sexuality* (1905), in which he claims: "Psycho-analytic research . . . has found that all human beings are capable of making a homosexual object-choice and have in fact made one in their unconscious" (145 n). I am suggesting that Schreiner's *African Farm* represents in fiction the same argument.

41. Such remarks anticipate T. E. Lawrence's *Seven Pillars of Wisdom: A Triumph* (1922; 1926), in which the author writes: "We had learned that there were pangs too sharp, griefs too deep, ecstasies too high for our finite selves to register. When emotion reached this pitch the mind choked; and memory went white till the circumstances were humdrum once more" (29–30). Later, when beaten and raped by Turkish soldiers, Lawrence remarks that "a delicious warmth, probably sexual, was swelling through me" (445).

42. See Kahane 82. For theoretical elaboration on the principle of stasis and death in literature, see Bersani and Dutoit 1–9.

43. That essay builds in turn on Freud's 1921–22 essay "Some Neurotic Mechanisms in Jealousy, Paranoia and Homosexuality," in which he began to assess the psychic relevance of sibling rivalry for the etiology of male homosexuality.

44. Here, as elsewhere, Freud considers in proper detail only the intricacies of this scenario for the boy. He writes, "In a precisely analogous way, the outcome of the Oedipus attitude in a little girl may be an intensification of her identification with her mother (or the setting up of such an identification for the first time)—a result which will fix the child's feminine character" (*Ego* 32).

45. And Fuss usefully cautions: "Any politics of identity needs to come to terms with the complicated and meaningful ways that identity is continually compromised, imperiled, one might even say *embarrassed* by identification" (10; original emphasis).

46. Concerning psychoanalysis and masculinity, the poet H. D. (Hilda Doolittle) recounts in *Tribute to Freud* (1945–46) that Freud had once told her: " 'And—I must tell you (you were frank with me and I will be frank with you), I do *not* like to be the mother in transference—it always surprises and shocks me a little. I feel so very masculine.' I asked him if others had what he called this mother-transference on him. He said ironically and I thought a little wistfully, 'O, *very* many' " (146–47; original emphases).

47. Were the cultural proscription against loving the father diminished, for instance, the internal contempt of the superego vis-à-vis the ego *might* be reduced. In adding this suggestion, however, I wish to echo Freud's contemporaneous caution, in *The Ego and the Id* (1923), that the superego is *not* a simple internal representative of cultural forces. The erroneous claim that the superego reproduces internally cultural expectations and demands has persisted despite Freud's claims to the contrary (26, 54).

48. Gregory Rose anticipates this statement when asking his sister, "have you ever known what it is to keep wanting and wanting and wanting to kiss someone's mouth . . . ?" (141).

CHAPTER 4

1. For elaboration on Hardy's "fatalism," see Elliott 15. Elaborating on Hardy's famous statement "Life offers—to deny!," L. Butler comments: "The point is that the Will is quite unaware of man's aspirations, and in the face of that fact man's best choice is withdrawal, resignation, learning not to desire" (7).

2. Elliott writes: "Hardy probably got from Hartmann the germ of that corollary for his Immanent Will—the melioristic belief that It may be gradually approaching a consciousness which will eventually reconcile contending elements of the earth. He asks William Archer, 'Do you know Hartmann's philosophy of the Unconscious? It suggested to me what

seemed almost like a workable theory of the great problem of the origin of evil—though this, of course, is not Hartmann's own theory—namely, that there may be a consciousness, infinitely far off, at the other end of the chain of phenomena, always striving to express itself, and always baffled and blundering, just as the spirits seem to be'" (27). Elliott immediately corroborates Hardy: "Certainly the idea is not Hartmann's; it is Schopenhauer's" (27).

3. Here I am departing from Elliott's argument that "Hardy's tragedy can be said to spring from within the human actor only in so far as this universal force fastens one of its tentacles within the very mind of man" (33). Such claims preempt Hardy's interest in psychological *determinants,* and not merely psychological effects. In "La nature humaine," in *Le pessimisme de Thomas Hardy* (73–112), Ridder-Barzin advances claims similar to Elliott's. For more sophisticated readings of determinism in Hardy's work, see Fussell 28 and Manning 58–60. And for a fine account of the way Hardy's "'culture'-heroes live out the collapse of Victorian secular idealism," see DeLaura, "Ache" 397.

4. "[T]he flaw exists within the very structure of the foundation," notes Meisel, adding that "twilight comes slowly, but with a relentless inner logic" (98). Such perspectives help us approach even the idea of "internal impediments" in Hardy with caution. As L. Butler notes, "Time and again Hardy's lovers are disappointed, but the disappointment of unrequited love, although painful, is in some ways less acute than the disillusionment of successful love" (10). This chapter is in part a meditation on this fascinating paradox in Hardy's work.

5. See also Copjec, *Read:* "Freud does not set social reality—civilization—*against* the pleasure principle, but rather defines the former as a product of the latter. Civilization does not test, but realizes our fantasies; it does not put us in touch with Fate (the real), but protects us from it" (40).

6. For a more elaborate reading of this dynamic, see Jacobus, "Sue" 305 and "Tess's" 319–20.

7. Milberg-Kaye dismisses as "simplistic" the assumption that Henchard's selling his wife is the sole cause of his ruin (64). Addressing the novel's interest in psychic predispositions to failure, Thurley adds: "Character is doomed out of its own strength. At the same time, personality tends towards an equally fatal instability. People [in Hardy's novels] . . . break down like filaments charged with too much current" (24). My point about hubris also applies to Phillotson, in *Jude the Obscure.* The narrator of Hardy's last novel tells us that "the schoolmaster's plans and dreams so long indulged in had been abandoned for some new dream with which neither the Church nor literature had much in common" (215).

8. Hardy, *Collected* 531. Seymour-Smith repeats the second quotation in his introduction to *Mayor* 12; see also Moore 16–17 and Narayanaswamy 70.

9. Schweik's important essay "Character and Fate in Hardy's *The Mayor of Casterbridge*" endorses my argument that Hardy's psychological emphasis shatters the suggestion that Fate is an absolute determinant of character and desire. To put this another way, Hardy's conception of the unconscious (inherited from Hartmann and Schopenhauer [see note 2 above]), in advancing a slightly different idea of agency, proves *nonidentical to his philosophi-*

cal emphasis on the Immanent Will. See Schweik 249–50; also Hennelly 94; Meisel 91; Edmond 111; and King: "If Michael Henchard is a 'man of character,' it is only because his character aids and abets those forces which destroy him" (42).

10. Hardy's thoughts about the reception of *Jude the Obscure* suggest that he *did* intend to represent such piquancy in his works. "In my own eyes," he writes, "the sad feature of the [critics'] attack was that the greater part of the story—that which presented the shattered ideals of the two chief characters, and had been more especially, and indeed almost exclusively, the part of interest to myself—was practically ignored by the adverse press of the two countries [England and the United States]" (qtd. in Orel 33).

11. This "antihumanist" perspective recurs at the end of the novel when Tess, running from afar to meet Angel Clare, is described as "a moving spot intrud[ing] on the white vacuity of its perspective" (473).

12. The stoicism we detect in Hardy's poem "He Fears His Good Fortune" rescinds neither this fascination with endings nor the implicit notion that failure is arranged to the subject's satisfaction: "Well . . . let the end foreseen / Come duly!—I am serene" (*Collected* 479).

13. L. Epstein's commentary on this scene usefully reminds us that "the sale that severs the alliance between Mr. and Mrs. Michael Henchard is also a wedding that creates a union between Mr. and Mrs. Richard Newson" (50). See also Beegel (esp. 109) for an interesting account of matrimony in *Far from the Madding Crowd.*

14. For instance, Ridder-Barzin: "Dans *The Mayor of Casterbridge,* Henchard est peut-être ambitieux, mais ce que Hardy nous a montré en lui, c'est avant tout le jouet d'un Destin implacable égorgeant peu à peu sa victime [Henchard is perhaps ambitious, but Hardy reveals him to be above all else the victim and toy of an implacable Destiny that slowly slaughters its victim]" (73; my trans.).

15. See Grindle 105–6. I also would dispute Thurley's claim that Henchard's "death . . . finally redeems the moody violence of his life, so that Hardy can take in his stride the dangerously self-conscious tragic image with which he attempts to define him" (149). For readings of Henchard's death appropriately emphasizing the repercussions of defeat, see D. Brown 62 and Stewart 124.

16. Perhaps the strongest example is "Michael Henchard's Will," which *The Mayor of Casterbridge* lists two pages before it concludes. Henchard's "Will" is of course the testament of his desire, surviving beyond his death, but it also attests to his ongoing *opposition* to the Immanent Will. In partial contrast to Henchard's death drive, Lucetta, the narrator tells us, is eventually "fairly mastered [by] an intoxicating *Weltlust,*" or lust for worldly pleasure and material advancement (343)—certainly rather an interesting substitution.

17. Hardy's notion of representing thought in this way may derive from Carlyle, who, in *On Heroes, Hero-Worship, and the Heroic in History* (1840; 1841), invokes "the greatest invention man has ever made, this of marking down the unseen thought that is in him by written characters. It is a kind of second speech, almost as miraculous as the first" (27).

18. I am greatly indebted to Copjec's fine reading of this passage in "Evil in the Time of the Finite World." Kant's argument differs greatly from Whitman's and Emerson's, for

whom homoerotic passion is tainted only by the intrusions of public life. For elaboration, see Christopher Newfield's excellent reading of Emerson's essay "Friendship" (34–37).

19. When anticipating the "expiration" of his oath that he abstain from alcohol for twenty-one years, Henchard declares: "in twelve days I shall be released from my oath . . . and then I mean to enjoy myself, please God!" (303). Those witnessing Henchard's binge describe him as "bust[ing] out" of this oath (303). The narrator later observes that when the ferocious drive had passed, "the volcanic fires of his nature had burnt down" (308).

20. For evidence of "miserabilism," whose source (following Novalis's remark) seems closer to the superego than to Fate, consider the following passage: "Misery taught him nothing more than a defiant endurance of it . . . He looked out at the night as at a fiend. Henchard, like all his kind, was superstitious, and he could not help thinking that the concatenation of events this evening had produced was the scheme of *some sinister intelligence bent on punishing him*" (197; my emphasis). In *Jude* Sue Bridehead invokes the same vindictive "intelligence" as one reason she must return to Phillotson—a return the narrator calls "her mental volte-face" (431); see 413 and *The Woodlanders* 428.

21. A related point emerges in *Tess* when the narrator remarks that Angel Clare's friends "could applaud or condemn each other, amuse or sadden themselves by the contemplation of each other's foibles or vices; men every one of whom walked in his own individual way the road to dusty death" (173–74).

22. See *Tess* 204, a passage I discuss toward the end of this chapter.

23. When Sue does eventually allow Phillotson to kiss her, for instance, we are told that "a quick look of aversion passed over her face, but clenching her teeth she uttered no cry" (479).

24. Sue herself immediately contradicts this characterization: "But I won't have it! Some of the most passionately erotic poets have been the most self-contained in their daily lives" (203).

25. That Hardy is invoking this play becomes clear when Farfrae, observing Lucetta, notes that "his Calphurnia's cheek was pale" (340). See also Ingersoll, "Troping" 65. For related interest in the novel's literary sources, see also Rabiger 101.

26. Kucich astutely remarks, "Honesty and fidelity are so imperilled by the encroachments of desire in Hardy's work—both social and sexual desire—that he can reimagine them only as a stringent distantiation from it" ("Moral" 234).

27. Langbaum's article also usefully—if inconsistently—engages with this difficulty, advancing a reading of Henchard's preoccupation with power and mastery that supposedly refutes Freudian emphases: "[Henchard's] violently explosive behaviour might be attributed to sexual repression. But that Freudian concept does not seem to apply, largely because we are not given a sense of charged-up sexual energy and because Henchard's two soaring expressions of love, for Farfrae and Elizabeth-Jane, are not apparently directed toward physical gratification though they might have been portrayed that way" (21). This point seems rather to beg the question. If Henchard's "repression" *had* been successful, it would betray no sign of difficulty; we witness the difficulty in sexual and symptomatic forms because the repression *fails*. Langbaum also seems unwilling to conceptualize this relation between love

and desire, preferring to claim that "[i]n Henchard the desire for power replaces sexuality" (22). The problem nonetheless resurfaces when Langbaum interprets the erotic constituents of power, arguing in the next paragraph: "In portraying Henchard's love of Farfrae, Hardy suggests if not homosexuality at least the inevitable homoerotic element in male bonding" (22). In this way, while Langbaum simply—and usefully—iterates Wright and J. Hillis Miller, his own argument is tautological.

28. "Whether owing to the barbarizing of taste in the younger minds by the dark madness of the late war," writes Hardy, in his "Apology" for the *Late Lyrics and Earlier* poetry collection, "the unabashed cultivation of selfishness in all classes, the plethoric growth of knowledge simultaneously with the stunting of wisdom, 'a degrading thirst after outrageous stimulation' (to quote Wordsworth again), or from any other cause, we seem threatened with a new Dark Age" (*Collected* 530). One might contrast Hardy's concern about "outrageous stimulation" with the passage in *Tess* I interpret below, which states that the young milkmaids who "palpitate with . . . hopeless passion" for Angel Clare are "ecstasiz[ed] . . . to a killing joy" (205, 206).

29. The narrator soon corrects this impression, again iterating the legal and affective principle of a "claim": "The mockery was, that he should have no sooner taught a girl to claim the shelter of his paternity than he discovered her to have no kinship with him" (197). This comment refers us back to Susan's remarks about the respective duties of kin and friendship, but Henchard's realization, we should add, is fundamentally an axiom in Hardy's work.

30. One thinks here of Freud's statement, in "On the Universal Tendency to Debasement in the Sphere of Love" (1912), about "psychical impotence," victims of which fail to sustain both sexual and affectionate regard for another: "Where they love they do not desire and where they desire they cannot love" (185, 183). And in "A Special Type of Choice of Object Made by Men" (1910), Freud reveals that homo- and heterosexual desires may be concomitant, rather than mutually exclusive, in the same subject (see 166–67).

31. I interpret this homoerotic fascination in *The Ruling Passion: British Colonial Allegory and the Paradox of Homosexual Desire* esp. 113–20.

32. When Heyst first sees Morrison on the island of Timor, he "accost[s]" him on a whim because Morrison seems to be "a man in trouble, expressively harassed, dejected, lonely" (*Victory* 114).

33. Indeed, the same degree of affective and symbolic uncertainty undermines both same- and different-sex relationships. Commenting on Henchard's relationship with Elizabeth-Jane, Grindle notes: "It is one of the most striking features of *The Mayor of Casterbridge* that the central relationship is not only *not* a sexual one, it is one which defies acceptable labelling altogether. . . . The novel plays repeatedly on this question of whether or no the possibility [of kinship] will be realised. Is she or isn't she his daughter? And, intertwined with that, does he or doesn't he care about her?" (95). We must note, however, that Hardy initially "suppressed" the novel's most explicit heterosexual content—Henchard's unmarried affair with Lucetta in Jersey—"until the publication of the first uniform edition of 1895" (Winfield 57).

34. Although Showalter's essay contains interesting insights, it seems uncertain about Hardyesque psychology. For instance: "For the heroes of [Hardy's] tragic novels—Michael Henchard, Jude Fawley, Angel Clare—maturity involves a kind of assimilation of female suffering, an identification with a woman which is also an effort to come to terms with their own deepest selves. . . . Hardy not only commented upon, and in a sense, infiltrated, feminine fictions; he also understood the feminine self as the estranged and essential counterpart of the male self" ("Unmanning" 101). Departing from this suggestion of psychic complementarity, I am arguing that Hardy's psychological wisdom stems from his suspicion, to quote Lacan, that "there is no sexual relation" without the *fantasy* of complementarity, and that the sexes fundamentally are riven by asymmetry. I base this claim on both my reading below and my interpretation above of various passages in *Jude* and *Tess*.

35. See Wright: "Hardy's novels . . . illustrate both the delights and the dangers of eroticism; they portray the impossibility of undistorted relationships between men and women" (2). I am also drawing on Millgate's and Dellamora's appraisal of Hardy's friendship with the Rev. Henry Moule. Millgate, in Dellamora's words, "believes that on the evening of Hardy's last conversation with Moule at Queens' College, Cambridge, in the following month [June 1873], the older man made an explicit approach to Hardy—an approach to which he responded with anger. Three months afterwards to the day, Moule committed suicide at Cambridge. Hardy was devastated, and from this time onward in his fiction 'never portrayed a man who was not, in some way, maimed by fate'" (Dellamora, "Male" 467; see Millgate esp. 156). To this, let us add "maimed by desire"; *The Mayor of Casterbridge* was published as a novel in 1886.

36. See Lacan, *Four* 184: "There is a *jouissance* beyond the pleasure principle."

37. See note 28 above regarding Hardy's concern about "outrageous stimulation" (as he observes, the phrase is Wordsworth's). See also chapter 2 for a brief account of Swinburne's interest in "over-much delight."

38. The narrator's account of Winterborne's internal struggle is instructive: "Winterborne, though fighting valiantly against himself all this while—though he would have protected Grace's good repute as the apple of his eye, was a man; and, as Desdemona said, men are not gods. In face of the agonizing seductiveness shown by her, in her unenlightened school-girl simplicity about the laws and ordinances, he betrayed a man's weakness" (355).

39. The narrator contrasts such claims with Fitzpiers's passion, telling us that the "man whom Grace's matrimonial fidelity could not keep faithful was stung into passionate throbs of interest concerning her by her avowal of the contrary . . . and, melancholy as it may be to admit the fact, his own humiliation and regret engendered a smouldering admiration of her. . . . To be the vassal of her sweet will for a time—he demanded no more, and found solace in the contemplation of the soft miseries she caused him" (400, 406).

40. Describing Henchard's remarriage to Susan, the narrator tells us later that "Henchard's . . . well-known haughty indifference to the society of womankind, his silent avoidance of converse with the sex, contributed a piquancy to what would otherwise have been an unromantic matter enough. . . . Nobody would have conceived from his outward de-

meanour that there was no amatory fire or pulse of romance acting as stimulant to the bustle going on in his gaunt, great house" (153–54).

41. "Speech betrayeth thee," remarks Elizabeth-Jane to Lucetta (223).

CHAPTER 5

1. For an account of the novel's aesthetic failure ignoring the conceptual value of these deficiencies, see Powers.

2. "Integrity": L. *integer*—"intact, . . . making up a whole" (Hoad 238).

3. For a related discussion of the woman's "masquerade" and the man's "parade," see Rivière; Heath; and Lacan, *Seminar II* 37, 227.

4. We might observe a similar principle in modern camp—an aesthetic that lays bare, and ruins, the semiotics of performance through exaggeration. Arguably, Nash similarly exaggerates by representing all life in aesthetic terms: "[T]o live is such an art; to feel is such a career!" (*Tragic* 27).

5. Consider the novel's frequent allusions to physical and artistic tumescence—for example, Rowland's remark: " 'Of course when a body begins to expand, there comes in the possibility of bursting; but I nevertheless approve of a certain tension of one's being. It's what a man is meant for' " (*Roderick* 81).

6. Compare James, preface to *Tragic* 90: "the multiplication of *aspects*" culminates in "a *usurping* consciousness" (original emphases). James's explanation for Nick's failure is also significant. Having acknowledged that he "strove in vain . . . to embroil and adorn this young man on whom a hundred ingenious touches are thus lavished" (97), James first concludes that the idea of an artist "in triumph" would be uninteresting; his triumph should exist as a matter of what he *produces*. In relation to the novel's ending and the profound ambivalence that Nash's portrait generates, however, this conclusion seemed curious and unworkable even to James, whose explanation for Nick's failure becomes elliptical: "The better part of him is locked too much away from us, and the part we see has to pass for—well, what it passes for, so lamentably, among his friends and relatives" (97).

One answer to the failure, which may also account for James's admission that Nick's "better part . . . is locked . . . away," surfaces in an earlier statement: "What he produces . . . is another affair. His romance is the romance he himself projects" (96). As I argue later in this chapter, this "romance" constitutes the "unsaid" (122) of the novel because Nick's intimacy with Nash (as a project and projection) is not successfully resolved. On this point, it is notable that James dramatically revised Nick and Nash's "romance." In the January 1889 issue of the *Atlantic Monthly*, for instance, he described his conception of the novel as "the history of an American aesthete (or possibly an English one) [Nick], who *conceives a violent admiration* for a French aesthete (a contemporary novelist) [Nash], and goes to Paris to make his acquaintance; where he finds that his Frenchman is so much more thorough-going a specimen of the day than himself, that he is appalled and returns to Philistinism" (qtd. in Baker 151; my emphasis).

The absence of all reference to women here—to Julia as Nick's partner or to Miriam as the novel's principal "object"—supports my argument that women are initially subordinate to the "violent admiration" prevailing between Nick and Nash. Moreover, this "violence" recurs in Nash's removal from the text and in the narrative's insistence that marriage constitutes its only possible closure.

7. Nick greeted him and said it was a happy chance—he was uncommonly glad to see him.

"I never come across you—I don't know why," Nick remarked, while the two, smiling, looked each other up and down, like men reunited after a long interval [. . .]

". . . But surely we've diverged since the old days. I adore what you burn; you burn what I adore." [. . .]

"How do you know what I adore?" Nicholas Dormer inquired.

"I know well enough what you used to."

"That's more that I do myself; there were so many things."

"Yes, there are many things—many, many; that's what makes life so amusing."

"Do you find it amusing?"

"My dear fellow, *c'est à se tordre!* [it's a scream!] Don't you think so? Ah, it was high time I should meet you—I see. I have an idea you need me."

"Upon my word, I think I do!" Nick said, in a tone which struck his sister and made her wonder still more why, if the gentleman was so important as that, he didn't introduce him. (*Tragic* 21–22; see also a scene that is comparable in style and homoeroticism, in *The Sacred Fount* 151–52)

8. Concerning the novel's opacity, the note on the text in the 1978 Penguin edition of *The Tragic Muse* claims that James "minutely revised [the novel] . . . for the New York 'Definitive' Edition of the *Novels and Tales,* published in 1908, making verbal changes in almost every paragraph. These changes are usually, by the introduction of a periphrasis, to make the sentences more allusive and less simple and direct" (*Tragic* 6).

9. The narrator of *The Sacred Fount* (1901), for example, describes his preoccupation with voyeurism as "my private madness" and a "ridiculous obsession" (118, 72).

10. For a different reading of Nick's ontological split, see Kimmey, who argues with a confidence the novel cannot sustain, "Of course, Nick conquers his double nature and learns 'to be continuous.' He rids himself of his hypocrisy, his fatal 'talent for appearance'" (525–26).

11. For an interesting textual connection that might also endorse this point, see George Santayana's sonnet "Gabriel" (c. 1885–93), which begins thus:

I know thou art a man, thou hast his mould;
Thy wings are fancy and a poet's lie,
Thy halo but the dimness of his eye,
And thy fair chivalry a legend old.
Yet I mistrust the truth, and partly hold
Thou art a herald of the upper sky,

Where all the truth yet lives that seemed to die,

And love is never faint nor virtue cold . . . (*Complete* 125)

Since Santayana had strong—if ambiguous—intellectual relations with *William* James (see chapter 6), he may have read *The Tragic Muse* and even found it an inspiration for this sonnet. And while such exact creative debts are difficult to determine, I reproduce parts of Santayana's sonnet simply to demonstrate that Santayana's Gabriel—like James's—is *conceptually* caught between "fancy" and deceit.

12. Concerning the "fading" of the beloved, see Barthes: "Fade-out": "Painful ordeal in which the loved being appears to withdraw from all contact, without such enigmatic indifference even being directed against the amorous subject or pronounced to the advantage of anyone else, world or rival" (*Lover's* 112). The psychoanalytic significance of *aphanisis* is also important to consider here: According to Lacan, the subject must relinquish "being" for "meaning" to grasp its symbolic position (*Four* 209–15; also Silverman, *Subject* 168–73).

13. Wilde had such an experience when he *seemed* to capture the sexual enigma inspiring Shakespeare's *Sonnets:* "Perhaps, by finding perfect expression for a passion, I had exhausted the passion itself. . . . How was it that it had left me? Had I touched upon some secret that my soul desired to conceal? Or was there no permanence in personality?" (*Portrait* 246–47). For interesting accounts of this text's elliptical homosexual meanings, see Dowling, "Imposture"; Danson; and W. Cohen 191–236. I return to these interpretive questions about Wilde's text in the afterword.

Chapter 6

1. See Freud, "Creative Writers and Day-Dreaming" (1907; 1908), and *Leonardo da Vinci and a Memory of His Childhood* (1910). For an overview of Freud's arguments, see Loewald; and for more specific readings, see Bersani, *Freudian* 43–47 and *Culture* 29–46; and Laplanche, "Situate." This chapter owes much to the work of Laplanche and especially Bersani.

2. As the many references below attest, I am greatly indebted to McCormick's superb biography of Santayana.

3. Mario comments explicitly on this tendency after *The Last Puritan* has concluded, telling Santayana (both appear in propria persona), in response to the latter's questions "What of the characters, and in the first place of your own? Are you satisfied with your portrait?," "It's no portrait; or so flattered that nobody would recognise it. . . . Moreover, in general, you make us all take in your own philosophical style, and not in the least as we actually jabber. Your women are too intelligent, and your men also" (*Last* 718–19).

4. Thus Arnett, engaging what Santayana calls "a life of reason": "Vital animal desires and impulses . . . , combined with peculiarly human needs and characteristics in their relation to the environment, are the foundation of all the goods man can pursue. . . . However, Santayana also observes that not all men love or seek harmony, because its achievement demands the sacrifice of vital passions and interests which some are not willing to make" (4–5).

5. For elaborations on this partial inheritance, see Santayana, *Persons* 426 as well as *Sense* 24–25 n. 1, where he calls Schopenhauer "a good critic . . . [whose] . . . psychology was . . . far too vague and general to undertake an analysis of . . . those mysterious feelings [arising in response to particular objects]." See also *The Last Puritan* 166.

6. This line invokes and significantly transforms Santayana's earlier claim in Sonnet XXXIII (1895): "A perfect love is *nourished* by despair" (*Complete* 33; my emphasis).

7. "All that seems certain," Freud writes in *Civilization and Its Discontents* (1929; 1930), "is [beauty's] derivation from the field of sexual feeling. The love of beauty seems a perfect example of an impulse inhibited in its aim. 'Beauty' and 'attraction [*Reiz*]' are original attributes of the sexual object" (83). (Notes Freud's translator, James Strachey: "The German '*Reiz*' means 'stimulus' as well as 'charm' or 'attraction'" [83 n].)

8. Arnett (32–33) overlooks most of Santayana's conceptual difficulties. Ashmore (17) is more accurate when summarizing the object's "indeterminacy" in Santayana's work. However, like Arnett, Singer (44), and Kirkwood (78), he attributes a coherence to Santayana's conception of passion, pleasure, and desire (10). For an overview of these texts and their impact on Santayana studies, see Conner and Sprigge. See also Rowse and Lynn for useful engagements with Santayana's politics, and Antor (esp. 40–48) for a significant account of Santayana's likely influence on T. S. Eliot.

9. I summarize some of these arguments in "Thoughts" and *Ruling;* see also Harpham; Bersani, *Culture* 32–33, 41–42. Although not contemporaneous with Santayana, Thomas Carlyle's *Sartor Resartus* (1833–34) is a crucial antecedent here, advancing all of these points about cost, worth, and utility in aesthetic terms (for elaboration, see DeLaura, "Ishmael"). For a useful—if theoretically dense—account of this earlier period, see Poovey, *Making* esp. 56, 132.

10. In addition to the material I reproduce in this essay, one of Santayana's letters to Russell, written in September 1923, is significant and worth quoting: "I don't believe that anything has really happened to alter our relations to one another which were always tacit and expressed in conduct rather than words. You say now more than you ever *said* to me, even in our young days, about being 'attached to me'; you *must* have been, in some way which in spite of my cold-blooded psychology I don't pretend to understand. In that case, why drop me now, when certainly there has been no change on my side except that involved in passing from twenty to sixty? Let me come, anyhow, once, and we can judge better whether everything is as usual or whether the barrier you speak of—which certainly is not 'Elizabeth' [Countess Russell] or her affairs—really exists" (*Letters* 203).

11. I call this claim "patently absurd" because although Russell survived threats of blackmail in 1892 that would publicly have revealed his ongoing affairs with men (throughout these years he was unhappily married to Mabel-Edith Scott), in 1896 he managed to involve Santayana in two court cases, the first brought by Russell's wife and mother-in-law, charging him with buggery and with assaulting his servants and two boys (Santayana testified twice in Russell's defense). On April 15, 1900, under a new law in Nevada, Russell attempted to divorce Scott and marry Mollie Cooke. But when he and Mollie returned to England, he was arrested for bigamy, tried in the House of Lords, and, after pleading guilty,

sentenced to three months in Holloway Prison. For these and similar fascinating details, see McCormick 120–21.

12. Since Santayana's relationship with Russell had cooled considerably by this point, the tone of his letter is wistful, sad, and somewhat accusatory: "You minimise even your friendship with Lionel, in this very book: and I quite understand how you come to do it. You obliterate very soon your own feelings, when the occasion is past, and you never understand the feelings of others—it is part of your strength" (*Letters* 242; original emphasis).

13. Santayana's most elaborate account of Platonism is *Platonism and the Spiritual Life* (1927), but see also his earlier *Scepticism and Animal Faith: Introduction to a System of Philosophy* 225–26, and "Apologia pro mente sua" 542–49.

14. I am indebted here to Vlastos's invaluable reading of love and friendship in Aristotle's *Rhetoric* and Plato's *Republic, Lysis,* and *Symposium;* see esp. 31–34.

15. Irwin implies this when arguing that Plato's "conception of what is beautiful or admirable will be reflected in his choice of persons to love, and what to love about them, and in his choice of offspring—the virtues, laws, and so on, he tries to propagate. Both of these desires are altered by the development of his conception of the beautiful through the ascent" (167). For an interesting counterargument engaging texts by Aristotle and Montaigne, see Derrida 641–44. As we saw above, when Freud argued in *Group Psychology and the Analysis of the Ego* that the "emotional tie" is the "*successor* to a completely 'sensual' object-tie with the person in question or rather with that person's prototype (or *imago*)" (138; my emphasis), he appears torn between a desire to reproduce the dynamism of Plato's conception of love and a theoretical bid to produce the nonsexual from sexual drives. We see this more clearly in his 1911 essay on Schreber ("Psychoanalytic Notes" 61); see also Nussbaum's fine argument about St. Jerome's Lucretius in *Therapy* 140–91.

16. In Diotima's discussion with Socrates about procreation and the beautiful object, those who pursue creativity and social involvement as their contribution to society are said to "enjoy a far fuller community with each other than that which comes with children, and a far surer friendship, since the children of their union are fairer and more deathless" (*Symposium* 209C). Diotima underscores Plato's claim that creativity derives from the erotic rather than the nonsexual—and thus that artistic production is truly a "begetting" of a kind that Freud would struggle to define in "On Narcissism," his unfinished *Papers on Metapsychology,* and *The Ego and the Id.*

17. See McCormick 91–93 on Santayana's related critique of Hegel and Josiah Royce, and Wenkart 323–25 on Santayana's aesthetic understanding of "experience."

18. My aim here is not to downplay Santayana's conceptual differences with Freud, but to show how ambivalent and undecided his relation to psychoanalysis was, and thus demonstrate that Santayana could not in any simple way reject psychoanalysis *tout court.* See for instance Santayana's essay on "Psychologism" (in *Physical Order* 119–35), his remarks in *Realms of Being* (223, 335, 376, and 469), and his intriguing essay "A Long Way Round to Nirvana: Development of a Suggestion Found in Freud's *Beyond the Pleasure Principle.*"

19. In addition to the works referenced in the note above, see Santayana's "Literary Psychology," written in the 1920s, esp. 400–401.

20. Posnock writes of "Santayana's fastidious, immaculate asexuality" (61–62), his excellent essay demonstrating that such fastidiousness ultimately could not veil Santayana's internal sexual tensions. And McCormick writes: "There can be no doubt that Santayana was the subject of a prolonged sexual conflict, one which challenges the accepted wisdom that he was cold, detached, and somehow lacking in humanity, a view that he himself did so much to affirm" (49).

21. Santayana's four elegiac sonnets "To W. P." appear in *The Complete Poems* 125–26. The poet writes: "But yet I treasure in my memory/ Your gift of charity, and young heart's ease,/ And the dear honour of your amity" (126). Holzberger explains that Potter, among Harvard's class of 1893, "became Santayana's constant companion" while Santayana was an instructor in philosophy at that school and the organizer of regular "poetry bees" (Santayana, *Complete* 41), and he continues: "recalling the friendship almost fifty years later, Santayana writes that he came to think of him 'as a younger brother and as a part of myself.' Warwick Potter graduated with his class, and later that summer, together with his brother Robert, went for an ocean cruise aboard a yacht owned by a wealthy friend [Edgar Scott]. In October of 1893, in the harbor of Brest, Warwick, who had been terribly seasick, contracted cholera and died. The sudden death of this young friend had a powerful effect on Santayana and contributed to the influences that were bringing about the spiritual crisis he would later call his *metanoia*" (*Complete* 41; see also 613).

22. Santayana was not alone in advancing this homoerotic motif. Four years after the publication of Santayana's first collection, F. Holland Day completed *Study for the Crucifixion* (1898), which includes the homoerotic photograph "Crucifixion with Roman Soldiers." See Ellenzweig 54.

23. According to Matthew 27:33–34, *Golgotha* means "The Place of the Skull."

24. Santayana expounds on paganism and desire in "The Dissolution of Paganism" and "The Poetry of Barbarism," in *Interpretations of Poetry and Religion* 49–75 and 166–216, respectively. See also McCormick 84, 133.

25. This possible allusion to Orpheus and Eurydice would also invoke Cerberus, the dog guarding the entrance to Hades, which Santayana may be invoking above, in *Realms of Being*, when describing "the chained dogs below keep on barking in their kennels" (689).

26. As Vlastos notes, this phrase also occurs in Plato's *Laws* 836B–C, serving as the cause of much recent debate and interpretive confusion. Vlastos argues that Plato—*despite* his homosexuality—saw "anal intercourse" as "a degradation not only of man's humanity, but even of his animality: even to brutes, Plato believes, 'nature' ordains heterosexual coupling" (25). Vlastos critiques Hackforth's claim that Plato "is . . . making here 'a contemptuous reference to heterosexual love,'" saying that Hackforth's interpretation is "sharply at variance with the whole notion of 'birth in beauty' in the *Symposium*" (25 n. 76). Vlastos also argues that Dover's translation of "'contrary to nature' as 'against the rules' will not do: something far stronger is intended" (25 n. 76). I agree that Vlastos's translation *is* more accurate than Dover's—there being no doubt that Plato's *Laws* often revised and contradicted his previous philosophical claims—but it seems to me misleading to represent this difficult, often obtuse text as representative of Plato's oeuvre. Further, Vlastos's assumption

that Hackforth's interpretation "would be sharply at variance with the whole notion of 'birth in beauty' in the *Symposium*" seems to me quite incorrect (25 n. 76): One need only revisit Diotima's argument in 209C (qtd. in note 16 above) to grasp why. There is no doubt that Diotima is *not* referring here to biological procreation, which she discusses earlier in 208E. Arguments against the lover degrading himself obviously prevail in Plato's *Phaedrus*, but in his discussion with Phaedrus Socrates represents degradation by conditions (mania, idolization, jealousy, and a foolish disposition to neglect all social responsibilities— 239B–C) rather than specific sexual acts, such as sodomy. See for instance 238A–B:

> Now when opinion leads through reason toward the best and is more power-
> ful [in each one of us], its power is called self-restraint, but when desire irra-
> tionally drags us toward pleasures and rules within us, its rule is called excess.
> Now excess has many names, for it has many members and many forms; and
> whichever of these forms is most marked gives its own nature, neither beauti-
> ful nor honourable, to him who possesses it.

Socrates' examples are gluttony and excessive "desire for drink," but the object or act alone is not his concern—what matters for Socrates (and Plato had no problem agreeing) is the absence of moderation concerning the use of an object such as food or drink.

27. In Sonnet V, the poet asks, "Of my two lives which should I call the dream?," before concluding: "Truth is a dream, unless my dream is true" (*Complete* 93). While such references to "two lives" do not necessarily represent homosexuality—they could for instance refer to Santayana's perception, in Robert Martin's words, of being "too English for Spain, too Spanish for England or New England" (*Homosexual* 112)—they point up a crucial internal gap within the poet, indicating his difficulty in distinguishing between truth and illusion.

28. Unfortunately, although we cannot discount this passage as exceptional we also cannot argue with certainty here that the narrator's voice is simply Santayana's (for a useful account of this problem, see Saatkamp; also *Last* 565).

29. Recall from the previous chapter that in James's *The Tragic Muse* (1889; 1890) the protagonist Nick Dormer experiences a comparable dilemma: "The difficulty is that I'm two men. . . . One man wins the seat—but it's the other fellow who sits in it" (166).

30. Nathan A. Scott, Jr., is invaluable on this point: "Santayana's 'essence' is not, of course, as he frequently found it necessary to insist, merely another version of the Platonic Idea, for Platonism, as he reminds us, materializes the Idea into a supernatural power capable of acting causatively upon the natural order. . . . Santayana's doctrine of essence is not unlike Gerard Manley Hopkins' doctrine of 'inscape'" (203).

CHAPTER 7

1. I must stress this curious about-turn in Levine's otherwise valuable analysis of Forster's short stories. Until the final pages of her article, Levine appears as skeptical of Forster's accounts of sexual equality and "lust" as is Stone (see esp. Stone 392–93). Toward the end of her article, however, as I show below, Levine curiously transforms Forster's narrative difficulties with love and "lust" into a redemptive anticipation of interpersonal harmony.

2. Stone is citing the narrator's rueful acknowledgment in Forster's *Maurice;* see also A. Wilde.

3. Thus: "We know Forster *is* Maurice, at least as a sexual being" (original emphasis). As a consequence of this reading, Stone represents *Maurice* and *The Life to Come* collection as a "program of self-discovery" (389). Considering this assumption, we should recall Lawrence's interesting observation on Forster: "He tries to dodge himself—the sight is painful. . . . He knows that *self-realisation is not his ultimate desire*" (letter to Barbara Low and Bertrand Russell, February 12, 1915, *The Letters of D. H. Lawrence* 283, my emphasis).

4. Forster's strategy differs from Edward Carpenter's argument that homosexuality in literature and life should be "no exception . . . to the law that sensuality apart from love is degrading and *something less than human*" ("Homogenic Love" [1894] 340; my emphasis). Given Forster's attempt to resolve Carpenter's decree, questions emerge about the price of this exception and the possibility that Forster's ensuing desire is "something less than human." By engaging these questions, this chapter considers this conceptual gap between "love" and "sensuality."

5. My focus on the "eroticism of betrayal" owes much to Bersani's superb account of this phenomenon in Jean Genet's writing; see *Homos* esp. 151: *"Betrayal is an ethical necessity."* Considering Forster's avowed ambivalence to representing sexuality in his novels, and that he wrote much of *The Life to Come* collection while completing *A Passage to India* (1924), these claims invoke Forster's complex publication history (for elaboration, see Lane, *Ruling* 147–50).

6. For an account of Forster's racism, see Lane, "Psychoanalysis" 16–18. For confirmation of this point about malice, however, consider Forster's admission in his *Commonplace Book:* "Resentment is a plant of tortuous growth. Middleton Murry patronises and attacks my work, and at first I seem uninfected by this contact with him, and see clearly enough that he is lamenting not my troubles but his own. And I think that my feelings remain friendly towards him, and that I pity him. But the pity is not genuine, and, having led me to take unusual interest in Middleton Murry, it evaporates. I now discover that my unusual interest has a hostile tinge, and my heart beats quicker in the hope of him making a mistake, and *I enjoy hearing his enemies speak against him, and am even happier when he loses another of his former friends.* But for appearing petty, I would patronise and attack him" (1–2; my emphasis).

7. In addition to Levine's and Herz's arguments, cited above, we note that Levine reads Lionel's murder of Cocoanut in "The Other Boat" in this way: "Lionel's revulsion is not homophobic but against the bigotry of his class" (86); according to Levine, the story is thus about "thwarted love" (84). Downplaying the issue of murder, Norman Page observes of the same characters: "Their mutual infatuation overrides differences of race and social background, so that in the cabin they inhabit a world different from that of the deck and the dining-room; as the boat retraces in reverse the route of the earlier voyage, the two recapture the relationship of their boyhood, except that the tentative and half-realized sexuality of that time is now fully explicit" (57). In light of the story's ending, it is difficult not to consider these readings somewhat idealistic.

8. Although published in 1957, the Wolfenden Report's recommendation that Britain's Parliament partly decriminalize homosexual sex between men was not enacted until 1967. In 1967, Parliament established the age of consent for male homosexual sex at twenty-one for England and Wales (that for heterosexual sex and, implicitly, lesbian sex remained unchanged at sixteen). Despite resistance, Parliament voted on February 21, 1994, to lower the age of consent for male homosexual sex to eighteen (the vote was 427–162). For elaboration on Wolfenden, see Weeks, *Coming Out* 156–82, and Mort, "Sexuality."

9. Forster's reference to "a lad dangling from a noose" may invoke Housman's account in *A Shropshire Lad* (1896), "The Immortal Part," XLIV, of a man's suicide because of his homosexuality. Though ironic, Housman's reference to "the household traitor" has valuable bearing on my chapter and his account is worth quoting at length:

> Shot? so quick, so clean an ending?
>   Oh that was right, lad, that was brave:
> Yours was not an ill for mending,
>   'Twas best to take it to the grave.
>
> Oh you had the forethought, you could reason,
>   And saw your road and where it led,
> And early wise and brave in season
>   Put the pistol to your head.
>
> Oh soon, and better so than later
>   After long disgrace and scorn,
> You shot dead the household traitor,
>   The soul that should not have been born. (*Collected Poems* 66)

Following my discussion of George Santayana's aesthetic theory in chapter 6, it seems useful to observe that Santayana met Housman at Cambridge University in 1896. Writing to Cyril Clemens on August 17, 1945, Santayana elaborates: "I dined with [Housman] again years later at Lapsley's . . . but he was amiably silent. However, I had meantime read the Shropshire Lad, and Last Poems, and now More Poems, always with tears. There is not much else than tears in them, but they are perfect of their kind" (qtd. in McCormick 118).

10. Regarding this scenario's historical frequency: Henry Labouchère's amendment to Britain's 1885 Criminal Law Amendment Act was commonly known as the "Blackmailer's Charter" (Weeks, *Coming Out* 14, 22).

11. I refer here to Forster's fictional and nonfictional accounts of sex. For an example of the latter, see his "Kanaya" 324, which I discuss below. See also Lane, *Ruling* 173–74.

12. Compare this with Forster's 1927 entry in his *Commonplace Book*: "Sketch for a character: a highly civilised man who has deep emotions but has prepared no one to respect them when they come out. Consequently he is reduced to casual lust where he is satisfied and happy until his civilisation has an elevating and redeeming influences [*sic*] upon his bedfellows. The 'better' he makes people the lonelier he feels. He need not be unattractive physically" (24). See also the entry for 1925: "Isolation is the sum total of wretchedness to man" (1).

13. See "Anonymity: An Enquiry" (1925): "[E]ach human mind has two personalities, one on the surface, one deeper down. . . . The lower personality is a very queer affair. In many ways it is a perfect fool, but without it there is no literature, because unless a man dips a bucket down into it occasionally he cannot produce first-class work" (*Two* 83).

AFTERWORD

1. David Halperin writes, "I may not have worshiped Foucault at the time I wrote *One Hundred Years of Homosexuality,* but I do worship him now. As far as I'm concerned, the guy was a fucking saint. Not that I imagine Foucault to have led either a sexually or a morally perfect life. In fact, I know almost nothing about his life beyond what I've read in three recent biographies . . . My relation to him is indirect and secondary: like my relation to virtually every other great writer, ancient or modern, that I have ever studied, it is entirely mediated, imaginary, and—why bother to deny it?—hagiographical" (*Saint* 6).

2. For a remarkable elaboration on this point, see Bersani, *The Freudian Body: Psychoanalysis and Art* 4–6, 66, 107. In his recent study, *Homos* (1995), Bersani slightly modifies this argument, giving narrative occasional (though still precarious) suggestions of political efficacy. As I point out in a review article on *Homos,* Bersani has not fundamentally retracted his argument about failure; he has, however, slightly reframed his understanding of the way that narratives *represent* this failure (see Lane, "Uncertain"; also Dean, "Sex and Syncope" esp. 80–81). This afterword is greatly indebted to Bersani's reading of literary and psychoanalytic texts.

3. In addition to Bersani's work, Rose, Edelman (esp. 3–23), Roth, and Yingling have considerably influenced my argument. For essays addressing related issues in feminism and lesbian studies, respectively, see Jacobus, "Is There a Woman in This Text?" and Findley.

4. After detailing how words such as *hidden* and *secret* function in Wilde's novella, Dowling astutely notes: "Our real clue to the secret of Willie Hughes and to the 'secret' of the narrator's own text is the picture that is not inside the chest, an image of absence. Like the empty chest, the hollow text can be filled only by imposture (Lat. *imponere,* to put in), by putting presence in the place of absence" ("Imposture" 27; see also 28). Wilde's text implies that we lose meaning precisely when we seem to retrieve it. The lesson is important, if paradoxical, and forms the basis of my argument here. Wilde endorsed this lesson elsewhere when, as Dowling notes, he wrote his friend and silent collaborator, Robert Ross, observing, "Now that Willie Hughes has been revealed to the world, we must have another secret" (qtd. 26).

5. Pointing up one effect of this eclipse of historical difference, Henry Abelove has written poignantly of his queer students' frequent uninterest in—and even studied distance from—the apparently passé and outmoded concerns of lesbian and gay history and literature ("Queering" 50).

6. The preface and introduction to this book enumerate some of the conceptual and political tensions between Foucauldian and Lacanian approaches to queer theory. In this afterword I am primarily concerned with the repercussions of these tensions for literary criticism and theory. For recent psychoanalytic work arguing that the concept of "sexual

identity" is politically misleading and even sexually repressive, see Dean, "Eve" 119–26; Davidson 54–58; Abelove, "Freud" 66–67; also Fuss 10–11.

7. Distinguishing between the Freudian ego and the Lacanian subject further indicates this discrepancy between psychic and political fields. Assumptions that egoic defeat is identical to political quietism are frequently and mistakenly used to suggest that psychoanalysis is commensurate with political conservatism. For an interesting reversal of this assumption, see Bersani and Dutoit, *Arts:* "[T]here is nothing to be lost in our foundering with the notion of getting lost, and there is even something exhilarating in the idea of a joyful self-dismissal giving birth to a new kind of power" (9).

8. Cyril Wilde wrote: "All these years my great incentive has been to wipe that stain away; to *retrieve,* if may be, by some action of mine, a name no longer honoured in the land. The more I thought of this, the more convinced I became that, first and foremost, I must be a *man*. There was to be no cry of decadent artist, of effeminate aesthete, of weak-kneed degenerate" (qtd. in Holland 140; first italics mine). Although Sinfield quotes these lines (126), Cyril Wilde's aim to "retrieve" his family name from his father's tarnish provides an interesting strategic parallel to Sinfield's concern to "deheterosexualize" Wilde for queer purposes.

9. Here, I am rereading the object of Sedgwick's essay, "Privilege of Unknowing," by implicating her essay's useful account of the privilege to avoid and not know sexual definition and oppression in the effect of her specification of this unknown for lesbian and gay criticism. As before, and however inadvertently, this specification renders all forms of sexual desire that resist representation or denomination as complicit with the privilege of ruling *doxa*. In these terms, it is easy to see how Sedgwick transforms psychoanalysis—with its insistence that aspects of *subjectivity* resist representation—into one of the agents consolidating the "privilege of unknowing." What we could consider here is the way this argument, despite Sedgwick's emphasis on the complexity of sexual definition, inevitably fosters the belief that all sexuality can be represented and explained. Surely this assumption about sexual clarity is more dangerous, socially manipulative, and oppressive than is the subject's (or more precisely, the *ego*'s) retention of the "privilege of unknowing"?

10. In Hardy's *The Mayor of Casterbridge* (1886), for instance, Michael Henchard tells Susan, the wife he sold many years earlier at a country fair, that he wants to remarry her in order to maintain a secret that "would leave my shady, headstrong, disgraceful life as a young man absolutely unopened; the secret would be yours and mine only" (144). Later believing that Henchard is her father, Elizabeth-Jane tells her friend Lucetta Templeman, "Ah—you have many many secrets from me!" (271). The narrator adds that Elizabeth strives to "keep . . . in all signs of emotion till she was ready to burst" (271) and, subsequently, to "cork . . . up the turmoil of her feeling with grand control" (290). Such signs of turmoil and anguish anticipate Hardy's later novel *Tess of the d'Urbervilles: A Pure Woman* (1891), in which Tess suffers extreme isolation while keeping secret the fact that Alec d'Urberville preyed upon her and trying to keep secret the death of their infant. In advancing this point, I am of course aware that Henchard and Donald Farfrae's relationship, in Hardy's *The Mayor of Casterbridge,* has been interpreted as homosexual in character (see my inter-

pretation of these arguments in chapter 4 above). My point concerns the exclusivity of Sedgwick's claim about homosexual secrets in nineteenth-century literature, which compels her to excise all related arguments about heterosexual secrets in the same writing. For other examples, see Hardy's *Woodlanders,* esp. 303, as well as George Eliot's *Silas Marner* (1861), in which Godfrey Cass initially keeps secret the existence of Eppie, his child with Molly Farren (30-32). Indeed, in Eliot's and Hardy's writing alone it would be difficult to exhaust the list of hetero- and nonsexual secrets.

11. Meyers's argument that "homosexuality became legal" in Britain in 1967 is technically incorrect: Male homosexuality was only partially decriminalized that year. Until the recent (February 1994) change in British law, consensual sex between more than two men—or sex in which one of the men was younger than the age of consent (21), or even sex between two men observed by an affronted witness—was technically illegal.

12. Many queer writers and activists advance the point above about social integration, but for slightly different reasons; see Signorile; Vaid; Wojnarowicz.

13. For elaboration on the example of E. M. Forster—especially concerning the reception of his posthumous, homosexual writing, see Lane, *The Ruling Passion* 147–52.

14. For critiques of this biography's interpretive work, see W. Brown 140–49 and Halperin, *Saint Foucault* 162–82.

15. Van Leer's critique of Sedgwick's work, quoted above, reproduces Sedgwick's own argument against the proposition "We Know What That Means." His essay appeared in *Critical Inquiry* in 1989 as a response to Sedgwick's published essay "The Beast in the Closet: James and the Writing of Homosexual Panic" (1986).

16. For an example of this criticism—notable because the text in question evades the critic's efforts at detective work—see Summers 62–77. For a longer reading of this narrative difficulty and critical presumption, see Acocella.

WORKS CITED

Abelove, Henry. "Freud, Male Homosexuality, and the Americans." *Dissent* 33.1 (1985–86): 59–69.

———. "The Queering of Lesbian/Gay History." *Radical History Review* 62 (1995): 44–57.

Acocella, Joan. "Cather and the Academy." *New Yorker* Nov. 27, 1995: 56–71.

Adams, James Eli. *Dandies and Desert Saints: Styles of Victorian Manhood.* Ithaca: Cornell UP, 1995.

Adams, Stephen. *The Homosexual as Hero in Contemporary Fiction.* London: Vision, 1980.

Allen, Dennis W. *Sexuality in Victorian Fiction.* Norman: U of Oklahoma P, 1993.

Anderson, Amanda. *Tainted Souls and Painted Faces: The Rhetoric of Fallenness in Victorian Culture.* Ithaca: Cornell UP, 1993.

Antor, Heinz. "Bloomsbury Aesthetics and Other Early Twentieth-Century Theories of Art." *Anglia: Zeitschrift für Englische Philologie* 107.1–2 (1989): 34–48.

Aristotle. *Poetics.* Trans. Richard Jenko. Indianapolis: Hackett, 1987.

Armstrong, Nancy. *Desire and Domestic Fiction: A Political History of the Novel.* New York: Oxford UP, 1987.

Armstrong, T. D. "An Old Philosopher in Rome: George Santayana and His Visitors." *Journal of American Studies* 19.3 (1985): 349–68.

Arnett, Willard E. *Santayana and the Sense of Beauty.* Bloomington: Indiana UP, 1955.

Arnold, Matthew. "The Function of Criticism at the Present Time." 1864. *The Complete Prose Works of Matthew Arnold.* Vol. 3. Ed. R. H. Super. Ann Arbor: U of Michigan P, 1962. 258–85.

Ashmore, Jerome. *Santayana, Art, and Aesthetics.* Cleveland: Western Reserve UP, 1966.

Auerbach, Nina. *Woman and the Demon: The Life of a Victorian Myth.* Cambridge: Harvard UP, 1982.

Austen, Jane. *Mansfield Park.* 1814. Harmondsworth: Penguin, 1966.

———. *Sense and Sensibility.* 1811. Harmondsworth: Penguin, 1969.

Baird, Julian. "Swinburne, Sade, and Blake: The Pleasure-Pain Paradox." *Victorian Poetry* 9.1–2 (1971): 49–75.

Baker, Robert S. "Gabriel Nash's 'House of Strange Idols': Aestheticism in *The Tragic Muse.*" *Texas Studies in Literature and Language* 15 (1973): 149–66.

Banerjee, Jacqueline. "The Impossible Goal: The Struggle for Manhood in Victorian Fiction." *Victorian Newsletter* 89 (1996): 1–10.

———. "Schreiner's *The Story of an African Farm.*" *Explicator* 48.1 (1989): 43–45.

Baral, Kailash Chandra. "George Santayana and the Sense of Beauty." *Punjab University Research Bulletin* 19.1 (1988): 59–67.

Barash, Carol L. "Virile Womanhood: Olive Schreiner's Narratives of a Master Race." *Speaking of Gender.* Ed. Elaine Showalter. New York: Routledge, 1989. 269–81.

Barbey d'Aurevilly, Jules-Amédée. *Dandyism.* 1845. Trans. Douglas Ainslie. New York: PAJ, 1988.

———. "Du Dandysme et de G. Brummell." 1845. *Œuvres romanesques complètes.* Vol. 2. Paris: Gallimard, 1966. 667–718.

Barret-Ducrocq, Françoise. *Love in the Time of Victoria: Sexuality, Class, and Gender in Nineteenth-Century London.* 1989. Trans. John Howe. New York: Verso, 1991.

Barrett, Dorothea. "The Politics of Sado-Masochism: Swinburne and George Eliot." In Rooksby and Shrimpton 107–19.

Barthes, Roland. *A Lover's Discourse: Fragments.* 1977. Trans. Richard Howard. New York: Hill and Wang, 1978.

———. *Roland Barthes by Roland Barthes.* 1975. Trans. Richard Howard. Berkeley: U of California P, 1994.

———. *S/Z.* 1970. Trans. Richard Miller. New York: Hill and Wang, 1974.

Bartlett, Neil. *Who Was That Man? A Present for Mr. Oscar Wilde.* London: Serpent's Tail, 1988.

Bataille, Georges. *Erotism: Death and Sensuality.* 1957. Trans. Mary Dalwood. San Francisco: City Lights, 1986.

Baudelaire, Charles. *Œuvres complètes.* Ed. Claude Pichois and Y.-G Le Dantec. Paris: Gallimard, 1961.

———. *The Painter of Modern Life and Other Essays.* 1863. Ed. and trans. Jonathan Mayne. New York: Da Capo, 1964.

Beaver, Harold. "Homosexual Signs (In Memory of Roland Barthes)." *Critical Inquiry* 8.1 (1981): 99–119.

Beegel, Susan. "Bathsheba's Lovers: Male Sexuality in *Far from the Madding Crowd.*" In Cox 108–27.

Beerbohm, Max. "No. 2 The Pines." 1914. *And Even Now.* London: Heinemann, 1920. 55–88.

Beeton, Ridley. "Turning to Olive Schreiner." *Contrast* (Cape Town) 12.3 (1979): 41–44.

Bellringer, Alan W. "*The Tragic Muse:* 'The Objective Centre.'" *Journal of American Studies* 4.1–2 (1970): 73–89.

Bennett, Arnold. *The Old Wives' Tale.* 1908. Harmondsworth: Penguin, 1983.

Bergman, David, ed. *Camp Grounds: Style and Homosexuality.* Amherst: U of Massachusetts P, 1993.

Berkman, Joyce Avrech. *The Healing Imagination of Olive Schreiner: Beyond South African Colonialism.* Amherst: U of Massachusetts P, 1989.

———. "The Nurturant Fantasies of Olive Schreiner." *Frontiers: Journal of Women Studies* 2.3 (1977): 8–17.

———. *Olive Schreiner: Feminism on the Frontier.* St. Alban's, VT: Eden, 1979.

Bernheimer, Charles. "The Decadent Subject." *L'Esprit créateur* 32.4 (1992): 53–62.

Bersani, Leo. *The Culture of Redemption.* Cambridge: Harvard UP, 1990.

————. *The Freudian Body: Psychoanalysis and Art.* New York: Columbia UP, 1986.

————. *A Future for Astyanax: Character and Desire in Literature.* Boston: Little, Brown, 1976.

————. *Homos.* Cambridge: Harvard UP, 1995.

————. "Is the Rectum a Grave?" 1987. *AIDS: Cultural Analysis/Cultural Activism.* Ed. Douglas Crimp. Cambridge: MIT P, 1988, 1993. 197–223.

————. "Representation and Its Discontents." *Raritan* 1.1 (1981): 3–17.

Bersani, Leo, and Ulysse Dutoit. *Arts of Impoverishment: Beckett, Rothko, Resnais.* Cambridge: Harvard UP, 1993.

Black, Joel. "The Aesthetics of Gender: Zeuxis' Maidens and the Hermaphroditic Ideal." *Fragments: Incompletion and Discontinuity.* Ed. Lawrence D. Kritzman. New York: New York Literary Forum, 1981. 189–209.

Bloch, Ernst, et al. *Aesthetics and Politics: Debates between Bloch, Lukács, Brecht, Benjamin, and Adorno.* Trans. Ronald Taylor. London: Verso, 1977.

Boone, Joseph Allen. *Tradition Counter Tradition: Love and the Form of Fiction.* Chicago: U of Chicago P, 1987.

Borch-Jacobsen, Mikkel. *The Freudian Subject.* 1982. Trans. Catherine Porter. Stanford: Stanford UP, 1988.

Boswell, John. *Christianity, Social Tolerance, and Homosexuality.* Chicago: U of Chicago P, 1980.

Bradford, Helen. "Olive Schreiner's Hidden Agony: Fact, Fiction and Teenage Abortion." *Journal of Southern African Studies* 21.4 (1995): 623–41.

Brandon, Ruth. *The New Women and the Old Men: Love, Sex, and the Woman Question.* London: Secker and Warburg, 1990.

Bray, Alan. *Homosexuality in Renaissance England.* London: Gay Men's, 1982.

Brenkman, John. *Straight Male Modern: A Cultural Critique of Psychoanalysis.* New York: Routledge, 1993.

Bristow, Joseph. *Effeminate England: Homoerotic Writing after 1885.* New York: Columbia UP, 1995.

————. Introduction. *The Story of an African Farm.* By Olive Schreiner. New York: Oxford UP, 1992. vii—xxxvi.

Brontë, Charlotte. *Jane Eyre.* 1847. Harmondsworth: Penguin, 1987.

————. *Villette.* 1853. Harmondsworth: Penguin, 1985.

Brown, Douglas. *Hardy: The Mayor of Casterbridge.* London: Edward Arnold, 1962.

Brown, Wendy. "Jim Miller's Passions." *Differences* 5.2 (1993): 140–49.

Buchanan-Gould, Vera. *Not without Honour: The Life and Writings of Olive Schreiner.* London: Hutchinson, 1948.

Buckley, Jerome Hamilton. *The Victorian Temper: A Study in Literary Culture.* Cambridge: Harvard UP, 1951.

Buckton, Oliver. "'An Unnatural State': Gender, 'Perversion,' and Newman's *Apologia pro vita sua.*" *Victorian Studies* 35.4 (1991–92): 359–83.

Bulwer-Lytton, Edward George. *Godolphin.* London: Blackwood and Sons, 1862.

———. *Pelham; or, The Adventures of a Gentleman.* 1828; 1835; 1840. Ed. and introd. Jerome J. McGann. Lincoln: U of Nebraska P, 1972.

Busst, A. J. L. "The Image of the Androgyne in the Nineteenth Century." *Romantic Mythologies.* Ed. Ian Fletcher. London: Routledge, 1967. 1–95.

Butler, Judith. *Bodies That Matter: On the Discursive Limits of "Sex."* New York: Routledge, 1993.

———. *Gender Trouble: Feminism and the Subversion of Identity.* New York: Routledge, 1990.

———. "Imitation and Gender Insubordination." *Inside/Out: Lesbian Theories, Gay Theories.* Ed. Diana Fuss. New York: Routledge, 1991. 13–31.

———. *The Psychic Life of Power: Theories in Subjection.* Stanford: Stanford UP, 1997.

———. *Subjects of Desire: Hegelian Reflections in Twentieth-Century France.* New York: Columbia UP, 1987.

Butler, Lance St. John. *Thomas Hardy.* New York: Cambridge UP, 1978.

Butler, Samuel. *The Way of All Flesh.* 1873; 1903. Harmondsworth: Penguin, 1986.

Calinescu, Matei. *Five Faces of Modernity: Modernism, Avant-Garde, Decadence, Kitsch, Postmodernism.* Durham: Duke UP, 1987, 1993.

Cameron, Sharon. *Thinking in Henry James.* Chicago: U of Chicago P, 1989.

Carassus, Emilien. *Le Mythe du dandy.* Paris: Librairie Armand Colin, 1971.

Carlyle, Thomas. *Critical and Miscellaneous Essays.* 5 vols. New York: Scribner's, 1904.

———. *On Heroes, Hero-Worship, and the Heroic in History.* 1840; 1841. Ed. and introd. Carl Niemeyer. Lincoln: U of Nebraska P, 1966.

———. *Sartor Resartus.* 1833–34. Ed. Charles Frederick Harrold. New York: Odyssey, 1937.

Carpenter, Edward. *Civilisation: Its Cause and Cure.* 2nd ed. London: Sonnenschein and Co., 1891.

———. *The Drama of Love and Death: A Study of Human Evolution and Transfiguration.* New York: Mitchell Kennerley, 1912.

———. "Homogenic Love." 1894. In Reade 324–47.

———. *The Intermediate Sex: A Study of Some Transitional Types of Men and Women.* 1908. London: Allen and Unwin, 1930.

Carter, Geoffrey. "Sexuality and the Victorian Artist: Dickens and Swinburne." In Cox 141–60.

Casey, Janet Galligani. "Power, Agency, Desire: Olive Schreiner and the Pre-Modern Narrative Moment." *Narrative* 4.2 (1996): 124–41.

Cassidy, John A. *Algernon C. Swinburne.* Boston: Twayne, 1964.

Castle, Terry. *The Apparitional Lesbian: Female Homosexuality and Modern Culture.* New York: Columbia UP, 1993.

Chadwick, Owen. *The Spirit of the Oxford Movement: Tractarian Essays.* New York: Cambridge UP, 1990.

Charlesworth, Barbara. *Dark Passages: The Decadent Consciousness in Victorian Literature.* Madison: U of Wisconsin P, 1965.

Childers, Joseph. *Novel Possibilities: Fiction and the Formation of Early Victorian Culture.* Philadelphia: U of Pennsylvania P, 1995.

Christ, Carol T. "'The Hero as Man of Letters': Masculinity and Victorian Nonfiction Prose." *Victorian Sages and Cultural Discourse: Renegotiating Gender and Power.* Ed. Thaïs E. Morgan. New Brunswick: Rutgers UP, 1990. 19–31.

———. *Victorian and Modern Poetics.* Chicago: U of Chicago P, 1984.

———. "Victorian Masculinity and the Angel in the House." In Vicinus 146–62.

Christensen, Allan Conrad. *Edward Bulwer-Lytton: The Fiction of New Regions.* Athens: U of Georgia P, 1976.

Cixous, Hélène. "The Character of 'Character.'" *New Literary History* 5.2 (1974): 383–402.

Clayton, Cherry. "Forms of Dependence and Control in Olive Schreiner's Fiction." In Smith and Maclennan 20–29.

———. *Olive Schreiner.* New York: Twayne, 1997.

———, ed. *Olive Schreiner.* Johannesburg: McGraw-Hill, 1983.

Coblence, Françoise. *Le dandysme, obligation d'incertitude.* Paris: PUF, 1988.

Cohen, Ed. *Talk on the Wilde Side: Toward a Genealogy of a Discourse on Male Sexualities.* New York: Routledge, 1993.

Cohen, Jonathan. "This Disease Called Man." *American Book Review* 17.4 (1996): 1, 30.

Cohen, William A. *Sex Scandal: The Private Parts of Victorian Fiction.* Durham: Duke UP, 1996.

Cominos, Peter T. "Late-Victorian Sexual Respectability and the Social System." *International Review of Social History* 8.1 (1963): 18–48; 8.2 (1963): 216–50.

Conner, Frederick W. "'To Dream with One Eye Open': The Wit, Wisdom, and Present Standing of George Santayana." *Soundings* 74.1–2 (1991): 159–78.

Connolly, Thomas E. *Swinburne's Theory of Poetry.* Albany: SUNY P, 1964.

Conrad, Joseph. *Victory: An Island Tale.* 1915. Harmondsworth: Penguin, 1989.

Cooper, Michael A. "Discipl(in)ing the Master, Mastering the Discipl(in)e: Erotonomies in James' Tales of Literary Life." *Engendering Men: The Question of Male Feminist Criticism.* Ed. Joseph A. Boone and Michael Cadden. New York: Routledge, 1990. 66–83.

Copjec, Joan. "Evil in the Time of the Finite World." *Radical Evil.* Ed. Copjec. New York: Verso, 1996. vii—xxviii.

———. *Read My Desire: Lacan against the Historicists.* Cambridge: MIT P, 1994.

Cory, Daniel. *Santayana: The Later Years: A Portrait with Letters.* New York: George Braziller, 1963.

Cox, Don Richard, ed. *Sexuality and Victorian Literature.* Tennessee Studies in Lit. 27. Knoxville: U of Tennessee P, 1984.

Craft, Christopher. *Another Kind of Love: Male Homosexual Desire in English Discourse, 1850–1920.* Berkeley: U of California P, 1994.

Creech, James. *Closet Writing/Gay Reading: The Case of Melville's "Pierre."* Chicago: U of Chicago P, 1993.

Crews, Frederick. "Beyond Repression: A Response to Jonathan Cohen." *American Book Review* 17.4 (1996): 1, 10–11.

Crews, Frederick, et al. *The Memory Wars: Freud's Legacy in Dispute.* New York: New York Review, 1995.

Crompton, Louis. *Byron and Greek Love: Homophobia in Nineteenth-Century England.* Berkeley: U of California P, 1985.

Daleski, H. M. *Thomas Hardy and the Paradoxes of Love.* Columbia: U of Missouri P, 1997.

Danson, Lawrence. "Oscar Wilde, W. H., and the Unspoken Name of Love." *ELH* 58 (1991): 979–1000.

Darwin, Charles. *The Descent of Man, and Selection in Relation to Sex.* 1871. Introd. John Tyler Bonner and Robert M. May. Princeton: Princeton UP, 1981.

Davidson, Arnold I. "How to Do the History of Psychoanalysis: A Reading of Freud's *Three Essays on the Theory of Sexuality.*" *The Trial(s) of Psychoanalysis.* Ed. Françoise Meltzer. Chicago: U of Chicago P, 1988. 39–64.

Dean, Tim. "On the Eve of a Queer Future." *Raritan* 15.1 (1995): 116–34.

———. "Sex and Syncope." *Raritan* 15.3 (1996): 64–86.

———. "Transsexual Identification, Gender Performance Theory, and the Politics of the Real." *Literature and Psychology* 39.4 (1993): 1–27.

Delaroche, Patrick. "Les Trois étapes de la sexuation." *L'Enfant et la psychanalyse.* Paris: Éditions Esquisses Psychanalytique, 1993. 472–80.

DeLaura, David J. "'The Ache of Modernism' in Hardy's Later Novels." *ELH* 34.3 (1967): 380–99.

———. *Hebrew and Hellene in Victorian England: Newman, Arnold, and Pater.* Austin: U of Texas P, 1969.

———. "Ishmael as Prophet: *Heroes and Hero-Worship* and the Self-Expressive Basis of Carlyle's Art." *Texas Studies in Literature and Language* 11.1 (1969): 705–32.

———. "Reading Inman Rereading Pater Reading." *Pater Newsletter* 26 (1991): 2–9.

de Lauretis, Teresa. *The Practice of Love: Lesbian Sexuality and Perverse Desire.* Bloomington: Indiana UP, 1994.

Dellamora, Richard. "Male Relations in Thomas Hardy's *Jude the Obscure.*" *Papers on Language and Literature* 27.4 (1991): 453–72.

———. *Masculine Desire: The Sexual Politics of Victorian Aestheticism.* Chapel Hill: U of North Carolina P, 1990.

D'Emilio, John. "Capitalism and Gay Identity." *Powers of Desire: The Politics of Sexuality.* Ed. Ann Snitow, Christine Stansell, and Sharon Thompson. New York: Monthly Review, 1983. 100–113.

de Rougemont, Denis. *Love in the Western World.* 1940. Trans. Montgomery Belgion. Princeton: Princeton UP, 1983.

Derrida, Jacques. "The Politics of Friendship." *Journal of Philosophy* 85.11 (1988): 632–44.

Dickens, Charles. *Little Dorrit.* 1855–57. Harmondsworth: Penguin, 1987.

Dike, D. A. "A Modern Oedipus: *The Mayor of Casterbridge.*" *Essays in Criticism* 2.2 (1952): 169–79.

Disraeli, Benjamin. *Coningsby; or, The New Generation.* 1844. Harmondsworth: Penguin, 1983.

Dollimore, Jonathan. *Sexual Dissidence: Augustine to Wilde, Freud to Foucault.* New York: Oxford UP, 1991.

Donald, Adrienne. "Coming out of the Canon: Sadomasochism, Male Homoeroticism, Romanticism." *Yale Journal of Criticism* 3.1 (1989): 239–52.

D[oolittle], H[ilda]. *Tribute to Freud.* 1945–46 (1944). Foreword Norman Holmes Pearson. New York: New Directions, 1974.

Dor, Joël. *The Clinical Lacan.* Ed. Judith Feher Gurewich. Trans. Susan Fairfield. Northvale, NJ: Jason Aronson, 1997.

Doty, Alexander. *Making Things Perfectly Queer: Interpreting Mass Culture.* Minneapolis: U of Minnesota P, 1993.

Dowling, Linda. "The Decadent and the New Woman in the 1890's." *Nineteenth-Century Fiction* 33.4 (1979): 434–53.

———. *Hellenism and Homosexuality in Victorian Oxford.* Ithaca: Cornell UP, 1994.

———. "Imposture and Absence in Wilde's *Portrait of Mr. W. H.*" *Victorian Newsletter* 58 (1980): 26–29.

———. "Ruskin's Pied Beauty and the Constitution of a 'Homosexual Code.'" *Victorian Newsletter* 75 (1989): 1–8.

Draper, R. P. "*The Mayor of Casterbridge.*" *Critical Quarterly* 25.1 (1983): 57–70.

Duggan, Lisa. "Making It Perfectly Queer." *Socialist Review* 22 (1992): 11–31.

Edelman, Lee. *Homographesis: Essays in Gay Literary and Cultural Theory.* New York: Routledge, 1994.

Edmond, Rod. "'The Past-Marked Prospect': Reading *The Mayor of Casterbridge.*" *Reading the Victorian Novel: Detail into Form.* Ed. Ian Gregor. London: Vision, 1980. 111–27.

Elfenbein, Andrew. *Byron and the Victorians.* New York: Cambridge UP, 1995.

Eliot, George. *The Mill on the Floss.* 1860. Harmondsworth: Penguin, 1985.

———. *Silas Marner: The Weaver of Raveloe.* 1861. Introd. David Carroll. Harmondsworth: Penguin, 1996.

Eliot, T. S. "The Metaphysical Poets." 1921. *Selected Essays, 1917–1932.* New York: Harcourt, Brace, 1932. 241–50.

———. "Swinburne as Poet." 1920. *Selected Essays, 1917–1932.* New York: Harcourt, Brace, 1932. 281–85.

———. *The Use of Poetry and the Use of Criticism: Studies in the Relation of Criticism to Poetry in England.* 1933. London: Faber and Faber, 1964.

Ellenberger, Henri F. *The Discovery of the Unconscious: The History and Evolution of Dynamic Psychiatry.* New York: Basic, 1970.

Ellenzweig, Allen. *The Homoerotic Photograph: Male Images from Durieu/Delacroix to Mapplethorpe.* New York: Columbia UP, 1992.

Elliott, Albert Pettigrew. *Fatalism in the Works of Thomas Hardy.* 1935. New York: Russell and Russell, 1966.

Ellis, Havelock. "Notes on Olive Schreiner." 1884. In Clayton 40–41.

———. *Sexual Selection in Man.* 1905. Philadelphia: F. A. Davis, 1925. Vol. 4 of *Studies in the Psychology of Sex.* 7 vols. 1928–31.

Epstein, Joseph. "George Santayana and the Consolations of Philosophy." *New Criterion* 5.10 (1987): 15–27.

Epstein, Leonora. "Sale and Sacrament: The Wife Auction in *The Mayor of Casterbridge.*" *ELN* 24.4 (1987): 50–56.

Favardin, Patrick, and Laurent Bouëxière. *Le dandysme.* Lyon: La Manufacture, 1988.

Federico, Annette. *Masculine Identity in Hardy and Gissing.* Cranbury, NJ: Associated UP, 1991.

Feldman, Jessica R. *Gender on the Divide: The Dandy in Modernist Literature.* Ithaca: Cornell UP, 1993.

Felman, Shoshana. "To Open the Question." *Literature and Psychoanalysis: The Question of Reading: Otherwise.* Ed. Felman. Baltimore: Johns Hopkins UP, 1977. 5–10.

Felski, Rita. *The Gender of Modernity.* Cambridge: Harvard UP, 1995.

Feuerbach, Ludwig. *The Essence of Christianity.* 1841. Introd. Karl Barth. Trans. George Eliot. New York: HarperTorch, 1957.

Findley, Heather. "Is There a Lesbian in This Text? Derrida, Wittig, and the Politics of the Three Women." *Coming to Terms: Feminism/Theory/Politics.* Ed. Elizabeth Weed. New York: Routledge, 1989. 59–69.

Firbank, Ronald. *The Complete Firbank.* London: Duckworth, 1961.

First, Ruth, and Ann Scott. *Olive Schreiner.* London: Deutsch, 1980.

Fisch, Marilyn Woroner. "Swinburne's Divine Bitches: Agents of Destruction and Synthesis." *Journal of Pre-Raphaelite Studies* 7.2 (1987): 1–11.

Fletcher, Ian, ed. *Decadence and the 1890s.* London: Edward Arnold, 1979.

Fletcher, John. "Freud and His Uses: Psychoanalysis and Gay Theory." *Coming On Strong: Gay Politics and Culture.* Ed. Simon Shepherd and Mick Wallis. London: Unwin Hyman, 1989. 90–118.

Forbes, Jill. "Two Flagellation Poems by Swinburne." *Notes and Queries* 22 (1975): 443–45.

Forster, E. M. *Albergo Empedocle and Other Writings.* Ed. George H. Thomson. New York: Liveright, 1971.

———. *Collected Short Stories.* 1947. Harmondsworth: Penguin, 1954.

———. *Commonplace Book.* Ed. Philip Gardner. Stanford: Stanford UP, 1985.

———. Diary. Unpublished manuscript. Cambridge: King's College Library.

———. *Howards End.* 1910. Harmondsworth: Penguin, 1954.

———. "Kanaya." c. 1922. *Hill of Devi, and Other Indian Writings.* Ed. E. Heine. London: Arnold, 1983. 310–24.

———. *The Life to Come and Other Stories.* 1972. Harmondsworth: Penguin, 1989.

———. *Maurice: A Romance.* 1913–14. London: Edward Arnold, 1971.

———. *A Passage to India.* 1924. Harmondsworth: Penguin, 1984.

———. *Selected Letters of E. M. Forster: 1879–1920.* Vol. 1. Ed. Mary Lago and P. N. Furbank. London: Collins, 1983.

———. *Two Cheers for Democracy.* New York: Harcourt, Brace and World, 1951.

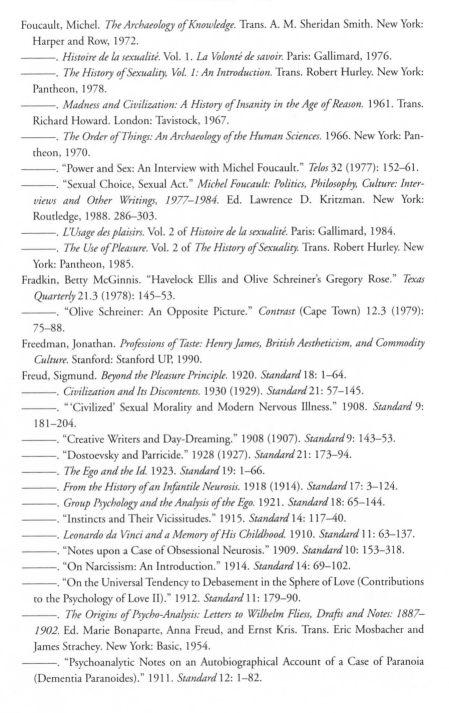

Foucault, Michel. *The Archaeology of Knowledge.* Trans. A. M. Sheridan Smith. New York: Harper and Row, 1972.

———. *Histoire de la sexualité.* Vol. 1. *La Volonté de savoir.* Paris: Gallimard, 1976.

———. *The History of Sexuality, Vol. 1: An Introduction.* Trans. Robert Hurley. New York: Pantheon, 1978.

———. *Madness and Civilization: A History of Insanity in the Age of Reason.* 1961. Trans. Richard Howard. London: Tavistock, 1967.

———. *The Order of Things: An Archaeology of the Human Sciences.* 1966. New York: Pantheon, 1970.

———. "Power and Sex: An Interview with Michel Foucault." *Telos* 32 (1977): 152–61.

———. "Sexual Choice, Sexual Act." *Michel Foucault: Politics, Philosophy, Culture: Interviews and Other Writings, 1977–1984.* Ed. Lawrence D. Kritzman. New York: Routledge, 1988. 286–303.

———. *L'Usage des plaisirs.* Vol. 2 of *Histoire de la sexualité.* Paris: Gallimard, 1984.

———. *The Use of Pleasure.* Vol. 2 of *The History of Sexuality.* Trans. Robert Hurley. New York: Pantheon, 1985.

Fradkin, Betty McGinnis. "Havelock Ellis and Olive Schreiner's Gregory Rose." *Texas Quarterly* 21.3 (1978): 145–53.

———. "Olive Schreiner: An Opposite Picture." *Contrast* (Cape Town) 12.3 (1979): 75–88.

Freedman, Jonathan. *Professions of Taste: Henry James, British Aestheticism, and Commodity Culture.* Stanford: Stanford UP, 1990.

Freud, Sigmund. *Beyond the Pleasure Principle.* 1920. *Standard* 18: 1–64.

———. *Civilization and Its Discontents.* 1930 (1929). *Standard* 21: 57–145.

———. "'Civilized' Sexual Morality and Modern Nervous Illness." 1908. *Standard* 9: 181–204.

———. "Creative Writers and Day-Dreaming." 1908 (1907). *Standard* 9: 143–53.

———. "Dostoevsky and Parricide." 1928 (1927). *Standard* 21: 173–94.

———. *The Ego and the Id.* 1923. *Standard* 19: 1–66.

———. *From the History of an Infantile Neurosis.* 1918 (1914). *Standard* 17: 3–124.

———. *Group Psychology and the Analysis of the Ego.* 1921. *Standard* 18: 65–144.

———. "Instincts and Their Vicissitudes." 1915. *Standard* 14: 117–40.

———. *Leonardo da Vinci and a Memory of His Childhood.* 1910. *Standard* 11: 63–137.

———. "Notes upon a Case of Obsessional Neurosis." 1909. *Standard* 10: 153–318.

———. "On Narcissism: An Introduction." 1914. *Standard* 14: 69–102.

———. "On the Universal Tendency to Debasement in the Sphere of Love (Contributions to the Psychology of Love II)." 1912. *Standard* 11: 179–90.

———. *The Origins of Psycho-Analysis: Letters to Wilhelm Fliess, Drafts and Notes: 1887–1902.* Ed. Marie Bonaparte, Anna Freud, and Ernst Kris. Trans. Eric Mosbacher and James Strachey. New York: Basic, 1954.

———. "Psychoanalytic Notes on an Autobiographical Account of a Case of Paranoia (Dementia Paranoides)." 1911. *Standard* 12: 1–82.

———. "Resistance and Repression." 1916–1917 (1915–1917). *Standard* 16: 286–302.

———. "A Seventeenth-Century Demonological Neurosis." 1923 (1922). *Standard* 19: 67–108.

———. "Some Character-Types Met with in Psycho-Analytic Work (II): Those Wrecked by Success." 1916. *Standard* 14: 316–31.

———. "Some Character-Types Met with in Psycho-Analytic Work (III): Criminals from a Sense of Guilt." 1916. *Standard* 14: 332–33.

———. "Some Neurotic Mechanisms in Jealousy, Paranoia and Homosexuality." 1922 (1921). *Standard* 18: 221–34.

———. "A Special Type of Choice of Object Made by Men (Contributions to the Psychology of Love I)." 1910. *Standard* 11: 163–75.

———. *The Standard Edition of the Complete Psychological Works of Sigmund Freud.* Ed. and trans. James Strachey. 24 vols. London: Hogarth, 1953–74.

———. "Thoughts for the Times on War and Death." 1915. *Standard* 14: 273–302.

———. *Three Essays on the Theory of Sexuality.* 1905. *Standard* 7: 123–245.

———. "The Unconscious." 1915. *Standard* 14: 161–215.

Freud, Sigmund, and Albert Einstein. "Why War?" 1933 (1932). *Standard* 22: 195–212.

Funston, Judith E. "'All Art Is One': Narrative Techniques in Henry James's *Tragic Muse*." *Studies in the Novel* 15 (1983): 353–55.

Fuss, Diana. *Identification Papers.* New York: Routledge, 1995.

Fussell, D. H. "The Maladroit Delay: The Changing Times in Hardy's *The Mayor of Casterbridge*." *Critical Quarterly* 21.3 (1979): 17–30.

Gallagher, Catherine. *The Industrial Reformation of English Fiction, 1832–1867.* Chicago: U of Chicago P, 1985.

Garber, Marjorie. *Vice Versa: Bisexuality and the Eroticism of Everyday Life.* New York: Simon and Schuster, 1995.

Gaskell, Elizabeth. *Mary Barton: A Tale of Manchester Life.* 1848. Ed. Stephen Gill. Harmondsworth: Penguin, 1985.

———. *Ruth.* 1853. New York: Oxford UP, 1981.

Gilbert, Sandra M., and Susan Gubar. *No Man's Land: The Place of the Woman Writer in the Twentieth Century.* Vol. 2. *Sexchanges.* New Haven: Yale UP, 1989.

Gilman, Richard. *Decadence: The Strange Life of an Epithet.* New York: Farrar, Straus and Giroux, 1975, 1979.

Gilmour, Robin. *The Idea of the Gentleman in the Victorian Novel.* London: Allen and Unwin, 1981.

Gissing, George. *The Odd Women.* 1893. Harmondsworth: Penguin, 1993.

Goetz, William R. "The Allegory of Representation in *The Tragic Muse*." *Journal of Narrative Technique* 8 (1978): 156–64.

Goldfarb, Russell M. *Sexual Repression and Victorian Literature.* Lewisburg, PA: Bucknell UP, 1970.

Gorak, Irene E. "Olive Schreiner's Colonial Allegory: *The Story of an African Farm*." *Ariel* 23.4 (1992): 53–72.

Graham, Peter W. "Bulwer the *Moraliste*." *Dickens Studies Annual* 9 (1981): 143–61.

———. "Pelham as Paragon: Bulwer's Ideal Aristocrat." *Victorians Institute Journal* 9 (1980–81): 71–81.

Gray, Stephen. "Schreiner's Trooper at the Hanging Tree." *English in Africa* 2.2 (1975): 23–37.

Greenberg, Robert A. "'Erotion,' 'Anactoria,' and the Sapphic Passion." *Victorian Poetry* 29.1 (1991): 79–87.

Grindle, Juliet M. "Compulsion and Choice in *The Mayor of Casterbridge*." *The Novels of Thomas Hardy*. Ed. Anne Smith. London: Vision, 1979. 91–106.

Gunter, Susan Elizabeth. "The Russian Connection: Sources for Miriam Rooth of James's *The Tragic Muse*." *South Atlantic Review* 53.2 (1988): 77–91.

Halberstam, Judith. *Skin Shows: Gothic Horror and the Technology of Monsters*. Durham: Duke UP, 1995.

Hall, Donald E., ed. *Fixing Patriarchy: Feminism and Mid-Victorian Male Novelists*. New York: New York UP, 1996.

———, ed. *Muscular Christianity: Embodying the Victorian Age*. New York: Cambridge UP, 1994.

Hall, Richard. "Henry James: Interpreting an Obsessive Memory." *Journal of Homosexuality* 8.3–4 (1983): 83–97.

Hall, William F. "Gabriel Nash: 'Famous Centre' of *The Tragic Muse*." *Nineteenth-Century Fiction* 21 (1966): 167–84.

Halperin, David M. *One Hundred Years of Homosexuality, and Other Essays on Greek Love*. New York: Routledge, 1990.

———. *Saint Foucault: Towards a Gay Hagiography*. New York: Oxford UP, 1995.

Hammond, Paul. *Love between Men in English Literature*. New York: St Martin's, 1996.

Hardy, Florence Emily. *The Life of Thomas Hardy, 1840–1928*. London: Macmillan, 1962.

Hardy, Thomas. "Candour in English Fiction." 1890. In Orel 125–33.

———. *The Collected Poems of Thomas Hardy*. New York: Macmillan, 1925.

———. *Far from the Madding Crowd*. 1874. Harmondsworth: Penguin, 1978.

———. *Jude the Obscure*. 1894; 1895. Harmondsworth: Penguin, 1983.

———. *The Mayor of Casterbridge*. 1886. Harmondsworth: Penguin, 1985.

———. *The Return of the Native*. 1878. Harmondsworth: Penguin, 1983.

———. *Tess of the d'Urbervilles: A Pure Woman*. 1891. Harmondsworth: Penguin, 1982.

———. *The Woodlanders*. 1886; 1887. Harmondsworth: Penguin, 1981.

Harpham, Geoffrey Galt. *The Ascetic Imperative in Culture and Criticism*. Chicago: U of Chicago P, 1987.

Harrison, Antony H. "The Aesthetics of Androgyny in Swinburne's Early Poetry." *Tennessee Studies in Literature* 23 (1978): 87–99.

———. "Eros and Thanatos in Swinburne's Poetry: An Introduction." *Journal of Pre-Raphaelite Studies* 2.1 (1981): 22–35.

———. "'Love Strong as Death and Valour Strong as Love': Swinburne and Courtly Love." *Victorian Poetry* 18 (1980): 61–73.

———. "Swinburne's Losses: The Poetics of Passion." *ELH* 49.3 (1982): 689–706.

———. "The Swinburnian Woman." *Philological Quarterly* 58.1 (1979): 90–102.

Harrison, Antony H., and Beverly Taylor, eds. *Gender and Discourse in Victorian Literature and Art.* DeKalb: Northern Illinois UP, 1992.

Hartsock, Mildred E. "Henry James and the Cities of the Plain." *Modern Language Quarterly* 29 (1968): 297–311.

Haynes, R. D. "Elements of Romanticism in *The Story of an African Farm.*" *English Literature in Transition* 24.2 (1981): 59–79.

Hazlitt, William. *The Complete Works of William Hazlitt.* 21 vols. Ed. P. P. Howe. London: Dent, 1930–34.

———. "The Dandy School." 1827. *Complete Works* 20: 143–49.

———. "On Effeminacy of Character." 1824. *Complete Works* 8: 248–55.

Heath, Stephen. "Joan Rivière and the Masquerade." *Formations of Fantasy.* Ed. Victor Burgin, James Donald, and Cora Kaplan. London: Methuen, 1986. 45–61.

Hennelly, Mark M. "The Unknown Character of *The Mayor of Casterbridge,* Parts I and II." *Journal of Evolutionary Psychology* 16.1–2 (1995): 92–101, 272–84.

Herz, Judith Scherer. *The Short Narratives of E. M. Forster.* New York: St. Martin's, 1988.

Heywood, Christopher. "Olive Schreiner's *The Story of an African Farm:* Prototype of Lawrence's Early Novels." *English Language Notes* 14 (1976): 44–50.

Higonnet, Margaret R., ed. *The Sense of Sex: Feminist Perspectives on Thomas Hardy.* Urbana: U of Illinois P, 1993.

Hilliard, David. "UnEnglish and Unmanly: Anglo-Catholicism and Homosexuality." *Victorian Studies* 25.2 (1981–82): 181–210.

Hoad, T. F., ed. *The Concise Oxford Dictionary of English Etymology.* Oxford: Clarendon, 1986.

Hobman, D. L. *Olive Schreiner: Her Friends and Times.* London: Watts, 1955.

Hoffman, Frederick J. *Freudianism and the Literary Mind.* 1945. 2nd ed. Baton Rouge: Louisiana State UP, 1957.

Holland, Vyvyan. *Son of Oscar Wilde.* London: Hart-Davis, 1954.

Holleran, Andrew. "(Artificial) Marble." *Ground Zero.* New York: Plume, 1988. 101–12.

Horton, Susan R. *Difficult Women, Artful Lives: Olive Schreiner and Isak Dinesen, In and Out of Africa.* Baltimore: Johns Hopkins UP, 1995.

Houghton, Walter E. *The Victorian Frame of Mind, 1830–1870.* New Haven: Yale UP, 1957, 1985.

Housman, A. E. *The Collected Poems of A. E. Housman.* New York: Holt, 1965.

Howells, Bernard. "Heroïsme, dandysme et la 'Philosophie du costume': Note sur Baudelaire et Carlyle." *Rivista di letteratura moderne e comparate* 41.2 (1988): 131–51.

Hughes, Randolph. Foreword. *Lesbia Brandon.* By Algernon Charles Swinburne. London: Falcon, 1952. iii—xxxv.

Hulme, T. E. "A Lecture on Modern Poetry." c. 1908. *Further Speculations.* Ed. Sam Hynes. Minneapolis: U of Minnesota P, 1955. 67–76.

———. "Romanticism and Classicism." c. 1911–12. *Speculations: Essays on Humanism and the Philosophy of Art.* 1924. Ed. Herbert Read. New York: Harcourt, Brace, 1936. 111–40.

Huysmans, J.-K. *Against Nature.* 1884. Trans. Robert Baldick. Harmondsworth: Penguin, 1959.

Hyder, Clyde K., ed. *Swinburne: The Critical Heritage.* London: Routledge, 1970.

Ingersoll, Earl G. "Troping and the Machine in Thomas Hardy's *The Mayor of Casterbridge.*" *University of Hartford Studies in Literature* 22.2–3 (1990): 59–67.

———. "Writing and Memory in *The Mayor of Casterbridge.*" *English Literature in Transition* 33.3 (1990): 299–309.

Irwin, T. H. *Plato's Moral Theory.* New York: Oxford UP, 1977.

Jacobson, Dan. Introduction. *The Story of an African Farm.* By Olive Schreiner. Harmondsworth: Penguin, 1971. 7–23.

Jacobus, Mary. "Is There a Woman in This Text?" *Reading Woman: Essays in Feminist Criticism.* New York: Columbia UP, 1986. 83–109.

———. "Sue the Obscure." *Essays in Criticism* 25.3 (1975): 304–28.

———. "Tess's Purity." *Essays in Criticism* 26.4 (1976): 318–38.

Jacoby, Russell. *The Repression of Psychoanalysis: Otto Fenichel and the Political Freudians.* New York: Basic, 1973.

James, Henry. *The Ambassadors.* 1903. Harmondsworth: Penguin, 1986.

———. "The Beast in the Jungle." 1903. *Novels and Tales of Henry James* 17: 61–127.

———. "The Great Good Place." 1900. *Novels and Tales of Henry James* 16: 225–63.

———. "The Jolly Corner." 1908. *The Jolly Corner, and Other Stories.* Ed. Roger Gard. Harmondsworth: Penguin, 1990. 161–93.

———. "The Liar." 1888. *Novels and Tales of Henry James* 12: 313–88.

———. "The Madonna of the Future." 1873. *Novels and Tales of Henry James* 13: 437–92.

———. *The Novels and Tales of Henry James: The New York Edition.* New York: Scribner's, 1908.

———. Preface. *Roderick Hudson.* By James. Harmondsworth: Penguin, 1986. 35–48.

———. "Preface to *The Tragic Muse.*" *The Art of the Novel: Critical Prefaces.* Introd. Richard P. Blackmur. New York: Scribner's, 1934. 70–97.

———. "The Pupil." 1891. *Novels and Tales of Henry James* 11: 511–77.

———. *Roderick Hudson.* 1874; 1875. Harmondsworth: Penguin, 1986.

———. *The Sacred Fount.* 1901. Ed. Leon Edel. London: Hart-Davis, 1959.

———. *The Tragic Muse.* 1889; 1890. Harmondsworth: Penguin, 1978.

Jeffers, Thomas L. *Samuel Butler Revalued.* University Park: Pennsylvania State UP, 1981.

Jeffreys, Sheila. *The Spinster and Her Enemies: Feminism and Sexuality 1880–1930.* London: Pandora, 1985.

Jenkyns, Richard. *The Victorians and Ancient Greece.* Cambridge: Harvard UP, 1980.

Johnson, Wendell Stacy. *Living in Sin: The Victorian Sexual Revolution.* Chicago: Nelson-Hall, 1979.

Jones, Ernest. "War and Individual Psychology." 1915. *Essays in Applied Psycho-Analysis.* London: Hogarth, 1951. 1: 55–76.

————. "War and Sublimation." 1915. *Essays in Applied Psycho-Analysis* 1: 77–87.

Jones, Tod E. "Michael Henchard: Hardy's Male Homosexual." *Victorian Newsletter* 86 (1994): 9–13.

Jordan, John O. "Closer Than a Brother: Swinburne and Watts-Dunton." *Mothering the Mind: Twelve Studies of Writers and Their Silent Partners.* Ed. Ruth Perry and Martine Watson Brownley. New York: Holmes and Meier, 1984. 204–16.

Jung, Carl G. *The Archetypes and the Collective Unconscious.* 1959. 2nd ed. Trans. R. F. C. Hull. Princeton: Princeton UP, 1969.

Kahane, Claire. *Passions of the Voice: Hysteria, Narrative, and the Figure of the Speaking Woman, 1850–1915.* Baltimore: Johns Hopkins UP, 1995.

Kains-Jackson, Charles. "The New Chivalry." 1894. In Reade 313–19.

Kant, Immanuel. *Religion within the Limits of Reason Alone.* 1793. Trans. Theodore M. Greene and Hoyt H. Hudson. New York: Harper and Row, 1960.

Kappeler, Susanne. *Writing and Reading in Henry James.* New York: Columbia UP, 1980.

Kellog, Stuart. "Introduction: The Uses of Homosexuality in Literature." *Literary Visions of Homosexuality.* Ed. Kellog. New York: Haworth, 1983. 1–12.

Kimmey, John L. "*The Tragic Muse* and Its Forerunners." *American Literature* 41 (1970): 518–31.

King, Jeannette. "*The Mayor of Casterbridge:* Talking about Character." *Thomas Hardy Journal* 8.3 (1992): 42–46.

Kinsey, Alfred C., Wardell B. Pomeroy, and Clyde E. Martin. *Sexual Behavior in the Human Male.* Philadelphia: W. B. Saunders Company, 1948.

Kipling, Rudyard. "Dray Wara Yow Dee." 1890. *The Writings in Prose and Verse of Rudyard Kipling, Vol. 4: In Black and White.* New York: Scribner's, 1897. 1–16.

————. *Kim.* 1901. Harmondsworth: Penguin, 1989.

————. "The White Man's Burden." 1899. *Rudyard Kipling's Verse: Definitive Edition.* Garden City: Doubleday, Doran and Co., 1942. 321–23.

Kirkwood, M. M. *Santayana: Saint of the Imagination.* Toronto: U of Toronto P, 1961.

Klevansky, Ruth. "Some Insights into the Nature of Lyndall's Idealism in *The Story of an African Farm.*" *Crux* (Pretoria) 19.1 (1985): 19–22.

Kopelson, Kevin. *Love's Litany: The Writing of Modern Homoerotics.* Stanford: Stanford UP, 1994.

Krige, Uys. "Introduction: Olive Schreiner: Poet and Prophet." *Olive Schreiner: A Selection.* Ed. Krige. Cape Town: Oxford UP, 1968. 1–30.

Kucich, John. "Moral Authority in the Late Novels: The Gendering of Art." In Higonnet 221–41.

————. *Repression in Victorian Fiction: Charlotte Brontë, George Eliot, and Charles Dickens.* Berkeley: U of California P, 1987.

Lacan, Jacques. *Écrits: A Selection.* Trans. Alan Sheridan. New York: Norton, 1977.

————. "L'Etourdit." *Scilicet* 4 (1973): 5–52.

————. *The Four Fundamental Concepts of Psycho-Analysis.* 1973. Ed. Jacques-Alain Miller. Trans. Alan Sheridan. New York: Norton, 1978.

———. "The Function and Field of Speech and Language in Psychoanalysis." 1953. In *Écrits: A Selection* 30–113.

———. *The Seminar of Jacques Lacan, Book I: Freud's Papers on Technique, 1953–1954*. Ed. Jacques-Alain Miller. Trans. John Forrester. Cambridge: Cambridge UP, 1988.

———. *The Seminar of Jacques Lacan, Book II: The Ego in Freud's Theory and in the Technique of Psychoanalysis, 1954–1955*. Ed. Jacques-Alain Miller. Trans. Sylvana Tomaselli. Cambridge: Cambridge UP, 1988.

———. "The Signification of the Phallus." 1958. In *Écrits: A Selection* 281–91.

Lafourcade, Georges. *La jeunesse de Swinburne*. 2 vols. Paris: Belles Lettres, 1928.

Laity, Cassandra. "H. D. and A. C. Swinburne: Decadence and Modernist Women's Writing." *Feminist Studies* 15.3 (1989): 461–84.

Lane, Christopher. Introduction. *The Psychoanalysis of Race*. Ed. Lane. New York: Columbia UP, 1998. 1–37.

———. *The Ruling Passion: British Colonial Allegory and the Paradox of Homosexual Desire*. Durham: Duke UP, 1995.

———. "The Testament of the Other: Abraham and Torok's Failed Expiation of Ghosts." *Diacritics* 27.4 (1997): 3–29.

———. "'Thoughts for the Times on War and Death': Militarism and Its Discontents." *Literature and Psychology* 41.3 (1995): 1–12.

———. "Uncertain Terms of Pleasure." *Modern Fiction Studies* 43.4 (1996): 807–26.

Lang, Cecil Y. "Lesbia Brandon." *Times Literary Supplement* Oct. 31, 1952: 716.

———. "Swinburne's Lost Love." *PMLA* 74 (1959): 123–30.

Langbaum, Robert. "The Minimisation of Sexuality in *The Mayor of Casterbridge*." *Thomas Hardy Journal* 8.1 (1992): 20–32.

Laplanche, Jean. *Life and Death in Psychoanalysis*. 1970. Trans. Jeffrey Mehlman. Baltimore: Johns Hopkins UP, 1976, 1990.

———. "To Situate Sublimation." Trans. Richard Miller. *October* 28 (1984): 7–26.

Lawrence, D. H. *The Letters of D. H. Lawrence*. Vol. 2. Ed. George J. Zytaruk and James T. Boulton. Cambridge: Cambridge UP, 1981.

———. *Women in Love*. 1920. Harmondsworth: Penguin, 1982.

Lawrence, T. E. *Seven Pillars of Wisdom: A Triumph*. 1922. Garden City: Doubleday, 1935.

Leavitt, David. *The Lost Language of Cranes*. New York: Knopf, 1986.

LeFew, Penelope A. "Schopenhauerian Pessimism in Olive Schreiner's *A Story of an African Farm* and *From Man to Man*." *English Literature in Transition* 37.3 (1994): 303–16.

Lenta, Margaret. "Racism, Sexism, and Olive Schreiner's Fiction." *Theoria* (Natal) 70 (1987): 15–30.

Lentricchia, Frank. "Philosophers of Modernism at Harvard circa 1900." *South Atlantic Quarterly* 89.4 (1990): 787–834.

Lerner, Laurence. "Olive Schreiner and the Feminists." In Smith and Maclennan 67–79.

———. *Thomas Hardy's The Mayor of Casterbridge: Tragedy or Social History?* London: Chatto and Windus, 1975.

Levine, June Perry. "The Tame in Pursuit of the Savage: The Posthumous Fiction of E. M. Forster." *PMLA* 99.1 (1984): 72–88.

Lewis, Simon. "Graves with a View: Atavism and the European History of Africa." *Ariel* 27.1 (1996): 40–60.

Litvak, Joseph. "Back to the Future: A Review-Article on the New Historicism, Deconstruction, and Nineteenth-Century Fiction." *Texas Studies in Literature and Language* 30.1 (1988): 120–49.

———. *Caught in the Act: Theatricality in the Nineteenth-Century English Novel.* Berkeley: U of California P, 1992.

Loewald, H. W. *Sublimation: Inquiries into Theoretical Psychoanalysis.* New Haven: Yale UP, 1990.

Lynn, Kenneth S. "Santayana and the Genteel Tradition." *Commentary* May 1982: 81–84.

Macey, David. *The Lives of Michel Foucault.* New York: Pantheon, 1993.

Macnaughton, W. R. "In Defense of James's *The Tragic Muse*." *Henry James Review* 7.1 (1985): 5–12.

Malek, James S. "Forster's 'Arthur Snatchfold': Respectability vs. Apollo." *Notes on Contemporary Literature* 10.4 (1980): 8–9.

Mangan, J. A., and James Walvin, ed. *Manliness and Morality: Middle-Class Masculinity in Britain and America, 1800–1940.* Manchester: Manchester UP, 1987.

Manning, F. "Novels of Character and Environment." 1912. *Hardy: The Tragic Novels.* Ed. R. P. Draper. London: Macmillan, 1975. 58–72.

Marcus, Steven. *Freud and the Culture of Psychoanalysis: Studies in the Transition from Victorian Humanism to Modernity.* New York: Norton, 1984.

———. *The Other Victorians: A Study of Sexuality and Pornography in Mid-Nineteenth-Century England.* New York: Basic, 1966.

Marcuse, Herbert. *Eros and Civilization: A Philosophical Inquiry into Freud.* New York: Random House, 1955.

———. *One-Dimensional Man: Studies in the Ideology of Advanced Industrial Society.* Boston: Beacon, 1964.

Marquard, Jean. "Hagar's Child: A Reading of *The Story of an African Farm*." *Standpunte* (South Africa) 121 (1976): 35–47.

Martin, Biddy. "Sexualities without Genders and Other Queer Utopias." *Diacritics* 24.2–3 (1994): 104–21.

Martin, Robert K. "The 'High Felicity' of Comradeship: A New Reading of *Roderick Hudson*." *American Literary Realism* 11 (1978): 100–108.

———. *The Homosexual Tradition in American Poetry.* Austin: U of Texas P, 1979.

———. "Roland Barthes: Toward an '*Écriture gaie*.'" In Bergman 282–98.

Martin, Robert K., and George Piggford. "Introduction: Queer, Forster?" *Queer Forster.* Ed. Martin and Piggford. Chicago: U of Chicago P, 1997. 1–28.

Mason, A. E. W. *The Four Feathers.* 1902. London: Smith, Elder, and Co., 1907.

Mason, Michael. *The Making of Victorian Sexual Attitudes.* New York: Oxford UP, 1994.

————. *The Making of Victorian Sexuality.* New York: Oxford UP, 1994.

Maugham, W. Somerset. *Of Human Bondage.* 1915. London: Mandarin, 1990.

Maynard, John. *Victorian Discourses on Sexuality and Religion.* Cambridge: Cambridge UP, 1993.

McClary, Susan. "Constructions of Subjectivity in Schubert's Music." *Queering the Pitch: The New Gay and Lesbian Musicology.* Ed. Philip Brett, Elizabeth Wood, and Gary C. Thomas. New York: Routledge, 1994. 205–33.

McClintock, Anne. *Imperial Leather: Race, Gender, and Sexuality in the Colonial Conquest.* New York: Routledge, 1995.

McCormick, John. *George Santayana: A Biography.* New York: Knopf, 1987.

McCracken, Scott. "Writing the Body: Edward Carpenter, George Gissing and Late-Nineteenth-Century Realism." *Prose Studies* 13 (1990): 178–200.

McGann, Jerome J. Introduction. *Pelham; or, The Adventures of a Gentleman.* By Edward George Bulwer-Lytton. Lincoln: U of Nebraska P, 1972. xi–xxv.

————. *Swinburne: An Experiment in Criticism.* Chicago: U of Chicago P, 1972.

McGhee, Richard D. "'Swinburne Planteth, Hardy Watereth': Victorian Views of Pain and Pleasure in Human Sexuality." In Cox 83–107.

McMurry, Andrew. "Figures in a Ground: An Ecofeminist Study of Olive Schreiner's *The Story of an African Farm.*" *English Studies in Canada* 20.4 (1994): 431–48.

McSweeney, Kerry. "Swinburne's Poems and Ballads (1866)." *Studies in English Literature* 11.4 (1971): 671–85.

Meisel, Perry. *Thomas Hardy: The Return of the Repressed: A Study of the Major Fiction.* New Haven: Yale UP, 1972.

Meredith, George. *The Egoist: A Comedy in Narrative.* 1879; 1897. New York: Norton, 1979.

————. *One of Our Conquerors.* 1891. London: Constable, 1910.

Meyers, Jeffrey. *Homosexuality and Literature, 1890–1930.* London: Athlone, 1977.

Milberg-Kaye, Ruth. *Thomas Hardy: Myths of Sexuality.* New York: John Jay, 1983.

Miller, D. A. "Austen's Attitude." *Yale Journal of Criticism* 8.1 (1995): 1–5.

————. *Bringing Out Roland Barthes.* Berkeley: U of California P, 1992.

————. *The Novel and the Police.* Berkeley: U of California P, 1988.

Miller, J. Hillis. *Thomas Hardy: Distance and Desire.* Cambridge: Harvard UP, 1970.

Miller, James. *The Passion of Michel Foucault.* New York: Simon and Schuster, 1993.

Millgate, Michael. *Thomas Hardy: A Biography.* New York: Random, 1982.

Moers, Ellen. *The Dandy: Brummell to Beerbohm.* New York: Viking, 1960.

Monneyron, Frédéric. "L'androgyne dans *Lesbia Brandon* de Swinburne." *Cahiers victoriens et édouardiens* 29 (1989): 55–65.

Monsman, Gerald. "The Idea of 'Story' in Olive Schreiner's *Story of an African Farm.*" *Texas Studies in Literature and Language* 27.3 (1985): 249–69.

————. "Olive Schreiner: Literature and the Politics of Power." *Texas Studies in Literature and Language* 30.4 (1988): 583–610.

————. "Olive Schreiner's Allegorical Vision." *Victorian Review* 18.2 (1992): 49–62.

————. "Patterns of Narration and Characterization in Schreiner's *The Story of an African Farm*." *English Literature in Transition* 28.3 (1985): 253–70.

————. "Writing the Self on the Imperial Frontier: Olive Schreiner and the Stories of Africa." *Bucknell Review* 37.1 (1993): 134–55.

Moon, Michael. "A Small Boy and Others: Sexual Disorientation in Henry James, Kenneth Anger, and David Lynch." *Comparative American Identities: Race, Sex, and Nationality in the Modern Text.* Ed. Hortense Spillers. New York: Routledge, 1991. 141–56.

Moore, Kevin Z. "Death against Life: Hardy's Mortified and Mortifying 'Man of Character' in *The Mayor of Casterbridge*." *Forum* 24.3 (1983): 13–25.

Morgan, Rosemarie. *Women and Sexuality in the Novels of Thomas Hardy.* New York: Routledge, 1988.

Morgan, Thaïs E. "Male Lesbian Bodies: The Construction of Alternative Masculinities in Courbet, Baudelaire, and Swinburne." *Genders* 15 (1992): 37–57.

————. "Mixed Metaphor, Mixed Gender: Swinburne and the Victorian Critics." *Victorian Newsletter* 73 (1988): 16–19.

————. "Reimagining Masculinity in Victorian Criticism: Swinburne and Pater." *Sexualities in Victorian Britain.* Ed. Andrew H. Miller and James Eli Adams. Bloomington: Indiana UP, 1996. 140–56.

————. "Swinburne's Dramatic Monologues: Sex and Ideology." *Victorian Poetry* 22.2 (1984): 175–95.

————, ed. *Victorian Sages and Cultural Discourse: Renegotiating Gender and Power.* New Brunswick: Rutgers UP, 1990.

Mort, Frank. *Dangerous Sexualities: Medico-Moral Politics in England since 1830.* New York: Routledge, 1987.

————. "Sexuality: Regulation and Contestation." *Homosexuality: Power and Politics.* Ed. Gay Left Collective. London: Allison and Busby, 1980. 38–51.

Mosse, George L. *The Image of Man: The Creation of Modern Masculinity.* New York: Oxford UP, 1996.

Narayanaswamy, K. R. "*The Mayor of Casterbridge:* A Reappraisal." *Literary Half-Yearly* 21.2 (1980): 68–77.

Newfield, Christopher. "Democracy and Male Homoeroticism." *Yale Journal of Criticism* 6.2 (1993): 29–62.

Northey, Margot. "Control and Freedom: Swinburne's Novels." *English Studies in Canada* 6 (1980): 292–306.

Nussbaum, Martha C. *The Therapy of Desire: Theory and Practice in Hellenistic Ethics.* Princeton: Princeton UP, 1994.

Oakley, J. W. "The Reform of Honor in Bulwer's *Pelham*." *Nineteenth-Century Literature* 47.1 (1992): 49–71.

Ogede, Ode. "The Tragic Vision in Olive Schreiner's *The Story of an African Farm*." *Kuka* (Nigeria) (1980–81): 26–33.

Orel, Harold, ed. *Thomas Hardy's Personal Writings: Prefaces, Literary Opinions, Reminiscences.* Lawrence: U of Kansas P, 1966.

Page, Norman. *E. M. Forster's Posthumous Fiction.* Victoria, BC: U of Victoria P, 1977.

Paglia, Camille A. "Nature, Sex, and Decadence." *Pre-Raphaelite Poets.* Ed. Harold Bloom. New York: Chelsea House, 1986. 219–37.

Parker, Christopher, ed. *Gender Roles and Sexuality in Victorian Literature.* Brookfield, VT: Scolar, 1995.

Parkin-Gounelas, Ruth. *Fictions of the Female Self: Charlotte Brontë, Olive Schreiner, Katherine Mansfield.* London: Macmillan, 1971.

Pater, Walter. *The Renaissance: Studies in Art and Poetry.* 1873; 1893. Ed. Donald L. Hill. Berkeley: U of California P, 1980.

Paxton, Nancy L. "*The Story of an African Farm* and the Dynamics of Woman-to-Woman Influence." *Texas Studies in Literature and Language* 30.4 (1988): 562–82.

Pearsall, Ronald. *Public Purity, Private Shame: Victorian Sexual Hypocrisy Exposed.* London: Weidenfeld and Nicolson, 1976.

———. *The Worm in the Bud: The World of Victorian Sexuality.* Toronto: Macmillan, 1969.

Pechey, Graham. "*The Story of an African Farm:* Colonial History and the Discontinuous Text." *Critical Arts* (South Africa) 3.1 (1983): 65–78.

Pecora, Vincent P. *Households of the Soul.* Baltimore: Johns Hopkins UP, 1997.

Phillips, Adam. *On Kissing, Tickling, and Being Bored: Psychoanalytic Essays on the Unexamined Life.* Cambridge: Harvard UP, 1993.

Pittick, Murray G. H. "Swinburne and the 'Nineties." In Rooksby and Shrimpton 120–35.

Plato. *Euthyphro, Apology, Crito, Phaedo, Phaedrus.* Trans. Harold North Fowler. Cambridge: Harvard UP/Loeb Classical Library, 1914, 1995.

———. *Lysis, Symposium, Gorgias.* Trans. W. R. M. Lamb. Cambridge: Harvard UP/Loeb Classical Library, 1925, 1991.

Poirier, Richard. "The Difficulties of Modernism and the Modernism of Difficulty." *Humanities in Society* 1.4 (1978): 271–86.

———. "Writing Off the Self." *Raritan* 1.1 (1981): 106–33.

Polhemus, Robert M. *Erotic Faith: Being in Love from Jane Austen to D. H. Lawrence.* Chicago: U of Chicago P, 1990.

Poovey, Mary. *Making a Social Body: British Cultural Formation, 1830–1864.* Chicago: U of Chicago P, 1995.

———. *Uneven Developments: The Ideological Work of Gender in Mid-Victorian England.* Chicago: U of Chicago P, 1988.

Porte, Joel. "Santayana's Masquerade." *Raritan* 7.2 (1987): 129–42.

Posnock, Ross. "Genteel Androgyny: Santayana, Henry James, Howard Sturgis." *Raritan* 10.3 (1991): 58–84.

Pound, Ezra. *Literary Essays of Ezra Pound.* 1954. Ed. T. S. Eliot. London: Faber and Faber, 1968.

Powers, Lyall. "James' *The Tragic Muse—Ave Atque Vale.*" *PMLA* 73 (1958): 270–74.

Praz, Mario. *The Hero in Eclipse in Victorian Fiction.* London: Oxford UP, 1956.

———. *The Romantic Agony.* 1933. Trans. Angus Davidson. New York: Oxford UP, 1951.

Rabiger, Michael. "Hardy's Fictional Process and His Emotional Life." *Alternative Hardy.* Ed. Lance St. John Butler. London: Macmillan, 1989. 88–109.

Rajchman, John. *Michel Foucault: The Freedom of Philosophy.* New York: Columbia UP, 1985.

Reade, Brian, ed. *Sexual Heretics: Male Homosexuality in English Literature from 1850 to 1900.* New York: Coward, McCann, 1971.

Reardon, Bernard M. G. *Religious Thought in the Victorian Age: A Survey from Coleridge to Gore.* 2nd ed. London: Longman, 1995.

Reed, John R. *Victorian Will.* Athens: Ohio UP, 1989.

Reich, Wilhelm. *The Function of the Orgasm: Sex-Economic Problems of Biological Energy.* 1968. Trans. Vincent R. Carfagno. New York: Farrar, 1973.

Richards, Jeffrey. "'Passing the Love of Women': Manly Love and Victorian Society." In Mangan and Walvin 92–122.

Richardson, Frank M. *Mars without Venus: A Study of Some Homosexual Generals.* Edinburgh: Blackwood, 1981.

Ridder-Barzin, Louise de. *Le pessimisme de Thomas Hardy.* Paris: PUF, 1948.

Riede, David G. "Bard and Lady Novelist: Swinburne and the Novel of (Mrs.) Manners." *Victorian Newsletter* 69 (1986): 4–7.

Rive, Richard. "New Light on Olive Schreiner." *Contrast* (Cape Town) 8.4 (1973): 40–47.

Rivière, Joan. "Womanliness as a Masquerade." 1929. *Formations of Fantasy.* Ed. Victor Burgin, James Donald, and Cora Kaplan. London: Methuen, 1986. 35–44.

Roof, Judith. *A Lure of Knowledge: Lesbian Sexuality and Theory.* New York: Columbia UP, 1991.

Rooksby, Rikky. "A. C. Swinburne's *Lesbia Brandon* and the Death of Edith Swinburne." *Notes and Queries* 40.4 (1993): 487–90.

———. "Upon the Borderlands of Being: Swinburne's Later Elegies." *Victorians Institute Journal* 20 (1992): 137–58.

Rooksby, Rikky, and Nicholas Shrimpton, eds. *The Whole Music of Passion: New Essays on Swinburne.* Ashgate, VT: Scolar, 1993.

Rose, Jacqueline. *Sexuality in the Field of Vision.* London: Verso, 1986.

Rosen, David. *The Changing Fictions of Masculinity.* Urbana: U of Illinois P, 1993.

Roth, Marty. "Homosexual Expression and Homophobic Censorship: The Situation of the Text." In Bergman 268–81.

Rowbotham, Sheila, and Jeffrey Weeks. *Socialism and the New Life: The Personal and Sexual Politics of Edward Carpenter and Havelock Ellis.* London: Pluto, 1977.

Rowse, A. L. "Santayana: A Prophet of Our Time." *Contemporary Review* 260.1517 (1992): 320–23.

Rubin, Gayle. "The Traffic in Women: Notes toward a Political Economy of Sex." *Toward an Anthropology of Women.* Ed. Rayna Reiter. New York: Monthly Review, 1975. 157–210.

Ruddick, Lisa. "Fluid Symbols in American Modernism: William James, Gertrude Stein, George Santayana, and Wallace Stevens." *Allegory, Myth, and Symbol*. Ed. Morton W. Bloomfield. Cambridge: Harvard UP, 1981. 335–53.

Ruskin, John. *Modern Painters:* 2. 1843; 1846. New York: Wiley, 1866.

———. "Of Queens' Gardens." 1864. *Sesame and Lilies: Three Lectures*. 1870. New York: Merrill and Baker, 1888. 83–133.

Ryan, Judith. *The Vanishing Subject: Early Psychology and Literary Modernism*. Chicago: U of Chicago P, 1991.

Saatkamp, Herman J. "Final Intentions, Social Context, and Santayana's Autobiography." *Text: Transactions of the Society for Textual Scholarship* 4 (1988): 93–108.

Salecl, Renata. "I Can't Love You Unless I Give You Up." In Salecl and Žižek 179–207.

Salecl, Renata, and Slavoj Žižek, eds. *Gaze and Voice as Love Objects*. Durham: Duke UP, 1996.

Salter, Donald. "That Is My Ticket: The Homosexual Writings of E. M. Forster." *London Magazine* Feb.-March 1975: 5–53.

Santayana, George. "Apologia pro mente sua." *The Philosophy of George Santayana*. Ed. Paul Arthur Schilpp. New York: Tudor Publishing, 1940. 497–605.

———. *The Complete Poems of George Santayana: A Critical Edition*. Ed. and introd. William G. Holzberger. Lewisburg, PA: Bucknell UP, 1979.

———. "Friendships." *Soliloquies in England and Later Soliloquies*. New York: Scribner's, 1922. 55–58.

———. *Interpretations of Poetry and Religion*. New York: Scribner's, 1900.

———. *The Last Puritan: A Memoir in the Form of a Novel*. London: Constable, 1935.

———. *The Letters of George Santayana*. Ed. and introd. Daniel Cory. New York: Scribner's, 1955.

———. "Literary Psychology." *Essays in Literary Criticism*. Ed. and introd. Irving Singer. New York: Scribner's, 1956. 394–401.

———. "A Long Way Round to Nirvana: Development of a Suggestion Found in Freud's *Beyond the Pleasure Principle*." *Some Turns of Thought in Modern Philosophy: Five Essays*. Cambridge: Cambridge UP, 1933. 87–101.

———. *Persons and Places: Fragments of Autobiography*. 1944. Ed. William G. Holzberger and Herman J. Saatkamp, Jr. Introd. Richard C. Lyon. Cambridge: MIT P, 1986.

———. *Physical Order and Moral Liberty: Previously Unpublished Essays of George Santayana*. Ed. John and Shirley Lachs. Nashville: Vanderbilt UP, 1969.

———. *Platonism and the Spiritual Life*. New York: Scribner's, 1927.

———. *Realms of Being*. 1927–38. New York: Scribner's, 1942.

———. *Scepticism and Animal Faith: Introduction to a System of Philosophy*. New York: Scribner's, 1923.

———. *The Sense of Beauty: Being the Outline of Aesthetic Theory*. 1896. New York: Dover, 1955.

Savran, David. *Cowboys, Communists, and Queers: The Politics of Masculinity in the Work of Arthur Miller and Tennessee Williams*. Minneapolis: U of Minnesota P, 1992.

Schopenhauer, Arthur. *Essays and Aphorisms.* Harmondsworth: Penguin, 1970.

———. *The World as Will and Idea.* 1818. Trans. R. B. Haldane and J. Kemp. New York: AMS, 1977.

Schreiner, Olive. *Dreams and Dream Life and Real Life.* 1890; 1893. London: T. Fisher Unwin, 1912.

———. *From Man to Man; or Perhaps Only . . .* 1873—c. 1909; 1926. Introd. Paul Foot. London: Virago, 1982.

———. *The Letters of Olive Schreiner.* Ed. S. C. Cronwright-Schreiner. London: Unwin, 1924.

———. *Olive Schreiner: Letters 1871–99.* Ed. Richard Rive. Cape Town: David Philip, 1987.

———. *The Story of an African Farm.* 1883. Ed. and introd. Joseph Bristow. New York: Oxford UP, 1992.

———. *Undine.* Introd. S. C. Cronwright-Schreiner. New York: Harper, 1928.

———. *Women and Labour.* London: Unwin, 1911.

Schweik, Robert C. "Character and Fate in Hardy's *The Mayor of Casterbridge.*" *Nineteenth-Century Fiction* 21.3 (1966): 249–62.

Scott, Nathan A., Jr. "Santayana's Poetics of Belief." *Boundary 2* 7.3 (1979): 199–224.

Scott, Bonnie Kime, ed. *The Gender of Modernism: A Critical Anthology.* Bloomington: Indiana UP, 1990.

Scott, Joan W. "The Evidence of Experience." *Critical Inquiry* 17.4 (1991): 773–97.

Sedgwick, Eve Kosofsky. "The Beast in the Closet: James and the Writing of Homosexual Panic." *Sex, Politics, and Science in the Nineteenth-Century Novel: Selected Papers from the English Institute, 1983–84.* Ed. Ruth Bernard Yeazell. Baltimore: Johns Hopkins UP, 1986. 148–86.

———. *Between Men: English Literature and Male Homosocial Desire.* New York: Columbia UP, 1985.

———. *Epistemology of the Closet.* Berkeley: U of California P, 1990.

———. "Privilege of Unknowing." *Genders* 1 (1988): 102–24.

———. *Tendencies.* Durham: Duke UP, 1993.

Shakespeare, William. *Julius Caesar.* 1599. The Arden Shakespeare. Ed. T. S. Dorsch. New York: Routledge, 1995.

———. *King Lear.* 1605. The Arden Shakespeare. Ed. Kenneth Muir. New York: Methuen, 1982.

Shand-Tucci, Douglass. *Boston Bohemia, 1881–1900. Ralph Adams Cram: Life and Architecture.* Amherst: U of Massachusetts P, 1995.

Shaw, W. David. *Victorians and Mystery: Crises of Representation.* Ithaca: Cornell UP, 1990.

Shires, Linda M., ed. *Rewriting the Victorians: Theory, History, and the Politics of Gender.* New York: Routledge, 1992.

Showalter, Elaine. *A Literature of Their Own: British Women Novelists from Brontë to Lessing.* Princeton: Princeton UP, 1977.

———. "Olive Schreiner: A Biography." *Tulsa Studies in Women's Literature* 1.1 (1982): 104–9.

————. *Sexual Anarchy: Gender and Culture at the Fin de Siècle.* New York: Penguin, 1990.

————. "The Unmanning of the Mayor of Casterbridge." *Critical Approaches to the Fiction of Thomas Hardy.* Ed. Dale Kramer. London: Macmillan, 1979. 99–115.

Signorile, Michelangelo. *Queer in America: Sex, the Media, and the Closets of Power.* New York: Anchor, 1993.

Silverman, Kaja. *Male Subjectivity at the Margins.* New York: Routledge, 1992.

————. *The Subject of Semiotics.* New York: Oxford UP, 1983.

Sinfield, Alan. *The Wilde Century: Effeminacy, Oscar Wilde, and the Queer Moment.* New York: Columbia UP, 1994.

Singer, Irving. *Santayana's Aesthetics: A Critical Introduction.* Cambridge: Harvard UP, 1957.

Smith, F. Barry. "Labouchère's Amendment to the Criminal Law Amendment Bill." *Historical Studies* 17 (1976): 165–73.

————. "Sexuality in Britain, 1800–1900: Some Suggested Revisions." In Vicinus 182–98.

Smith, Malvern V. W., and Don Maclennan, eds. *Olive Schreiner and After: Essays on Southern African Literature in Honour of Guy Butler.* Cape Town: David Philip, 1983.

Snodgrass, Chris. "Swinburne's Circle of Desire: A Decadent Theme." In I. Fletcher 60–87.

Snyder, Charles W. *Liberty and Morality: A Political Biography of Edward Bulwer-Lytton.* New York: Peter Lang, 1995.

Spivak, Gayatri Chakravorty. "More on Power/Knowledge." *Outside in the Teaching Machine.* New York: Routledge, 1993. 25–51.

Sprigge, Timothy L. S. *Santayana: An Examination of His Philosophy.* New York: Routledge, 1974, 1995.

Stanton, Domna C. *The Aristocrat as Art: A Study of the* Honnête Homme *and the Dandy in Seventeenth- and Nineteenth-Century French Literature.* New York: Columbia UP, 1980.

Steele, Murray. "A Humanist Bible: Gender Roles, Sexuality, and Race in Olive Schreiner's *From Man to Man.*" In Parker 101–14.

Steiner, George. "Under the Greenwood Tree." *New Yorker* Oct. 9, 1971: 158–69.

Stewart, Garrett. *Death Sentences: Styles of Dying in British Fiction.* Cambridge: Harvard UP, 1984.

Stockinger, Jacob. "Toward a Gay Criticism." *College English* 36.3 (1974): 303–10.

Stoler, Ann Laura. *Race and the Education of Desire: Foucault's "History of Sexuality" and the Colonial Order of Things.* Durham: Duke UP, 1995.

Stone, Wilfred. "'Overleaping Class': Forster's Problem in Connection." *Modern Language Quarterly* 39 (1978): 386–404.

Summers, Claude J. *Gay Fictions: Wilde to Stonewall: Studies in a Male Homosexual Literary Tradition.* New York: Continuum, 1990.

Sussman, Herbert L. *Victorian Masculinities: Manhood and Masculine Poetics in Early Victorian Literature and Art.* New York: Cambridge UP, 1995.

Swinburne, Algernon Charles. *The Complete Works of Algernon Charles Swinburne.* 20 vols. Ed. Sir Edmund Gosse and Thomas James Wise. London: Heinemann, 1926.

————. *Lesbia Brandon.* 1864. Ed. and fwd. Randolph Hughes. London: Falcon, 1952.

————. *Love's Cross-Currents: A Year's Letters.* 1862–63. New York: Harper and Brothers, 1905.

————. *Poems and Ballads, First Series.* 1866. *The Poems of Algernon Charles Swinburne.* Vol. 1. London: Chatto and Windus, 1904. 6 vols.

————. *The Swinburne Letters.* 6 vols. Ed. Cecil Lang. New Haven: Yale UP, 1959–62.

————. *Swinburne Replies: Notes on Poems and Reviews; Under the Microscope; Dedicatory Epistle.* Ed. Clyde K. Hyder. Syracuse: Syracuse UP, 1966.

Tanner, Tony. "Joseph Conrad and the Last Gentleman." *Critical Quarterly* 28.1–2 (1986): 109–42.

Tennyson, Alfred, Baron. *The Poems of Tennyson.* Ed. Christopher Ricks. Harlow, Essex: Longman Group, 1969.

Thackeray, William Makepeace. *The History of Pendennis: His Fortunes and Misfortunes, His Friends and His Greatest Enemy.* 1848–50. Ed. Peter L. Shillingsburg. New York: Garland, 1991.

————. *The Letters and Private Papers of William Makepeace Thackeray.* Ed. Gordon N. Ray. 4 vols. Cambridge: Harvard UP, 1946.

————. *Lovel the Widower.* London: Smith, Elder, 1861.

Thomas, Ronald R. *Dreams of Authority: Freud and the Fictions of the Unconscious.* Ithaca: Cornell UP, 1990.

Thurley, Geoffrey. *The Psychology of Hardy's Novels.* St. Lucia: U of Queensland P, 1975.

Toth, Emily. "The Independent Woman and 'Free' Love." *Massachusetts Review* 16 (1975): 647–64.

Ulrichs, Karl. *The Riddle of "Man-Manly" Love: The Pioneering Work on Male Homosexuality.* 2 vols. Trans. Michael A. Lombardi-Nash. Fwd. Vern L. Bullough. Buffalo, NY: Prometheus, 1994.

Vaid, Urvashi. *Virtual Equality: The Mainstreaming of Gay and Lesbian Liberation.* New York: Doubleday, 1995.

Vance, Norman. *The Sinews of the Spirit: The Ideal of Christian Manliness in Victorian Literature and Religious Thought.* Cambridge: Cambridge UP, 1985.

Vanden Bossche, Chris R. *Carlyle and the Search for Authority.* Columbus: Ohio State UP, 1991.

Van Leer, David. "The Beast in the Closet: Homosociality and the Pathology of Manhood." *Critical Inquiry* 15 (1989): 587–605.

Vicinus, Martha, ed. *A Widening Sphere: Changing Roles of Victorian Women.* Bloomington: Indiana UP, 1977.

Vlastos, Gregory. "The Individual as an Object of Love in Plato." *Platonic Studies.* Princeton: Princeton UP, 1973, 1981. 3–34.

Warner, Michael. "Homo-Narcissism; or, Heterosexuality." *Engendering Men: The Question of Male Feminist Criticism.* Ed. Joseph A. Boone and Michael Cadden. New York: Routledge, 1990. 190–206.

Webster's Third New International Dictionary of the English Language Unabridged. Editor-in-chief Philip Babcock Grove. Springfield, MA: G. and C. Merriam, 1961.

Weed, Elizabeth. "The More Things Change." *Differences* 6.2–3 (1994): 249–73.

Weeks, Jeffrey. *Coming Out: Homosexual Politics in Britain, from the Nineteenth Century to the Present.* London: Quartet, 1977.

———. "Discourse, Desire, and Sexual Deviance: Some Problems in a History of Homosexuality." *The Making of the Modern Homosexual.* Ed. Kenneth Plummer. London: Hutchinson, 1981. 76–111.

———. *Sex, Politics, and Society: The Regulation of Sexuality since 1800.* London: Longman, 1981.

———. "'Sins and Diseases': Some Notes on Homosexuality in the Nineteenth Century." *History Workshop* 1 (1976): 211–19.

Weil, Kari. *Androgyny and the Denial of Difference.* Charlottesville: UP of Virginia, 1992.

Weir, David. *Decadence and the Making of Modernism.* Amherst: U of Massachusetts P, 1995.

Wenkart, Henny. "Santayana on Beauty." *Analecta Husserliana.* Vol. 12. *The Philosophical Reflection of Man in Literature.* Ed. Anna-Teresa Tymieniecka. Dordrecht: Reidel, 1982. 321–26.

Wharton, Edith. *The Custom of the Country.* New York: Scribner's, 1913.

White, Allon. *The Uses of Obscurity: The Fiction of Early Modernism.* London: Routledge, 1981.

Whyte, Lancelot Law. *The Unconscious before Freud.* New York: Basic, 1960.

Wilde, Alan. "Desire and Consciousness: The 'Anironic' Forster." *Novel* 9.2 (1976): 114–29.

Wilde, Oscar. *The Decay of Lying.* 1891 (1885–90). *The Artist as Critic: Critical Writings of Oscar Wilde.* Ed. Richard Ellmann. New York: Random House, 1969. 290–320.

———. *De Profundis.* 1905. New York: Philosophical Library, 1950.

———. *The Picture of Dorian Gray.* 1890; 1891. Harmondsworth: Penguin, 1982.

———. *The Portrait of Mr. W. H.* 1889; 1893. *The Riddle of Shakespeare's Sonnets.* Ed. E. Hubler, et al. New York: Basic, 1962. 163–255.

[Wilde, Oscar, and others]. *Teleny; or, The Reverse of the Medal.* 1893. Ed. John McRae. London: Gay Men's, 1986.

Wilson, Edmund. "Introduction: Swinburne of Capheaton and Eton." *The Novels of A. C. Swinburne: Love's Cross-Currents and Lesbia Brandon.* New York: Farrar, Straus and Cudahy, 1962. 3–37.

Wilson, F. A. C. "Swinburne in Love: Some Novels by Mary Gordon." *Texas Studies in Literature and Language* 11 (1970): 1415–26.

———. "Swinburne's Prose Heroines and Mary's *Femmes Fatales.*" *Victorian Poetry* 9.1–2 (1971): 249–56.

Wilson, William. "Behind the Veil, Forbidden: Truth, Beauty, and Swinburne's Aesthetic Strain." *Victorian Poetry* 22.4 (1984): 427–37.

Winfield, Christine. "The Manuscript of Hardy's *Mayor of Casterbridge.*" *Papers of the Bibliographical Society of America* 67 (1973): 33–58.

Wojnarowicz, David. *Close to the Knives: A Memoir of Disintegration.* New York: Vintage, 1991.

The Wolfenden Report: Report of the Committee on Homosexual Offenses and Prostitution. 1957. Introd. Karl Menninger. New York: Stein and Day, 1963.

Wollheim, Richard. "Identification and Imagination: The Inner Structure of a Psychic Mechanism." *Freud: A Collection of Critical Essays.* Ed. Wollheim. Garden City: Anchor, 1974. 172–95.

Woodward, Anthony. *Living in the Eternal: A Study of George Santayana.* Nashville: Vanderbilt UP, 1988.

Woolf, Virginia. "Olive Schreiner." 1925. *Women and Writing.* Ed. Michèle Barrett. London: Women's, 1988. 180–83.

Wright, T. R. *Hardy and the Erotic.* London: Macmillan, 1989.

Yeats, W. B. *The Letters of W. B. Yeats.* Ed. Allan Wade. London: Hart-Davis, 1954.

———. *Per amica silentia lunæ.* New York: Macmillan, 1918.

Yingling, Thomas E. "Homosexuality and the Matter of Style." *Hart Crane and the Homosexual Text: New Thresholds, New Anatomies.* Chicago: U of Chicago P, 1990. 24–56.

Young, Robert M. *Mind, Brain, and Adaptation in the Nineteenth Century: Cerebral Localization and Its Biological Context from Gall to Ferrier.* 2nd ed. New York: Oxford UP, 1970, 1990.

Zima, Peter V. "From Dandyism to Art; or Narcissus Bifrons." *Neohelicon* 12.2 (1985): 201–38.

Žižek, Slavoj. "There Is No Sexual Relationship." In Salecl and Žižek 208–49.

Zyl, John van. "The Liberal Dilemma: Uncle Otto in *The Story of an African Farm.*" *Bulletin of the Association for African Literature in English* (Sierra Leone) 3 (1965): 48–53.

———. "Rhodes and Olive Schreiner." *Contrast* (Cape Town) 21 (1969): 86–90.

INDEX

Abbot, Henry Ward, 179, 186
Abelove, Henry, 8, 249n. 4, 284n. 5,
  285n. 6
Ackerley, J. R., 206
Acocella, Joan, 238, 286n. 16
Adams, James Eli, 75, 255n. 39,
  256n. 45, 257n. 2, 258n. 11
Adams, Stephen, 206–9, 222–23
Adorno, Theodor, 251n. 15
Allen, Dennis, 251n. 12, 255n. 39
Anderson, Amanda, 10, 99
Aristotle, 165, 279n. 14; *Poetics,* 165
Armstrong, Nancy, 249n. 6, 251n. 12,
  253n. 29, 254n. 32, 256n. 43
Armstrong, T. D., 187
Arnett, Willard E., 277n. 4, 278n. 8
Arnold, Matthew, 165–66, 175–76,
  248n. 12; "The Function of Criticism
  at the Present Time," 175
Ashmore, Jerome, 278n. 8
Atlantic Monthly, The, 146
Auden, W. H., 202
Auerbach, Nina, 256n. 40
Austen, Jane, 70; *Mansfield Park,* 70

Bain, Alexander, 247n. 3
Baird, Julian, 78
Baker, Robert S., 275n. 6
Balzac, Honoré de, 75
Banerjee, Jacqueline, 116
Baral, Kailash Chandra, 175
Barash, Carol L., 98
Barbey d'Aurevilly, Jules-Amédée, 57,
  64–65, 71, 108; "Du Dandysme et de
  G. Brummell," 65, 71, 108
Barret-Ducrocq, Françoise, 5
Barrett, Dorothea, 80
Barthes, Roland, 239–42, 277n. 12;
  Camera Obscura, 239; *A Lover's Dis-
  course,* 239, 277n. 12; *Roland Barthes,*

239–40; *S/Z,* 239; *Writing Degree
  Zero,* 239
Bartlett, Neil, 230–32
Bataille, Georges, 32–34
Baudelaire, Charles, xiii, 57, 64, 70–71,
  255n. 38; *Les Fleurs du mal,* xiii; *Mon
  cœur mis à nu,* 255n. 38; "Le Peintre
  de la vie moderne," 64, 70–71
Beaty, Jerome, 257n. 3
Beaver, Harold, 238
Beckett, Samuel, 70, 114
Beegel, Susan, 124
Beerbohm, Max, 261n. 4
Bellamy, Edward, 95
Bellringer, Alan W., 154
Bennett, Arnold, xiv, 252n. 16; *The Old
  Wives' Tale,* xiv, 252n. 16
Berkman, Joyce Avrech, 95–96, 265n. 8
Bernheimer, Charles, 260n. 22
Bersani, Leo, xviii, 7, 13, 30, 32, 66,
  144, 198, 218, 223, 228, 233,
  277n. 1, 282n. 5, 284nn. 2, 3; *Arts of
  Impoverishment,* 223, 269n. 42,
  285n. 7; *The Culture of Redemption,*
  277n. 1; *The Freudian Body,* 13, 30,
  198, 218, 228, 284n. 2; *A Future for
  Astyanax,* 144; *Homos,* 66, 284n. 2; "Is
  the Rectum a Grave?," 32; "Represen-
  tation and Its Discontents," 233
Bieber, Irving, 264n. 26
Binswanger, Ludwig, 14
Black, Joel, 263n. 23
Boone, Joseph Allen, 95
Borch-Jacobsen, Mikkel, 115
Boswell, James, 172
Boswell, John, 17
Bouëxière, Laurent, 58
Bradford, Helen, 94
Brandon, Ruth, 107
Bray, Alan, 254n. 32

313